"Your Communication Model for Business and

P9-EGN-655

Each chapter begins with an intriguing opening vignette, *"Communicating Without a Strategy."* These opening scenarios emphasize that communicating without a systematic strategy or overall thinking process can cause problems and challenges to effective communication.

COMMUNICATING WITHOUT A STRATEGY

A Strategy Beats "Winging It"

A 19-year-old sophomore, Robert already has a full-page résumé. He is confident that his experience and abilities far exceed those of his peers. When a recruiter from a well-known company comes to his campus to interview candidates for internships, Robert signs up, but he refuses offers of information and counseling about the job search process. After all, he knows all about himself, and that is what the recruiter wants to know, right? Needless to say, Robert's lack of preparation is obvious. The recruiter is insulted that a job candidate would think he could be successful by "winging it."

Kim is a junior taking an introductory communication class at a major urban school. Her first assignment is an oral presentation on a controversial issue. Kim tries to make up for her weak public speaking skills by conducting in-depth research and giving a clearly organized speech, targeted directly at the needs and interests of her listeners. When preparing, she writes every word of her speech, but she never once practices it out loud. The day of the...

At the end of each chapter, the authors revisit the opening scenarios in a special section, *"Applying the Strategic Communication Model."* They emphasize how applying the Strategic Communication Model (SCM) would increase effectiveness in the described communication tasks. This modeling approach prepares future communicators to develop their problem-analysis skills so they can effectively create and deliver appropriate and effective messages via a variety of media and in a wide range of contexts.

APPLYING THE STRATEGIC COMMUNICATION MODEL

Let's take a final look at how using the Strategic Communication Model might help the three people we described in the opening story of the chapter. Robert's self-confidence in his interviewing ability may be well founded, but his failure to *define the context* (especially to understand his audiences and their needs) would cost him dearly in a job interview. Had he taken the time to gather information about the company, Robert may have landed a job. Kim's extra effort to *select and organize information* for her presentation is laudable, but her lack of attention to good *delivery skills* hurt her badly. Learning to combine good preparation with a professional presentation will help Kim make her message that much better. And finally, Sam's assumption that the company he was writing to was a tire company made him look uninformed and reflects a failure to *define the context* of his communication effort. Had he done a bit of research, Sam would have realized that his cover letter was inappropriate. In all cases, application of the Strategic Communication Model would have made the likelihood of their communication success much greater.

Application Activities

Activity 1-1 Defining a Context

A good way to start understanding the Strategic Communication Model is to apply it to real situations in your communications class. Let's work our way through the first step of the model with typical questions that you might ask yourself when you are planning to communicate in this class. For the purpose of this activity, focus on this class in general, not on a specific assignment.

Analyze the following and write your responses. (Writing is the best way to develop critical thinking skills. Just thinking about these factors will be far less valuable.) You need not follow any specific writing format, but a question-answer pattern works well for many people.

Interactive CD-ROM Exercises

1. **Define the Situation.** To accurately define the context, first define the situation. In this case, your situation is what you must communicate in this communication class, including everything involved with taking a particular class. To effectively define the situation, you must understand the culture of your class.
   a. **Limit the problem.** Identify the important issues of this class so that you can limit the problem. For example, what is the outcome you hope to achieve through the messages in this class? To fulfill a class requirement? To get an A in this class? To express genuine opinions that you want to share? What else?
   b. **Evaluate the problem within the external climate.** What have you heard about business communication classes in general? What have you heard about other communication classes at your school? What other classes and activities are you involved in this semester? What else?

Each chapter includes selected CD-ROM exercises. This exclusive Strategic Communication Model CD-ROM provides an interactive format for key end-of-chapter material. Students will apply what they have learned to a variety of hands-on activities along with benefiting from additional valuable student resources to reinforce and enhance their business communication skills. In addition, the CD-ROM offers a powerful, interactive grammar assessment that helps students and instructors to reinforce appropriate language usage. Grammar reinforcement exercises simultaneously develop the student's ability to work with communication software, to learn about the strategic role of communication in the business enterprise, and to develop appropriate language skills.

Business Communication

DISCOVERING STRATEGY, DEVELOPING SKILLS

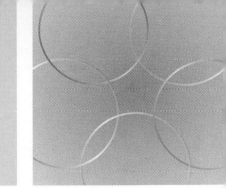

Business Communication

DISCOVERING STRATEGY, DEVELOPING SKILLS

Sherron Bienvenu, Ph.D.
Associate Professor in the Practice of Management Communication
Goizueta Business School
Emory University

Paul R. Timm, Ph.D.
Professor of Management Communication
The Marriott School of Management
Brigham Young University

Upper Saddle River, NJ 07458

Library of Congress Cataloging-in-Publication Data

Timm, Paul R.
  Business communication: discovering strategy, developing skills / Paul R. Timm,
Sherron Bienvenu.--1st ed.
    p. cm.
  Includes bibliographical references.
  ISBN 0-13-091313-8
    1. Business communication. I. Bienvenu, Sherron. II. Title.

HF5717 .T56 2001
658.4'5--dc21

2001036674

Acquisitions Editor: David Parker
VP/Editor-in-Chief: Jeff Shelstad
Assistant Editor: Jennifer Surich
Editorial Assistant: Virginia Sheridan
Media Project Manager: Michele Faranda
Senior Marketing Manager: Debbie Clare
Marketing Assistant: Brian Rappelfeld
Managing Editor (Production): Judy Leale
Production Editor: Theresa Festa
Production Assistant: Dianne Falcone
Permissions Coordinator: Suzanne Grappi
Associate Director, Manufacturing: Vincent Scelta
Production Manager: Arnold Vila
Design Manager: Patricia Smythe
Designer: Blair Brown
Interior Design: Karen K. Quigley
Cover Design: Michael Fruhbeis
Cover Illustration/Photo: Michael Fruhbeis
Illustrator (Interior): Electra Graphics, Inc.
Associate Director, Multimedia Production: Karen Goldsmith
Manager, Print Production: Christy Mahon
Composition: Carlisle Communications, Ltd.
Printer/Binder: Courier/Kendallville

Credits and acknowledgments borrowed from other sources and reproduced, with permission, in this textbook appear on appropriate page within text.

10 9 8 7 6 5 4 3 2 1
ISBN 0-13-091313-8

To our spouses for their inspiration and support.

BRIEF CONTENTS

REFERENCE TOOLS

CONTENTS

PART 2: DEVELOPING STRATEGY-BASED WRITING AND SPEAKING SKILLS 73

PART 3: DELIVERING POWERFUL MESSAGES   169

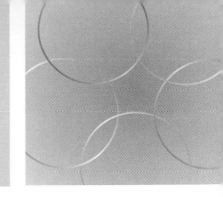

INTRODUCTION

COMMUNICATION AND CAREER SUCCESS IN THE TWENTY-FIRST CENTURY

> The most important thing I learned
> in school was how to communicate.
> —Lee Iacocca, Former CEO, Chrysler Corp.

Successful Twenty-First Century Careers Require Excellent Communication Skills

Career success comes to people who are good at giving correct information, developing strong working relationships, attracting and satisfying customers, working in teams, solving disputes, building consensus for decisions, picking other people's brains for useful insights, conveying ideas, listening, and building networks of friends and co-workers. What is the common denominator in all these activities? They all involve the functions of *business communication:* writing, speaking, interviewing, and group interaction skills. In fact, excellent communication skills can do more to jump-start a promising career than almost any other factor.

More than ever before, the ability to communicate well determines an employee's capability to thrive in today's business world. Organizations cannot function without effective communication. Businesses must communicate in a number of different contexts. They must communicate with their customers through advertising, sales, public relations, and customer service activities. They must share ideas, apply new knowledge and information, and motivate and train employees. Without these kinds of functions, organizations will be less productive and companies may fail. People with well-developed communication skills are crucial to organizational success. Such people are always in demand.

How do your skills measure up against the requirements of today's workplace? What skills will best serve you as you begin your career and contribute your skills to the businesses and organizations of the twenty-first century? How confident are you in your ability to devise a communication strategy, write effectively, prepare and deliver a good oral presentation, participate in meetings and interviews, and gather feedback? This book will help you develop those skills.

Five Barriers That Hinder Business Communication Success

What are some of the hurdles to building communication competence? We have found five typical barriers that make the process difficult for many people. A major function of this book is to teach you ways to overcome these barriers, so let us begin our study by looking at five common barriers to effective personal communication.

Barrier 1: The "I-Already-Know-How" Attitude

We have all been communicating since we were children, and most of us think we are pretty good at it. We assume that because what we say and write makes sense to us, it also makes sense to—and should be accepted by—others. Unfortunately, this attitude may cause us to bumble along the way we always have, thus missing the opportunity to improve the quality of our communication. This can be the worst form of tunnel vision. The reality is that none of us are perfect communicators, and most of us aren't nearly as good as we think we are—or could be.

Barrier 2: An Oversimplified View of How Communication Works

We mistakenly see communication as a controllable, mechanical activity in which a speaker or writer says something and a listener or reader responds in some predictable way. The reality is that, in most cases, the process is nowhere near that simple and we cannot fully *control* communication. We can, and should, seek to *influence* other people with our messages, but ultimately it will be those other people who determine our success. This reality is frustrating for people who want to be dictators, persuaders, or motivators. We all want to get people to do what we ask, to get our peers to accept our point of view, to get customers to buy, and to get our bosses to be impressed with us. But whether such things happen or not is ultimately determined by our readers or listeners. The fact is that *those who receive our messages determine the meaning of our messages.*

Real communication improvement often means letting go of old assumptions and getting out of the comfortable rut of communicating-as-usual. Improvement has little to do with talking louder, more emphatically, or more earnestly. Improvement has little to do with increasing the amount of information we project to others or with making the message sound better and better to *ourselves*. Improvement has *everything* to do with understanding our message receivers and developing more understanding for them. This means looking at the world through the eyes of others, walking the proverbial mile in another's shoes. Most of us are hesitant to do this, even though this kind of empathizing brings meaningful communication improvement. Understand that the message receiver determines communication success.

As with any skill development, great communicators are willing to do that which poor communicators are unwilling to do. Great communicators understand the process and work at the problem without being slaves to the ways they have always done things in the past.

Barrier 3: Too Little Communication

Too little communication is often a cause of crumbling relationships and dysfunctional families. Similiarly, countless business relationships fail because employees and managers withhold appreciation, concern, or ideas. Groups of people who cannot express their ideas and share their feelings with each other seldom succeed as an organization.

Similarly, companies that do too little to get useful feedback from customers and employees run the risk of flying blind. Such organizations may go along and be oblivious to the missed opportunities and poor market acceptance of their products or services. They fail to realize their potential because they don't get the feedback they need to correct and improve. Employees in successful organizations work hard to avoid the problem of too little communication by seeking input from customers and co-workers, by keeping other people informed, and, when appropriate, by involving others in ongoing communication.

Barrier 4: Too Much Communication

People who receive enormous amounts of irrelevant information may collapse under the load. This is the organizational equivalent of the old quip: "I asked him what time it was, and he told me how to build a watch." Smart businesspeople keep others informed of things they need to know or may want to know but don't bombard them with trivia. Smart communicators carefully select information for their messages based on the needs and wants of their target audiences. They don't overload their readers or listeners with trivia. They are aware of the potential problem of communication overload.

We all receive hundreds or even thousands of messages every day. As a student, you may often feel overloaded by the stack of textbooks you need to read or the classroom information you should remember. You face the everyday challenge of busy people—that of having to cut through the clutter of communication overload. To deal with this challenge, effective business communicators need to select and convey the truly important messages, target the right audiences, and express ideas clearly.

Barrier 5: Failure to Use a Strategy

Many unsuccessful communicators fail because they have no sensible plan for creating and delivering their messages. We all may be tempted to "wing it" at times, but communications delivered without a plan run a serious risk of failing or even backfiring. The use of a strategy will greatly improve your likelihood of success. A key characteristic of this book is that it teaches you a strategic approach to planning and executing any communication situation. We will introduce you to this approach in Chapter 1 and build the remainder of the book around it. Using a strategic communication model will help you overcome the temptation to communicate without a plan.

Three Tactics to Overcome the Barriers

We have suggested some personal barriers to effective communication. Now we offer you three general suggestions on how to overcome them. We will, of course, elaborate on these in the remainder of the book.

Tactic 1: Discover the Power of Communication Strategy

You can distinguish yourself from the many haphazard communicators who just improvise—or "wing it"—by applying a communication strategy. Planning your messages with the help of a strategic communication model is not difficult. Applying an appropriate model and making it a part of your daily thinking will dramatically set you apart from less successful communicators.

Do not think that using a strategic model limits your creativity. A strategy is not a cookbook, a set of rigid rules, or a foolproof formula. Instead, a strategy is an approach using sound communication principles and basic procedures. The Strategic Communication Model discussed in this book provides you with a systematic plan that you can complement with countless personal variations and creative flourishes. We will show you how to use your personal skills and capabilities to your best advantage within the framework of a strategy.

Tactic 2: Develop the Critical Skills Required for Business Communication Success

As you work through this book, you will grow to appreciate that developing strong communication skills really is worth the effort—that it is of critical importance to your career and your life. This book will provide you with concrete ways to improve the full range of business communication skills you will use every day in your career.

Tactic 3: Maintain Realistic Expectations

Keep your skill development efforts grounded in reality. You can do much to improve your abilities, but always remember that *communication is susceptible to the reactions of other people and you cannot absolutely control what happens.* Acknowledge this lack of total control and remain realistic about what you can accomplish as a communicator. Your realistic picture can begin with two constructive expectations:

- Expect *to be misunderstood* by at least some of your listeners and readers. This is inevitable.
- Expect *to misunderstand* others at least some of the time. This, too, is a reality of life—you, as a message receiver, will misunderstand others at times.

With those expectations firmly in mind, you get a clearer picture of the task that lies before every communicator—that of striving to *reduce the degree of such misunderstanding.* Some might argue that expecting misunderstanding is a negative attitude. However, such expectations are healthy and realistic. Communicators who keep these expectations in mind accept their share of responsibility for reducing possible confusion or ambiguity in their messages. They accept the reality that miscommunication often happens, and they acknowledge the need to put themselves in the shoes of their message receivers and anticipate what they might possibly misunderstand. These actions are important and fundamental to building communication competency.

Take the Challenge

Are you ready to take the challenge? Are you ready to jump-start your career with powerful communication skills? If so, this book will help you think more effectively. It will give you many new ideas about communication behaviors that work for people. Try them and then look at your results. Think about what went well, what did not go well, and how to try it a little differently next time. This constant process of experimentation and learning will pay large dividends.

Improving the ways you communicate can be a challenging task because your communication style is a natural part of your personality. When someone says, "You should change the way you communicate," that person is asking you to change your normal behaviors—something that is often not easy. But you can improve your communication effectiveness if you thoughtfully apply the steps of the Strategic Communication Model. These steps are:

1. Define the context in which you are communicating.
2. Consider your media and timing options.
3. Select and organize the information you wish to convey.
4. Deliver your messages effectively.
5. Evaluate feedback for ongoing improvement.

The strategy and skills you will learn from this book—covering a full range of business communication skills, including written, oral, interpersonal, and graphic (or visual)—can dramatically improve your likelihood of achieving maximum communication effectiveness. The abilities you develop will be transferable to virtually any career position. We encourage you to build upon your personal uniqueness.

How to Use This Book

As you work through this book, you will find a logical progression to the material presented. In Part 1 you will discover and apply the Strategic Communication Model. Chapter 1 presents an introduction to the model. Chapter 2 introduces foundation skills for business writing, and Chapter 3 introduces foundation skills for business speaking. In Part 2, you will develop strategy-based writing and speaking skills. Chapter 4 covers defining the context, Step 1 of the Strategic Communication Model. Chapter 5 shows you how to consider media and timing options, the second step of the model. Chapter 6 discusses selecting and organizing information for your messages, Step 3 of the model, and Chapter 7 presents ideas for creating effective visual support materials.

In Part 3, we look at ways you can improve the delivery of your message, the fourth step of the model. In Chapter 8, you will build on the writing foundation skills introduced in Chapter 2 and learn how to deliver your message with effective business writing. Similarly, in Chapter 9, you will build on the writing foundation skills introduced in Chapter 3 and learn to deliver your message with effective oral presentations. In Chapter 10, you will learn ways to apply the model to meetings and group activities, and, in Chapter 11, you will gain insights on participating in effective conversations and interviews. Finally, in Chapter 12 (Part 4), you will learn ways to evaluate feedback for continued success, Step 5 of the Strategic Communication Model.

The reference tools provide additional information for quick review. Reference Tool A shows how to avoid common grammar, punctuation, and usage mistakes. Reference Tool B overviews approaches to researching your topic and documenting your findings. Reference Tool C will help you recognize tendencies in gender differences in workplace communication. Reference Tool D shows tips on the formatting of written documents, and Reference Tool E provides useful editing symbols.

If you are ready to learn, this book is ready to coach you. We think you will find the book practical and user friendly. We do not mandate any simplistic, "one-best-way" formulas for communicating. We do, however, provide you with a foundation that, when blended with your flexibility and creativity, can give your communication credibility and impact.

When developing this new book, we also realized a set of well-written and well integrated teaching supplements can often be the difference between an average and an excellent teaching experience. The *Business Communication: Discovering Strategy, Developing Skills* supplements are completely integrated with the text and seamlessly support the Bienvenu/Timm communication strategy. The supplements provide instructors with the materials to effortlessly plan and teach classes, as well as provide student assignments, quizzes, and tests. The supplements equip students with the tools to master and immediately benefit from the communication strategy.

The supplements, author, Molly Epstein, a colleague and friend of the book authors, coordinated with Sherron Bienvenu and Paul Timm throughout the creation of the text and the supplements. Professors Timm and Bienvenu directed the creation of all supplements to ensure that they simplify both the teaching process for instructors and learning process for students. Therefore, these supplements enable instructors to effortlessly present a fully integrated semester of business communication training.

The supplements' author combination of business and English degrees enables her to create materials that focus on the macro business issues while helping students develop the micro language skills necessary to succeed in business. Professor Epstein has taught undergraduate business communication classes for seven years, so she understands how to create interactive exercises that facilitate learning. The instructors' package includes:

Instructor's Manual
Test Bank
PowerPoint Slides
Study Guide
myPHLIP Companion Web site
Interactive CD-ROM

So let's get started with *Business Communication: Discovering Strategy, Developing Skills.*

Acknowledgments

Every book is the collective work of many people who influence, enlighten, and motivate the authors. We are fortunate to have an exceptional team of professional friends and colleagues who have put their imprint on this project. We thank and commend them.

Reviewers:

- Robin Breault, Georgia State University
- David Buckner, University of Washington Business School
- Glenna A. Dod, Wesleyan College
- Diana Green, Weber State University
- Ruth Ellen Greenwood, Humber College of Applied Arts & Technology
- Christine A. Jonick, Gainesville College
- Bobbie Krapels, University of Mississippi
- Shirley Kuiper, University of South Carolina
- Sally Lawrence, East Carolina University
- Terrell Manyak, Nova Southeastern University
- Leanne Maunu, San Diego State University
- Mary Meredith, University of Louisiana
- Lynda Money, Weber State University
- Cheryl Nixon, Babson College
- Mary Ellen Nourse, University of Idaho
- Betty Schroeder, Northern Illinois University
- Judith Smith, University of Maryland
- John C. Sutton, Francis Marion University
- Jie Wang, University of Illinois
- William Wardrope, Southwest Texas State University

Colleagues:

Marriott School of Management, Brigham Young University:

- Colleagues William H. Baker, Michael Thompson, Kristen DeTienne, Ray L. Young, and the Management Communication team in the Department of Organizational Leadership and Strategy.

Goizueta Business School, Emory University:

- Dean Thomas S. Robertson and Associate Dean Joseph F. Porac.
- Communication Team colleagues Molly Epstein and Deborah Valentine.
- Research Assistants Vicki Travis, Leslie Wexler, and Nicki Marshek.

Members of the Association of Business Communication.

The Prentice Hall team, especially:

- David Parker, Acquisitions Editor, who inherited this project but still treated us like his first born.
- Theresa Festa, Production Editor, who cheerfully crossed every last t, dotted every last i, and beat every deadline.
- Debbie Clare, who was our consistent, unfailing champion (and we hope always will be).
- Linda Schreiber, who encouraged us to undertake this project.
- Shannon Leuma, Developmental Editor, who never tired, never lost her spirit, and never forgot anything.

- Danielle Meier and Mary Fernandez, our marketing reps, who were always there to cheer us on.
- Jeff Shelstad, Virginia Sheridan, and Donna Mulder, whose enthusiasm and hard work helped us finally cross the finish line.

Special thanks to Dr. Molly Epstein, our Supplements Editor, who contributed to the development of this project over the years by teaching the material in her own classes. She then used that experience and expertise to design a complete set of supplements that are cutting edge, real world, and precisely focused to immeasurably enhance the value of this book for both student and teacher.

Some material in this book was adapted from Paul R. Timm and James A. Stead, *Communication for Business and the Professions* (Upper Saddle River, NJ: Prentice Hall, 1996).

A variation of the Context Analysis Worksheet was introduced by Sherron Bienvenu in *The Presentation Skills Workshop* (New York: AMACOM, 2000) and is a derivation of the Audience Analysis Worksheet introduced by Sherron Bienvenu Kenton and Deborah Valentine in *CrossTalk: Communicating in a Multicultural Workplace* (Upper Saddle River, NJ: Prentice Hall, 1997).

A variation of the Outline Worksheet was introduced by Sherron Bienvenu Kenton and Deborah Valentine in *CrossTalk: Communicating in a Multicultural Workplace* (Upper Saddle River, NJ: Prentice Hall, 1997). A variation also appeared in *The Presentation Skills Workshop* by Sherron Bienvenu (New York: AMACOM, 2000).

A variation of the Presentation Evaluation was introduced by Sherron Bienvenu in *The Presentation Skills Workshop* (New York: AMACOM, 2000).

A B O U T T H E A U T H O R S

Sherron Bienvenu, Ph.D.

Dr. Sherron Bienvenu is Associate Professor in the Practice of Management Communication at the Goizueta Business School of Emory University. She also teaches in the International MBA Program at the Helsinki School of Economics and Business Administration in Finland.

Dr. Bienvenu authored *The Presentation Skills Workshop* (AMACOM Books, 2000) and co-authored *CrossTalk: Communicating in a Multicultural Workplace* (Prentice Hall, 1997). She also wrote and appears as an on-camera spokesperson in two training videos.

An active consultant and trainer, Dr. Bienvenu's corporate clients include Lockheed Martin Aeronautical Systems, AT&T, Weeks Corporation, Home Depot, American Cancer Society, Fleet Capital, BellSouth International, Centers for Disease Control, Vegsauki (Iceland), and others. Her workshops and seminars apply communication principles to functional areas including sales, marketing, and management. She has worked with a wide variety of industries including health care, consulting, broadcasting, real estate, law, education, banking, finance, law enforcement, fund-raising, manufacturing, public utilities, and telecommunications.

Paul R. Timm, Ph.D.

Dr. Paul R. Timm is a Professor in the Marriott School of Management at Brigham Young University. An active author, he has written some 34 books dealing with management and business communication, customer loyalty, human relations, supervision, and self-management. Selected books have been translated into eight languages and are sold worldwide.

Dr. Timm writes content for Internet training modules as well as magazine and journal articles. He also wrote and appears in eight videotape training programs produced by Jack Wilson Video, Chicago.

He served as Assistant Dean and Department Chair at the Marriott School's Department of Organizational Leadership and Strategy. He teaches communication and organizational behavior courses to graduate and undergraduate students as well as Executive Education programs. His consulting clients include organizations in the United States and Europe, where he trains in communication skills, self-management, and strategies for building customer loyalty.

Discovering and Applying the Strategic Communication Model

Part 1

Step 1. Define the Context

A. Define the situation.
  1. Limit the problem.
  2. Evaluate the problem within the external climate.
  3. Evaluate the corporate culture that impacts the problem.

B. Define your audience.
  1. Identify all potential audiences (distinct or overlapping).
  2. Learn about each audience.

C. Define your objectives with each audience.
  1. Define your overall goal.
  2. Identify the specific purpose of the communication.
  3. Acknowledge your hidden agenda.

Step 2. Consider Your Media and Timing Options

A. Select media options that are most appropriate for your message.
B. Evaluate your timing options.

Step 3. Select and Organize Your Information

A. Review your analysis of your situation, audiences, and objectives.
B. Compare key organizational patterns and select the most effective one.
C. Limit your main points.
D. Enhance your message with powerful support material (visual aids, numbers, and examples).

Step 4. Deliver Your Message

A. Develop your writing, speaking, interpersonal, and group skills.
B. Prepare thoroughly (rehearse your presentations and edit your writing).
C. Express confidence in your topic and in yourself.
D. Be yourself (but adapt your style to your audience and situation).

Step 5. Evaluate Feedback for Continued Success

A. Give feedback.
B. Solicit feedback.
C. Receive feedback.
D. Evaluate yourself with the Credibility Checklist:
  1. Goodwill: your focus on and concern for your audience
  2. Expertise: your education, knowledge, and experience
  3. Power: your status, prestige, and success
  4. Confidence: the way you present yourself and your message

SKILL OBJECTIVES

After you have studied this chapter, you should be able to:

- Identify the five steps in the Strategic Communication Model.
- Describe the advantages of using a systematic communication strategy.
- Explain what is meant by the *context* of a communication event.
- Identify how media and timing options can affect messages.
- Understand how to select the appropriate information for any given audience and organize that information in an effective manner.
- Recognize some elements of your message delivery style.
- Know the basics of giving, soliciting, and receiving feedback.
- Identify the four dimensions of credibility that have an impact on your communication effectiveness.

Introduction to the Strategic Communication Model: Discovering a Strategic Approach

CHAPTER 1
SKILL
FOCUS:

Discovering the Foundations

of Message Planning

and Delivery

Communication is the only

task you cannot delegate.

—Roberto C. Goizueta,

Chairman and CEO,

The Coca-Cola Company

$\mathscr{C}$OMMUNICATING WITHOUT A STRATEGY

A Strategy Beats "Winging It"

A 19-year-old sophomore, Robert already has a full-page résumé. He is confident that his experience and abilities far exceed those of his peers. When a recruiter from a well-known company comes to his campus to interview candidates for internships, Robert signs up, but he refuses offers of information and counseling about the job search process. After all, he knows all about himself, and that is what the recruiter wants to know, right? Needless to say, Robert's lack of preparation is obvious. The recruiter is insulted that a job candidate would think he could be successful by "winging it."

Kim is a junior taking an introductory communication class at a major urban school. Her first assignment is an oral presentation on a controversial issue. Kim tries to make up for her weak public speaking skills by conducting in-depth research and giving a clearly organized speech, targeted directly at the needs and interests of her listeners. When preparing, she writes every word of her speech, but she never once practices it out loud. On the day of the presentation, she stands up, looks down, and almost incoherently reads word for word off the page. She speaks softly and with little variety, which makes her sound unenthusiastic and nervous. Her excellent preparation is wasted because her delivery sounds like she is "winging it."

Sam, a recently graduated senior, is on the lookout for a job. Ignoring the advice of his college career counselor, Sam decides not to research the companies to which he is applying. Instead, he writes a generic cover letter to each company. In one cover letter, Sam writes, "I have been interested in the tire business, and especially your company, ever since my father ran a small tire store when I was young. I think I would be an ideal candidate for any position at your company." What Sam doesn't know is that the company he has written to has long ago divested itself of its tire business and is now an aerospace company. When the company receives Sam's letter, it's obvious he has not done his research and that he is "winging it."

Students and businesspeople often feel so confident in their ability to communicate that they see little need to prepare. They have had success in past attempts to write or speak and assume that they can use the same techniques regardless of the audience or purpose. Without thinking the situation over, they rely on style over substance—or substance with no style—and the results are disastrous. So, if you have been told that you are articulate and smooth as a writer or speaker, beware! You still need to prepare for a speech. Or if you have been told that your material is excellent, again, beware! Poor delivery or a sloppy-looking letter can ruin a well-prepared message.

This chapter will introduce you to the five-step Strategic Communication Model,[1] which forms the blueprint for this book's approach to better business communication. As you read, keep in mind that this chapter presents a very broad overview of the model. The rest of the book will develop the model and show you how to add the layers of detail that will help you better communicate.

The Strategic Communication Model

The Strategic Communication Model offers you a systematic plan. However, you can still personalize your approach when you use the model.

Good strategies help people solve problems in functional, creative ways. The same is true whenever you communicate: Using a good strategy will help you get your point across effectively and efficiently. The Strategic Communication Model that we will be using in this book provides just such a working plan for the preparation and delivery of oral and written messages. This five-step strategic process is suitable for all types of workplace communication and allows you to personalize your approach while following one basic master plan. It allows for plenty of creativity and opportunities to project your unique personality and makes you more credible and persuasive when you present, write, interview, or interact in teams and groups. In short, the Strategic Communication Model makes you a more effective communicator.

The Strategic Communication Model includes the following five steps:

When we use the term *audience* in this book, we mean anyone who could potentially read or hear your message, whether you want them to or not.

1. **Define the context.** Learn everything you can about the context in which you are communicating—the current situation, your target audiences, and your objectives with each of those audiences.
2. **Consider your media and timing options.** Decide on the communication medium that is most appropriate and effective for your message and the best time for the message to arrive.
3. **Select and organize information.** Make sure you have organized your information so that it will meet your objectives with your audiences. Base your organizational plan on the information you have collected about the context and your media and timing options.
4. **Deliver your message.** When it is time to deliver your message, do so appropriately and correctly with a confident, personal style.

5. Evaluate feedback for continued success. Give and gather feedback so that you may continue to learn and grow as a communicator.

Figure 1-1 presents an illustration of the Strategic Communication Model. Notice that each of the five steps just mentioned can be broken down into detailed substeps. Don't be overwhelmed or try to digest every step just yet—we will look

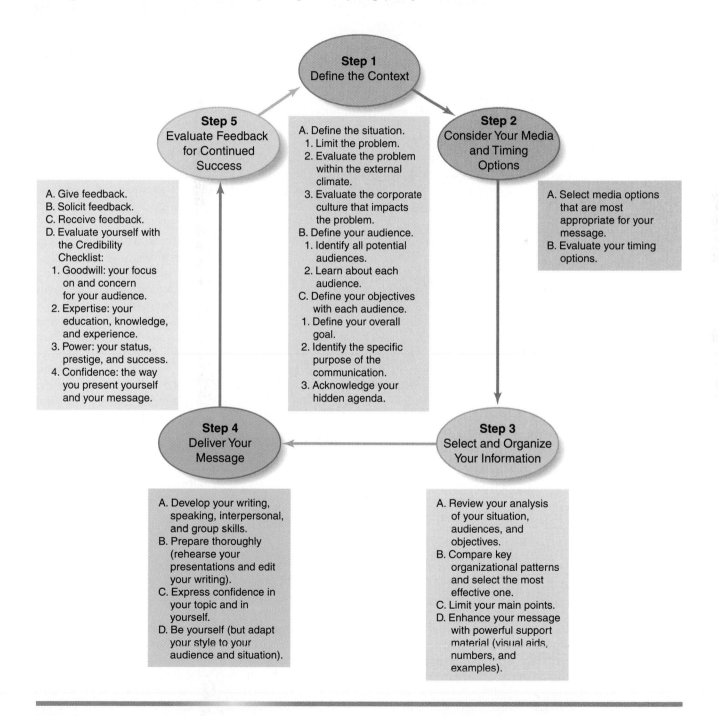

Step 1
Define the Context

Step 5
Evaluate Feedback
for Continued
Success

Step 2
Consider Your Media
and Timing
Options

A. Define the situation.
1. Limit the problem.
2. Evaluate the problem within the external climate.
3. Evaluate the corporate culture that impacts the problem.
B. Define your audience.
1. Identify all potential audiences.
2. Learn about each audience.
C. Define your objectives with each audience.
1. Define your overall goal.
2. Identify the specific purpose of the communication.
3. Acknowledge your hidden agenda.

A. Give feedback.
B. Solicit feedback.
C. Receive feedback.
D. Evaluate yourself with the Credibility Checklist:
1. Goodwill: your focus on and concern for your audience.
2. Expertise: your education, knowledge, and experience.
3. Power: your status, prestige, and success.
4. Confidence: the way you present yourself and your message.

A. Select media options that are most appropriate for your message.
B. Evaluate your timing options.

Step 4
Deliver Your
Message

Step 3
Select and Organize
Your Information

A. Develop your writing, speaking, interpersonal, and group skills.
B. Prepare thoroughly (rehearse your presentations and edit your writing).
C. Express confidence in your topic and in yourself.
D. Be yourself (but adapt your style to your audience and situation).

A. Review your analysis of your situation, audiences, and objectives.
B. Compare key organizational patterns and select the most effective one.
C. Limit your main points.
D. Enhance your message with powerful support material (visual aids, numbers, and examples).

Figure 1-1
The Strategic Communication Model

more closely at, and give you examples of, each step as the chapter develops and throughout the rest of the book.

Step 1: Define the Context

Define the situation.
Define your audience.
Define your objectives with each audience.

Defining the context of your message is vital to its success.

When we talk about the communication *context,* we are referring to three key factors that form the foundation for your strategic planning:

- The situation or problem that causes you to produce your message (*Why* are you communicating?)
- Your target audiences (*To whom* are you communicating?)
- Your desired objectives with those audiences (*What* do you want your readers or listeners to do or think?)

Start your message preparation with specific knowledge about what you are dealing with, whom you are presenting to, and what you want them to do or think.

You greatly improve the odds of getting what you want if you thoroughly understand the situation, your audiences, and your objectives before you communicate. Novice communicators often fail to spend enough time defining their situation, audience, and overall objectives. They prefer to jump into preparing what they want to say without sufficiently thinking about what their message receivers need or want. Defining the context is a critical step in any communication effort, whether you are planning a class presentation, an interview for an internship, or a written report for a directed study. On the job, your first responsibility might be to arrange a meeting for your supervisor or to research current market trends and deliver your findings in a report or presentation. You will always need to start with specific knowledge about what you are dealing with, whom you are presenting to, and what you want them to do or think. In fact, defining the context may well be the single most important thing you can do to achieve your goals.

As we look closer at the communication context, we find that it includes three major parts: your situation, your audience, and your objectives. Our strategic approach analyzes each aspect separately and systematically. We'll start with the existing situation, because the situation usually creates the reason to communicate. In Chapter 4 we will build on these ideas and provide many more examples.

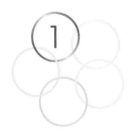

Define the Situation

The first part of defining the context involves looking at the scope of the problem you are planning to communicate about, evaluating the external climate in which the problem exists, and evaluating the corporate culture. The *external climate* is a composite of business, economic, political, or social pressures being faced by similar businesses or organizations. For example, the external climate of small high-tech companies may be viewed as risky or unlikely to generate an immediate profit. Or the same companies may be seen as exciting, high-growth organizations. This viewpoint will change based on what is happening in the external climate. *Corporate culture* refers to the predominant values, attitudes, and beliefs of the company that are consciously or subconsciously agreed upon by most members and result in shared behaviors.

The *external climate* is a composite of business, economic, political, or social pressures being faced by similar businesses or organizations.

Corporate culture refers to the predominant values, attitudes, and beliefs of the company.

Unfortunately, no one is going to hand you a complete description of the corporate culture or a full explanation of the problems and issues surrounding a company's external climate. Your job as a business communicator is to carefully research information that will help you develop your message. Our friends Robert and Sam, in our opening story, seem oblivious to this need to understand the context for their job search. In order to define the situation completely, they, and we, should follow the steps explained in the next few sections.

Limit the Problem   This step may sound simple, but isolating the significant issues at the root of a problem is often difficult. Focus on the distinct cause of your message. Then, if necessary, break your problem into smaller parts and work on them one at a time. For example, if you are going to talk about ways to prepare a group report for a class, be clear about each person's specific assignment. Divide the work up to avoid omitting important topics, duplicating efforts, or wasting time on issues that don't really relate to your purpose.

Messages arise from problems. Problems arise from issues or areas of concern that need to be addressed.

Evaluate the Problem Within the External Climate   As we noted earlier, it's important to look at the climate in which your particular communication problem or issue exists to determine how this climate affects the problem. Whatever your topic, be aware of factors that influence the organization and your audiences. Find out what's going on in the specific field, in related industries, and in the local and global markets. Keep current on issues that affect you, and update your research regularly.

For example, if your communication challenge is to negotiate a starting salary or hourly rate for your first job, you should find out in advance what other companies are paying and what other students are earning for similar positions in the same industry and geographical area. You can be sure employers offering you jobs have researched what they should expect to pay. Be prepared!

Keep up-to-date on issues that affect you and your message. Industries change quickly, so don't be caught unaware!

Evaluate the Corporate Culture That Impacts the Problem   Keep in mind that the culture of an organization derives from agreed-upon attitudes, values, and beliefs that result in shared behaviors. These accepted behaviors are often

The way people in a company interact, dress, and work can tell you a great deal about its corporate culture.

The culture of an organization is often established by the leader of the group.

established by the leader of the group, such as the president of a company or the professor in a class. For example, the culture of your accounting class may be more formal than the culture of your marketing class, based on the personality and behaviors of the respective professors. Tangible indicators of culture found in any company include:

- Formal versus informal communication styles
- Professional versus casual dress codes
- Rigid versus flexible work hours
- Entrepreneurial risk-taking versus conservative, "safe" attitudes

A communication strategy that would be appropriate in a small, informal, flexible organization might be completely inappropriate in a larger one that is more formal and structured.

Define Your Audience

Most people spend too little time on careful audience analysis.

The second part of defining the context includes identifying and learning about your target audiences. Too often people do an inadequate job of analyzing their audience. The more specific information you have about your readers or listeners, the better you can tailor your message to their needs and achieve your goals. The most common mistakes people make are *generalizing* and *assuming* things about their audiences. The following are some steps you can take to be assured that your audience analysis is thorough.

Three types of potential audiences are: the primary audience, the hidden audience, and the decision makers.

Identify All Potential Audiences (Distinct or Overlapping)   This includes the primary audience, the hidden audience, and the decision makers. The *primary audience* is the actual individual(s) to whom you speak or write. This is the person to whom your letter is addressed or the people sitting in front of you when you make a presentation. The *hidden audience* is an indirect receiver of your message, such as a person who hears the message secondhand. This audience may not be directly connected with your communication purpose or process but may have some power over you. For example, a powerful hidden audience can be a significant family member of your primary audience who has considerable influence at home. The *decision maker* is your most important audience. This is the person who has authority to approve your idea, course of action, or project. Since these audiences can overlap, the decision maker might be your primary audience (hearing your speech or reading your letter) or your hidden audience (a manager from another department).

For example, if you are giving a presentation to your class to persuade them to vote for you for a student government office, your primary audience would be the members of the class. They would also be the decision makers, since they have the ability to cast a vote in your favor at election time. Your hidden audience might be other students who know you in other classes and influence your classmates. Your instructor, who evaluates you and grades your presentation, is also a decision maker in this example.

You don't always have a hidden audience, but you should be aware that there is always a possibility of one.

Learn About Each Audience

Collect information about the personal and professional facts, attitudes, wants, and concerns of your audience.

Focus on facts, attitudes, wants, and concerns. To do so, first gather both professional and personal facts about audience members, such as their age, gender, ethnicity, cultural background, education, job responsibilities and status, civic and religious affiliations, and their knowledge of your topic. Ask yourself many questions about your audience to determine what kind of information is likely to get a

Audience "memberships" can overlap and be hidden, so you should take into account all possible audiences when you communicate.

response from them. Talk to anyone who may know the people with whom you are about to communicate, and ask for their opinions. Dig for the answers.

Next, discover your audience's attitudes about you, about your topic, and about actually being present as a receiver of your message. As disillusioning as it may be, the reality is that many people would rather be somewhere else, with someone else, doing something else than listening to your presentation or reading your proposal or report. The hard questions that you must ask yourself are: "What does my audience think about me? What do they think about my topic? What do they think about spending time listening to my speech or reading my letter?"

Next, determine exactly what your audience wants to know. In the Introduction, we mentioned the problems of giving the audience too much or too little information. Your job is to balance between the two. Give your audience what they want to know before you ask them to meet your needs. For example, a problem can arise when a supervisor tells employees only what they *need to know* to do their specific jobs, without regard for information that will motivate them to perform their tasks well. The employees might do as they are instructed but without enthusiasm or commitment. What they may *want to know* is how the project will impact the company or how the customer uses the product. Keeping employees informed about the company in general makes people feel more a part of a team, even if the specific information is not absolutely crucial to their job performance.

Finally, recognize *consistent audience concerns*. Most people with whom you interact on a regular basis express continuing interest in the same issues, such as cost or time constraints. When you have several individuals in your target audience, remember to consider that each might have his or her *own* consistent concerns. At school, for example, you quickly learn what's important to your instructors. Some may be fussy about the appearance of a paper whereas others may stress content or creativity. This learning can be transplanted into any communications atmosphere. At work, you may also quickly learn that one manager is consistently impressed by your client visits whereas another manager appreciates you more when you are in the office. In Chapter 4 we show you a Context Analysis

Ask yourself what your audience thinks about you, about your topic, and about spending time reading your memo or listening to your presentation.

Until you tell your audience what they *want to know* (provide them with some motivation), they will not enthusiastically hear what you *need them to know.*

Consistent audience concerns are those issues that the people you interact with express on a regular basis.

Worksheet with specific questions that will help you get the answers to the kinds of questions addressed here.

Define Your Objectives with Each Audience

The third part of defining the context concerns your objectives with each of your audiences. Most messages, no matter how apparently simple, encompass three objectives: defining your overall goal, identifying the specific purpose of the communication, and acknowledging your hidden agenda.

Define Your Overall Goal

Your overall goal is your ultimate purpose or your long-term plan.

The overall goal reflects your ultimate purpose or long-term plan. You may not actually refer to this goal in your message, but you should recognize where your specific message fits in that overall plan. For example, getting a job in a brokerage firm might be your overall goal, but your specific purpose would be to impress a particular person in a particular interview during the job search process.

Identify the Specific Purpose of the Communication

Your *specific purpose* is what you want your readers or listeners to *do* after you've communicated with them.

The specific purpose of the communication is what you want your reader or listener to do after receiving the message. Identify the specific purpose by combining your needs with your analysis of the target audiences. Pay particular attention to your audience's level of knowledge about your topic. Remember that your primary audience may know a lot about your subject, but your decision maker may need a review of the background information. As a result of this communication, ask yourself exactly what you want your reader or listener to *do*.

Acknowledge Your Hidden Agenda

Finally, as you clarify your intentions about your objectives with the members of your audience, keep in mind that you probably also have hidden agendas—personal goals you want to achieve but don't necessarily talk about. Everybody has hidden agendas, especially successful people. Each time you speak or write, you have an opportunity to work toward your goals. Acknowledge this opportunity and factor it into your planning.

Acknowledge that you probably have hidden agendas—personal goals you want to achieve but don't necessarily talk about.

For example, one hidden agenda might be that you want your internship supervisor to write a letter of recommendation for you at the end of the summer. You wouldn't ask for that favor in advance, but throughout the summer, you can demonstrate the qualities that you would like expressed in your letter when you speak, write, or interact in teams and groups. Then, when it's time to ask, you have a better chance of getting a good recommendation.

In summary, Step 1 of the Strategic Communication Model involves thinking through all relevant information about your situation, audiences, and objectives.

Step 2: Consider Your Media and Timing Options

Select media options that are most appropriate for your message.
Evaluate your timing options.

Now that you understand Step 1, your communication context—the situation, your audience, and your objectives—you can explore the second step in the model: "which" and "when" options.

- Which medium is most appropriate for your message?
- When should the message arrive?

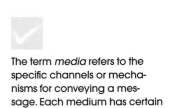

It's important to look at these options in any communication context. Failure to do so may result in the meaning of your message being drowned out by an inappropriate medium or being undermined by awkward timing. The next few sections outline these two substeps, which we will build on in Chapter 5.

Select Media Options That Are Most Appropriate for Your Message

Technology is providing an almost daily increase in media options. In addition to the traditional presentation, letter, memo, interview, meeting, and telephone call, we also have fax, e-mail, teleconferencing, and even multimedia from which to choose when deciding how to send a message. An effective communicator evaluates the pros and cons of each option in relation to the situation, the audience, and the resulting goals. Some issues to consider when choosing a medium include:

The term *media* refers to the specific channels or mechanisms for conveying a message. Each medium has certain advantages, disadvantages, and ground rules.

- The nature of the content (personal or confidential)
- The preparation time and cost involved
- How convenient it will be for the listener or reader to receive the message
- The delivery time required
- Whether there are multiple receivers with different concerns
- The necessity of maintaining a permanent record of the communication
- The appropriateness of nonverbal interaction
- The required response time

Each medium has certain advantages, disadvantages, and ground rules that make it more or less appropriate for a specific purpose. Unfortunately, we too often make our choices about how the message is to be sent based on our *own* communication

Think carefully about how you want to send your message.

habits—what's most comfortable for us—rather than on the preferences of our target audiences or the needs of the situation.

Evaluate Your Timing Options

The timing of a message can have an impact on its effectiveness. For example, a thank-you note sent months late or a sales presentation given before the customer is ready to buy may have little positive effect. Thus, you should consider the needs of your audience in conjunction with your own communication goals when deciding when to send the message. It is important not to communicate only at your own convenience but instead to take into account the convenience of your audience.

Timing is important in delivering any message.

Also think about the sequencing and spacing of your messages, particularly with multiple audiences. Decide which audience is to receive which message and in what order. Also consider how much time to allow between messages. The very process of selecting which audience to tell first communicates a strong message in itself. For example, you wouldn't annoy a senior manager with a question that your direct supervisor could answer. Conversely, the senior manager would never tell you about a policy change before telling your supervisor.

Step 3: Select and Organize Your Information

Review your analysis of your situation, audiences, and objectives.

Compare key organizational patterns and select the most effective one.

Limit your main points.

Enhance your message with powerful support material (visual aids, numbers, and examples).

After you have defined the context of your message and have considered your media and timing options, you can move on to the next step of our Strategic Communication Model—selecting and organizing information. But before you start pulling material and making an outline, make sure you take a moment to follow the first step in the process—that of reviewing your situation, audience, and objectives. The next few sections discuss this step as well as the other steps involved in effectively selecting and organizing your information. Chapter 6 elaborates on this process.

Review Your Analysis of Your Situation, Audiences, and Objectives

Only after you have completed the first two steps in the model should you select an appropriate organizational plan.

As we mentioned previously, a common mistake of inexperienced business communicators is to receive an assignment and immediately begin selecting and organizing information. They overlook or ignore the first two steps in the model. These are the fly-by-the-seat-of-the-pants communicators we talked about earlier. They may be able to get by with a lack of analysis some of the time; however, in today's business environment, "getting by" does not provide you with a competitive advantage. And choosing the wrong information because of poor situation and audience analysis can seriously damage your credibility. Thus, this step includes making sure your assumptions to this point have been correct. Only after you have analyzed your context, considered your options, and are comfortable with your decisions should you select an appropriate organizational plan for the information.

Compare Key Organizational Patterns and Select the Most Effective One

Compare key organizational patterns for the body of your message, select one, and include a complete introduction and conclusion. The introduction grabs your audience's attention, explains what's coming, and establishes the benefit for the receiver. The body of your message follows through on your stated plan. The conclusion summarizes and reinforces your main points and asks for action. Planning an organized message, complete with an introduction and conclusion, ensures that you follow through with the purpose of your communication.

A well-planned message grabs attention and previews what is coming up. It then presents the body, followed by a review of key information in a conclusion.

Limit Your Main Points

Limit the information in the body of your message, focusing on material that offers specific, personal benefit to the individuals receiving the message. Too many people focus on the benefit for the organization, such as increased profits, rather than the benefit for the actual receiver, such as increased salaries or bonuses. In addition, cognitive psychologists tell us that on average, people can only remember between three and seven items. Busy businesspeople are more likely to remember only three. If you give too many reasons to hire you or buy your product, your reader or listener may only remember a few of them, and those may not be your most persuasive points. Fewer main points work better.

Don't try to tell your readers or listeners everything you know—be selective!

Enhance Your Message with Powerful Support Material (Visual Aids, Numbers, and Examples)

No matter how brilliantly you speak or write, your audience will remember your points better when you use interesting support materials. Provide appropriate support with visual aids, numbers, and examples. Good visual aids will draw your audience into your presentation and make it more interesting to them.

Step 4: Deliver Your Message

Develop your writing, speaking, interpersonal, and group skills.

Prepare thoroughly (rehearse your presentations and edit your writing).

Express confidence in your topic and in yourself.

Be yourself (but adapt your style to your audience and situation).

Now that you have defined the context of your message, have considered media and timing options, and have selected and organized your information, you are ready for Step 4 in the model: deliver the message. The term *deliver* is often associated with oral presentations or speeches, but in this book it refers to the more generic process of getting a message to its receivers. Delivery may take the form of spoken messages, writing, nonverbal cues (such as gestures and facial expressions), or visuals and graphics. If you have completed the previous three steps well, delivering your message will be that much easier. However, keep in mind that collecting your information and presenting it are equally important. A good solid presentation can be ruined by poor delivery. Kim, in our opening story, is guilty of failure to deliver effectively. The following are steps you can take to make your delivery more

Delivery may take the form of spoken messages, writing, nonverbal cues, or visuals and graphics.

effective. Chapters 8 through 11 will elaborate on delivering effective messages in writing, oral presentations, meetings, and interviews.

Develop Your Writing, Speaking, Interpersonal, and Group Skills

Developing your writing, speaking, interpersonal, and group skills is a lifelong process of continual improvement. Start with the basics. Learn to speak and write clearly and expressively. Actively look for opportunities to speak, write, and interact in teams and groups. Continually work to develop and display a professional visual image, such as how you dress, how you research and present your support materials, and how you design documents and visual aids.

Prepare Thoroughly (Rehearse Your Presentations and Edit Your Writing)

Research your topic so that your delivery is dynamic and articulate.

Demonstrate the accuracy of your research and analysis with dynamic, articulate delivery. Rehearse presentations and edit written messages. Be prepared to answer questions. Write like you talk—in your own words (but avoid grammatical errors and use common sense about slang or expletives). Avoid reading to your audience or mimicking another person's writing style.

Express Confidence in Your Topic and in Yourself

Your readers and listeners will appreciate your enthusiasm.

Show confidence in your material because you are well-prepared. Exhibit confidence in yourself in all kinds of communication situations, even when things go wrong, such as unexpected interruptions or equipment failure. Let your audience know how enthusiastic you are about your topic.

Allow your personality to show in all your communication.

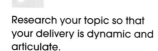

Be Yourself (But Adapt Your Style to Your Audience and Situation)

Most of all, be yourself. Allow your personality to show in all your communication. You are the most important part of your message, and your unique personality is your most valuable delivery skill. However, keep in mind that you may need to adapt your style to meet each audience's expectations in their corporate culture.

You are the most important part of your message, so be yourself!

Step 5: Evaluate Feedback for Continued Success

Give feedback.

Solicit feedback.

Receive feedback.

Evaluate yourself with the Credibility Checklist.

Effective communication is an ongoing process of practice and improvement. Yes, you have to get feedback, and no, you won't get any better by communicating the same way over and over. If you always do what you've always done, you'll always get what you've always gotten. Feedback-based changes are crucial to improvement. With good feedback, Robert, Kim, and Sam would see how they were hurt by the lack of research, preparation, and practice.

You won't improve your communication skills without applying feedback.

Improvement in communication skills is based on realistically evaluating feedback from your target audiences and trusted colleagues. Apply all four parts of the feedback process—giving, soliciting, and receiving feedback, and evaluating yourself with the Credibility Checklist—as described in the following sections. Chapter 12 provides a great deal more information about how to give, get, and use feedback—a crucial aspect of the Strategic Communication Model.

Give Feedback

If you only offer positive feedback to other people, you are cheating everyone. The speaker or writer will miss the opportunity to learn from matching your perceptions—what you heard or read—with his or her intentions—what the speaker or writer meant for you to hear or read. You, as an evaluator, will miss the opportunity to learn from recognizing your own shortcomings that you may see in someone else's work.

Learn about your own communication skills by reading other people's writing and watching other presentations.

Truly useful feedback points out a need for improvement and offers suggestions for how to make that improvement without discouraging the person who prepared the message. The following are some basic guidelines for giving good feedback:

- Describe something positive first (such as, "Your letter made a lot of good points . . .")
- Express constructive criticism in terms of "I" (such as, "I needed to know more about . . ." or "I didn't understand . . .")
- Give a specific example (such as, "For example, I couldn't follow your description of . . .")
- Offer an option for a solution (such as, "Perhaps if you could show me that information on a chart . . .")
- Close with another positive statement (such as, "Your idea shows promise. With a bit more clarification of the budget, I think we'll be ready to make a decision.")

You'll learn more from constructive feedback than you will from an insincere pat on the back.

Cartoon by Bradford Veley, Marquette, Michigan.

Solicit Feedback

To be an effective business communicator, you need to ask for feedback.

The individual who gives feedback is not the only person responsible for improving communication. To be an effective business communicator, you also need to reach out for feedback. "So, how'd I do?," however, may not be the best question to ask if you really want thoughtful feedback. You may hear "Great!" and feel better, but you won't get the information you need to learn and grow. Instead, ask open-ended questions that avoid single-word responses.

The following are three simple guidelines for soliciting the kind of feedback that will help you improve your communication:

- Identify individuals—people you trust—who can provide you with the feedback you need.
- Ask them *in advance* to evaluate your presentation or document.
- Specify areas where you need them to pay close attention.

Receive Feedback

Be responsive to feedback from others; don't be overly defensive and don't overreact.

Try to avoid behaviors that are not constructive when receiving feedback, such as over-reacting, disregarding, or blaming others. None of these reactions will help you improve as a communicator. Instead, use the following positive attitudes and behaviors:

- Develop a feedback-receptive attitude—be open.
- Listen carefully to comments and take notes in detail if appropriate.

- Ask for specific information and examples; then repeat these back to the person giving the feedback for clarification.
- Notice nonverbal messages from your audience. (These can tip you off as to how well you are *really* doing.)
- Correct in the direction of the evaluation—don't overreact.
- Accept responsibility for any needs and changes.
- Recognize that whatever your audience perceives, real or not, is very real to them—show appreciation for their point of view.

Evaluate Yourself with the Credibility Checklist

The most important element of your communication strategy is to project credibility. If your audience perceives that you are credible—if they believe you, trust you, have confidence in you—you will be more persuasive as a communicator. And if you are persuasive, you will get what you want: You will achieve the specific purpose of your message.

Your credibility is based on your audience's perception of four key characteristics—your goodwill, expertise, power, and confidence.[2] These four characteristics make up what we will call the Credibility Checklist. This checklist is your way of double-checking your decisions throughout the Strategic Communication Model process. The following are the four major characteristics that make up the Credibility Checklist. Chapter 12 discusses the Credibility Checklist in greater detail.

In any communication, the only reality is the perception of the audience—your intention and how credible you think you are don't count.

1. Goodwill: Your Focus on and Concern for Your Audience

Let your audience know that you are aware of their personal and professional facts, their attitudes, and their consistent concerns.

Goodwill is your audience's perception of what you think of them. If you don't convince your audience of your goodwill, they will not believe in you as a speaker. You can best project goodwill by thoughtfully selecting information based on your analysis of your audience, situation, and objectives. If you haven't thought carefully about the people hearing your presentation, reading your e-mail, or conducting your interview, you won't come off as credible or earn their goodwill. By demonstrating your goodwill to your audience, you help them decide what you think about them—how unique they are, how special they are, and how important they are to you.

2. Expertise: Your Education, Knowledge, and Experience

You can best project expertise through illustrative examples that demonstrate your knowledge, education, and experience.

Expertise is your audience's perceptions of facts about you. This characteristic can be a little difficult to convey because you don't want to appear arrogant or brag about what you know. Thus, you can best project expertise through illustrative examples that demonstrate your knowledge, education, and experience. Share work, school, or personal experiences to convey relevant and impressive facts about yourself.

3. Power: Your Status, Prestige, and Success

Power is your audience's perception of what other people think about you.

Power is your audience's perception of what other people think about you. Power arises from formal positions, associations with others who have power, authority you have earned, and your accomplishments. You will best project power by selecting material that refers to your rank (for instance, you can use an example that reminds your audience that you are their supervisor) and illustrates your successes (for instance, you can use an example of a successful decision you made elsewhere). Look for opportunities to tactfully mention any recognition that would illustrate power to this specific audience. Keep in mind that success is "transferable"—for example, an accomplishment as president of a student organization illustrates leadership ability that you can apply on the job, such as being the project leader of a self-directed work team.

You will be confident if you carefully and thoroughly prepare.

4. Confidence: The Way You Present Yourself and Your Message

People who are perceived as confident are generally thought to have more goodwill, expertise, and power.[3] You will best project confidence through excellent communication skills, which always include doing your homework and preparing messages tailored to your audiences' needs and concerns. Once your material is right, it will be easier for you to feel confident. When you feel confident, the audience "sees" that confidence and responds positively.

APPLYING THE STRATEGIC COMMUNICATION MODEL

Let's take a final look at how using the Strategic Communication Model might help the three people we described in the opening story of the chapter. Robert's self-confidence in his interviewing ability may be well founded, but his failure to *define the context* (especially to understand his audiences and their needs) would cost him dearly in a job interview. Had he taken the time to gather information about the company, Robert may have landed a job. Kim's extra effort to *select and organize information* for her presentation is laudable, but her lack of attention to good *delivery skills* hurt her badly. Learning to combine good preparation with a professional presentation will help Kim make her message that much better. And finally, Sam's assumption that the company he was writing to was a tire company made him look uninformed and reflects a failure to *define the context* of his communication effort. Had he done a bit of research, Sam would have realized that his cover letter was inappropriate. In all cases, application of the Strategic Communication Model would have made the likelihood of their communication success much greater.

Summary of Key Ideas

So that's it—an overview of the Strategic Communication Model. We realize that we have thrown a lot of information at you in this chapter, and you may not remember all the details or how the steps flow from one to another. That's okay. The remainder of this book builds on the blueprint described here, and as you read further, you will get a clearer picture of how to use the Strategic Communication Model. What is important at this point is that you remember the five basic steps in the model:

Step 1. **Define the context** of the current situation, your target audiences, and your objectives with each of those audiences.

Step 2. Consider **your media and timing options** and select the communication medium that is most appropriate and effective for your message and the best time for the message to arrive.

Step 3. Use that knowledge to **select and organize specific information** to meet your objectives with your audiences.

Step 4. **Deliver your message** with a confident, personal style.

Step 5. **Evaluate feedback** for continued growth and success.

If you apply the Strategic Communication Model to all of your business communications, you will be more credible and more persuasive when you write, present, interview, or interact in teams and groups.

Application Activities

Activity 1-1 Defining a Context

A good way to start understanding the Strategic Communication Model is to apply it to real situations in your communications class. Let's work our way through the first step of the model with typical questions that you might ask yourself when you are planning to communicate in this class. For the purpose of this activity, focus on this class in general, not on a specific assignment.

Interactive CD-ROM Exercises

Analyze the following and write your responses. (Writing is the best way to develop critical thinking skills. Just thinking about these factors will be far less valuable.) You need not follow any specific writing format, but a question-answer pattern works well for many people.

1. **Define the Situation.** To accurately define the context, first define the situation. In this case, your situation is what you must communicate in this communication class, including everything involved with taking a particular class. To effectively define the situation, you must understand the culture of your class.

   a. **Limit the problem.** Identify the important issues of this class so that you can limit the problem. For example, what is the outcome you hope to achieve through the messages in this class? To fulfill a class requirement? To get an A in this class? To express genuine opinions that you want to share? What else?

   b. **Evaluate the problem within the external climate.** What have you heard about business communication classes in general? What have you heard about other communication classes at your school? What other classes and activities are you involved in this semester? What else?

c. **Evaluate the corporate culture that impacts the problem.** Each class you take has a distinct culture based on the class format, the tone set by the professor, and the mix of students in the class. How is this class different from, and the same as, other classes? What seem to be some shared values, attitudes, and behaviors of the class members? How do your instructor's personality, teaching style, and stated expectations affect the class? What else?

2. **Define Your Audience.**
   a. **Identify all potential audiences (distinct or overlapping).**
      ■ Primary: To whom will you actually present your point of view?
      ■ Decision maker: Who picks you for teams? Who makes class assignments or grades you? Anyone else?
      ■ Hidden: Are there any hidden audiences? Who might influence the perspective of your other audiences?
   b. **Learn about each audience.**
      ■ Professional and personal facts: How much do you know about your instructor's and your classmates' age, gender, education, work experience, extracurricular activities and interests, civic and religious affiliations, ethnicity, and cultural background? List as much information as possible.
      ■ Attitudes about you, your topic, and whether your audiences want to receive your message: How do you think your classmates feel about you? How do you think their opinions will influence their response to the topics you will write and speak about? How do you think your instructor feels about having you in class? What else?
      ■ Their wants and your needs: What do you think your classmates want from you? What does your instructor want? What do you need from them?
      ■ Consistent concerns: In general, what do students want to get from a class and from each other? How about what your instructor wants?

3. **Define Your Objectives with Each Audience.**
   a. **Define your overall goal.** By the end of this class, what would you like to have achieved with your instructor? With your classmates?
   b. **Identify the specific purpose of the communication.** This will vary with each assignment, but how do you think you will combine what you want to achieve with a particular assignment with what you know about the wants and needs of your instructor and classmates?
   c. **Acknowledge your hidden agenda.** What kinds of private goals do you have? How do you think a business communication class can help you reach these goals?

If you take the time to carefully define your context, you are well on your way to discovering the value of using the Strategic Communication Model. If you have difficulty answering some of these questions, don't worry too much. The remainder of the book will give you much deeper insight into the model.

Activity 1-2 Considering Your Media and Timing Options
Working with three to five other students, complete the following:

1. Make a list of all the various media people use to communicate.
2. List the pros and cons for choosing each medium. (Hint: What's good for one situation and audience may be bad for another situation and audience.)
3. List examples or personal experiences in which choosing the wrong medium or sending a message at the wrong time had a negative effect on the communicator's success.

4. Compile a master list of media and compare experiences among all the groups in the class. What do these experiences say about the importance of selecting appropriate media and timing for messages?

Bonus activity: After you have completed the activity, think about the other members of your group. What did you learn from working with them that would help you conduct an audience analysis of your class?

Activity 1-3 Selecting and Organizing Information and Delivering Your Written Message

Please visit the interactive CD-ROM included with your text to take advantage of the grammar assessment tool. Not only will you identify the areas within grammar and punctuation where you need work, you will also be given an opportunity to do several exercises to improve your skill in that area.

Grammar Assessment

1. Review the parts of your context analysis from Activity 1-1 that asked you to analyze your instructor.
2. Write a memo to your instructor identifying three issues that are challenges to you when you communicate. Do your best to select communication challenges you face or anticipate facing that relate to school or work rather than home and family.
3. Your memo should be one page and should follow a standard memo format. Examples of memo formats are available in Reference Tool D, "Formatting Written Documents," or you may use the standard templates in your word processing software (Word™, WordPerfect™, etc.). Review Step 3 (Select and Organize Information) of the Strategic Communication Model for hints on what information to include in your introduction and conclusion. The body of your memo should list the three issues and the reason why each is a communication challenge. Figure 1-2 is an example of a memo that would fulfill this assignment.
4. Your instructor will evaluate your memo on content (three issues and the reasons), clarity (how easy it is to read), correctness (grammar and punctuation—see Reference Tool A, "Avoiding Common Grammar, Punctuation, and Usage Mistakes," if you have questions), organization (introduction, body, and conclusion), and professional appearance (see Reference Tool D, "Formatting Written Documents," for memo formats).

Activity 1-4 Selecting and Organizing Information and Delivering Your Oral Message

1. Review your entire context analysis of your class and your instructor.
2. Prepare a two-minute presentation to the class. Your specific purpose is to persuade the class that you would be a good team member for a communication class project. Therefore, you should select information about yourself that would benefit a team of your peers who are working together toward a common goal.
3. Organize your presentation to include an introduction, body, and conclusion. Your introduction should grab your audience's attention, state your purpose, preview your main points, and show some personal and specific benefit for the listeners. The body of your presentation should contain two to four facts about you with stories that explain those facts. Illustrate each fact with a prop. (For example, a day planner might illustrate that you are organized. A phone might illustrate that you stay in touch. A photo of your dog might illustrate that you are loyal. Your Greek organization T-shirt might illustrate that you are social and popular. A keepsake from a foreign city might illustrate that you have had

Figure 1-2
Example Memo

Memorandum

To: Professor Epstein
From: Leslie Dillon
Date: April 1, 2001
Subject: My Three Communication Challenges

Even though I have been communicating one way or another since I was born, I still have communication challenges. The three that I would like to explain are the ones that I will work on in this business communication class.

Talking Without Thinking
My first communication challenge is that my mouth sometimes works ahead of my brain. This is a problem when I say the wrong thing because I didn't take the time to consider the potential results of saying the wrong words. I need to learn that I don't always have to have the first answer or the quickest comeback.

Writing Without Reading
My second communication challenge is that I sometimes fire off e-mails too quickly. This is a problem when I don't proofread what I have written. It is also a problem when the words that I write look different on the screen than how they sounded in my head. It's also a problem when the wrong person receives my e-mail, either because I sent it by mistake or because the person I sent it to forwarded my message. I need to learn to take time to read my written messages carefully and to think about everyone who might read them.

Doing Without Listening
My third communication challenge is that I often act too fast. This is a problem when I get an idea and race off to do something about it without paying attention to all the details. Right now, I do this most often in classes when I do my homework without really paying attention to all the instructions from the teacher. I need to learn to listen very carefully and ask questions about what I don't understand before I start to work on something. If I don't, even if I get a good job when I graduate, I won't keep it.

I hope to work on thinking, reading, and listening so that my talking, writing, and doing will improve. Otherwise, I suppose I will have the communication skills I had as a baby: crying a lot.

international exposure.) Your conclusion should tell your audience what you want them to remember (a summary of your main points), confirm what you want them to do (select you for their group), and close with a strong final statement (which may refer back to your attention-grabber).

4. Practice your presentation so that you can deliver it by referring to an outline. Do not write it word for word. Look at all the members of your audience, and talk directly to each of them. Be yourself, show enthusiasm, and have fun.

5. Your instructor will evaluate you on content (how relevant it is for your audience), organization (all the points in the introduction, body, and conclusion), and delivery (spontaneity and enthusiasm).

Activity 1-5 Evaluating Feedback

1. As you listen to your classmates' two-minute presentations, make a list of one good aspect of each speech and one aspect that needs work. Try to consider elements of content, organization, and delivery.
2. Review the "Give Feedback" section of Step 3 in the Strategic Communication Model. When your instructor asks for areas that you identified as needing work, practice the pointers for giving useful and motivating feedback to your peers.
3. Review the "Receive Feedback" section of Step 3 in the Strategic Communication Model. When your classmates discuss areas that need work that might pertain to you, practice the pointers for responding to this useful feedback.

Career Activity

Career Activity 1-1 Following Up on an Internship Opportunity

Juan was happy to learn that his business communication professor had scheduled Charita Miles as a guest speaker. Ms. Miles was an advertising account executive at Jarrett Advertising, and Juan was eager to learn about her career. Ms. Miles was a dynamic speaker who captivated the audience by showing popular advertisements and then explaining the strategy behind them. Juan was fascinated by what he learned and spoke with Ms. Miles after the presentation. She encouraged Juan to apply for a summer internship at Jarrett and gave him her card.

Juan wanted to make sure that Ms. Miles remembered him, so he immediately picked up the phone and called her voice mail. This is what he said:

> "Hi, Charita. You probably don't remember me, but this is Juan Mendoza from Parker Business School. I really, really enjoyed your presentation today and hope that you will consider me for a summer internship. Chicago is the perfect place for me to spend the summer because I have family there. Um . . . I really like advertising and I think an internship with Jarrett Advertising would look great on my résumé. Hey, I look forward to seeing you this summer."

The voice mailbox interrupted: "If you are satisfied with your message, press 1. If you would like to delete and rerecord, press 2." Juan breathed a sigh of relief and quickly deleted the message. "That wasn't what I intended to say at all!" Juan thought, "I'd better think this through."

After the near-disaster with the voice mail, Juan reviewed his communication model and wrote the letter in Figure 1-3 to Ms. Miles.

After reading Juan's letter, answer the following questions:

1. Did Juan accurately define his audience in the voice mail? In the letter?
2. Does Juan have a clear objective in the voice mail? In the letter?
3. What are the benefits of the voice-mail medium for Juan? What are the benefits of the written medium?
4. Was Juan's timing appropriate?
5. Did Juan provide enough information in the voice mail? In the letter?
6. In the voice mail, what evidence does Juan provide that will persuade Ms. Miles that he will be a contributing intern? What about in the letter?
7. What benefit does Juan offer Ms. Miles? In the letter? In the voice mail?
8. Was Juan's tone appropriate in the voice mail? In the letter?
9. What feedback would you give Juan on his voice mail? On his letter?

Figure 1-3
Juan's Letter to Ms. Miles

Juan Mendoza
123 Main Street
Hillsboro, TX 76645
876.458.9887

September 3, 2001

Ms. Charita Miles
Senior Account Executive
Jarrett Advertising
327 Michigan Avenue
Chicago, IL 60657

Re: Request for Summer Internship

Dear Ms. Miles:

Jarrett Advertising's slogan, "Reach for the stars," summarizes my approach to life. Like your company's founder, Martin Jarrett, I believe that success can only come through hard work and creativity. Please consider me as a candidate for a summer internship at Jarrett Advertising.

As an intern at Jarrett, I will contribute my knowledge of the Latin American community. During your presentation, you mentioned that Jarrett recently added two new products that are marketed to the Latin American community. I have lived in Latin American communities in both Dallas and Miami, so I am familiar with the domestic Latin American community. As the son of a U.S. Army officer, I have lived in both Puerto Rico and Santiago, Chile. I speak and read Spanish fluently.

Ms. Miles, thank you for speaking at Parker Business School and sharing your story with us. I have enclosed my résumé to tell you more about myself. I will call you on Monday, September 12, to answer any questions you may have.

Sincerely,

Juan Mendoza

Juan Mendoza

myPHLIP Companion Web Site

Learning Interactively

Visit the myPHLIP Web site at www.prenhall.com/timm. For Chapter 1, take advantage of the interactive "Study Guide" to test your chapter knowledge. Get instant feedback on whether you need additional studying. Read the "Current Events" articles to get the latest on chapter topics, and complete the exercises as specified by your instructor. Expand your learning with a visit to the "Research Area." There you will find a wealth of information you can use to complete your course assignments.

Notes

1. A variation of the Strategic Communication Model was introduced by Sherron Bienvenu in *The Presentation Skills Workshop* (New York: AMACOM, 2000). This model is a derivation of the CrossTalk Communication Model, introduced by Sherron Bienvenu Kenton and Deborah Valentine in *CrossTalk: Communicating in a Multicultural Workplace* (Upper Saddle River, NJ: Prentice Hall, 1997).
2. Sherron Bienvenu introduced the first version of the four-dimensional credibility model in "Speaker Credibility in Persuasive Business Communication," *The Journal of Business Communication*, Spring 1989, pp. 143–158. A derivation appeared in *CrossTalk: Communicating in a Multicultural Workplace* (Upper Saddle River, NJ: Prentice Hall, 1997). Bienvenu introduced the current version in *The Presentation Skills Workshop* (New York: AMACOM, 2000).
3. D. K. Berlo, J. B. Lemert, and R. J. Mertz, "Dimensions for Evaluating the Acceptability of Message Sources," *Public Opinion Quarterly*, 33, (1969), 563–575.

Step 2. Consider
Your Media and
Timing Options

Step 1. Define
the Context

SKILL OBJECTIVES

After you have studied this chapter, you should be able to:

- Define what is meant by the *functional* nature of business communication.
- Recognize elements of the situation, audience, and objectives that will have an impact on your message's success.
- Choose appropriate media and timing options for a given message.
- Select and organize message information to create an effective introduction, body, and conclusion.
- Strengthen your message's introduction by using clear content preview, gaining the readers' attention, and establishing specific and personal benefits to them.
- Tell readers which information is most important by using three types of access techniques for emphasis.
- Present your message in a lively, economical manner using simple, familiar wording, uncomplicated sentence structure, and short paragraphs.
- Use feedback to proofread and edit your document as well as to determine the success of your message.

Step 3. Select
and Organize
Your Information

Step 5. Evaluate
Feedback for
Continued Success

Step 4.
Deliver
Your
Message

Introduction to Business Writing: Foundation Skills for Writing Well

CHAPTER 2
SKILL
FOCUS:

Applying the Strategic Communication Model to Written Communication

2

COMMUNICATING WITHOUT A STRATEGY

The Message That Doesn't Quite Do It

"Look at these letters I get," Jason said to Maren as they sorted through a day's correspondence in his office. "My in-box runneth over—and some of these letters are ridiculous. Just yesterday I received a neatly addressed envelope with nothing in it! I've received so many strange letters and memos, I actually keep a file called 'stupid writing examples.' It can be pretty amusing."

He pulled out a letter and showed it to Maren. "Here's one from an office machine manufacturer. It's dated November 30 and it starts with 'In response to your letter of August 3. Nice quick response, huh? And then all it says is 'please contact the VWA Corp. of America."

"I don't get it," said Maren.

"Me, neither. I have no idea what the August letter asked for, and I have even less idea why I should contact VWA! Oh, here's another of my personal favorites—I just got this one from the benefits office. I think it is trying to say something about changes in our benefits, but it lost me with this great phrase buried in the second paragraph. 'nonexempt employees should bring documentation of their 401K distribution preferences and all account identification numbers.' Does that make sense to you?" Maren laughed and shook her head.

"My all-time favorite bad writing example is the instruction manual I got with my computer," said Maren. "I bought a basic personal computer, and the manual is aimed at a computer scientist. I could swear it was written in some alien tongue posing as English. I would read paragraphs over and over again, and I'd still have absolutely no idea what I was supposed to do."

Jason nodded. "I wonder why some writers just don't get it. If only they'd think about their readers once in a while."

Have you ever read a letter or a document that just doesn't make sense? The message clearly tells you that the writer has done little to make the document useful or has failed to enclose something necessary to convey the message. The time and effort spent on the "communication" are utterly wasted. In the business world, this is not terribly uncommon. Perhaps it is because organizations produce so many letters, memos, and other documents. More likely, it is because the people who write them are not applying good communication principles.

This chapter will teach you how to apply the five-step Strategic Communication Model to business writing. It will lay out the basic foundation skills, discussing how you can apply each step in the model to your business writing to make it more effective. Chapter 8 will build on the foundation skills you learn in this chapter to help you write with accuracy and professionalism.

Business Writing Is Functional Writing

Business writing is functional writing—it seeks specific results.

Business writing—the kind of writing that serves the needs of organizations and their customers—is *functional* writing; it seeks to accomplish specific tasks. Therefore, business writing is obviously different from other types of writing, such as personal letters, poetry, or fiction. The difference between literature and business writing is similar to the difference between culture and agriculture. In business you're concerned with the *yield*. This is not to say that your writing should be so utilitarian as to be abrupt, abrasive, or overly blunt. Such writing could damage your credibility. As a business writer your challenge is to be functional—accomplish a specific task—while also projecting favorable credibility. If you don't know precisely what you are trying to accomplish, your reader will not know what to do with your message.

Since your task is *functional* writing, your challenge is to get readers to *do* something or to *think* in some way they would not had they not received the message. One way to ensure that your writing is indeed functional is to apply the Strategic Communication Model. Each step in the model supports the process of maintaining a functional focus in your writing by having you ask yourself some important questions. Let's review the steps and questions:

Each step in the Strategic Communication Model supports the process of maintaining a functional focus.

- **Step 1: Define the context.** Is this message necessary? Does it respond to a particular need or problem? Do you have a clear idea of what you want to accomplish? Is your big idea something you can realistically achieve? Is your message addressed to the right person(s)? Have you thought carefully about your target audience(s)?
- **Step 2: Consider your media and timing options.** Is this message best delivered via written media? Are you certain that you need to write this? Would other ways of communicating be more effective? Is this a good time to write?

- **Step 3: Select and organize your information.** Does this writing contain the right information, and is it well organized for understanding? Have you covered all necessary points? Do you have a reasonable number of main ideas that can be arranged in ways the reader will comprehend?
- **Step 4: Deliver your message.** Have you prepared thoroughly? Can this writing deliver your message appropriately? Is your planned message one that can be produced to look and sound professional?
- **Step 5: Evaluate feedback for continued success.** Have you polished and edited the message before you sent it? Did you seek input from others to be sure the message is effective? Do you offer the receiver an easy way to respond to you?

If you make the Strategic Communication Model an integral part of your message planning and delivery, these five steps will determine the functional quality of your writing—whether it accomplishes its tasks or not. Now let's look more closely at each step as it applies to written communication.

Step 1: Define the Context for Your Written Message

To determine whether your document is necessary and appropriate, you need to consider the specific situation, your target audiences, and your objectives. To whom should you send the message in addition to the primary receiver? Do people in the organization typically provide copies of written messages to people other than the target reader? Might it perhaps be advantageous to address secondary or hidden audiences for additional impact? Are your communication objectives clear? Do you fully understand what you are trying to accomplish? This may seem like a lot of questions, but such questions can be important in determining your message's effectiveness.

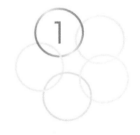

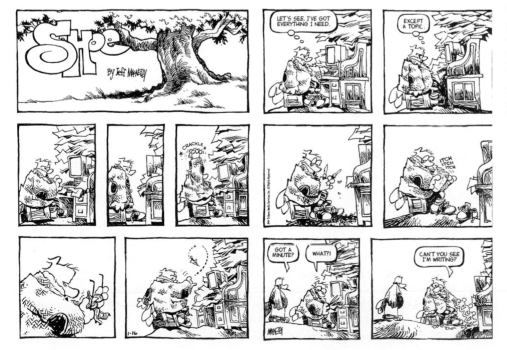

Defining the context can help you write better messages—and break through writer's block!

We knew one young man named Ben who took the time to write a letter thanking the college recruiter who had recommended him for a position he received with BellSouth. Ben sent the letter after he had been working at BellSouth for about six months. His letter included these lines:

> I just wanted to let you know how rewarding my work with BellSouth has been and thank you for helping me get launched. Since you were the very first company person I met, I thank you for setting the stage for my career and for being such a positive role model for me.

The main point of the message was to say thank you and make the recruiter feel a sense of satisfaction in his work. The receipt of an unexpected letter had a powerful impact. The recruiter called Ben and thanked him for the note, expressing surprise that he had taken the time to write it.

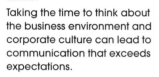

Taking the time to think about the business environment and corporate culture can lead to communication that exceeds expectations.

Before starting to write his letter, Ben took some time to think about his company's business environment and corporate culture. He considered what was expected of him and found a way to exceed those expectations in a positive way. The BellSouth recruiter didn't expect such a positive note because most employees he recruited didn't bother to thank him, especially in writing. Ben was sincere in wanting to thank the recruiter, but he was also aware that his message may have secondary or hidden audiences as well. As it turned out, the recruiter was a good friend of Ben's boss. You can bet the thoughtful letter was mentioned to the boss, providing a positive ripple effect for Ben.

Step 2: Consider Your Media and Timing Options Before Writing

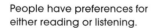

People have preferences for either reading or listening.

As you define the context (Step 1 in the Strategic Communication Model), also consider that some people prefer written documents over oral conversations and vice versa. These preferences can help you in Step 2 of the model. Management guru Peter F. Drucker observes that people have preferences for either reading or listening.[1] Very few people are both reading and listening oriented. Drucker says that quite a few great leaders have risen to the top because they were effective as writers but then failed because their new leadership positions required them to be listeners. When Dwight D. Eisenhower, for example, was a successful speechwriter for General Douglas MacArthur, he could "describe a situation or explain a policy in two or three beautifully polished and elegant sentences." However, Eisenhower as president "was held in open contempt by his former admirers" who considered him a buffoon because he rambled on endlessly with incoherent and ungrammatical sentences.

Reading-oriented people prefer to learn from reading and analyzing written material. The reader type is more comfortable thinking through ideas and expressing arguments in writing. These types of people may lose arguments because they don't come back with the best response as quickly as the listener types. Listener types prefer to pick up information from listening and conversations. They often prefer spoken media. As you define the context for your message, you may want to look for cues that indicate such preferences in your message receiver.

If a communication situation deals with sensitive or personal issues (for example, you need to express dissatisfaction with someone's behavior) or is likely to require an extensive two-way exchange of ideals or impressions, don't rely on writing alone—call or visit. Select a carefully written document, however, if the situation needs to accomplish the following:

- Convey fairly complex, but not highly emotional, information (a list of costs and serial numbers of parts, for example)
- Retain a permanent record of what was said (a proposal for services with prices quoted, for example)
- Project a somewhat formal message (a proposal or a contractual agreement, for example)

FOCUS ON

Visual Versus Auditory People[2]

A field in psychology called neurolinguistic programming (NLP) studies people's information-receiving preferences. Although we all use a variety of senses to perceive and digest information, we each tend to have a preferred way of making sense of the world. About 55 percent of businesspeople prefer to receive information visually. These would be the *reading-oriented* people Peter Drucker refers to in his research. A slightly smaller percentage prefers to receive information through hearing—they have an auditory preference. These are Drucker's *listening-oriented* people.

Paying attention to what people say can give you tips to their preference. Comments such as "How do you think this will *look?*" "I *see* what you are getting at," or "The reports *show* me that . . ." tend to indicate a visual preference. Comments such as "I *hear* what you are saying," "That *sounds* like a good idea," or "I need someone to *talk* to me about this," may indicate an auditory preference for information.

If you want to identify more cues that can indicate a person's preferred way of receiving information, conduct a search on the Internet to get more information about NLP.

Although Dwight D. Eisenhower was a successful speechwriter, he was not regarded as an effective oral communicator.

Reading-oriented people prefer to learn from reading and analyzing written material whereas listener types prefer to learn from spoken messages.

If a communication situation deals with sensitive or personal information or requires an extensive two-way exchange of ideals or impressions, don't rely on writing alone—call or visit.

Disadvantages of written media include high cost and the lack of immediate feedback. In most cases, writing a document is harder work—and more costly—than just talking. Nevertheless, when you need these advantages and can live with the disadvantages, writing makes sense.

Be sure to write promptly. Remember the letters Jason and Moren looked at? The one written almost 4 months after the original request did a poor job of timing and sent an unspoken message by this delay.

Step 3: Select and Organize Your Information

Once you have decided that writing is the best medium for your message, you need to decide the most effective method for organizing and formatting your document, Step 3 in our Strategic Communication Model. In this chapter, as we look at writing basics, we will consider a generic introduction, body, and conclusion. In later chapters, we will show you many ideas for developing effective patterns of organization, different writing styles, and graphic techniques appropriate to various situations.

Write Introductions That Get Attention, Preview Content, and Suggest Reader Benefit

You create expectations about a message and its writer even before you read the entire message.

When you are clear about your main point, put yourself in the shoes of your reader, who may be very busy and is probably being bombarded with many different messages. How can you motivate that person to pay attention to and digest your message? How can you make it easy for the reader to get your message? The answer lies in *reader expectations*.

When readers pick up a memo, letter, or other paper document, or receive an e-mail, they immediately begin to *anticipate*—to form expectations—about the message. These expectations are guesses about the message even before they read it. They also make guesses about the credibility, motives, and intentions of the person writing the message. Psychologists tell us that expectations can have a strong influence on what we hear or read. What we expect is often what we "get"—even when we have to change our perception of the real message to fit our preconceived ideas. In other words, we may psychologically distort or misunderstand a message that says something we did not expect to read. Such distortion damages communication effectiveness.

Expectations, however, can also work in a positive way for the communicator. If what a reader anticipates is confirmed, he or she will better understand the message. It makes sense, then, for the writer to create the most appropriate and positive expectations early in the communication. One of the most effective ways to set the right expectations is simply to tell the reader what the message (or the next section of the message) is about. We do this with *content preview*. Content preview can be general or specific. In either case, it sets the stage for what will follow. The following is an example of general content preview:

> This memo is to provide you with some background ideas on how various campus organizations recruit students.

A more specific content preview gives more details. For example:

> This memo describes your team's product-by-product sales results for last month and the year to date.

In both cases, content preview helps readers focus on what the message will be about and alludes to the value of that information. Readers who have a preview of what the message is about and why it may be valuable to them are more likely to read the message.

In longer documents, the last paragraph of a section can be used to create content preview for the section to follow. This description of the specific items that will be coming up links the parts of the document and helps the overall message flow better. Here is an example:

> This report on our Future Business Leader's club recruiting results will give you an idea of the major challenges we face. The next section of this report will identify the three most significant problems and provides several recommendations for changing our approach to student recruiting.

As these examples show, the easiest way to create content preview is by simply telling the reader what's coming up next. This can be easily done when the message is direct and to the point—when the main point of the message is presented early. However, if your message would work better in an indirect arrangement (such as when conveying bad news or trying to sell the reader), use only general content preview. For example, you would not want to start a sales message by directly saying, "I want to sell you some insurance." That previews the content but may also turn off the reader before you can offer your reasoning. But for most other messages, you can use direct content preview.

Here are some more examples of direct content preview statements:

- *The following report recommends renting the warehouse in the Westside Industrial Park.*

The Expense of Memos[3]

The cost of writing memos has a high price tag, according to a recent study by IWCC Training in Communications, a Toronto consulting firm. Planning, composing, and editing a routine memo takes an average of 54 minutes. This means that writing a memo costs almost $82, based on an annual employee salary of $35,000. And the annual cost of writing one memo per week? $4,258.60.

A good introduction should get your readers' attention and prepare them for the message.

Content preview prepares the reader for the message to follow.

The easiest way to create content preview is by simply telling the reader what's coming up next.

- *This performance review cites three incidents of substandard performance.*
- *In response to your request for a transfer, here are the procedures you'll need to follow.*
- *This business plan shows how an investment of only $5,000 can create a viable vending route that will produce monthly income of at least $600.*

In many cases, the *subject line* serves as the content preview. E-mail has a standard template that includes a subject line. Memos and some letters also use subject lines. A typical memo format with a subject line is shown in Figure 2-1.

To get the most benefit from a subject line, make its wording *informative* rather than simply *topical*. An informative subject line conveys a complete thought; a topical subject line does not. In some cases, a topical subject line is no more than a category for filing the memo. Notice the difference between topical and informative subject lines:

The subject line is an excellent place to create content preview.

Topical Subject Line	Informative Subject Line
Guest Speaker	Sen. Diane Feinstein to be guest speaker at November luncheon
Advanced Management Program	Congratulations on your selection for the Advanced Management Program on May 28
New Policy on Rental Car Insurance	Do not buy the $12 per-day insurance when renting a car
Staff Meeting	April 26 staff meeting at 2 P.M. in room 37

In each preceding case, the informative subject line conveys a complete thought. It need not be a complete sentence but should be an independent clause, that is, a clause that can stand alone in conveying an idea. Using an informative subject line creates clear content preview for the reader.

Informative subject lines convey a complete thought to the reader.

In cases when you choose to place the main point of your message later (such as in bad news messages), you can still use informative subject lines. They will not

Figure 2-1
Typical Memo Format

MEMORANDUM

To: All college seniors

From: Harrison Ford

Subject: New class on anthropology and violence to be offered spring semester

Date: October 15, 2001

[Body of the message]

explicitly reveal the main purpose of the message but still create content preview. Examples:

- *Policy change will affect sales compensation*
- *Update on new pricing schedule effective January 2002*
- *Further details on last week's staff meeting*

Presenting clear content preview is one of the simplest ways for a writer to create realistic expectations in the reader's mind. By doing this, you reduce misconceptions and improve the accuracy of your communication.

A final but equally important function of the introduction is to motivate readers to read the rest of the document. You can best get readers' attention by appealing to their *needs*—establishing some personal benefit that readers will get from reading your message. Phrasing your opening remarks in terms of what readers will gain from this message is often a good strategy. Statements such as, "This memo will give you the data needed for your performance review," or "Here are three proven sales tips for handling customer objections about our new model #223" establish why reading the message will be beneficial to the readers. Then use their expectations to move them toward accomplishing your specific purpose.

Presenting clear content preview is a simple way to create realistic expectations in your reader's mind.

Get readers' attention by appealing to their *needs*. Establish some personal benefit that readers will get from reading your message.

Access Key Information in the Body of the Message

In the body of any message, certain ideas or bits of information are more important than others. One common mistake made in functional writing is the failure to point out which bits of information are, in fact, more important. The following sections explain how you can avoid that mistake.

In business communication, you need to make key ideas obvious.

Give Important Information a Position of Prominence   The more the reader will need to understand certain information, the more *accessible* you should make it. In literary writing, a reader is expected to read through the whole story to find the important material. The author doesn't normally help the reader to do that efficiently. In business communication, you need to make the key ideas obvious. Ideally, a report, letter, or memo should be written so that it need not be read word for word but can be skimmed. The key bits of information should jump out at the reader.

Use Accessing   Virtually any message will include key pieces of information needed for accurate communication and also additional verbiage or "word-packaging." *Accessing* is the process by which a writer points to certain bits of information, helping the reader easily identify the most important parts of a message. Your written message can use three types of accessing: *verbal, psychological,* and *visual.* Each of these will point to the key ideas of the message. Some are subtler than others, and, of course, you can use a variety of accessing techniques within the same document.

Verbal accessing.   Verbal accessing is the use of *word cues* to indicate that a key idea is coming up or has been stated. One way of doing this is to say such things as:

Verbal accessing uses words to point to the most important information.

- *"The most important aspect is . . ."*
- *"This last part is particularly important . . ."*
- *"Please read these instructions carefully . . ."*
- *"Of all the options suggested, one stands out . . ."*

Psychological accessing.   Psychological accessing entails deciding how to arrange information in the message. Three ways to achieve psychological emphasis are order, space, and freshness.

Psychological accessing entails deciding how to arrange information in the message.

The *order of information*—when clearly pointed out to the reader—can help the reader anticipate what is coming next and to remember what has been said. This form of psychological emphasis helps separate the key ideas from the extraneous. The following is an example of ordering information:

> *This report will give you a chronological look at the history of the problem from 1998 to present.* (THIS SENTENCE PROVIDES CONTENT PREVIEW.)
>
> (THE FOLLOWING ARE HEADINGS THE REPORT MIGHT HAVE:)
>
> *1998 to 2000 Gradual Reduction in Market Share*
>
> *2001 Premature Introduction of the Abacus Product Line*
>
> *2002 Resources Spent to Solve Abacus*
>
> *2003 Loss of Key Management Personnel*

Other orders of arrangement that your reader will readily recognize are place comparison ("This report compares districts in the Midwest Region . . .") and cause and effect.

The amount of space that has been devoted to a particular topic helps to indicate its relative importance.

When we talk about *space* in terms of psychological emphasis, we are referring to the relative amount of space devoted to a particular topic. If, for example, a sales letter for a piece of machinery spends several paragraphs describing reliability and only one short line indicating something about its ease of operation, we psychologically determine that reliability is more important than ease of operation.

Finally, psychological emphasis can be achieved through *freshness* by suggesting that the message is a new approach, a catchy idea, or a particularly innovative notion. Imaginative wording such as identifying a problem by a clever phrase can give psychological emphasis to it.

Visual accessing. This form of accessing includes the use of lists, icons, spacing, and so on to allow the reader to skim through the message and gather its important ideas. The following list offers suggestions on visual techniques you can use. We will talk more about design skills and how you can use creative visual design techniques for better accessing in Chapter 7. Visual accessing techniques can include:

Appealing to the reader's curiosity about the freshness of your message helps to make the material more interesting.

- Enumeration: 1, 2, 3, or I, II, III, or a, b, c
- Listing: Such lists are put in columns and can have these notations:
  1. Numerals
  A. Letters
  • Bullets
- "wingdings" (such as ✂ ⊠ ☺)
- CAPITALIZING or **bolding**
- Headings and captions
- <u>Underlining</u> or *italics*
- Borders around paragraphs, pages, or other sections
- Typeface variations using different **FONTS**, *styles,* and SIZES
- Icons, clip art, and simple illustrations
- Colored paper and design borders (which can be purchased at office supply stores ready for your computer printer or photocopier)
- Graphics
- Varied margins and line justifications to "frame" the message
- Use of white space to provide contrast and give audiences a break

Visual accessing uses layout and design techniques to point to key information.

Today's word processing software gives writers a wide variety of accessing capabilities once available only to artists and designers. Take the time to learn about such capabilities, and you'll give added professionalism to your documents while providing better access for your reader. However, be careful not to use too many different visual techniques in the same document. Too much variety gives a busy, cluttered look.

Limit Your Main Points Be sure to keep the number of main points in your message to a manageable number. People can seldom digest more than five main points. Messages with three to five points should be the norm. Some audiences can deal with more complexity, of course, but it is best to strive for the fewest number of main points possible to convey your specific purpose.

Avoid using too many main points.

Write Strong, Action-Oriented Conclusions

The third part of any business message is the conclusion. Business writing almost always requires a conclusion. The most common functions of concluding remarks are to:

- **Summarize:** A summary of main ideas provides a good review for readers. Don't repeat the whole document, of course, but an abbreviated recap can be very helpful.
- **Motivate action:** Since business writing seeks to get readers to do something, you should also motivate them to act. Make the requested action easy for the readers. Say what you want them to do or think in the conclusion of your message. Often, adding a few words about the urgency to act now can get readers to avoid procrastinating.

Voice recognition software allows a computer to translate your spoken words into text.

Concluding remarks function to summarize, motivate action, and leave the reader with something to remember.

■ **Leave the reader with something to remember:** The end of the document is a strong emphasis position, and you should take advantage of that fact. Add a final comment that may recap your theme, add additional motivation, or otherwise reinforce your big idea. Common examples of this are found in many sales letters that include "P.S." comments designed to reinforce or further motivate the reader. For example, a sales letter may close by saying "If you call within a week, you will receive an additional . . .," or an instructional memo may recap the three steps needed to accomplish the specific purpose.

FOCUS ON

Voice Recognition Software[4]

One of the major drawbacks to written communication is the cost of producing messages. It is simply more difficult and time consuming to write than to speak. Many of us who are less than excellent typists look forward to the day we can speak into our computer and have it produce flawlessly written text. To some extent we can do that today with *voice recognition software*—software that allows a computer to translate your spoken words into text. Some software packages claim 98 percent accuracy rates when converting sound to type. However, this isn't as good as it sounds. Business writer Joseph E. Garber comments:

Unfortunately, even 98% is pretty lousy . . . [because] the more words spoken, the bigger the chance of a screw-up. If your computer's odds of getting a single word right are 98%, its odds of getting two words right are 98% of that 98%—or 96%. And the probability of your dictating 200 words into a computer with no problems is not quite 2%.

Still, as technology advances, look for increased performance in voice recognition software and in other software tools.

Step 4: Deliver Your Message with an Appropriate Writing Style

Unless you have a boss or an organizational culture that dictates something else, the vast majority of your business writing is likely to use efficient sentence structure and vigorous, economical language. As always, it is important to use good judgment and to keep your audience in mind when writing any message. The following sections provide useful suggestions and discuss important elements of writing style. Chapter 8 will build on these suggestions to help you write with increased accuracy and professionalism.

Use Efficient Sentence Structure and Short Paragraphs

Long, complex, or compound sentences can damage message efficiency. They slow down both reader and writer. Therefore, use efficient sentence structure in the body of your message. (If you are unclear about sentence structure, Reference Tool A, "Avoiding Common Grammar, Punctuation, and Usage Mistakes," provides a good review.)

Use good judgment and to keep your audience in mind when writing any message.

Sentences should convey bite-sized pieces of information that can be digested by your reader, one piece at a time. The rule of thumb is that, for most adult readers, sentences should average about 16 to 18 words in length. Of course, some sentences may have only two or three words, whereas others can run to 30 or so. This guideline is not intended to be a hard-and-fast formula, but for general readability shorter sentences work better than longer ones.

Shorter, direct sentences deliver clearer messages to your readers.

Another consideration in dealing with sentence length is that different lengths have different effects on readers. Short sentences have punch. They emphasize. They hit hard. However, the potential disadvantage of using only exceptionally short sentences is that they may sound like you are talking down to the reader. Too many very short sentences can create a dogtrot rhythm and sound like a children's book.

Longer sentences, on the other hand, can be useful in deemphasizing information that may be objectionable or unpleasant for your reader. Such information can get "buried" in a longer sentence, which is a good place to put information that you do not want to dwell on, but which may be necessary for understanding. The following is an example of a sentence attempting to hide information:

Longer sentences can be useful in deemphasizing information that may be objectionable or unpleasant for your reader.

> The company is well aware of the unique requirements of this job, which, unfortunately, you have not yet had the opportunity to attain thoroughly, despite your admirable willingness to learn.

The essence of this sentence is "you are not qualified," but the longer construction tries to deemphasize that harsh reality.

Finally, in business and professional writing, paragraphs are often shorter than you'd expect to find in literature, unless you are trying to deemphasize a bit of information. People prefer to read information presented in manageable bits. When people receive a written message with long, heavy-looking paragraphs, they are likely to conclude that the message is going to be hard to read. No one wants to face a page covered with a huge mass of words.

Shorter paragraphs make a document easier to read.

Grammatically, a paragraph should develop one theme, but we have considerable flexibility in choosing when to break to a new paragraph. For functional business writing, paragraphs should rarely exceed six or seven lines. Figure 2-2 shows the visual effect of different paragraph lengths. Which would you prefer to read?

Sentences should convey bite-sized pieces of information that can be digested by your reader, one piece at a time. The rule of thumb is that, for most adult readers, sentences should average about 16 to 18 words in length. Of course, some sentences may have only two or three words while others can run to 30 or so. This guideline is not intended to be a hard-and-fast formula, but for general readability, shorter sentences work better than longer ones. Another consideration in dealing with sentence length is that different lengths have different effects on readers. Short sentences have punch. They emphasize. They hit hard. However, the potential disadvantage of using only exceptionally short sentences is that they may sound like you are talking down to the reader. Too many very short sentences can create a dogtrot rhythm and sound like a children's book. Longer sentences, on the other hand, can be useful in de-emphasizing information that may be objectionable or unpleasant for your reader. Such information can get "buried" in a longer sentence, which is a good place to put information that you do not want to dwell on, but which may be necessary for understanding.

Sentences should convey bite-sized pieces of information that can be digested by your reader, one piece at a time.

The rule of thumb is that, for most adult readers, sentences should average about 16 to 18 words in length. Of course, some sentences may have only two or three words while others can run to 30 or so. This guideline is not intended to be a hard-and-fast formula, but for general readability, shorter sentences work better than longer ones.

Another consideration in dealing with sentence length is that different lengths have different effects on readers. Short sentences have punch. They emphasize. They hit hard. However, the potential disadvantage of using only exceptionally short sentences is that they may sound like you are talking down to the reader. Too many very short sentences can create a dogtrot rhythm and sound like a children's book.

Longer sentences, on the other hand, can be useful in deemphasizing information that may be objectionable or unpleasant for your reader. Such information can get "buried" in a longer sentence, which is a good place to put information that you do not want to dwell on, but which may be necessary for understanding.

Figure 2-2
Long Paragraphs Versus Short Paragraphs

Use Vigorous and Economical Language

Be certain that each word or phrase in your writing carries its weight.

Look carefully at your writing to be certain that each word or phrase carries its weight. Some phrases that show up in poorly thought-out business writing are there because people think that's the way business writing should sound. When inexperienced writers check the correspondence files to see how others have written in the past, they perpetuate what is often poor writing. They may end up using antiquated business phrases such as the ones in the following rhyme:

> We beg to advise you and wish to state
> That yours has arrived of recent date.
> We have it before us; its contents noted.
> Herewith enclosed are the prices we quoted.
> Attached you will find, as per your request,
> The forms you wanted, and we would suggest,
> Regarding the matter and due to the fact
> That up to this moment your order we've lacked,
> We hope that you will not delay it unduly.
> We beg to remain, yours very truly.[5]

Many phrases formerly thought of as good business etiquette are too wordy.

Although an exaggeration, this rhyme illustrates how vitality can be sapped out of a message when buried under these kinds of expressions. In fairness, we should point out that many of these phrases have evolved over time from what was once considered accepted business etiquette. Commerce was rich with formal and excessively polite and flowery phrases in years past. In some cultures, it continues to be so. A recently received letter from a consulting client in Brazil ended with this sentence: "Staying at your disposal, we look forward to hearing from you." In the American business culture, we seldom use such expressions, preferring more economical, conversational language. In fact, led by the expansion of e-mail, business writing is getting increasingly direct, concise, and virtually absent of ornate or flowery expressions.

To achieve economy of language, also work to reduce unneeded repetition and cluttered phrasing. The following sections present some ideas for boosting the vitality of your writing.

Avoid Unnecessary Repetition   Although repeating an idea can be an effective teaching device (especially in oral communication) and a useful form of verbal accessing, unnecessary repetition distracts the reader. Here are some examples:

Needless Repetition	Repetition Eliminated
The general rules for internship participants *will be enforced equally for each and every person.*	The rules will apply to all interns.
In my opinion I think the plan presents a reasonable picture.	I think the plan is reasonable.

Use Economical Wording   Surplus words and cluttered phrases that add nothing to the meaning of the sentence should be dropped. Phrases that can be replaced by a single word or shorter expression should be changed. Here are some examples:

Cluttered	More Concise
In the event that payment is not received . . .	If we do not receive payment . . .
The report is *in regard to the matter of* our long-term obligations . . .	The report is about our long-term obligations . . .
I have just received your letter and wanted to respond quickly.	I wanted to respond quickly to your letter.
The quality of his work is so good that *it permitted us to* offer him a long-term contract.	His work was so good that we offered him a long-term contract.
In this letter we have attempted to answer any possible questions you may have, but if you have further questions, please *do not hesitate to contact us.*	If you have additional questions, please call us.

To achieve a lively and economical language tone, write the way you would talk in a planned, purposeful conversation. For example, if you hand a document to a coworker in your office, you wouldn't *say,* "Enclosed herewith please find the report I've written." In conversation you would be more likely to say, "Here's the report I prepared on . . ." So why not write that way? Conversational language gets to the point and conveys your message efficiently.

Conversational language is usually the most efficient way of phrasing ideas.

Don't bore your audience with vague, abstract language. Write the way you would talk.

Use Clear, Concrete Wording   You improve language efficiency by using clear, specific words rather than vague or abstract ones. Clear wording creates vivid, specific mental images in the mind of your reader. Here are some examples:

Clear words create specific images and ideas in the mind of the reader.

Vague, Abstract Wording	Clear, Specific Wording
Leading student	Top student in a class of 80
Most of our people	87 percent of our employees
In the near future	By noon Wednesday
Lower cost than . . .	$43 less than . . .
Low energy consumption	Uses no more power than a 60-watt light bulb
The cost would be significant	Every student will pay $286 per year

Use Active Voice   You improve language efficiency by using active voice. The grammatical term *voice* refers to whether the sentence is constructed such that the subject of a sentence *acts* or is *acted upon*. If the subject *does the acting*, you are writing in the active voice. If the subject of the sentence is *acted upon*, the passive voice is being used. (Can you hear the difference in the last two sentences?) Here are some examples:

Passive Voice	Active Voice
Each tire *was inspected* by a mechanic.	A mechanic *inspected* each tire.
A gain of 41 percent *was recorded* for paper product sales.	Paper product sales *gained* 41 percent.

Passive Voice	Active Voice
A full report *will be sent* to you by the supervisor.	The supervisor *will send* you a full report.
All figures in the report *are checked*.	The accounting department *checks* all figures in the report.

Active voice tends to be more efficient because it makes your sentences more *explicit, personal, concise,* and *emphatic*:

Most business writing should be in active voice.

- **Explicit:** "The board of directors decided" is more explicit than "A decision has been made." With active voice you know who did what.
- **Personal:** "You will receive our decision" is both personal and specific; "The decision will be mailed" is impersonal.
- **Concise:** The passive voice requires more words and thus slows down both the writing and reading. Compare "Exhibit 2 shows" with "It is shown by Exhibit 2."
- **Emphatic:** Passive verbs dull action. Compare "An analysis was prepared by the intern" with "The intern analyzed . . ."

The clearer relationship between subject and verb in active voice adds force and momentum to your writing. By closely associating the *actor* (noun) and the *action* (verb), you help your reader visualize more clearly what is happening. In some cases, of course, you may intentionally want to deemphasize this association (or remove the actor entirely) by using passive voice. For example, which would you rather report?

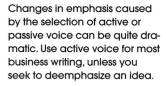

Changes in emphasis caused by the selection of active or passive voice can be quite dramatic. Use active voice for most business writing, unless you seek to deemphasize an idea.

I just deleted your proposal. (ACTIVE)

or

Your proposal has been deleted. (PASSIVE)

Use Simple, Everyday Wording Often a common word can do the job of a multisyllable jawbreaker. A clear correlation exists between how many syllables are in a word and how difficult it is to read and understand. Using many big words slows down both the writer and the reader, as the example in our opening story illustrates. In addition, longer words usually don't communicate any more effectively than shorter ones, despite the increased effort. In the following examples, listen to the differences:

Long and Heavy Wording	Everyday Wording
Polysyllabic verbiage obfuscates comprehension.	Big words block clarity.
Our *analysis* of the *situation* suggests needed *experiential* training to *optimize* the job performance of our employees.	We think our people need more job training.
John *acceded* to the demands for *additional compensation.*	John agreed to pay them more.

Long and Heavy Wording	Everyday Wording
My investment recommendations were *predicated* on the *anticipation* of additional *monetary funds* being made available.	I based my investment recommendations on an expected increase in money available.
Ramifications of our *performance shortfall* included *program discontinuation.*	Since we didn't reach our goal, management discontinued the program.

Some business writers feel they must use technical or formal language to convey the appropriate *image.* You serve only your *illusions* of status with language so technical and stilted that it loses meaning for your receiver. Talk in terms that your reader is sure to understand.

Using many big words slows down both the writer and the reader.

FOCUS ON

Incomprehensible Instructions[6]

The following instructions appeared on actual products. Obviously, these writers did not use the Strategic Communication Model in preparing their messages.

On a Sears hairdryer: *Do not operate while sleeping.*

On a bag of Fritos: *You could be a winner! No purchase necessary. Details inside.*

On some Swanson frozen dinners: *Serving suggestion: Defrost.*

On packaging for a Rowenta iron: *Do not iron clothes on body.*

On Boot's Children's Cough Medicine: *Do not drive car or operate machinery.*

On Nytol sleep aid: *Warning: may cause drowsiness.*

On a Korean kitchen knife: *Warning: keep out of children.*

On Sainsbury's peanuts: *Warning: contains nuts.*

On Tesco's tiramisu dessert (printed on bottom of box): *Do not turn upside down.*

Step 5: Evaluate Your Feedback for Continued Success

The final step in the Strategic Communication Model deals with feedback—giving, soliciting, and receiving it. This feedback will help you evaluate your credibility and, as such, has a bearing on continuous communication improvement. In Chapter 12 we will take an in-depth look at these critical functions, but for now we will mention some ways to get feedback for your written communication.

When writing, you can get two kinds of feedback: that received *before* you send the message and that received *as a result of* sending the message. Before sending a letter, memo, or report, reread it and keep in mind the writing suggestions we discussed earlier in the chapter. (The computer manual Maren describes in our opening story was apparently not reviewed by typical readers). Have you written to the appropriate audience and used the appropriate medium of communication? Is your message well organized? Have you written a strong introduction, a clear body, and a solid conclusion? In doing so, have you used vigorous and economical wording? Have you used the best word in every instance? Are your sentences too long or overly complicated? Have you avoided unnecessary repetition?

When writing, you can get two kinds of feedback: that received *before* you send the message and that received *as a result* of sending the message.

After you have finished looking over your own writing, ask someone else to read your message. The best way to do this is to volunteer to review or proofread other people's documents so that you create a team. Other readers will almost always see something you missed. Typos, missing words, grammar errors, unintended tone problems, or simply confusing language will jump out at another reader while you may miss them. Accept such criticism objectively, and use it to help you write better messages.

Keep in mind also that it is never a good idea to rely only on your word processing program to catch all your spelling or grammar errors. Although these features are very helpful, they do not catch every mistake, so don't let them substitute for careful proofreading. And remember, even important e-mail messages can also benefit from a quick review by a fresh pair of eyes.

The second kind of feedback is the results you get from your message. If you write a request for information and get no responses, you are receiving feedback! Something isn't working, and you may want to revisit your message. The ultimate feedback in business communication is whether your readers do what you want them to do.

One final comment about writing and feedback: No one writes letter-perfect prose the first time around. Writing is a process of drafting and revising, often several times. Plan to revise, revise, and revise. Don't make the mistake of "pride in authorship" in which you feel that because you wrote it and it sounds good to you, it must be perfect. Be open to suggestions, and be willing to rewrite, perhaps several times.

Always proofread your messages before sending them out. If possible, get someone else to check them, too.

No one writes perfect documents on the first attempt. Assume the first time is a rough draft and then edit and polish your work.

Electronic Editing Tools

Word processing programs such as Microsoft Word allow another person to edit your document and insert suggested changes in another color. Using Microsoft's Track Changes tool, you can then look at the changes and decide which changes to accept and which to reject. If a third (or fourth, or fifth, and so on) person wants to add his or her edits, these edits will appear in another color, making it clear who is giving what feedback. Readers can also use the Insert Comment tool to communicate with you. Both of these tools are extremely helpful and can save you time. Figure 2-3 shows an example of a paragraph that has been edited by a number of different users. Comments are indicated by the bracketed and numbered initials.

A. Different colors signify that two different people have edited this document.

Fast Facts: Electronic Editing Features

Word processing programs such as Microsoft Word allow another person to edit your document and type in his or her suggested changes in red or another color. Using Microsoft's Track Changes tool, you can then look at the changes and decide which changes to accept and which to reject. If a third (or fourth, or fifth, and so on) person wants to add his or her edits, these edits will appear in another color, making it clear who is giving what feedback. Readers can also use the Insert Comment tool to communicate with you. Both of these tools are extremely helpful and can save you time.

B. Brackets enclosing an editor's initials signify that a comment has been inserted. Double-click on the bracketed box to view the comment's contents or select View, Comment.

C. A vertical line in the margin indicates that changes have been made to the corresponding line of text.

Figure 2-3   Example of the Track Changes and Insert Comment Tools in Action

APPLYING THE STRATEGIC COMMUNICATION MODEL

Think back on the opening story of Jason and Maren and the "stupid writing examples." The writers of those documents could benefit from using the Strategic Communication Model by carefully *defining the context* (especially thinking about their audience—the reader), *considering their media and timing options* (not waiting four months to answer a letter), and *selecting and organizing appropriate information.* The empty envelope reflects simple carelessness, but other messages may have been better delivered with a phone call (instead of a letter) or even a presentation (the benefits department instructions). Use of written media precludes most immediate feedback, and these writers may never know that these writing efforts were wasted.

When applying the Strategic Communication Model to your own writing, remember that, regardless of the message, information must be *selected, organized,* and *delivered* with the reader clearly in mind.

Summary of Key Ideas

- Business writing is *functional* writing. It should always focus on a particular result.
- Good writers learn to adjust their message and writing style as dictated by their situation, their audiences, and their objectives with each audience. They should carefully consider their overall goal, specific purpose, organizational environment, and the nature and characteristics of readers (primary, secondary, and hidden) when preparing their communication.
- A strong introduction should include clear content preview that creates appropriate expectations in the minds of the readers, grabs their attention, and establishes reader benefit.
- The body of a message should be limited to main points that are relevant to the audience and that they can remember. Typically, three to five main points are ideal.
- The conclusion of most business documents should summarize, include a clear action step, motivate action, and provide a memorable close.
- Accessing adds verbal, psychological, and visual emphasis to important ideas in a message, thus helping your reader understand the main point.
- Most of today's business writing calls for an efficient, conversational style using simple sentence structure.
- Message efficiency is achieved through economy of language, simple conversational wording, and active voice.
- Message effectiveness is determined by the degree to which the letter clearly conveys the message, projects a favorable image of the writer, and accomplishes the specific purpose.
- Feedback for the writer takes two forms: that received when proofing the draft message and that received after the message is sent.

Application Activities

Activity 2-1 Applying Information Sharing and Image Building
Every letter does two jobs: (1) It *conveys a message,* and (2) it *projects an image* of its writer. Writers should normally be concerned with both information sharing and image building in their documents. Going back to our earlier discussion of word

choices, people who insist on using professional jargon in an attempt to feed their sense of elitism may convey a learned image but will soon turn off readers who can't figure out what they are saying. Such "impressive-sounding" letters may stroke the writer's ego, but they only frustrate the reader.

Interactive CD-ROM Exercises

Conversely, the writer who spits out cold, heartless, but fact-filled sentences with great precision may seem like a well-programmed android. Good business letters are more than pure information transfer; they also involve impressions and expressions of humanity. Even when mass-printed by a computer, professional letters can sound like you are chatting over the back fence with your neighbor. Letter effectiveness arises from both the informational and the "human" content of the message. With these thoughts in mind, complete the two steps in the following assignment:

1. Figures 2-4, 2-5, and 2-6 (pages 48, 49) present three sample letters. We have deleted the addresses and present only the body of the messages. Review these three letters.
2. In light of what we have discussed in this chapter, describe your impressions of the relative clarity and image projected by these letters. Look for writing that reinforces or varies from what we have discussed. Suggest how you could improve each letter. Pay special attention to the quality of the letter's attention-grabber, benefit for reader, content preview (or lack of it), accessing, closing remarks, and language use.

Activity 2-2 Searching for the Message's Critical Information

Review the sample letters in Figures 2-4, 2-5, and 2-6 on pages 48 and 49. Look for the words or phrases that communicate the most essential information—that is, the information without which the message would not work. Identify these words or phrases using a highlighter. Where does the writer position these? Are these key bits of information well accessed? Is this the way you would write the letters? If not, what would you do differently? Why?

Activity 2-3 Completing Letter Rewrites

Please visit the interactive CD-ROM included with your text to take advantage of the grammar assessment tool. Not only will you identify the areas within grammar and punctuation where you need work, you will also be given an opportunity to do several exercises to improve your skill in that area.

Grammar Assessment

Select one of the sample letters in Figures 2-4, 2-5, and 2-6 and rewrite it based on the ideas discussed in this class. Be prepared to explain why you rewrote it as you did.

Activity 2-4 Making a Case for Accessing

Please visit the interactive CD-ROM included with your text to take advantage of the grammar assessment tool. Not only will you identify the areas within grammar and punctuation where you need work, you will also be given an opportunity to do several exercises to improve your skill in that area.

Grammar Assessment

1. Write a short report (two to three pages) discussing why accessing is important in business communication. (Review Reference Tool D, "Formatting Written Documents," for information on formatting a short business report.)
2. Address your report to your peers at school who have not taken a business communication class yet. Remember that your instructor is both your hidden audience and the decision maker who will grade your paper.
3. Include your thoughts on when you may want to avoid accessing key ideas. Describe some examples that will be relevant to your primary audience.

Figure 2-4
Sample Letter 1

Was it something we said? Or didn't say?

You've been one of our most valued customers, and we've been committed to serving you well. If we haven't completely satisfied you, please let me know what we might have done differently. I can assure you that when an important customer like you hasn't called on us recently, we take a fresh look at the way we do business.

If it wasn't something we said, did one of our competitors woo you away? If so, I'm certain we can provide you with a level of service that no one else can match. Your satisfaction is our goal, and we have expanded our staff and broadened our product selection to better meet your needs. This illustrates our undying commitment to preserve our most valued business relationships.

We miss you. So tell me—what can we do to regain your business? Please call me or visit soon.

Sincerely,

[signature]

Figure 2-5
Sample Letter 2

Thank you for your interest in ZelCo Manufacturing. We appreciate your letting us know of your availability, and we're glad you think ZelCo is worth it.

The problem is that we don't have a position open right now that matches your background and experience. We are a fast-growing company offering tremendous employment benefits, as you know. But for now we don't see a fit for your qualifications. We have, however, started a file in your name for future reference. We will call you for an interview should our needs change within the next year.

We are pleased to expand our pool of potential employees with someone as well qualified as you are. Good luck in your current job search.

Sincerely,

[signature]

Career Activity

Career Activity 2-1 Researching a Company for an Internship

Using the Internet and any other sources available to you, research a company or organization you may want to work for or have an internship with. Then prepare a one-page written message to your instructor covering the following:

1. Describe the organization's products or services.
2. Define the context of that organization by describing the current business environment and whatever information you can find that describes the corporate culture.
3. Explain what makes this organization attractive to you.
4. Identify any aspects of the organization that might cause you to not like working there.

Figure 2-6
Sample Letter 3

You were chosen to be part of the Bama Software Shops team partly because of your willingness to strive for excellence in performing your job. So far, you are not totally succeeding as indicated by dropping sales volume.

Our customers can get similar software from any one of hundreds of other companies. Some of them are closer to home and may offer more attractive pricing. Some are just a few keystrokes away on the Internet. How do we compete? By offering the best, most consistently pleasant and professional service available in our area. Service is what sets us apart and distinguishes us from the competition.

Customers must believe they're getting value for their money here at Bama. As we grow, it becomes increasingly difficult to give all customers the level of personalized service they expect from us. And yet, it's ever more critical that customers perceive our service to be superior.

To accomplish this, it will take every employee making the effort every day. It will take our unified dedication to finding ways to improve, even when that means changing old ways. I'm asking you to seek out those things that may inhibit our ability to deliver quality service—together we can change them for the better.

Let's get together next week after our Tuesday staff meeting and do some brainstorming about ways we can give customers better service.

Let's make quality a priority!

Sincerely,

[signature]

myPHLIP Companion Web Site

Learning Interactively

Visit the myPHLIP Web site at www.prenhall.com/timm. For Chapter 2, take advantage of the interactive "Study Guide" to test your chapter knowledge. Get instant feedback on whether you need additional studying. Read the "Current Events" articles to get the latest on chapter topics, and complete the exercises as specified by your instructor. Expand your learning with a visit to the "Research Area." There you will find a wealth of information you can use to complete your course assignments.

Notes

1. Peter F. Drucker, *Management Challenges for the 21st Century* (New York: HarperBusiness, 1999), p. 170.
2. An excellent book on NLP in business is Michael Brooks, *The Power of Business Rapport* (New York: HarperCollins, 1991).
3. Cynthia E. Griffin, "Bad Words," *Entrepreneur* (February 2000), p. 34.
4. Joseph R. Garber, "Speak for Yourself," *Forbes,* November 15, 1999, p. 244.
5. P. D. Hemphill, *Business Communications* (Englewood Cliffs, NJ: Prentice-Hall, Inc., 1976), p. 27.
6. *Uncle John's Absolutely Absorbing Bathroom Reader* (Ashland, OR: The Bathroom Reader's Institute, 1999), p. 103.

SKILL OBJECTIVES

After you have studied this chapter, you should be able to:

- Identify and distinguish among four types of briefings commonly used in organizations.
- Determine whether an oral presentation is appropriate considering the specific situation, your target audiences, and your communication objectives.
- Anticipate the kinds of questions your listeners are likely to ask.
- Prepare an effective introduction that gains the listeners' attention while establishing specific benefits for them to listen.
- Apply five different techniques for introducing a talk and describe three ways to avoid wasting introduction time.
- Describe the basic patterns of arrangement for the body of a message.
- Recognize the need to support each key idea and identify five forms of support.
- Use transitions and a strong conclusion that includes a summary, an action step, and a memorable closing statement.
- Deliver a message with skill and confidence by using effective wording and verbal and nonverbal platform skills.
- Evaluate yourself when you rehearse and appreciate both immediate and delayed feedback from others.

Introduction to Business Speaking: Foundation Skills for Speaking Well

CHAPTER 3 SKILL FOCUS:

Applying the Strategic Communication Model to Oral Communication

 OMMUNICATING WITHOUT A STRATEGY

Many Ideas in Need of Focus

"I have a whole bunch of great ideas for our new business," said Terry enthusiastically. "My mind is swimming with the possibilities. Where should I begin?"

"I really appreciate your excitement, Terry," responded Marilyn. "That's why we wanted to bring you on board. Marcus and I aren't as creative as you are. We're good at administering the company but really need your fresh thoughts. Let's schedule a time tomorrow morning when you can give us your game plan."

"That'll be great," Terry answered. "I'll spend the afternoon organizing my thoughts. We can take this company in so many directions! Let me sort out my thinking and recommend a course of action."

"Sounds great. We'll schedule the conference room for an hour tomorrow at 9 A.M."

That afternoon, Terry did "swim" in thoughts. She quickly realized that she had more ideas than Marcus and Marilyn could possibly digest in one presentation. The challenge she faced was how to extract the best ideas and present them clearly.

In another office, a phone rings. It's Sean's boss asking him to take a few minutes at the staff meeting to bring everyone up-to-date on the program to convert the office's product-ordering system. Just as he ponders how he'll do this, one of the newer clerks comes to his office door. "I'm having a heck of a time figuring out this filing system, Sean. Where do we keep the completed orders? How can I tell if an order is completed or pending? Everybody seems to be doing things a different way. I'm confused."

This sounds like just another day for two typical business communicators.

Business professionals are often asked to present proposals, explain new products, and give progress reports. Often the best medium for conveying such information is the business presentation. However, the thought of giving a talk in front of others has a way of unraveling even the most self-confident individual. Surveys have indicated that of all human fears, giving a public speech is at the top of the list, right up there with spiders, snakes, and, oh yes, death. Although business presentations are somewhat different from public speeches, they can sometimes produce just as much anxiety.

This chapter discusses the foundation skills for preparing an effective business presentation. These skills provide the basics needed to develop and deliver a talk, a briefing, or even an impromptu pitch for an idea or suggestion. In Chapter 9 we will build on the skills discussed in this chapter to explore delivering powerful presentations in greater detail.

Business Speaking Differs from Public Speaking

An oral presentation in business is often called a briefing, a presentation, or a talk.

Business presentations answer important questions by providing digestible information for listeners.

Persuasive presentations seek specific action from listeners. What do you want them to *do*?

Some types of oral business communication are second cousins to public speaking. They share some common characteristics but differ in several ways. Both business speaking and public speaking are (or should be) *purposeful* communications that involve planning, careful preparation, and skillful delivery using the spoken word. However, public speakers tend to be more oratorical, appealing to a mass audience, whereas business communicators are much more likely to talk to audiences they know or to people whose views are clearly understood (such as potential clients), not the general public.

An oral presentation in business is often called a briefing, presentation, or, simply, a talk. In addition, the business world presents many opportunities for rather spontaneous oral delivery of messages in meetings, interviews, or face-to-face chats with associates and company leaders. The points covered in this chapter can apply to any form of oral communication in varying degrees.

The purpose of effective presentations and briefings is to provide people with digestible information. In other words, *business presentations answer questions*. The four types of presentations commonly used in business communication situations are:

- Persuasive
- Explanatory
- Instructional
- Progress reports

The key feature of a *persuasive* presentation is that it attempts to get others to "buy" an idea, plan, or recommendation. Although an element of persuasion can be found in any presentation, persuasive briefings focus on this aspect extensively. An attempt to sell your colleagues or boss on an idea for accomplishing a goal, a different method of handling a process, or the need for a different work schedule are all types of persuasive presentations.

Effective presentations and briefings should provide an audience with digestible information.

In *explanatory* and *instructional* briefings or presentations you do not try to sell anything, but you do provide opportunities for the listener to gain knowledge, understanding, or skills. *Explanatory* briefings generally present a "big picture" overview, such as orienting new employees to the company, acquainting staff members with what is involved in creating a new department in the company, or showing how each function of the organization fits in with others. *Instructional* briefings are more specific. They teach others how to do or use something, such as a new software program, machine, procedure, or system. This usually entails more audience involvement, such as testing listeners to see whether they have achieved the skill or knowledge needed.

Explanatory briefings generally present a "big picture" overview. *Instructional* briefings are more specific. They teach others how to do or use something.

A *progress report* brings the audience up-to-date on some project with which they are already familiar. Examples of this may be reports on the development of a new product, findings of an ongoing research project, or a comparison of a department's success against its objectives or goals.

Progress reports bring the audience up-to-date on some project with which they are already familiar.

Good communicators make educated guesses—before they deliver their message—about how listeners are likely to react to it. Business communicators have an advantage over public speakers in that they are more likely to know the people to whom they speak. Their audiences will often be employees or staff from within their own company or customers whose preferences and motivations the speakers understand. The fact that the speaker knows the audience makes its analysis a more manageable task, but defining the context for the message is still an important step. This leads to the first step of the Strategic Communication Model in which you ask many questions about your situation, audiences, and objectives with each audience.

Step 1: Define the Context for Your Spoken Message

To determine whether an oral presentation is appropriate, consider the specific situation, your target audiences, and your communication objectives with those audiences, Step 1 of the Strategic Communication Model. Does the situation lend itself to oral communication? Does your organization normally use oral media for the kind of information you wish to present? If not, could it perhaps be advantageous to use a presentation even though it is not expected? Is immediate feedback from your audience likely to be helpful? Is the message one that can be given to several people at once, or does it need to be tailored for each receiver?

The more you know about your audience, the better you can answer these kinds of questions and improve your chances of communicating effectively. Inexperienced speakers too often jump to their presentation without doing a thorough job of defining the context of their presentation. By making some careful judgments or guesses about the people you will talk to, you can adjust your message for maximum impact.

The process of defining the context is not mysterious; we all make guesses about others' behaviors every day. When we walk down a busy street, we guess that others will go to one side of the sidewalk. We anticipate the possibility that the person walking in front of us may suddenly stop to look in a shop window. More to the point, when we bring a message to someone, we picture mentally how that person is likely to react. When you inform your roommate that a friend is coming to visit for a few weeks or that the kitchen sink is clogged up again, you can pretty well predict the kind of reaction you'll get. Similarly, salespeople learn to anticipate buyer objections ("A notebook computer might be stolen from my dorm room") and deliver carefully prepared responses ("But you can secure it to any desk surface with a handy lock."). Students learn to anticipate the reaction from their professor when an assignment is turned in late. Audience analysis and the prediction of responses are normal and natural daily activities for all of us.

As you prepare an oral presentation, like Terry in our opening story, you should sort your ideas and list all possible questions your topic might provoke in the minds of your listeners. Don't just write the obvious ones; dig a little deeper to anticipate what else might be on the minds of your listeners—those in your primary and hidden audiences and, especially, the decision makers. Remember that you are interested in personal and professional facts, attitudes about yourself and your subject, and consistent concerns that you have heard your listeners express in the past. A talk that fails to address relevant listener concerns is likely to fall flat.

You can learn to predict listener responses by carefully considering:

- Your own experiences with situations or topics similar to the one about which you will be speaking.
- Your understanding of the actions, attitudes, wants, and concerns of your listeners or other people who are similar to your listeners.

Of course, since each communication situation and each person are unique, you cannot predict listener responses with 100 percent accuracy, but you can improve the prediction of likely responses with careful audience analysis. Remember that defining the context for a business presentation is a *questioning* process. The answers aren't always clear, but the process is essential to effective presentations.

We all participate in audience analysis and the prediction of responses daily.

List all potential questions that might be asked by your audiences: primary, hidden, and decision makers.

Audience analysis helps us better predict audience responses. The more you know about your audience, the better.

Finally, as you define the context for your talk, you need to ask yourself some questions, too. What is your overall goal? What is the specific idea for the talk? What hidden agenda do you have in making this presentation? For example, if you were working for the campus computer store, your overall goal with a customer would be to sell a computer. But on the first visit, your specific purpose might be to sell the importance of purchasing the best technology. Your hidden agenda would be to appear knowledgeable and charming so the customer will ask for you on a return visit.

Step 2: Consider Your Media and Timing Options Before Speaking

Step 1 will then lead to Step 2 of the model as you think about media and timing. The major advantages of oral presentations are that they allow more dynamic, interactive ways to exchange ideas. Giving a talk lets you:

- Speak to a number of people at the same time.
- Project your personality and enthusiasm for your ideas better than most of us can do in writing.
- Get immediate feedback in the form of listener reactions to your message.

Because of these characteristics, presentations are a useful medium when you want to control the timing of an announcement and when you need to immediately see what the reaction to your message will be.

The drawbacks to oral media are that they:

Business speaking is a good way to control the timing of a message, to project your personality, and to get immediate feedback.

- Do not provide a permanent record of the communication (unless you video- or audio-tape the speech).
- May not be as effective when conveying complex data (although you can supplement a talk with handouts or other documents).
- Are not likely to be convenient for all the members of the audience.
- Can seem less formal than written communication.
- Often elicit audience response, which can be challenging if you have bad news to report.

Once you've anticipated your listeners' likely concerns and determined that an oral presentation is your best medium, you are ready to select and organize information for your presentation. The next sections will focus on the important function of developing solid message content.

You are ready to select and organize information for your presentation only after you have anticipated your listeners' likely concerns and determined that an oral presentation is your best medium.

Step 3: Select and Organize Your Information

Both Terry and Sean, in our opening story, need to sort through a lot of ideas and potentially confusing data. Planning any message's content involves writing. Jotting down notes on a blank sheet or entering thoughts into your computer is critical to creative thinking. We all know of people who say they have planned something carefully "in their heads." That doesn't work for anyone we know. You may have heard the saying that the shortest pencil is better than the longest memory. We strongly recommend that you write your ideas and thoughts and don't rely on your memory alone.

The use of content preview and accessing can be applied to both written and spoken messages.

The use of content preview and accessing that we discussed in Chapter 2 can be applied to spoken messages as well. In a presentation, your content preview will be a part of your introduction, which we will discuss in the next section. Verbal accessing (using phrases to point to the most important information) and psychological accessing (using clear wording, simple sentence structure, and repetition) are virtually the same for spoken and written messages. Visual accessing, used in written messages (enumeration, white space, bullets, font variations, etc.), has a nonverbal counterpart in presentations, which we will talk about when we discuss delivery of the message later in this chapter.

Once your purpose is clear and you have analyzed your situation, determined the specific objective that you want to achieve with your audience(s), and decided on your media options, your next task is to sort out the main ideas of your presentation. Main ideas are the concepts that your listeners must understand for your talk to succeed. These ideas should be stated in the form of conclusions you want your listeners to reach. For example, your main ideas that support the thesis, "Our small business should hire a freelance Internet Web site designer," may be:

1. Our company could profit dramatically from e-commerce, but we do not have the expertise needed to get online.
2. The costs of hiring a freelance designer would be lower than if we dedicated inexperienced employees to the project.
3. Several freelance designers with excellent reputations are available to our company.
4. Attracting a small number of new customers could offset the start-up costs of a Web site.

Main ideas are the concepts that your listeners must understand for your talk to succeed. State in the form of conclusions you want your listeners to reach.

When developing these main ideas or concepts—those the audience *must* understand if you are to be successful—be sure to:

- State the main ideas as conclusions, preferably in complete sentences.
- Be sure each idea leads to a specific objective, such as securing agreement, convincing, or gaining a desired action.
- Express ideas in thought-provoking ways.
- Use only a few main ideas. (Three is an ideal number; listeners generally have a hard time remembering more than five.)

Since you are still in a planning stage at this point, don't be overly concerned with the supporting details of the talk. Do be sure that you have focused on the main ideas. Once this overall planning is complete, it is time to assemble the contents of your presentation—the introduction, body, and conclusion.

Grab Listener Attention and Interest with Your Introduction

Your introduction should grab the listener's attention and interest. It should also preview your purpose and main points and tell your audience what they will get from listening to your presentation.

An effective introduction grabs the listener's attention and creates appropriate expectations.

The introduction that only gets attention does just part of the job. You can get attention by pounding on the desk, shouting obscenities, or telling an unrelated joke, but none of these devices does what an introduction should do. An effective introduction also creates appropriate expectations in the minds of your listeners, prepares them to receive your message, and gives some indication of the benefit they can expect to receive from listening to your message.

Grab Audience Attention   The following are some effective ways to grab your audience's attention as you introduce your topic:

- **Use a statement of topic or reference to the occasion to which you are speaking.** If you are certain that your audience is already interested in what you'll be saying, a simple statement of your topic may be sufficient, such as, "I am going to outline the new sales representative compensation program." Referring to the occasion for which you are speaking may sound like this: "As you know, Tom has asked me to take a few minutes at each staff meeting to update you on our newest employee additions." Remember to be very careful about assuming audience interest. Others rarely care as much about the topic as you do. Assuming that they do can lead to complacency and lack of sufficient preparation.

- **Use a startling statement or statistic.** Select a provocative statement or statistic that your audience may not know, such as, "The river behind our assembly plant has been declared a fire hazard," or "By the year 2007, 3 billion people will be using the Internet on a regular basis," or "Today, on May 10, you begin working for yourself and your family. Since the first of the year, you've been working to pay your taxes."

Attention Spans

Typically, audiences are alert as a speaker begins to talk. Their attention span curves downward as the presentation goes on and then perks up as the speaker gives his or her conclusion. Keep this attention span in mind, and prepare a strong introduction that draws your listeners in and a solid conclusion that captures their interest a final time.

Selecting information that your audience doesn't know will grab their attention.

A rhetorical question—if you are sure that it will elicit the desired response—can be a good way to start a speech.

A short story, quote, or light remark can effectively lead into the body of your talk.

Asking a few questions of listeners or having the group participate in an activity can be a good way to start a presentation.

People will not listen to your message if they see no personal benefit.

- **Ask a rhetorical question.** This introduction technique uses a thought-provoking question for which you don't expect an answer, such as "Just how many more price increases can our company take?" or "How would you feel if you were turned down for a promotion because you had a physical handicap?" Be sure to refer to your audience analysis to be certain that your question will elicit the desired response.

- **Use a quotation, definition, or short narrative.** Often a short story, quote, or light remark can effectively lead into the body of your talk—if it makes a relevant point. A talk about the challenge of reorganizing a group of independent-minded employees could start by comparing the task to "herding alligators." Speaking about prompt responses to customer needs could start with the quote, "Nothing impresses so significantly as immediate follow-up." The narrative or short anecdote, especially if a personal example, often works beautifully. Don't drag out the story; use it only as a lead-in to the meat of your presentation. Two words of caution: (1) Always practice a story *out loud* several times to be sure it *sounds* as good as it reads. Pay special attention to the exact wording of the punch line; and (2) remember that your story should reflect both the theme and the tone of the presentation.

- **Employ audience participation.** Asking a few key questions of specific listeners or having the group take a quiz or participate in a simple activity can be a good way to get them in tune with your presentation. You might want to say something such as, "I'd like to ask for your candid remarks about the office relocation proposal. Martha, what concerns do you have?" However, be sure you don't put people on the spot. Also be sensitive to your tone of voice in asking the questions. Don't do anything that's likely to embarrass your listeners or make them uncomfortable. Don't drag it out too long, and be sure to show your listeners how this relates to your theme and purpose.

Preview Your Purpose and Establish Listener Benefit   As we have discussed, in addition to getting attention, a good introduction will give listeners some sense of what the rest of your talk will be about. It will state, specifically and personally, why this information is useful to them. After all, people won't want to spend time listening to you if your message offers no personal benefit to them. The following are some effective ways to establish listener benefit:

- **Preview your purpose.** As we discussed in Chapter 2, previewing the purpose of your message helps people psychologically prepare to receive it. An example of this would be to say, "I will give you four specific ideas you can use to improve your customer service."

- **Set the agenda.** Let your listeners know what you will be covering and, perhaps, what you will *not* be talking about. Again, this helps them prepare for your message. An example of this would be to say, "I will cover the new sales compensation plan but will not be giving you any information about profit sharing at this time."

- **Establish listener benefit.** Let people know why this information will be useful or important to them. Review your audience analysis and identify their potential motives for listening. We all want to know why we should listen to a presentation— what's in it for us. An example of this would be to say, "With this training, you can eliminate those pesky word processing problems that keep popping up and save time every day."

Avoid Wasting Introduction Time   An inadequate introduction can seriously damage your talk by failing to gain attention, setting an inappropriate tone, or damaging your credibility. The following are some opening comments you should avoid:

- **Avoid the apologetic beginning.** Avoid the "unaccustomed-as-I-am-to-public-speaking" type of remark. Never use opening statements such as, "I'm here to bore you with a few more statistics," or "I'm pretty nervous, so I hope you'll bear with me." If you haven't prepared well enough to be effective, it will become obvious to your audience soon enough. Don't announce it.
- **Avoid the potentially offensive beginning.** Avoid off-color jokes, sarcastic or ridiculing statements, or any remarks that are inappropriate for the audience or occasion. Someone is almost always the target of such remarks, and he or she might be your decision maker!
- **Avoid the gimmicky beginning.** Resist the temptation to blow a whistle, sing a song, role-play a scene from a play, or write the work *sex* on the blackboard saying, "Now that I have your attention . . . ." Such embarrassing and distracting gimmicky beginnings put your audience on the spot when they don't know how to respond. They can also quickly damage your credibility.

The introduction is, arguably, the single most important segment of your talk, so plan it carefully. If you don't gain attention and stimulate listener interest, the rest of your talk may fall on deaf ears.

Telling a joke is not a good way to begin most business presentations. It may gain attention, but it is not likely to create appropriate expectations.

Apologetic, offensive, overused, and gimmicky openers often fail and may damage your credibility.

Develop the Body of Your Message

The introduction sets the stage for the body of your presentation. The body presents the main points and organizes and elaborates on them so that your listeners will remember what you say. The number of main points should be limited to as few as will cover the material adequately. Research shows that most people's short-term memory is limited to about five items. To be safe, try to keep main points to three or four if possible. If you must cover more than that number, provide listeners with a written list or an outline.

The body presents the main points and organizes and elaborates on them so that your listeners will remember what you say.

Organize Your Main Points   The arrangement of the main points will vary depending on your purpose. The following sections describe some of the most commonly used options.

The arrangement of the main points will vary depending on your purpose.

Chronological order.   A *chronological order* organization pattern arranges points as they occur in time. This is a good choice when it is important that your audience understands the time progression of your topic. A presentation to new employees on the company's history or a progress report would probably use a chronological ordering pattern. An instructional presentation about a new process, for example, might cover:

A chronological order organization pattern arranges points as they occur in time.

1. How to gather the correct information for the new forms
2. How to fill out the forms properly
3. How to route the completed forms to the desired recipients

Topical or spatial order.   *Topical order* moves from one topic to another in a systematic manner. For example, a presentation about the skills needed in newly hired employees may talk first about computer competency, then about communication skills, and finally about the ability to drive a truck. Each of these categories of skills is a topic. Details would explain the specifics of each of these categories of skills.

Topical order moves from one topic to another. Spatial order moves from examples that are nearby to those that are far away or vice versa.

Spatial order moves from examples that are nearby to those that are far away or vice versa. For example, a report on computer system upgrades may begin with the local branch and move to outlying branches or to other cities.

Direct or indirect.   The *direct pattern* of arrangement begins with the main idea or the general conclusion of the briefing followed by supporting information. The following is an example of a direct organizational plan:

—*Main point:*

If we maintain current sales rates, the coming year should be our most profitable year since 1998. (Now the listener is probably asking why)

—*Supporting details:*

1. In the last six months, orders for our main products increased 86 percent.

2. Costs of materials stabilized; projected increase not more than 2 percent in coming year.

3. Union wages and benefits frozen at present levels for next 18 months with recent contract. (Now the listener understands why)

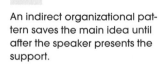

A direct order arrangement puts the main idea first followed by supporting points that answer listener questions.

Organize details under their main point. The main points should be prioritized so that the most important, dramatic, or significant point comes first. (In our example, this is the sharp increase in orders.) The decision about which points are most attractive should be based on your audience analysis. Notice that the supporting details are phrased as notes, not necessarily complete sentences, and that they answer potential questions the listeners may ask. Using phrases or outline form rather than complete sentences makes it easier to speak spontaneously and avoid reading your speech. The direct organizational pattern is appropriate for most business presentations. It is efficient and hits the main point immediately while the audience's attention level is high.

The opposite of the direct organizational pattern is (surprise!) the *indirect pattern*. The indirect or inductive pattern starts with details or supporting information and builds up to the conclusion. Main points are arranged in ascending order of importance so that the main idea or conclusion comes last. You would choose the indirect pattern if you need to explain your reasoning *before* getting to the main point. (We will discuss this further in Chapter 6.) Here is how the example above would look if arranged inductively:

—*Supporting details:*

1. Union wages and benefits frozen at present levels for the next 18 months with the current contract.

2. Costs of raw materials stabilized; projected increases not more than 2 percent in coming year.

3. Orders for main products increased by 86 percent in last 6 months. (Now the listener wants to know what these points are leading up to)

—*Main point:*

If we maintain current sales rates, the coming year will be our most profitable year since 1998. (Now the listener knows what the main point is)

An indirect organizational pattern saves the main idea until after the speaker presents the support.

Problem-solution. In a *problem-solution* order, the speaker clarifies and amplifies some need or issue in order to concern the listener about the problem in personal terms. Once listeners reach this point, they are likely to welcome and accept the introduction of your solution. Television advertisements often use an abbreviated form of this pattern. They introduce—even create—a problem (an upset stomach, unreliable product, or that embarrassing dandruff) and then solve the dilemma by introducing their product.

In a problem-solution order, the speaker clarifies and amplifies some need or issue and offers a solution.

Cause-effect. The *cause-effect* pattern of arrangement looks at (no surprise!) causes and effects. By clarifying how one event or action causes another, you can recommend changes in one to bring about corresponding changes in the other. This arrangement can be useful in explanatory or informational presentations or, when followed by a call for action, in persuasion. The following is an example of a cause-effect pattern:

> The steady rise in the number of incoming students has resulted in an overload in the required courses and has caused a drop in student satisfaction with those courses. Here are the enrollment figures and the course evaluation numbers that support this theory.

The cause-effect pattern of arrangement looks at causes and their effects.

STAR(R). The *STAR(R)* pattern of arrangement has five elements (situation, task, action, results, and recommendations) that spell out the acronym STAR(R). Progress reports can use this pattern effectively by describing a situation you or the company faced, what task this situation required, what you or the company did, what happened as a result, and (sometimes) what you or the company recommend next. The following is an example:

1. **Situation:** Several competitors have created Web sites that are attracting our customers.
2. **Task:** My assignment was to evaluate the use of web marketing for our company.
3. **Action:** I solicited proposals from several Web site developers and evaluated them based on the criteria established by the review committee.
4. **Result:** Based on my analysis of these proposals, I am convinced that a Web site would be profitable.
5. **Recommendation:** The company should hire WebBuddies, Inc. to develop and manage our Web site.

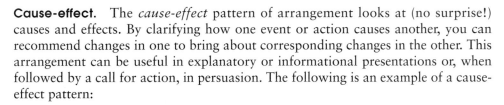

The STAR(R) pattern of arrangement has five elements: situation, task, action, results, and recommendations.

Support Each Main Point   Most main points take the form of simple declarative statements. Few of these can stand alone without further elaboration. Support, clarification, and proof can shore up these themes and result in audience acceptance and agreement. The following sections outline several types of support.

Key ideas can seldom stand alone. You need to provide evidence to support your assertions.

Specific details or explanation.   Here you simply explain in other words what you have asserted. This support may be prefaced by remarks such as "Let me explain why I've said that . . ." or "Another way to say this might be . . ." Generally, this is not the strongest form of support, nor the most creative.

Giving specific details or explanations is not the strongest or most creative way to support a key idea.

Examples.   As we mentioned earlier, personal examples can be especially powerful. They add support to main points and also lend credibility to the speaker. Some speakers are unduly hesitant about using personal experiences, but these provide support of a first-hand nature that can be very convincing.

Personal examples can add support to main points and lend credibility to the speaker.

Be certain that your example is typical of, and pertinent to, the point being supported. For example, let's say that your main point is "Morale in the office is low." If you support that point with just a single example of one employee's complaints about working conditions, you run the risk of distorting the picture. Perhaps that one person has a special problem and his or her dissatisfaction is not indicative of other workers. If, however, you string together a series of separate examples, you develop support for your theme:

—Main point:

Employee morale is low.

—Supporting details:

1. Six different workers have complained about the excessive heat in the office.
2. Absenteeism is up 20 percent over last month.
3. Three workers quit, citing unbearable work conditions.
4. Four grievances have been filed with the union.

Statistics can provide support so long as they are used ethically.

Statistics. Statistics provide support when they are used ethically. Information can be distorted when statistics are misused or misunderstood. You can often choose how to word a statistic to make it sound bigger or smaller. You could say, for example, that a training seminar for employees will cost $10,000, or you could say that it will cost "only $58 per employee."

The following guidelines will help you use statistics appropriately:

1. Round off large numbers so your listeners can digest them. Make 3.97 percent into "almost 4 percent." (Of course, you wouldn't do this if that .03 percent was enough to change the statistical significance of your arguments, which would be unethical.)
2. Interpret the numbers in some meaningful way. Say "One family in four" or use easy-to-understand percentages.
3. Be sure to compare apples to apples. We once heard a speaker express relief that the U.S. unemployment rate was only 6 percent, whereas in Israel, "one person in 18 is unemployed." That is virtually the same percentage!
4. Use charts and graphs to help your audience understand the statistics.

Formal quotations or testimonials can be powerful if the source is seen as credible by your target audience.

Formal quotations or testimonials. Formal quotations or testimonials can be very effective forms of support. If you choose to quote an authority, be sure that person is:

- A recognized expert
- In a position to know about the specific point you are trying to support
- In general agreement with other authorities on the subject
- Free from prejudice that would distort his or her view

The person quoted need not be a world-renowned expert; he or she may well be someone within the organization with considerable experience or training in the area being discussed.

Audiovisual aids. Audiovisual aids may be used in conjunction with several other types of support. Visuals can range from a simple chalkboard or flip chart to highly sophisticated multimedia productions involving slides, video clips, special lighting

FOCUS ON

Ethical Persuasion

Any discussion of persuasion always includes reminders to analyze your audience and determine their wants, needs, and concerns so that you can position your appeal as a solution to the problem. Ethical persuasion is a sincere appeal based on what the audience really does want, need, or is concerned about—and is a true solution. Unethical persuasion—or manipulation—occurs in two ways:

1. **The need is not real.** Advertising provides many examples of persuasion based on nonexistent problems—people selling products that are really not necessary.

2. **The reasoning is not sound.** From the kindergarten room to the boardroom, you will hear variations on "everybody's doing it!" Common persuasive arguments include how "everyone" owns a particular product, thinks a particular way, or acts in a particular fashion.

Of course, if you are found out, your persuasive attempts with the audience you attempted to mislead will be much more difficult in the future. So, to protect your reputation and your future communication effectiveness with your target audiences, be sure that your solutions are valid, reliable responses to real wants, needs, and concerns.

---

effects, and elaborate sound systems. In most business presentations you can use a wide variety of devices, such as charts, graphs, overhead projectors, slides, movies or videotapes, tape recordings, and models.

One more point about types of support: Speakers can often get into a rut by using the same types of support over and over. People who use a variety of support types are usually more interesting. Varying support types adds *texture* to the message and holds listener interest better. We will spend more time on designing visuals in Chapter 7.

Varying the types of support used creates better *texture* in a message and is more likely to hold listener interest.

Present a Strong Conclusion

Conclusions serve to help your listener remember important information. You should try to accomplish three things as you conclude most presentations. (The exception may be the simple progress report.) You should:

Conclusions help your listener remember important information.

1. Summarize your main points and restate your main idea.
2. Provide your audience with a clear action step, a prescribed behavior, or mental activity they should *do,* and remind them of the urgency (or at least the importance) of that action.
3. Close with a strong final statement.

Summarize Your Key Ideas and Restate Your Main Points Summaries are especially useful to recap the key ideas (but not too many of the details) of your talk. Repetition helps us remember, so use this important tool as you lead into your close. Avoid introducing any new material at this point. It may confuse your listeners or get them thinking about something other than your concluding remarks.

Provide Your Audience with a Clear Action Step Action steps are appropriate for all kinds of presentations. As we have mentioned, the action step tells your

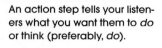

An action step tells your listeners what you want them to *do* or think (preferably, *do*).

listeners what you want them to *do* or think (preferably, *do*). It should reflect—and sometimes exactly repeat—the specific purpose that you stated in your introduction. If the action you are requesting requires immediate response, now is the time to stress that urgency.

Your audience has a right to expect and receive guidance from all your research and preparation. If you don't provide such guidance in the form of a clear request for specific action, you have probably shortchanged your listeners.

Most business presentations need a strong closing statement.

Close with a Strong Final Statement   Never end on a weak or confusing note. If you decide to take audience questions, conclude the question-and-answer session by recapping your strongest point. Don't just let the talk fizzle out. Use a powerful final statement. Remember that your conclusions need not be elaborate or drawn out. If the rest of the talk is well done, the conclusion will fall into place and bring a sense of finality.

Step 4: Deliver Your Message with an Appropriate Speaking Style

If you apply these ideas to developing a business presentation that has a clear purpose, that is right for your context (audience, situation, and business environment), and that can best be accomplished with an oral medium, you will be well on your way toward mastering the preparation skills for business speaking. You are now ready to focus on Step 4 of our model. When you finally think about delivering your message, your focus will be on your verbal and nonverbal platform skills. However, you should consider the actual wording of your material first.

Use Words That Ensure Delivery Success

The wording of your presentation will affect your speaking style. Therefore, you should apply the same basic principles we discussed in Chapter 2. Specifically, we recommend that you use:

Because we retain only a small portion of what we hear, you should use repetition when speaking.

- Efficient sentence structure
- Vigorous, economical wording (especially clear, concrete language)
- Mostly simple, everyday wording

One main difference in wording a spoken message versus wording a written one is that in speaking you should use more repetition. By repeating key information, speakers increase the likelihood that their audiences will remember and, hopefully, use the information given to them.

Use Platform Skills That Ensure Delivery Success

Of course, a good oral presentation involves more than just the words used. Project your research and analysis with dynamic, articulate delivery. Rehearse presentations, preferably in front of a live audience—someone you trust to provide you with good feedback.

In Chapter 9, we will talk in more detail about the issues that affect delivery of a good business presentation. For now, however, let's consider four basic methods you can use to get your oral message across with professionalism and style.

Use Verbal Skills   Speak clearly and expressively. Use variations in volume, pitch, and pace to emphasize key points and to convey enthusiasm. Avoid a "stage voice" that sounds artificial or a monotone that fails to convey emotion. Don't try to sound like an orator; just speak naturally and conversationally. Avoid reading to your audience or mimicking another person's delivery style. Talk *to* your audience, not *at* them.

Speak clearly, use variation, and avoid a "stage voice" that fails to convey emotion.

Use Nonverbal Skills   Exhibit physical control so that your audience believes that everything you are doing with your face, hands, feet, and the space around you is a result of conscious decisions. Avoid contrived or exaggerated gestures, but let your hand and facial expression project naturally. Also, project a professional visual image by dressing appropriately. Most importantly, avoid wearing anything that is distracting. For men this can mean loud ties with odd patterns or belt buckles with unusual designs. For women, distractions can come from mismatched clothing, bright nail polish, or unusual makeup colors.

Exhibit physical control so that your audience believes that you are in control of everything you are doing.

Express Confidence   Express confidence in your material—based on your preparation—and in yourself. You now know more about this topic than anyone in the room! *You* are the expert. Be prepared for when things go wrong, such as unexpected interruptions or equipment failure. Let your audience know how enthusiastic you are about your topic. (Such enthusiasm need not be rah-rah cheerleading but should convey sincerity and conviction that what you are saying is important.)

Your listeners will appreciate your preparation, clarity, and confidence.

Be Yourself   Allow your personality to be reflected in your communication. However, adapt your style to meet each audience's expectations in their corporate culture. You are the most important part of your message, and your unique personality is your most valuable delivery skill.

You are the most important part of your message, so be yourself!

When giving a presentation, use visual aids and project a professional visual image by dressing appropriately.

Step 5: Evaluate Your Feedback for Continued Success

Immediate feedback flows to you as you talk. Delayed feedback is provided by what your receivers *do* with the message.

Speakers get two kinds of audience feedback: immediate and delayed. *Immediate feedback* flows to the speaker as she or he talks. An effective speaker will monitor the audience and look for verbal and nonverbal cues that indicate whether the message is getting through. If audience behaviors, especially nonverbal responses, indicate that they are confused, worried, bored, or otherwise distracted, adjust your message, ask questions, or test for understanding. As we have discussed, the ability to get immediate feedback and to make quick adjustments are major advantages of oral media.

Delayed feedback is provided by what your receivers do with the message. To what extent do they do what you want them to do? If your talk is informative or instructional, how well do they understand and apply what you have said? If your speech is persuasive, to what degree do they agree with you or fulfill a commitment to do what you've asked?

Sales presentations result in great feedback: The decision maker either buys your product or does not. Instructional talks, likewise, give clear feedback when you determine whether the listeners can do what you have taught them to do. You may want to test for such understanding by asking your audience to demonstrate or summarize what you have said.

Use Feedback When Practicing Your Presentation

Never go into a presentation without practicing. As we have mentioned, the best kind of practice is rehearsing in front of someone whose opinions you trust. When your rehearsal audience gives you feedback, avoid reacting in ways that are not constructive. We talked about accepting feedback in Chapter 1, but the key points bear repeating:

Be responsive to feedback from others and accept and appreciate it; don't defend yourself or overreact.

- Be open and receptive to feedback.
- Listen carefully to comments and take notes.
- Ask for specific information and examples, then repeat these back to the person giving the feedback for clarification.
- Look for nonverbal messages from your audience and ask them about these ("You looked confused when I talked about . . .").
- Don't overreact or defend yourself with the reasons why you did or said something.
- Accept responsibility for any needs and changes.
- Recognize that whatever your rehearsal audience perceives is real to them and may represent what your "real" audience will see.

Finally, remember to evaluate yourself so that your audience will believe that you are credible. Double-check your material to be certain that your audience will perceive your goodwill, expertise, and power. Rehearse several times out loud so that you sound confident. Practice in front of a mirror to confirm that you *look* confident.

APPLYING THE STRATEGIC COMMUNICATION MODEL

Let's take a look at how using the Strategic Communication Model might help Terry and Sean, the two people we talked about at the beginning of this chapter. Terry had already realized that she had more ideas than Marcus and Marilyn could digest in one presentation. If she carefully *defines her context,* particularly thinking about the concerns that Marcus and Marilyn will have with her suggestions, she can *select material* that is more likely to get a positive response. By considering what else Marcus and Marilyn are likely to have on their schedules, Terry can use *timing* to her benefit by asking to present on a day that is less hectic than usual.

Sean's challenge is to prepare quickly and respond succinctly. His *context analysis* will reveal important information about the needs of his two target audiences. Since he has very little time to update the staff on the new ordering system, he will likely choose the *STAR(R) pattern* and report on why the system is being changed (situation), his specific assignment (task), the progress he is making (action), and when the ordering system will be ready (result). He might also include suggestions for training the employees on the new system (recommendations). He will *deliver his message* using computer-generated slides and with a degree of formality, as expected for staff meetings.

For his quick instructions to the clerk, Sean will remember that this employee is new and confused, so he will use a simple *chronological pattern* to explain the filing system. He will be informal, personal, and direct in his *delivery style* to make this new employee more comfortable. Based on the questions he receives at each occasion, Sean will know how effectively he has communicated his message. Both Terry and Sean will save time and increase their chances for success by working through the Strategic Communication Model.

Summary of Key Ideas

- Business speaking is less oratorical than public speaking and is often addressed to an audience the speaker knows.
- Carefully define the specific situation (including the business environment and corporate culture), your target audiences (primary, secondary, and hidden), and your communication objectives with those audiences to determine whether an oral presentation is appropriate.
- Defining the situation should include anticipating the kinds of questions your listeners are likely to ask. Plan your message content in writing, not by relying on memory alone.
- When assessing your media and timing options, remember that an oral presentation allows you to speak to a number of people at the same time (you control the timing), to project your personality and enthusiasm, and to get immediate feedback in the form of listener reactions to your message.
- Apply content preview and accessing to oral presentations in much the same way as in written communication.
- An effective introduction gains the listeners' attention and interest while showing them the specific, personal benefits of listening to your message.

- The body presents main points and elaborates on them with support such as details or explanations, stories, examples, statistics, quotations or testimonials, and audiovisual aids. Keep main points to three or four, if possible.
- Prepare an effective conclusion that includes a summary, an action step, and a strong final comment.
- Delivery of your presentation is affected by preparation and word choice as well as verbal and nonverbal skills. The first steps to developing dynamic platform skills are preparation, speaking clearly and expressively, projecting confidence, and being yourself.
- Appreciate both immediate and delayed feedback as well as feedback received while rehearsing. Evaluate your content and delivery to ensure audience perceptions of credibility.
- Evaluate your feedback by checking audience behaviors and nonverbal cues and by determining if your listeners do what you advocate in your presentation. React to feedback in constructive ways.

Application Activities

Activity 3-1 Articulating Specific Purposes and Key Ideas

Following are some central themes (main ideas) for presentations. Based on your own experience (no research is needed), see if you can come up with several key ideas for each. We have completed the first one as an example.

Specific Purpose:
Recycling of aluminum and newspapers should be a high priority of our company.

Key Ideas:
1. Recycling demonstrates social conscience.
2. Recycling takes very little time.
3. Income generated from recycling could be used to fund employee events.

Specific Purpose:
The company should (or should not) provide free gym membership (or flexible work hours, extended vacation, cell phones, notebook computers) for employees.

Key Ideas:
1.
2.
3.

Specific Purpose:
Starting a new business venture as soon as possible is (or is not) the best way for college students to achieve financial security.

Key Ideas:
1.
2.
3.

Specific Purpose:
The best career opportunities for business students are (or are not) found in Internet-based businesses.

Key Ideas:
1.
2.
3.

Bonus Activity:

After completing your list of key ideas, gather supporting information for each by searching the Internet. Find at least one supporting example for each key idea.

Activity 3-2 Pinpointing Potential Questions

Following are some key ideas. For each key idea, write one or more potential questions a listener is likely to ask about it. (We will discuss context analysis and suggest ways to *answer* the questions in Chapter 4. For now, see what questions spring to mind for each of these key ideas.) We have completed the first one as an example.

Key Idea:

An after-hours, mandatory first-aid course should be required for all employees.

Potential Audience Questions:
1. Who would provide and pay for such training?
2. Does the number of accidents or injuries justify the costs of providing such training?
3. Is requiring such training an infringement on people's free time?
4. Why should this training apply to all employees?
5. Why can't this be done during work hours or lunch hour?

Key Idea:

Our school should (or should not) issue a credit card that must be used for all school-related purchases. It would be the only card accepted on campus.

Potential Audience Questions:
1.
2.
3.
4.

Key Idea:

An internship in an established company should (or should not) be required for earning a degree from our school.

Possible Audience Questions:
1.
2.
3.
4.

Key Idea:

Classes should (or should not) use only online readings and handouts, thus eliminating the use of textbooks.

Possible Audience Questions:

1.
2.
3.
4.

Interactive CD-ROM Exercises

Activity 3-3 Getting It Down on Paper

Select a current business-related presentation topic from a newspaper, business periodical, or media site (such as CNN.com, CNBC.com, FoxNews.com, or others) and identify a primary target audience. Identify your specific purpose, three to five key ideas, and at least two possible audience questions for each key idea. To best anticipate audience questions, be sure to consider Step 1 in the Strategic Communication Model.

Using your best critical thinking, determine how your audience is likely to respond to what you say. Then develop answers and support, completing the following sentences:

1. My specific purpose is:
2. My primary target audience is:
3. The most important information I have about this audience is:
4. My hidden or decision-making audience (if different) is:
5. The most important information I have about this audience is:
6. My three to five key ideas are:
   - Key Idea 1:
   - Key Idea 2:
   - Key Idea 3:
   - Key Idea 4:
   - Key Idea 5:

Next, return to each key idea and write the possible questions your audience may have about that idea. Then list the supporting data you plan to use for each key idea. These data should answer the audience's potential questions.

Activity 3-4 Teaching a Simple Skill

Think of a fairly simple task that you could teach the members of your communication class. Outline a four-step training presentation, using the Outline Worksheet that follows. If you can't think of a topic, try one of these:

- How to use your favorite Internet search engine
- How to negotiate rent and expenses with a roommate
- How to create an Excel spreadsheet
- How to manage your time in an overloaded semester
- How to dress for "casual day" at work

OUTLINE WORKSHEET
Introduction

- **Attention-grabber.** Based on what I know about my primary audience, what will get his, her, or their attention (and also relate to my topic and situation)?

_____

_____

- **Purpose.** As a result of this message, what do I want my audience to *do*?

_____

_____

- **Agenda.** How am I going to accomplish my objectives; that is, what is my *agenda* for delivering the message?

  _____

  _____

- **Benefit for audience.** What's in it for my audience, specifically and personally?

  _____

  _____

Body

- Point 1: _____

  Support Material (such as statistics or examples):

  _____

  _____

- Point 2: _____

  Support Material: _____

  _____

- Point 3: _____

  Support Material: _____

  _____

- Point 4: _____

  Support Material: _____

  _____

Conclusion

- **Summary.** Exactly what do I want my audience to *remember* (the essence of my main points)?

  _____

  _____

- **Specific action.** Exactly what do I want my audience to *do?*

  _____

  _____

- **Strong final statement.** What is the *last thought* I want to leave with my audience?

  _____

  _____

Career Activity

Career Activity 3-1 Designing a Presentation for a Company Recruiter

Access the Web site of a company in an industry that appeals to you. Scan pages on employment opportunities until you find a description of an internship or entry-level job that looks interesting. Write three main requirements for that position, as listed in the description. Using these three requirements as your main points, design a short presentation to the company recruiter to inform him or her that you are qualified to be considered for the position. The only information you have on your audience (the recruiter) is based on the job description. To complete the exercise, use the Outline Worksheet.

myPHLIP Companion Web Site

Learning Interactively

Visit the myPHLIP Web site at www.prenhall.com/timm. For Chapter 3, take advantage of the interactive "Study Guide" to test your chapter knowledge. Get instant feedback on whether you need additional studying. Read the "Current Events" articles to get the latest on chapter topics, and complete the exercises as specified by your instructor. Expand your learning with a visit to the "Research Area." There you will find a wealth of information you can use to complete your course assignments.

Developing Strategy-Based Writing and Speaking Skills

Part 2

Step 1. Define the Context

A. Define the situation.
  1. Limit the problem.
  2. Evaluate the problem within the external climate.
  3. Evaluate the corporate culture that impacts the problem.

B. Define your audience.
  1. Identify all potential audiences (distinct or overlapping).
  2. Learn about each audience.

C. Define your objectives with each audience.
  1. Define your overall goal.
  2. Identify the specific purpose of the communication.
  3. Acknowledge your hidden agenda.

Step 2. Consider Your Media and Timing Options

A. Select media options that are most appropriate for your message.

B. Evaluate your timing options.

Step 3. Select and Organize Your Information

A. Review your analysis of your situation, audiences, and objectives.

B. Compare key organizational patterns and select the most effective one.

C. Limit your main points.

D. Enhance your message with powerful support material (visual aids, numbers, and examples).

Step 5. Evaluate Feedback for Continued Success

A. Give feedback.

B. Solicit feedback.

C. Receive feedback.

D. Evaluate yourself with the Credibility Checklist:
  1. Goodwill: your focus on and concern for your audience
  2. Expertise: your education, knowledge, and experience
  3. Power: your status, prestige, and success
  4. Confidence: the way you present yourself and your message

Step 4. Deliver Your Message

A. Develop your writing, speaking, interpersonal, and group skills.

B. Prepare thoroughly (rehearse your presentations and edit your writing).

C. Express confidence in your topic and in yourself.

D. Be yourself (but adapt your style to your audience and situation).

Step 2. Consider
Your Media and
Timing Options

Step 1. Define
the Context

SKILL OBJECTIVES

After you have studied this chapter, you should be able to:

- Recognize the importance of defining the context for any business message.
- Describe the factors that comprise the communication context.
- Limit the topic of a message to make it more effective.
- Identify key elements in the business environment and corporate culture that may affect your business message.
- Name seven characteristics of organizational culture that can have an impact on how a message is received in that organization.
- Distinguish among three groups of target audiences and explain why each audience may have different needs and wants.
- Use listening skills, observation techniques, and secondary sources to gather information.
- Define the overall objective, specific purpose, and hidden agenda of any message.
- Complete a Context Analysis Worksheet.

Step 3. Select
and Organize
Your Information

Step 5. Evaluate
Feedback for
Continued Success

Step 4.
Deliver
Your
Message

Defining the Context: Articulating the Message Situation, Audiences, and Objectives

4

CHAPTER 4
SKILL
FOCUS:

Analyzing Audiences,

Communication Environments,

Organizational Culture, and

Message Objectives

COMMUNICATING WITHOUT A STRATEGY

Poor Audience Analysis Can Sink a Book

Two hundred people crammed into a Manhattan Barnes & Noble store to hear first-time novelist Jonathan Tropper read from his debut work, *Plan-B*. The crowd was so big that the store had to send out for more copies. How did Mr. Tropper manage to attract so much attention? With the power of e-mail. He sent personal messages about his novel to friends, family, and even strangers whose names and electronic addresses he culled from book-selling sites such as Amazon.com. But four months later, instead of counting sales, Mr. Tropper was counting the things he would have done differently to avoid an expensive lesson in the pitfalls of Internet marketing.

High on the success of his in-store reading, Mr. Tropper took what he thought was the next logical step. He hired an online marketing company. In stark contrast to his own tiny e-mail campaign, the marketing company unleashed a torrent of e-mail promoting *Plan-B* to influential people and chat groups in the Web's sprawling book and publishing communities.

That campaign touched off a remarkably potent backlash. Several incensed Web purists scrawled angry replies on Amazon.com's review page for *Plan-B*, instructing people not to buy the book. Sales collapsed.

"Please do not support an author who would send unsolicited e-mail to advertise his book," one e-mail recipient wrote. David Douglass, an illustrator who came across the company's e-mail in a kite-enthusiast chat group, complains it "wasn't even dimly related to the content of the site." He posted a reply: "I hate spammers."[1] (*Spam* is unwanted e-mail. It is the electronic equivalent of junk mail. A *spammer* is one who distributes such mass e-mailings.)

What went wrong? Surely advertising communication is a good way to sell products, isn't it? So why the backlash?

Effective business communication requires understanding your audiences. The more specific that understanding, the more likely you will succeed. The Strategic Communication Model, around which this book is designed, stresses the importance of defining the context for your messages, including the needs and wants of your audiences. Spammers (and more than a few other business communicators) use a shotgun approach, shooting in the general direction of the target and hoping to hit a few. Professional business communicators today must use a narrow, targeted focus—a rifle approach.

This chapter looks in more depth at the processes involved in defining the context for a given message. Your challenge is to learn everything you can about the context in which you are communicating, including the current situation, your target audiences, and your objectives with each of those audiences.

Understand the Three Factors of Communication Context

This chapter focuses on step 1 of the Strategic Communication Model: defining the context. As we discussed in Chapter 1, the communication context includes:

- The *situation or problem* that causes you to produce your message. (*Why* are you planning to communicate?)
- Your *target audiences:* primary, hidden, and decision makers. (To *whom* are you communicating?)
- Your *desired objectives* with those audiences. (*What* do you hope to accomplish with your message? What do you want your readers or listeners *to do* or *think?*)

Understanding the situation, your target audiences, and your desired objectives at the beginning of your preparation provides you with the foundation for a successful communication strategy.

Understanding these three factors at the beginning of your preparation will provide you with the foundation for a successful communication strategy. We'll start with the existing situation, because the situation often creates the motivation to communicate. For example, the quarterly sales meeting might be the situation that precipitates the preparation of your sales report. A desire to schedule a presentation or an assignment to write a letter addressing a company need are the triggers for analyzing the communication situation.

At the end of this chapter, you will find two Context Analysis Worksheets (Figures 4-6 and 4-7). One has been completed as an example; the other is blank for you to copy and use as you plan messages. Within each section of the chapter, we have also included the portions of the Context Analysis Worksheet that deal with the step of the Strategic Communication Model at hand. As you read through the material, try to fill out the portions of the worksheet, using a recent example in which you received or sent a message within an organization. You may want to review an announcement or policy change at your school or a message you communicated to someone else in your study group. If you cannot think of an applicable situation, try applying the worksheet to the opening story in this chapter.

Define the Situation

As you remember from Chapter 1, three tasks comprise the process of defining the situation: limiting the problem, evaluating the problem within the external climate, and evaluating the corporate (or organizational) culture that affects the problem. Figure 4-1 shows the portion of the Context Analysis Worksheet that deals with this process. We look at each of these tasks in the following sections.

Limit the Problem

Limiting the scope of your message is critical to good communication for the simple reason that you could go on and on about almost any topic (and some people do!). We know a professor who stands before his class, holds up a piece of chalk, and asks the class to respond to the question, "What could you say about this piece of chalk?" Once the students begin to respond, they identify a wide range of topics associated with a simple piece of chalk. They suggest talking about uses for chalk, descriptions of its shape and size, the comparative advantages of chalk versus ink markers, its chemical composition, and even the history of the chalk industry. In short, any number of topics for messages could come from focusing on even a simple object.

Limiting the problem makes the message more manageable and reduces the likelihood of you going on with irrelevant information.

Your first challenge as a communicator, therefore, is to determine what you want to say and what aspects of the topic you will avoid. As easy as this may sound, isolating the specific issues that you want to address can be difficult unless you focus on the distinct reason for the message. Specify the parameters and simplify the situation to manageable proportions.

For example, if a labor union in your industry is threatening a strike, you might choose to limit your discussion to reasons for the current dispute and your opinions about how to resolve it. You should probably avoid discussing the history of labor relations, the pros and cons of having a unionized company, or the personalities of individuals involved. Don't get sidetracked onto other subjects, even if they may be interesting to you. Limit your message to information that may best solve the problem or address the concerns arising from the situation—in this case, limit the topic to issues that may have an impact on the decision to strike.

Limit your message to relevant information or concerns that focus on the situation.

Evaluate the Problem Within the External Climate

As we have mentioned, the best way to evaluate the external environment is to be current on what is happening in your specific industry, in related industries, and in the local and global markets that influence your organization and your audiences.

CONTEXT ANALYSIS WORKSHEET

[DEFINING THE SITUATION]
How should I limit the problem or topic of my message?

What factors in the business environment may influence my audience's response to my message?

What key elements in the corporate culture should I take into account as I prepare my message?

Figure 4-1
Context Analysis Worksheet: Defining the Situation

If business is to be your career, stay abreast of information about your industry.

Commit to staying current on what is happening in your industry so that you may best evaluate any problem within its external climate.

Watch business television, read and clip articles from business publications, and simply stay well informed about issues and events that could affect your company. If business is to be your career (and the vast majority of us work in business-related enterprises), commit to staying abreast of what is happening.

The issue of spamming described in our opening example is a current business concern that is widely discussed in the media. The communicator should have been aware of the possible negative effects of mass e-mailing to unrelated audiences. This is a real hot-button issue with businesspeople who feel inundated with junk messages that waste their time and reflect negatively on their industry (in the preceding case, publishing).

FOCUS ON

Industry Publications[3]

Keep current with what's happening in your profession and industry. Read the latest information. Then clip or photocopy articles that can be of interest to your boss or work associates. Develop a system to file such clippings, and tag copies to other people who may be interested. The result: You will be perceived by colleagues and supervisors as someone who is truly interested in the business and is involved in sharing ideas of value.

The lower your job level in the organization, the more impact this can have. As an entry-level worker, for example, few bosses would expect you to work so hard to stay current. That poses a perfect opportunity to exceed your boss's expectations by showing that you are aware of and concerned about your business environment. This information gathering and sharing can also make you a more effective communicator by increasing your awareness of the external business climate.

Evaluate the Corporate Culture That Has an Impact on the Problem

In Chapter 1 we briefly described corporate culture factors such as formal versus informal communication styles, professional versus casual dress codes, rigid versus flexible work hours, and risk-taking versus conservative attitudes. In this section we will look a bit deeper at this concept of corporate culture.

As you have learned, the culture of an organization derives from its shared attitudes, beliefs, and meanings, which result in shared behaviors. Recent research summarized by Stephen Robbins shows seven primary characteristics that capture the essence of an organization's culture.[3]

The culture of an organization derives from its shared attitudes, beliefs, and meanings, which result in shared behaviors.

- **Innovation and risk taking:** The degree to which employees are encouraged to be creative, innovative, and to take risks.
- **Attention to detail:** The degree to which employees are expected to exhibit precision, careful analysis, and attention to detail.
- **Outcome orientation:** The degree to which management focuses on results or outcomes rather than on the techniques or processes used to achieve those outcomes.
- **People orientation:** The degree to which management decisions consider the effects of outcomes on people within the organization.
- **Team orientation:** The degree to which work activities are organized around teams rather than individuals.
- **Aggressiveness:** The degree to which people are aggressive and competitive rather than easygoing.
- **Stability:** The degree to which organizational activities emphasize maintaining the status quo in contrast to growth or change.

Some organization's cultures are more team based than others.

Organization A

This organization is a manufacturing firm. Managers are expected to fully document all decisions, and "good managers" are those who can provide detailed data to support their recommendations. The organization does not encourage creative decisions that incur significant change or risk. Because managers of failed projects are openly criticized and penalized, managers try not to implement ideas that deviate much from the status quo. One lower-level manager quoted an often-used phrase in the company: "If it ain't broke, don't fix it."

Employees in this firm are required to follow numerous rules and regulations. Managers supervise employees closely to ensure there are no deviations. Management is concerned with high productivity regardless of the impact on employee morale or turnover.

Work activities are designed around individuals. There are distinct departments and lines of authority, and employees are expected to minimize formal contact with other employees outside their functional area or line of command. Performance evaluations and rewards emphasize individual effort, although seniority tends to be the primary factor in the determination of pay raises and promotions.

Organization B

This organization is also a manufacturing firm. Here, however, management encourages and rewards risk taking and change. Decisions based on intuition are valued as much as those that are well rationalized. Management prides itself on its history of experimenting with new technologies and its success in regularly introducing innovative products. Managers or employees who have a good idea are encouraged to "run with it," and failures are treated as "learning experiences." The company prides itself on being market driven and rapidly responsive to the changing needs of its customers.

The firm has few rules and regulations for employees to follow, and supervision is loose because management believes that its employees are hardworking and trustworthy. Management is concerned with high productivity but believes that this comes through treating its people right. The company is proud of its reputation as being a good place to work.

Job activities are designed around work teams, and team members are encouraged to interact with people across functions and authority levels. Employees talk positively about the competition between teams. Individuals and teams have goals, and bonuses are based on achievement of those outcomes. Employees are given considerable autonomy in choosing the means by which the goals are attained.

Figure 4-2
Contrasting Organizational Cultures[4]

Figure 4-2 contrasts the cultures of two organizations. As you read these descriptions, think about the impact on communication styles in each. As you can see, a communication strategy that would be appropriate for Organization A will likely be less successful in Organization B. For example, in Organization A, people would probably be expected to follow standard communication procedures (letter or memo formats, formal meetings, strict adherence to chain of command, etc.). Communicators in Organization B, on the other hand, have much more latitude to be creative, informal, and perhaps to work around the normal chain of command to get things done.

Define Your Audience

The second step in defining the context includes identifying and learning about your target audiences. The more specific information you have about your readers or listeners, the better you can tailor your message to their needs and achieve your specific purpose. As we discussed in Chapter 1, the most common mistakes we make are generalizing and assuming things about our audiences. The Strategic Communication Model provides questions to ask about your audiences that will take you beyond generalizing and assuming. Figure 4-3 shows the portion of the Context Analysis Worksheet that deals with this step.

The more specific information you have about your readers or listeners, the better you can tailor your message to their needs and achieve your objectives.

Identify All Potential Audiences (Distinct or Overlapping)

Let's take a moment to review the three kinds of audiences—primary, hidden, and decision makers—that we discussed in Chapter 1.

- **Primary audience.** The primary audience is easy to identify because they are the individual(s) to whom you address your memo or talk. The primary audience is critical to the success of your communication. However, you should not limit your audience analysis to just these people. In almost every case, you need to think about other audiences as well.

Do not limit your audience analysis to your primary audience. Keep in mind other audiences also.

- **Hidden audience.** The hidden audience is composed of the indirect receivers of your message. This audience may not be directly connected with your communication purpose or process but may have some power over you. An example is your supervisor, who may not directly receive your message but who is likely to hear about it. Another example of a hidden audience may be a peer in your class who is asked by her internship employer to suggest other qualified students for positions. Your reading the opening story in this chapter makes you a hidden audience witnessing Mr. Topper's e-mail message.

Hidden audiences are not always obvious but can have a real impact on your overall goals or objectives.

CONTEXT ANALYSIS WORKSHEET

[DEFINING THE PRIMARY AUDIENCE]
Who is my primary audience (actual receiver of my message)?

- What do I know about him, her, or them personally and professionally (age, gender, educational level, job responsibility and status, civic and religious affiliation, knowledge of subject, and cultural background)?
- What are his, her, or their key attitudes about me?
    - About my subject?
    - About receiving my message?
- What does my primary audience *want* to know about my subject?
- What do I *need* my primary audience to know?
- What is the *consistent concern* that I always hear from such primary audiences?
- What specific information addresses those concerns?

[DEFINING OTHER POSSIBLE AUDIENCES]
Who is my hidden audience?

- What do I know about him, her, or them?
- What is the *consistent concern* of my hidden audience?
- What specific information addresses that concern?

Who is the decision maker?

- What do I know about him or her?
- What is the *consistent concern* of the decision maker?
- What specific information addresses that concern?

Figure 4-3
Context Analysis Worksheet: Defining Your Audience (Primary and Other)

Audience memberships can overlap, and you may have only a primary audience, but a message can fail if you neglect hidden audiences or decision makers.

Oversimplifying your view of the audience can damage your success.

- **Decision maker.** The decision maker is your most important audience, even in situations in which this audience gets information secondhand from your primary audience. In classroom presentations, this is likely to be your instructor. Your classmates may be the primary audience, but the instructor will be assigning a grade. Likewise, someone outside the primary audience may well make a final decision on your proposal. (Often organizations observe a chain of command, whereby you are limited to communicating with only your immediate boss. He or she then takes your ideas to his or her boss who holds the authority to decide. In such cases, the decision maker may not even hear or read your message firsthand.)

An example of these three types of audiences might be illustrated by a situation in which customers come to your office for a sales presentation. Your primary audience is that group of customers. Your hidden audience might be your manager, who tends to drop in on sales presentations and who has power over your career advancement. Your decision maker may be someone in the customer's organization who did not attend your presentation but who will make a decision based on the reports of the employees who did attend. Therefore, your primary audience must clearly understand your message in order to interpret it later for the absent decision maker.

This may all seem complicated, but these are the realities of the business world. Communicators who simplify too much and think only of the obvious primary audience often fail to accomplish their objectives.

Learn About Each Audience

Focus on the facts, attitudes, wants, and concerns of each audience. To the extent possible, learn as much as you can about each audience using the kinds of questions on the Context Analysis Worksheet. Make an effort to focus on the following four activities:

1. Gather personal and professional facts.
2. Consider audience attitudes.
3. Evaluate audience "wants" and your "needs."
4. Look for consistent concerns.

Gather as many professional and personal facts about audience members as you possibly can.

Gather Personal and Professional Facts   First, gather as many professional and personal facts about audience members as you possibly can. (Remember that you may have multiple audiences and need to gather information about each.) Gather information about your audience's age, gender, education level, cultural background, religious preferences, personal values, job responsibilities and status, as well as their knowledge of your topic. Consider these and any other personal data that may be useful in better understanding your audiences.

- **Age, gender, and education level.** Your message may be phrased much differently for an audience of young, ambitious college students than for a group of senior citizens. Younger, ambitious audiences may be more likely to be motivated by opportunities to make money or start a business, whereas senior citizens may find that much less relevant.

  Recognize, too, that both your gender and that of your target audience can influence your communication effectiveness. Studies consistently show that men and women often communicate differently. And even when they communicate the *same* way, men and women are often *perceived* differently by their target audiences. Gender communication differences in workplace communication are discussed in more detail in Reference Tool C, "Recognizing Gender Differences in Workplace Communication."

- **Cultural background, religious preferences, and personal values.** The national culture in which people live, as well as the cultures their families may have brought with them through the generations, have an impact on their values and, thus, on what motivates them. Similarly, people who are involved in religious activities may base their thinking on how an idea fits with their view of ethics or appropriate behaviors.

- **Job responsibilities and status.** People from different levels in an organization may look at issues in different ways. In traditional organizations, the higher the position a person holds, the better he or she may be at dealing with complex problems and taking a larger view of the implications of recommended actions. Lower-level employees tend to see issues through the lens of their limited experience.

  As modern organizations become less hierarchical and more team oriented, this distinction between so-called levels becomes blurred. Many of today's organizations downplay status differences and work hard to be sure employees throughout the company are fully informed about all aspects of the business.

- **Knowledge of your topic.** How much people already know about your topic will have a dramatic impact on how you should develop your message. If your audience has sufficient background experience with your topic, you might be able to move more quickly through your material or ask for a greater commitment to your objectives. If your audience knows little about your topic, you will have to inform before you can persuade.

Generation Gaps

Today's senior citizens tend to hold work values that have traditionally revolved around hard work, conservative behaviors, and loyalty to their work organizations. Generation Xers (people born since the early 1970s) tend to value flexibility, job satisfaction, and adequate leisure time. They are loyal to relationships but less so to organizations.

People from different levels in an organization may look at issues in different ways.

Consider your audience's age when communicating.

Key Dimensions in Assessing Cultures

In the 1990s, organizational culture researcher Geert Hofstede studied data looking at work-related values of more than 100,000 employees in 40 countries. He found that managers and employees differ on five value dimensions of national culture. As you read these, think about how each might influence a person's communication behaviors.

- **Power distance.** Some cultures put strong emphasis on social classes or socioeconomic levels. People in higher positions would rarely be approached by those in lower circumstances. These class differences are quite rigid. Conversely, some cultures put little emphasis on such status and treat all people equally. The culture of the United States exhibits lower power distance.
- **Individualism versus collectivism.** Some cultures accept or encourage individualism. Others frown on it, instead stressing the value of collective behaviors. People who rate individualism highly tend to look after themselves and their families; people who rate collectivism highly tend to belong to groups and look after each other in exchange for loyalty.
- **Quantity of life versus quality of life.** Quantity of life is the degree to which the society values the accumulation of material things, skills, and attributes. Quality-of-life cultures focus on the value of relationships and showing concern for the welfare of others.
- **Uncertainty avoidance.** Some cultures value predictable and stable structure (individuals tend to become nervous and stressed when the routine is upset). Others encourage innovation and risk taking, even when it may undermine traditional ways of doing things.
- **Long-term versus short-term orientation.** Some cultures are simply more patient than others, looking to the long run rather than pressing for more rapid changes. Figure 4-4 shows how some countries compare on these cultural dimensions.

Country	Power Distance	Individualism*	Quantity of Life**	Uncertainty Avoidance	Long-Term Orientation***
China	High	Low	Moderate	Moderate	High
France	High	High	Moderate	High	Low
Germany	Low	High	High	Moderate	Moderate
Hong Kong	High	Low	High	Low	High
Indonesia	High	Low	Moderate	Low	Low
Japan	Moderate	Moderate	High	Moderate	Moderate
Netherlands	Low	High	Low	Moderate	Moderate
Russia	High	Moderate	Low	High	Low
United States	Low	High	High	Low	Low
West Africa	High	Low	Moderate	Moderate	Low

Figure 4-4
Examples of Cultural Dimensions That Impact Audience Values[5]

* A low score is synonymous with collectivism.

** A low score is synonymous with high quality of life.

*** A low score is synonymous with a short-term orientation.

Knowing this information can give you hints as to how audience members may react to what you say. For example, as we mentioned, older workers may be more loyal to the ways things have always been done and resistant to changes you are recommending. Audience members who are active in religious organizations may respond well to your recommendation of a charitable activity. People in lower levels of responsibility may resist additional overtime work whereas higher-level personnel may accept the need to work longer hours in order to maximize their bonuses. Be careful, however, to remember that these generalizations are just that—generalizations. Communicators run the risk of stereotyping when they take an oversimplified view of groups of people. Ultimately, the best option is to come to understand people as individuals, not as categories.

Communicators run the risk of stereotyping when they take an oversimplified view of groups of people. Understand people as individuals, not as categories.

Ask yourself many questions about each listener. Think carefully about past experiences with the people with whom you will communicate. If you don't know them personally, consider your experience with similar people in similar situations. The longer you have worked with individuals, the more you are likely to know about them. Review all pertinent information and make notes. Then make your best guesses about how they are likely to respond to your ideas or proposals. You cannot predict with 100 percent accuracy how people will react, but the more information you have, the better your predictions will be.

Gather as much information about each audience and make some educated guesses as to how they are likely to respond to your message.

Consider Audience Attitudes   Next, make some realistic inferences about your audience's attitudes about you, about your topic, and about being there to receive your message. This recognition of your audience's attitudes can be humbling. Honesty may force you to acknowledge that your audience doesn't want to deal with you or your topic. They may prefer to never receive your letter, read your report, hear your presentation, or attend your meeting. They may be very turned off by your unsolicited e-mail as our author friend discovered.

Make some realistic inferences about your audience's attitudes about you, about your topic, and about being there to receive your message.

Always consider your history with your audience!

MR. TWEEDY   by **Ned Riddle**

"You're not still sore that we voted you 'Least Likely To Succeed' in Eastside High, are you, Ed?"

Managers often deal with challenging audiences when they require employees to take training courses. A classic example is when a company hires consultants to teach presentation skills. The consultants need to ask themselves questions such as, "What are likely to be our audience's attitudes about us or the topic of our message (i.e., attending a training program)?" Most employees know little about the consultants personally, but they hate the idea of going to a speaking course. They may have a desk full of work and a to-do list a mile long, and they may resent their bosses telling them to attend the course. Honest consultants would probably conclude that their primary audience would rather be thrown into a pit of snakes than attend speech training.

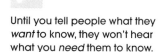

Be realistic about audience attitudes. Acknowledge negative feelings they may hold toward you or your topic and arrange your message to deal with those feelings.

Realistic audience analysis prepares you for handling reluctant message receivers and likely listener objections. As disillusioning as it may be, you *will* face times when your audience would rather be somewhere else, with someone else, doing something else rather than reading your document or listening to your presentation. Don't assume that just because it's part of their job to receive and respond to your message that they really care. You have to anticipate their needs and give them something to *motivate* them to care. Don't downplay these facts or hide from the truth. Accept this as good audience data and face it head on with excellent preparation.

Evaluate Audience Wants and Your Needs

Your next step is to determine exactly what your audience wants to know. Your job is to give them their "wants" before you ask them to do something that meets your "needs." In other words, you must satisfy their information hunger before you ask them to change their beliefs or behavior. Until you tell people what they *want* to know, they will never hear what you *need* them to know to fulfill the purpose of your message.

Until you tell people what they *want* to know, they won't hear what you *need* them to know.

For example, your supervisor might ask you to draft an outline for a presentation and a follow-up memo to employees to explain changes in job responsibilities after a reorganization. However, employees may not be willing to focus on the details of their job descriptions until you tell them about the security of their jobs or the status of their benefit plans. Satisfy your audience's information needs first.

Look for Consistent Concerns

Your next step is to recognize consistent audience concerns. As we discussed in Chapter 1, most people with whom you interact regularly express continuing interest in the same issues or themes. Remember to consider that each individual in your target audience might have his or her own consistent concerns.

Keep consistent audience concerns at the top of your mind. Don't waste time with issues that your audience considers irrelevant.

If you are recommending a change in the way you will handle assignments as an intern, for example, you may be wise to include justifications based on how the department you work in can benefit from your experience. However, the same recommendation made to the company's internship coordinator might need to focus on how it would result in an improved learning experience for you.

Define Your Objectives with Each Audience

Most messages have three objectives: an overall goal, a specific communication purpose, and a hidden agenda.

The third part of the first step in the Strategic Communication Model is to specify your objectives with each of your audiences. Most messages, no matter how apparently simple, encompass three objectives: an overall goal, a specific communication purpose, and a hidden agenda. Figure 4-5 shows the portion of the Context Analysis Worksheet that deals with this step. We will look at each of these objectives in the following sections.

CONTEXT ANALYSIS WORKSHEET

[DEFINING OBJECTIVES WITH EACH AUDIENCE]
What are my objectives with my primary audience?
What are my objectives with other possible audiences?

Figure 4-5
Context Analysis
Worksheet: Defining
Your Objectives with
Each Audience

Define an Overall Goal

The overall goal is your long-range plan or major desired result. For example, as a student, your overall goal might be to graduate with a specific degree. Your overall goal for your first job would be to get hired by a good company or to launch your own business. Your overall goal for a career would probably be to move into higher levels of responsibility in an organization or to build your company to a certain size. In corporate communication, the overall goal is often based on the mission statement of the organization. For example, the overall goal of a presentation about the budget for the next quarter might reflect the company's commitment to increase the value of its stock, or your luncheon speech at a civic club might focus on the president's initiative to "give something back" to the community.

Mission Statements

A *mission statement* is a definition of an organization's vision and values—where it is going and what it cares about. This statement typically emerges from a strategic planning process and is often printed and widely publicized to company employees, customers, and others. If used effectively, it helps companies make consistent decisions.

Identify the Specific Purpose of the Communication

The specific purpose of the communication depends on your needs and on your analysis of target audiences. Ask yourself, "As a result of this communication, exactly what do I want to occur?" Failing to articulate a clear purpose is an all too frequent pitfall for ineffective communicators. Too often they are not specific enough. For example, the specific purpose of your cover letter is to get the interview. The specific purpose of a first interview is to be invited back for a second interview. The specific purpose of the quarterly budget report might be to clearly explain each department's responsibilities for cutting expenses. The specific purpose of a civic club speech might be to garner community support for a new business.

Be sure that you clearly understand how you want your audience to react to your message—specifically.

Be realistic about how much you can accomplish with a single communication attempt. Persuasion, especially, is a process that is seldom fully accomplished with one message. Most audiences consist of people with various levels of willingness to accept your ideas.

Sales professionals talk about the sales cycle as a series of steps customers go through before actually buying. If, for example, you are in the market for a new computer, an effective salesperson would typically:

Work toward a realistic goal and move your audience toward the next step in accomplishing your overall goal.

- Give you information about the computer orally and offer a brochure
- Invite you to see the computer in the store or a demonstration room
- Encourage you to try the computer, using some of its features
- Prepare the paperwork for the purchase
- Deliver and possibly install the computer

Each of these actions is a step in the sales cycle. A typical buyer would go through all the steps. Few, if any, would simply read a brochure and then write a check to

The Persuasion Continuum

Since your goal in functional business communication is most often to persuade others, you need to be realistic about your chances. The process of your communicated message can be visualized as a continuum from 0 to 10, where 0 represents "I know (or care) *nothing* about this," and 10 represents "I'm ready to sign on the dotted line!" (Or 0 is "Who is this Pat person applying for the sales position?" and 10 is "Let's hire Pat for the job!")

Business communicators hurt their efforts when they assume that their audience knows or cares more than they actually do and ask those audiences to move too quickly up the continuum. You must work to accurately assess where your audi-ence is on the continuum and then set a reason-able, specific objective. You generally can't get your audience from 0 to 10 in one message. A more realistic goal would be to move them from complete ignorance to partial knowledge of an issue. For example, your specific purpose might be to take your audience from a 0 ("We don't need interns in our department") to a 3 ("An intern would be a low-cost solution for the extra help we need on our summer projects"). This is much the way a car salesperson moves a customer from browsing through the lot (2), to sitting inside a car (4), to taking a test drive (6), to going inside to dis-cuss terms (7), to signing a contract (10).

buy the computer. Each step in the process has a specific communication objective: to move the target audience to the next step in the sales cycle.

Acknowledge Your Hidden Agenda

Having a hidden agenda is perfectly normal and should be considered as you plan your message.

Finally, as you specify your objectives, keep in mind that you have a hidden agenda—personal goals to which you are aspiring. Everybody has them. This is perfectly nor-mal. Acknowledge that you have a hidden agenda and factor it into your planning.

For example, your hidden agenda may be to be perceived by your peers in class as a leader, to be offered a full-time job after your internship, or to be considered for management training after a few months into your first job. If you factor these goals into your planning, you can make a conscious effort to include information that would demonstrate your leadership potential or value to the company.

Gather the Information You Need

The most common information-gathering approaches are lis-tening, observing, and reading secondary sources.

The process of defining your communication context requires gathering good infor-mation and using that information to tailor your message. This is where all the parts of your Context Analysis Worksheet come together. Getting this information is not always easy, but it is generally worth the effort. In this section, we will talk about ways of gathering such data. Following that discussion, we will show you a sample of a completed Context Analysis Worksheet.

The most common information-gathering approaches are listening, observing, and reading secondary sources. Let's talk a bit about each of these.

Use Listening as an Information-Gathering Technique

Listening may well be the most important of all communica-tion skills.

Ironically, of the four basic communication skills—reading, writing, speaking, and listening—only listening is rarely taught in formal classes. Yet, of all the communi-cation skills, listening may actually be the most important. In any case, it deserves more attention than it typically gets.

Some people think that listening is passive—really just a matter of sitting back and letting the talker have his or her say. In reality, it is a highly active mental process that takes two forms: support listening and retention listening. *Support listening* consists of giving people enough feedback so that they thoroughly express their thoughts. *Retention listening* emphasizes techniques for capturing information from what is said. Let's look at each listening approach.

Use Support Listening   The intent of support listening is to learn what a person thinks and feels. When gathering information with support listening, avoid speaking except to encourage the other person to elaborate. Support listening seeks to draw out people's feelings and ideas by using nonevaluative responses such as:

Support listening consists of giving people enough feedback so that they thoroughly express their thoughts.

- **Open questions or "uh-huh" responses.** An open question is one that cannot be answered with a simple yes or no statement. "Uh-huh" is the simplest kind of oral response and consists of saying "uh-huh" or "hmmm" as other people talk to encourage them to continue to clarify their comments.
- **Content reflection (repeating the person's answer).** Content reflection involves repeating, mirroring, or echoing the statement made by another person in the form of a question. This is done without using a tone of voice that implies a judgment. You simply repeat what was said in essentially the same words and wait for further elaboration or clarification.

Support listening places the responsibility for continuing a conversation, dialogue, or interview on the other person.

Use Retention Listening   Retention listening calls for techniques that help you remember and use information gathered. The following are some tips for improving your retention:

Retention listening is a process of gathering and storing information for future use.

- **Minimize distractions.** Concentrate on the speaker. Force yourself to keep your mind on what the speaker is saying, and avoid multitasking. Trying to do other things while listening simply does not work.
- **Be an opportunist.** Do your best to find areas of interest between yourself and the speaker. Ask yourself, "What's in it for me? What can I get out of what this person is saying?"
- **Stay alert.** Avoid daydreaming if the person you are listening to is a bit boring. Force yourself to stay alert. If your thoughts run ahead of the speaker, use the extra time to evaluate, anticipate, and review.
- **Identify the speaker's purpose.** Is this person trying to inform you, or persuade you, or is he or she perhaps just trying to entertain you?
- **Listen for central themes rather than for isolated facts.** Too often people get hopelessly lost as listeners because they focus on unimportant facts and details and miss the speaker's main point.
- **Plan to report the content of a message to someone within eight hours.** This forces you to concentrate and to remember. It is a good practice technique.
- **Take notes efficiently.** The simple process of writing key ideas as you hear them helps you retain information. Learn ways to do this efficiently.

Use Observation as an Information-Gathering Technique

The best observations are structured and systematic. You may not be getting good information based on one or two haphazard observations.

Legendary baseball manager Yogi Berra once said, "You can observe a great deal by watching." Well put, Yogi. Much of the information needed to tailor your business communications can be gathered by observation. This is particularly true when considering the corporate culture (many facets of which are readily observable) and the external climate. We learn about these things by systematically observing and carefully reading.

Of course, be aware that you may not get good information based on one or two haphazard observations. A better technique is to plan to systematically observe in certain ways over a period of time so that what you see is more likely to be common occurrences, not fluke behaviors. Multiple observations of the same or similar behaviors are better than just one look.

If you suspect a problem or sense that an issue needs to be researched, make the effort to observe relevant behaviors systematically. For example, if a particular product in your store is not selling as well as it should, you may schedule systematic observations of customer behaviors. Select random times to observe how people look at or touch the product. Observe customer traffic patterns in your store. Do people seem to walk past the product without looking at it? Are customers hesitant to pick up the product or look more closely at it? Do they seem to react negatively when they see the price? Is the packaging hard to hold or so dull that people don't seem to notice it? These are the kinds of questions that can be answered in part by observation of customer behavior.

FAST FACTS

Traffic Patterns

Traffic patterns in retailing are the activities of potential customers as they move through the store. Supermarkets, for example, are set up in ways that encourage customers to move from one section of the store to another. Displays and shelves are designed to attract customers to the kinds of products that are most profitable. These patterns are subtle communication devices.

Read Secondary Sources as an Information-Gathering Technique

Use secondary information to enrich your knowledge of a company or industry and to better define the context of your message.

A *secondary source* of information is an article, report, statistic, or other document already written about a topic. Researchers almost always look first at such sources to see what has already been discovered rather than starting from the beginning and repeating someone's efforts. Reading such printed materials or studying information on the Internet are excellent ways to gather information about the context of your communication. In the past, reviewing secondary sources required library research, but today your "library" exists in cyberspace. With the Internet you have a wealth of information available at the stroke of a few keys.

With a little effort, you can become very familiar with the kinds of issues facing any industry or company. Using an Internet search engine, you can simply type in the name of a company and find a wealth of articles about it. Use this secondary information to enrich your knowledge of the company or industry and to better define the context of your message. If your research reveals that the industry is facing serious profit problems due to increased competition, for example, you need to consider that fact as you plan your messages.

You may choose to use other data-gathering methods, of course. In Reference Tool B, "Researching Your Topic and Documenting Your Findings," we show you other ways to gather useful information. For now, these three approaches will meet most needs: listening, observing, and reading secondary sources.

Use the Context Analysis Worksheet

Figure 4-6 is a completed Context Analysis Worksheet for a business report. The writer's assignment is to prepare a persuasive report encouraging workers in the company to accept a proposed company reorganization. Let's see how this might look:

Figure 4-7 (see pages 94–96) is a blank Context Analysis Worksheet that you may photocopy for your own use (you will be returning to this worksheet throughout the course of the book). This worksheet pulls together all the separate worksheet elements you have seen throughout the chapter. As you review it, be sure that you understand what information should be placed in each section. If you are unclear about any section, review the material in this chapter.

Figure 4-6
A Completed Context Analysis Worksheet (Based on the Strategic Communication Model)

CONTEXT ANALYSIS WORKSHEET

[DEFINING THE SITUATION]

How should I limit the problem or topic of my message?
Limit topic to the proposed three-phase reorganization plan. Do not introduce other possible variations. Present enough supporting data from consulting firm recommendations. Show advantages to employees throughout.

What factors in the business environment may influence the audience's response to my message?
Another local company, ABC Corporation, reorganized two years ago and went out of business within 10 months, resulting in 300 people being unemployed. The industry is going through difficult economic times due to increased foreign competition.

What key elements in the corporate culture should be taken into account as I prepare my message?
Stable, low risk-taking, traditional manufacturing environment. Management is very slow to change existing procedures. Workers prefer stable environment. Old-line company has not had a significant reorganization in more than 10 years.

[DEFINING THE PRIMARY AUDIENCE]

Who is my primary audience (actual receiver of my message)?
Employees, most of whom are hourly paid workers with specialized skills. They do repetitious tasks on an assembly line and tolerate the boring jobs by enjoying strong friendships with co-workers.

• What do I know about him, her, or them personally and professionally (age, gender, educational level, job responsibility and status, civic and religious affiliation, knowledge of subject, cultural background)?
They don't have a lot of employment options. Average age is mid- to late forties. Forty percent of workforce is over 55. Blue-collar experience. Very skilled in what they do but could not find other jobs easily. About half male and half female. Strong work ethic, good people. High school education; many have worked for company all their adult lives. Have lived in community for generations. Multicultural mix but predominantly Hispanic.

• What are his, her, or their key attitudes about me?
I'm a new person; they see me as a college hot-shot. Some fear that I will be a "hatchet man" and that I don't have the same loyalty to the company that they do. They are suspicious of me.

Figure 4-6
A Completed Context
Analysis Worksheet (Based
on the Strategic
Communication Model)

CONTEXT ANALYSIS WORKSHEET (continued)

• What are their attitudes about my subject?
They know little about organizational design and will be concerned about
how each new department will impact their work life. They fear any
changes that may make their employment less secure or take them away
from friends at work. The proposed changes are threatening to them.

• What are their attitudes about receiving my message? (Actually taking the time to
  attend my presentation, read my memo, etc.)
They seem eager to see my report because they have heard rumors, know
that a change is coming, and want to see something more concrete. They
are very willing to make the time to read it.

• What does my primary audience *want* to know about my subject?
What changes are being proposed and how these changes will affect their
lives. Also want to know why the company is doing this.

• What do I *need* my primary audience to know?
That their jobs are secure and that the changes will improve the overall
stability of the company. Every effort is being made to keep work groups
intact.

• What is the *consistent concern* that I always hear from such primary audiences?
Why change? Why rock the boat? Things have been the way they are for
a long time, and we like them this way.

• What specific information addresses those concerns?
Explain the competitive pressures that make the changes necessary.

[DEFINING OTHER POSSIBLE AUDIENCES]
Who is my hidden audience?
My boss. She wants to see if I can convince the employees of the need for
such changes and get them to agree with or at least not fight against the
proposed reorganization.

• What do I know about him, her, or them?
She is looking for the next generation of leadership for the company and
considers this assignment very important.

• What is the *consistent concern* of my hidden audience?
Cost-effectiveness while maintaining a stable workforce. Increasing
competition is a constant challenge.

• What specific information addresses that concern?
The plan includes additional opportunities for the workers to be involved
in the change process and to understand the need to keep costs low.

CONTEXT ANALYSIS WORKSHEET (continued)

Who is the decision maker?
The union leaders who must be won over to convince the workers that the plan is a good deal.

• What do I know about him or her?
They have been tough but fair. They are smart enough to recognize competitive pressures and the need for accepting some or all of the proposed changes. They are worried about some of the job changes.

• What is the *consistent concern* of the decision maker?
Economic stability of the company. The union boss has high concern for the workers. Workers are more important than the overall company.

• What specific information addresses that concern?
The report is based on extensive economic data gathered with the help of a respected consulting firm. The outlook for the company is bright if we successfully reorganize. If not, the company will not remain competitive.

[DEFINING OBJECTIVES WITH EACH AUDIENCE]

What are my objectives with my primary audience?
Explain reasons for organizational changes and reduce their fears about the impact of these changes. Gain their trust.

What are my objectives with other possible audiences?
Impress the boss with my ability to handle this task and demonstrate my management skills.

Figure 4-6
A Completed Context Analysis Worksheet (Based on the Strategic Communication Model)

Figure 4-7
Blank Context Analysis
Worksheet (Based on the
Strategic Communication
Model)

CONTEXT ANALYSIS WORKSHEET

[DEFINING THE SITUATION]
How should I limit the problem or topic of my message?

What factors in the business environment may influence the audience's response to my message?

What key elements in the corporate culture should be taken into account as I prepare my message?

[DEFINING THE PRIMARY AUDIENCE]
Who is my primary audience (actual receiver of my message)?

• What do I know about him, her, or them personally and professionally (age, gender, educational level, job responsibility and status, civic and religious affiliation, knowledge of subject, and cultural background)?

• What are his, her, or their key attitudes about me?

• What are his, her, or their attitudes about my subject?

CONTEXT ANALYSIS WORKSHEET (continued)

• What are his, her, or their attitudes about receiving my message? (Actually taking the time to attend my presentation, read my memo, etc.)

• What does my primary audience *want* to know about my subject?

• What do I *need* my primary audience to know?

• What is the *consistent concern* that I always hear from such primary audiences?

• What specific information addresses those concerns?

[DEFINING OTHER POSSIBLE AUDIENCES]
Who is my hidden audience?

• What do I know about him, her, or them?

• What is the *consistent concern* of my hidden audience?

• What specific information addresses that concern?

Figure 4-7
Blank Context Analysis Worksheet (Based on the Strategic Communication Model)

Figure 4-7
Blank Context Analysis
Worksheet (Based on the
Strategic Communication
Model)

CONTEXT ANALYSIS WORKSHEET (continued)

Who is the decision maker?

• What do I know about him or her?

• What is the *consistent concern* of the decision maker?

• What specific information addresses that concern?

[DEFINING OBJECTIVES WITH EACH AUDIENCE]
What are my objectives with my primary audience?

What are my objectives with other possible audiences?

APPLYING THE STRATEGIC COMMUNICATION MODEL

Let's look back at our opening story about the author who used mass e-mail (spam) to hype his book. Based on what we covered in this chapter, what should Jonathan Tropper have done differently?

Perhaps at the root of Tropper's problem was the early success he experienced with the bookstore crowds. He inferred from that success that he could use a different medium and have the same success. He generalized to all potential book buyers from a small sample who came to the store. But his e-mail audience was very different from the walk-in bookstore fans.

In reality, the bookstore audience was self-selected—that is, they *chose* to come into the store because they were interested in books. His e-mail message receivers were very different in that they were not primed to buy books at the time they got the message. On the persuasion continuum, they were perhaps at 1 or 2s, whereas the bookstore visitors were at 6 or 7 or higher.

More importantly, the author violated the "culture" of book selling. He used a mass-marketing approach to send a message that needed to be much more personalized and focused. His personal, in-store efforts were considered normal and appropriate for selling novels. His mass-marketing efforts were seen as high pressure and were, thus, rejected. In short, he seriously misread the context of his communication. This misreading cost him dearly. A more careful analysis of the audience and context would have suggested a personal, low-keyed presentation of his book and hoped-for word-of-mouth recommendations.

Summary of Key Ideas

- Message effectiveness is dramatically affected when you take the time and make the effort to carefully define the context for your business messages.
- The communication context consists of the specific problem or issue, the audiences, and your specific objectives with each audience.
- Limiting the problem, evaluating the external climate, and evaluating the corporate (or organizational) culture are important planning activities.
- Factors such as age, gender, and national cultures have an impact on people's work values.
- Key dimensions of different national cultures include power distance (status differences), individualism, quantity of life (materialism), uncertainty avoidance (versus risk taking), and long-term versus short-term orientation.
- Three groups of target audiences should be considered as you define your context: primary, hidden, and decision makers. These may be different people who have different informational needs and wants. These groups can also overlap.
- Context analysis information can be gathered by careful listening, systematic observation, and review of secondary sources.
- Two types of listening can be effective: support listening and retention listening.
- The Context Analysis Worksheet is a useful tool for planning any message.

Application Activities

Activity 4-1 Defining the Context

Complete a Context Analysis Worksheet for one of the following situations:

1. You have been asked to give an oral presentation to sell a product or service you are familiar with to your class.
2. You want to prepare a written document advocating a zoning change that will permit a recreation center to be built in an area where several senior citizen apartment complexes are located. You will distribute this to the seniors.
3. You are preparing a speech or written document to advocate voting for or against a current law or rule change. (This may be for an apartment residents' association, a rule in some organization you are familiar with, or a legislative issue.)

4. You have been asked to speak to a high school young entrepreneurs club that focuses on teaching young people to start and run their own businesses.

Interactive CD-ROM Exercises

Activity 4-2 Determining How Well Others Define Their Contexts

Do an Internet search of current business magazines to find companies that are experiencing unfavorable publicity. These may be companies whose products are defective, whose services practices are substandard, or whose sales results are poor. Review the ways they are communicating with their various audiences in light of the material discussed in this chapter. Write a brief report (two pages or less) on why these companies have been effective or ineffective and how they have used or failed to use effective context analysis.

Activity 4-3 Gathering Information on Corporate Culture

Recent graduates from your school are a valuable resource for information on the corporate culture in which they work. Plan to conduct an interview with a recent graduate to gather information about an organization's corporate culture. Design questions that you can ask to discover the seven primary culture characteristics of the company.

- Innovation and risk taking (Example question: *Can you tell me about a time when an employee was rewarded for innovating thinking or risk taking?*)
- Attention to detail
- Outcome orientation
- People orientation
- Team orientation
- Aggressiveness
- Stability

Activity 4-4 Practicing Listening Skills

Prepare to interview a business executive and explore ways in which communication strategy has contributed to his or her success. You will have the greatest opportunity to create a strong impression during an interview if you have thoroughly researched the organization before the interview. Outline the specific information-gathering sources you will use for an upcoming interview.

- **Company:** List the name of the company with which you would like to interview.
- **Listening strategy:** During the interview, what information do you hope to gather? When will you begin gathering information? Who can be sources of information?
- **Support questions:** List some open-ended questions you will ask. Describe how you will reflect the content of this statement: "When I graduated from college, I thought that all that strategy stuff was only theoretical. But once I began working in business, I realized that I needed to use communication strategy on a daily basis."
- **Retention tactics:** What will you do if there is a noisy distraction in the hallway? What materials will you bring to ensure that you can take notes? How will you locate central themes? What form will your "report" take and when will you write it?
- **Observation strategy:** What opportunities will you have to observe the organization? Whom will you observe? When will your observation begin?
- **Secondary source strategy:** What secondary sources are available to you? List at least four. Where will you find them? When will you access the sources? How will you let your interviewer know that you have researched the company?

Activity 4-5 Analyzing Your Peer as Your Audience

Since your peers will make up the audience for your in-class presentations, it is helpful to analyze your peers. Pair up with a classmate and analyze him or her as an audience member, including personal and professional facts, attitudes, "wants," and consistent concerns. Write a memo to your professor detailing what you have discovered in your analysis. Remember to copy your peer on the memo.

Career Activity

Career Activity 4-1 Analyzing a Potential Employer

Complete a Context Analysis Worksheet to analyze a potential employer. Select a company or industry and research it carefully using secondary sources (primarily the Internet). Your overall goal is to sell yourself to a company for which you want to work (either as an intern or full-time employee). From this analysis, describe how you might approach the company or organization to sell yourself.

myPHLIP Companion Web Site

Learning Interactively

Visit the myPHLIP Web site at www.prenhall.com/timm. For Chapter 4, take advantage of the interactive "Study Guide" to test your chapter knowledge. Get instant feedback on whether you need additional studying. Read the "Current Events" articles to get the latest on chapter topics, and complete the exercises as specified by your instructor. Expand your learning with a visit to the "Research Area." There you will find a wealth of information you can use to complete your course assignments.

Notes

1. Matthew Rose, "Author Learns E-mail Can Sell or Sink a Book," *Wall Street Journal,* August 7, 2000, p. B1.
2. Stephen P. Robbins, *Essentials of Organizational Behavior,* 6th ed. (Upper Saddle River, NJ: Prentice-Hall, Inc., 2000), p. 235.
3. Adapted from Paul R. Timm, *51 Ways to Save Your Job* (Hawthorne, NJ: Career Press, 1992), p. 22.
4. Ibid., p. 236. Reprinted with permission.
5. Adapted from G. Hofstede, "Cultural Constraints in Management Theories," *Academy of Management Executive* (February 1993), p. 91.

SKILL OBJECTIVES

After you have studied this chapter, you should be able to:

- Recognize the advantages and disadvantages of different business communication media.
- Select appropriate media rather than using them out of habit.
- Describe how communication media trigger certain expectations in message receivers, present trade-offs between efficiency and effectiveness, and have unique capabilities.
- Explain the distinction between communication efficiency and communication effectiveness.
- Apply appropriate media based on characteristics such as speed, feedback capacity, hard-copy availability, message intensity and complexity, formality, and relative costs.
- Identify some of the unspoken ground rules associated with different communication media.
- Describe ways to mix media to improve effectiveness.
- Identify a variety of communication tools used in organizations.

Consider Your Media and Timing Options: Making the How and When Decisions for Your Message

CHAPTER 5
SKILL
FOCUS:

Identifying and Using

Appropriate Media and

Timing Options to Increase

Communication Effectiveness

COMMUNICATING WITHOUT A STRATEGY

Wilbur Jackson's Blistering Memo

The following memo is fairly clear, but it fails miserably to accomplish its goal. Read it and see if you can determine why.

MEMORANDUM

TO: All employees
FROM: Wilbur Jackson, Supervisor
DATE: August 14, 2001
RE: COFFEE BREAK ABUSE
It has recently come to my attention that department employees are taking excessively long coffee breaks. These violate company policy. Employees caught taking more than fifteen minutes in the morning and afternoon will be terminated. If things don't improve, the manager of the Roach Coach, Inc., will be told to not send their snack and coffee truck to our company anymore. I trust you will obey policy in the future regarding this matter.

What problems do you see with this memo? You could cite its tone and format, but a more basic problem arises from the writer's decision to use a memo in the first place. This is an ineffective communication medium for this message. Wilbur chose the "easy way" to deal with a problem and, in so doing, probably created more problems than he solved.

Suppose that you work for Wilbur and that you have been very careful to limit your coffee breaks to less than fifteen minutes. Further suppose that you often forgo breaks to meet the demands of your job. How would you react to this memo? Suppose Wilbur sent this message shortly after you had put in large amounts of volunteer overtime to meet heavy production demands. How would that make this reprimand even worse?

A critical step when initiating a message is to consider media and timing options. The term *media* refers to the channels or mechanisms for conveying a message. Each medium has certain characteristics, advantages, and disadvantages that make it more or less effective under various circumstances. We introduced the concept of considering your options in Chapter 1. This chapter builds on that introduction by giving you more information about media and timing options. The decisions you make at this phase of your planning can have a considerable impact on the overall effectiveness of your communication.

Be Aware of the Many Media and Timing Choices

Don't just communicate at your convenience. Be sensitive to your audience.

Awareness of media and timing options can greatly improve the likelihood of successful communication with multiple audiences.

This chapter focuses on Step 2 of the Strategic Communication Model, consider your media and timing options. Never before have business communicators had so many media options available. If you are new to the business world, you may not realize how dramatically things have changed in recent years. Traditional media such as letters, presentations, memos, interviews, meetings, and telephone calls are now supplemented with faxes, e-mail, teleconferencing, Web pages, videos, and DVDs, to name a few changes. You can use any of these or combine several to deliver your messages. Effective communicators evaluate the pros and cons of each option in relation to the message context, their audience, and their objectives. Less effective communicators too often make media choices out of habit or based on what's easiest instead of considering the needs and preferences of their target audiences.

Similarly, some people fail to think about the timing of their messages: When should the message arrive for maximum impact? Timing of a message can have an impact on its effectiveness. For example, a thank-you note sent months after a gift is received or a persuasive presentation given before the receiver is ready to make a decision may have little positive effect. Again, consider the needs of your audience in conjunction with your own communication goals as you decide when to send the message. Don't just communicate at your convenience. Be sensitive to whether your audience is capable of understanding and available to receive your message.

Timing questions can be further complicated when you communicate with multiple audiences. You need to think about the sequencing and spacing of your messages. With whom should you talk first? How much time should you allow between messages? In companies, you are normally expected to go through channels of authority. You would not, for example, go directly to a senior manager with a question that your direct supervisor could answer. Conversely, the senior manager should not tell you about a decision before telling your supervisor.

Also, certain audiences should receive information before others. For example, an employee who is being promoted or reassigned should get this message before others do. The supervisor of that employee should also be informed of changes in advance of a public announcement. Violating these timing issues can lead to embarrassment and the feeling of being "out of the loop" in the organization.

Never before have business communicators had so many media and timing options available.

Casual Messages with an Impact

A dean at a university wrote to a number of prominent people to see whether they would consider speaking on campus. One such person was a man who had run for president of the United States a decade earlier. The man's response illustrates the impact of media and timing choices. This prominent politician answered the request within a week using a handwritten letter indicating his willingness to speak. Although he had secretaries who could have typed the letter, he chose to personalize this message and use a medium that is often reserved for correspondence between personal friends. The impact on the receiver was dramatic. The thought that such a busy and prominent man would handwrite a letter conveyed a sincerity and generosity that the dean will never forget.

Consider Your Media Options

Having defined the context of your message by understanding the situation, your audiences, and your objectives, you are ready to use this information to choose from the many media options, Step 2 of our model. Your choice can dramatically impact the message's outcome. Resist the temptation to skip this phase of the Strategic Communication Model. An otherwise effective message can fall flat (or even backfire) if you use an inappropriate medium or have poor timing.

Beware of information overload when sending business messages.

Each communication medium:

- Triggers certain expectations in the message receivers
- Presents a trade-off between efficiency and effectiveness
- Has unique capabilities
- Plays within certain ground rules

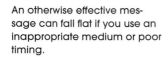

The strategic model reminds you to consider the timing of your messages.

The combined effect of all this is that the medium you select for a particular message becomes a part of the message—it conveys information about the message.

FOCUS ON

Communication Overload

A common challenge for today's businesspeople is communication overload. With the increasing use of e-mail and voice mail (phone messaging), people often feel bombarded with an enormous amount of information. Because of overload, some messages may be ignored. Businesspeople face the challenge of trying to communicate through all the clutter of competing messages. Keeping messages concise and focused is one way to reduce overload.

An otherwise effective message can fall flat if you use an inappropriate medium or poor timing.

Consider Your Receivers' Media Expectations

People expect certain types of messages to be communicated via certain media. Habits of communicating develop and become the norm. With this in mind, a business communicator may try using a different medium or combination of media to give a message extra impact. If, for example, a change in work schedule is normally posted on a bulletin board, a supervisor may get better audience attention by calling a meeting or talking with each worker individually about an unusual change. A letter sent to a worker's home will have a different impact than will a general public address system announcement. Customers who expect little or no follow-up after a sale may be impressed by a personal, handwritten note. Apply creativity, a consideration of media characteristics, and some educated guesses about the likely effects of messages, and you may see some real opportunities to develop an interesting and effective media mix.

Consider Media Efficiency and Effectiveness

The cost of communicating is an important consideration. In a broad sense, cost can best be calculated by distinguishing between communication *efficiency* and communication *effectiveness*. These are very different things.

Communication *efficiency* is a simple ratio between the resources expended to generate a message (including time, materials, and effort) and the number of people to whom the message is sent. To improve efficiency, simply increase the number of people reached or reduce the message preparation costs. The widely distributed memo, mass mailing, or large meeting can be *efficient*. Wilbur Jackson's memo was efficient in our opening story.

Communication *effectiveness* is quite another matter. To remember the four-part definition of communication effectiveness, use the acronym RURU. Business and professional communication may be said to be *effective* when a message is:

- *Received* by its intended audience
- *Understood* essentially the same way by the recipients as intended by the sender
- *Remembered* over a reasonable period of time
- *Used* when appropriate occasions arise.[1]

The dilemma for the message sender is that, in most cases, the communication methods that are most efficient are least effective, and vice versa. In almost every case, for example, face-to-face conversation with individuals is the least efficient, least convenient, and most costly method of communication. It is also the most effective. And, for some types of messages, including Wilbur's problem with the coffee breaks, it is essential. Wilbur's efficient memo results in a shotgun approach that is likely to hit the wrong people (violating the first effectiveness condition mentioned earlier) by striking the innocent as well as the guilty. This could cause huge resentment.

Another efficiency-versus-effectiveness example comes from a business manager in a large corporation, who tells this story:

> I once attended a meeting that was called by the general manager for about 200 employees, midlevel managers, supervisors, and office staff. A meeting room was rented at a hotel near the main office, since we had no conference room large enough. The purpose of the meeting was for the general manager to explain, in a broad sense, the need to economize in our everyday operations. After stating that need and explaining how it related to the company's profit picture, the executive asked if anyone had any comments or suggestions.
>
> One secretary spent approximately ten minutes explaining how she had developed a system to save paper clips and make scratch pads out of used paper. Several others took the opportunity to impress the boss with their success stories at recycling containers or cutting down on photocopying.
>
> But no one seemed to notice the cost of that meeting! By the time the people drifted back to their offices, the company had spent over 300 employee-hours in direct labor costs alone. In addition, the company incurred the cost of the meeting room and the cost of reduced efficiency back at the offices while all the supervisors were gone. The company also faced the incalculable cost of possible lost business or customer resentment

Communication efficiency equals the number of people reached divided by the cost of producing the message.

Communication effectiveness is not the same as communication efficiency.

created when people wanting to speak to an employee simply had to wait until our meeting ended.

What was the return on this communication investment? Participants learned that the company would like to make a profit (a real eye-opening notion!), and they picked up some tips on saving paper clips and making scratch pads. The corporation used a thousand-dollar medium to convey nickel-and-dime ideas. The point, of course, is that selection of appropriate communication media can have a considerable effect on communication costs and effectiveness.

In some cases, of course, a message is very simple or not important enough to discuss in individual, face-to-face interaction. In many cases, organizational size or complexity forbids it. You need to strike a balance between efficiency and effectiveness. Unfortunately, many business communicators choose a medium out of habit, without considering the merits or drawbacks of possible alternatives. They also tend to select what is easiest for *them* to do—rather than thinking about the preferences of their audiences. For example, some people e-mail extensively because they are at their computer all day. Others prefer to work with cell phones, drop in on people to communicate in person, or call frequent meetings. These media may be fine as long as they are chosen purposefully, not just used out of habit.

Consider Media Capabilities

Each medium has specific advantages and disadvantages based on its capabilities and limitations. Let's look at some of the capabilities of business communication media that make one preferable to others in a given situation.

Many business communicators get into the habit of using the same media without regard to how effective they are.

Speed   The speed of a medium depends on several factors, including preparation time, delivery time, and assimilation time (the time it takes for the receiver to comprehend the message being delivered). A letter is generally slow getting from sender to receiver (although overnight services and faxes have reduced delivery time), but an oral presentation of the same information may take considerably more preparation time. The time-consuming work of producing a videotape or slide presentation may be offset when repeated showings can efficiently present the same information to many audiences. Normally, the spoken word is faster than a print medium, except when we are comparing a formal oral presentation with a handwritten note.

The spoken word is generally faster than print media.

Feedback Capacity   The amount and promptness of feedback are important media considerations. Written media elicits no feedback from your audience while you are writing the message. By the time you get a response, it is too late to adjust and clarify the original message. Telephone conversations provide immediate feedback in the form of questions, comments, tone of voice, pauses, hesitations, and so on. Face-to-face communication situations provide all this plus nonverbal feedback in facial expressions, body movements, and postures.

Verbal and face-to-face media provide the most immediate feedback.

Hard-Copy Availability   Whether a tangible, permanent record of the message is *normally* retained or not is another media characteristic. Ordinarily, interviews, informal conversation, and telephone messages leave no record. (Of course, these

can be recorded, but that is not routine practice in most organizations.) E-mail messages can be printed or maintained in electronic files but otherwise do not leave an easily accessible hard copy. Written communications such as letters, reports, and most memos are often maintained on file. An informal note, however, may be discarded and is, therefore, usually a nonrecord medium. Of course, a nonrecord medium can have advantages where candid, off-the-record expression is called for. Putting it in writing seems to make the message more formal or official, a situation that may also call for less openness in expression.

Putting something in writing makes the message more formal, which may also lead to less openness in expression.

Message Intensity and Complexity   Some media are more appropriate for conveying complex or highly intense messages. A high-intensity message may be one that conveys unpleasant information or in some way plays on the receiver's emotions. Examples are messages that criticize the receiver's behavior or complex information about price changes or legal interpretations. Persuasive messages that require careful explanation of underlying reasoning are often best communicated by a medium that can carry complex data in a relatively structured format. Typically, a formal letter, a carefully planned oral presentation with handouts, or a written report would meet these requirements. Casual conversation or a brief memo would be less appropriate.

Complex messages may require media that can carry detailed information in a structured manner.

Formality   Some media are more appropriate for formal occasions, and others fit well in informal settings. A letter of congratulations to an employee seems more formal and has a rather different effect than, say, a casual, unplanned remark conveying the same information. The letter makes it official. An informal handwritten note sent to the board of directors by a worker may be considered out of line. When the message is intended for internal consumption only (within the organization), its format may be less formal than if it were to be publicly disseminated outside the company. For this reason, memos are used internally, whereas written correspondence sent outside the organization takes the form of letters—a slightly more formal format.

Letters are generally more formal than memos.

Figure 5-1 summarizes key characteristics of some common business communication media. The bolded items suggest characteristics that may be the most significant reason for choosing a particular medium.

Consider Media Ground Rules

Another way to determine the best media is to think about the ground rules—the underlying assumptions associated with each option. These ground rules for use of a particular medium are usually assumed by participants rather than prescribed in advance. Communication professor Richard Hatch illustrates, for example, that

When the ground rules are broken, the medium becomes ineffective.

Media	Speed	Feedback Capacity	Hard Copy Available	Formal/ Informal	Can Handle Complex/ Intense Messages	Cost (High/Low)
Informal conversation	**Fast**	High	No	Informal	No	Low
Telephone conversation	**Fast**	Medium	No	Informal	No	Low– Medium
Voice mail	**Fast**	Low	No	Informal	No	Low
Formal oral presentation	Medium	Medium	Maybe	**Formal**	**Yes**	Medium– High
Informal note	Medium	**Low**	Yes	Informal	No	Low
Memo	Medium	Low	**Yes**	Either	Possible	Medium– High
E-mail	Fast	Low	**Yes**	Informal	Possible	Medium
Fax	**Fast**	Low	Yes	Either	Yes	Medium
Letter	Slow	Low	Yes	Formal	**Yes**	Medium– High
Formal report	Very slow	Low	Yes	Very formal	**Yes**	High

Figure 5-1
Characteristics and Costs of Business Communication Media

the medium called "polite conversation" usually works under the following ground rules:[3]

- Whoever is talking may continue to talk until he or she appears to be finished.
- No speaker should talk for "very long" at a time, which may vary from a few seconds to two or three minutes, depending on the circumstances.
- Nobody may interrupt the speaker unless he or she agrees to be interrupted.
- When a silence occurs, each participant has an equal opportunity to begin talking; that is, nobody is intentionally excluded.
- Anybody who is talking may change the subject without getting permission from other participants.

When such ground rules are violated, participants in the communication situation are thrown off. Imagine a polite conversation in which any of the rules listed are violated—let's say, for example, that interruptions abound—and you are likely to picture an ineffectual and decidedly impolite conversation.

Figure 5-2 suggests additional examples of the kinds of ground rules (which are often unspoken) for several spoken and written/graphic media.

Obviously we don't consciously consider each rule every time we communicate, but these ground rules can provide a rational basis for making decisions about what

Ground rules can provide a basis for making decisions about what medium to use for messages.

Even in polite conversation, there are certain ground rules that must be covered.

Some Possible Ground Rules	Spoken Media				Written/Graphic Media		
	Conversation (Telephone or Face-to-Face)	Interview	Meeting	Presentation	Letter/ Memo/ E-Mail	Report	Slides/ Display
Receivers may interrupt and/or seek clarification	Yes	Yes	Yes	No	No	No	No
Participants may change the subject	Yes	Sometimes	Yes	No	No	No	No
One person may talk for extended periods	No	No	No	Yes	No	Yes	No
Participants have equal opportunity to initiate ideas	Yes	Sometimes	Yes	No	No	No	No
Sender presents messages in a standard arrangement or format	No	Sometimes	No	Yes	Usually	Yes	Sometimes
Sender presents supporting data of considerable detail with conclusion	Sometimes	No	Sometimes	Yes	Sometimes	Yes	Sometimes
Medium conveys artistic or aesthetic qualities	No	No	No	Somewhat	No	Sometimes	Yes

Figure 5-2
Examples of Ground Rules for Media[4]

medium to use for specific messages. If, for example, you need to convey some highly technical, intricate, and complex information, you would likely avoid the friendly conversation medium. Such messages may involve talking for very long periods of time, and listeners would be expected to refrain from changing the topic. Recognizing the ground rules in operation may alert you to potential communication failures.

Consider Media Mixing: A Sound Alternative

The Grapevine as a Medium

The term *grapevine* refers to the unofficial path of verbal communication. Rumors or scuttlebutt spread from person to person through an informal network. Surprisingly, the grapevine can be quite accurate with some kinds of messages.

Bear in mind that you are certainly not limited to the use of a single medium for a given message. Often a combination of several media does the job very nicely, since disadvantages of one medium can be offset by another. For example, the slow-feedback characteristic of written media can be offset by an accompanying oral medium. Figure 5-3 suggests some ways to combine commonly used media to offset such disadvantages.

Experiments studying the effects of combining media have produced inconclusive results, primarily because of the difficulty of accounting for all possible variables—especially nonverbal ones. Nevertheless, some tentative findings have emerged. In one classic experiment, specific factual information was transmitted using each of the following media or combinations of media:

- Oral only
- Written only
- Posted on a bulletin board
- The grapevine (no formal message sent)
- Both oral and written

Figure 5-3
Combining Media for Effectiveness

Medium	Major Limitations	Supplemental Media
Conversation (phone or live)	No record; little nonverbal feedback with phone use	Record notes; send additional written material; tape record
Formal oral presentation	Preparation time; no record	Written handouts; outline of presentation; supplemental readings
Informal note	Low feedback; may look overly casual or unimportant	Telephone or conversation follow-up; insert with printed card
Memo	Low immediate feedback; medium often overused	Telephone follow-up to check for understanding
E-mail	Informal; may get lost among overload	Follow-up hard copy or supplemental information; telephone or conversation follow-up
Formal report	Preparation time; low feedback; cost of printing, etc.	Meeting or presentation to discuss, clarify, and provide/receive feedback

Several days after the messages were delivered, researchers tested the recipients to see how much content they could accurately remember. The results showed that the written-plus-oral message combination resulted in the greatest retention. Oral exchange alone was second in recall accuracy, followed by the written message used alone. The bulletin board was next, and the grapevine came in last in this study.[5]

In a later study of communication within a company, researchers asked supervisors to rate the effectiveness of (1) written, (2) oral, (3) written and then oral, and (4) oral and then written communication for different types of situations. In general, the oral-followed-by-written technique came out best. Supervisors saw it as most effective for situations that required immediate action, passed along a company directive, communicated an important policy change, reviewed work progress, called for praising a noteworthy employee, or promoted a safety campaign. The written-only technique was judged best for passing along information that required action in the future or was of a general nature. An oral-only message was suggested for informal reprimands or to settle a dispute among employees.[6]

Research has shown that a written-plus-oral message combination results in the greatest retention.

FOCUS ON

Tools Used in Business Communication

Today's businessperson is bombarded with enormous amounts of information. So how can the effective communicator be heard above the din of competing messages? Try creativity in media selection. Creativity and innovation start with a look at what's being done now. The following presents a brief review of the kinds of communication media and tools used in businesses. This listing represents popular use, not necessarily the optimum use of communication tools. The intent of this listing is to create awareness about the breadth of media options available to today's business communicator.

Tools to Convey Job-Related Information

Organizations use the following tools to convey information, such as work directives and policy clarification, that people must have to be effective:

- Published job descriptions, procedures, practices, or policy manuals
- Instructional interviews, performance reviews, briefings, or training sessions

- Newsletters and in-house magazines
- Benefits statements (individual accounting of the value of an employee's benefit package)
- Reprints or summaries of technical articles

Tools to Convey "For-Your-Information" Messages

Companies use for-your-information tools to convey messages that are likely to be of some interest but are not crucial to the job functions of employees. (For-your-information messages are often abbreviated as FYI. Messages described as FYI generally don't require a reply.) Such FYI messages serve to keep organization members "in the loop."

- Announcement memos (used to explain personnel changes, promotions, appointments, etc.)
- Information/reading racks (stocked with pamphlets, how-to booklets, and magazines or journals of varying topics)
- Bulletin boards

Continued

Tools to Motivate Employees

Companies use the following tools to build and strengthen organizational identification and loyalty:

- Auto windshield decals, bumper stickers, or license plate frames
- Open houses, family nights (programs including tours of the plant, exhibits, demonstrations, samples, and refreshments), and alumni or retiree activities
- Letters and cards (sympathy, birthday, anniversary, etc.)
- Recreational and social activities (such as athletic leagues, picnics, and outings)
- Uniforms, coveralls, hard hats, and name badges marked with the company logo
- Displays and exhibits (photos, artwork, videotape, or slide presentations on subjects such as company history, company products, or statistical data regarding employees, management, and stockholders)

Tools to Convey Upward Feedback

Companies use certain media to encourage upward feedback from subordinates or customers to management. Examples of these media include:

- Advisory councils, focus groups, or similar groups to identify employee or customer concerns
- Grievance interviews in which employees or customers can speak face-to-face with a company representative
- Exit interviews (interviews with employees who are leaving the company, attempting to understand why they are leaving or what concerns they have about the company)
- Suggestion systems

These listings represent only a sample of tools used in organizations to communicate and create understanding.

Consider Your Timing Options

Poor timing can ruin even the most carefully crafted message. This can occur when we communicate at our own convenience rather than being sensitive to our audience. Timing of messages can also have a dramatic effect on their acceptance and understanding. The following sections offer some suggestions for making good decisions about media timing.

Be Aware of Competing Audience Concerns

You can best avoid timing mistakes by knowing your audiences and being sensitive to their needs.

Sometimes leaders deliver their messages at poor times. One manager sent an e-mail message to subordinates asking them to call his secretary to schedule a meeting to talk about "performance issues." The e-mail arrived at 5 P.M. on a Friday, giving the receivers all weekend to wonder and worry about this vaguely threatening message. In another case of poor timing, a manager told a subordinate that his contract was not going to be renewed on a day that marked the three-year anniversary of a tragic auto crash that killed the man's wife.

You best avoid such timing mistakes by knowing your audiences and being sensitive to their needs. Put yourself in their shoes and ask, "Is this a good time to receive such a message?"

 Sometimes you cannot control the timing of a message. This advertisement appeared in magazines across the country just days after the August 2000 Concorde crash in Paris.

Avoid Communicating When You Are Upset

Many of us have fired off a blistering memo, made an angry phone call, or spouted off in a meeting while upset. And many of us have had to eat our words later. If a situation prompts you to send an emotionally charged message, write or draft your thoughts but hold on to them for a day or two. Letting the message ferment and then editing it carefully can help you avoid embarrassment and serious credibility damage.

Wait a day or two before sending an emotionally charged message so that you can think about and edit it.

Be Aware of Message Sequencing

Additional timing considerations are sequencing and spacing of your messages, especially with multiple audiences. Sequencing means deciding who will get the message first, second, and so on. An effective communicator will decide which audience is to receive which message in what order.

Also consider how much time to allow between messages. For example, if you are given the task of training people in all your company's locations about a benefits change, you need to decide whom you will present to first, second, and so on. If the message is about retirement program changes, you may well choose to talk first to older workers, who will be affected soonest by the change. In addition, organizations generally want information to follow the chain of command. You may need to get approval from your supervisor or even that person's manager before distributing a message. Sending out unapproved messages is a serious social blunder that can hurt your career.

 Consider the sequencing and spacing of your messages.

APPLYING THE STRATEGIC COMMUNICATION MODEL

The medium that communicators choose for their messages sends important signals to the receivers. In the case of Wilbur Jackson in our opening story, he chose a routinely distributed, photocopied memo. The effect was to convey some possible unspoken messages such as:

- This message isn't very important. If it were, I'd present it more formally.
- You are not important enough to receive this information from me personally.
- I am too busy to convey this information to you in a more personal way.
- I don't care about the appearance of my message; this "quick-and-dirty" approach is good enough.
- This matter is so urgent, I had to sacrifice personalizing and professionalism to get out the information quickly.
- This is routine information that you will readily understand.

Unfortunately, Wilbur apparently gave little thought to the medium he chose. In failing to look at his options, he did not consider the fact that the medium itself makes a comment about the contents of the message. When criticizing personal behavior, other media are almost always superior to a quick memo. If he were really interested in changing the behavior of his employees, Wilbur would have met with people individually in an interactive conversation. This would cost more (in time and effort), but if the message is truly important and demands behavior changes, conversations are a far superior medium.

Summary of Key Ideas

- The medium you select to communicate your message will have an impact on the meaning the receiver attaches to the message.
- The media, methods, or approaches we choose when communicating can enhance or detract from our communication success.
- Each communication medium triggers certain expectations in the message receivers, presents a trade-off between efficiency and effectiveness, and has unique capabilities.
- What receivers might expect should be factored into media choice decisions. At times you will want to use the expected media; at times you may want to use unexpected media to direct special attention to your message.
- Efficiency and effectiveness are different and should be weighed in your media decision. Communication efficiency is a simple ratio between the total costs of a message and the number of people reached by that message. Communication effectiveness is determined by the degree to which a message is *received* by the intended audience, *understood* correctly, *remembered* for a reasonable period of time, and *used* when appropriate occasions arise. (The acronym RURU can help you remember this.)
- Capabilities inherent in a given medium should be considered when selecting that medium. Among the salient characteristics are speed, feedback capacity, hard-copy availability, message intensity and complexity, and formality.

- A communication medium operates within a generally accepted set of ground rules. These ground rules play a large part in determining the medium's effectiveness in a given situation.
- Mixing several media can offset the disadvantages of one of them, resulting in more effective communication.
- Consider timing options for your message by being aware of your audience's competing concerns, avoiding communicating when upset, and being sensitive to message sequencing.
- A wide range of communication tools is available to you. Creativity and innovation will help your message stand out from the massive amount of information bombarding people today.

Application Activities

Activity 5-1 Experiencing Media Choice Problems
Recall an experience you have had in which an inappropriate medium was used to convey an important message to you. Describe what happened in a memo to your instructor.

Activity 5-2 Recognizing Media Ground Rules
List eight communication media you use regularly. Then try to articulate as many ground rules as you can for each medium. Finally, identify the most important characteristic that would cause you to choose each medium.

Media I Use	*Ground Rules*	*Strongest Reason for Use*
1.		
2.		
3.		
4.		
5.		
6.		
7.		
8.		

Activity 5-3 Applying Media Choices in Your Class
Write a memo to your professor detailing the role that each of the forms of media will play in your relationship with both your professor and classmates. Address peer-related issues of team projects, peer feedback, and study groups. Address instructor-related issues of graded assignments, individual questions, and feedback. You may want to organize your memo using two major headings: Spoken Communication and Written Communication.

Activity 5-4 Compensating for a Less Than Ideal Medium
As a reporter for the university newspaper, you have scheduled an interview with a local public official, Ms. Washington. When you arrive for the interview, the receptionist informs you that Ms. Washington missed her flight and is still in another city. She will not be able to do the interview in person but has requested that you leave a list of questions. She will answer the questions via e-mail as soon as she returns. The

Interactive CD-ROM Exercises

receptionist requests that you e-mail your questions to Ms. Washington by 5:00 P.M. that day.

To help you write the interview, answer these questions:

1. What disadvantages does the written medium have compared to face-to-face spoken communication?
2. What must you do to compensate for the disadvantages?
3. What benefits does the written medium have compared to face-to-face communication?
4. What can you do to capitalize on the benefits?
5. How will your communication strategy differ now that the interview format has changed?
6. What must you do to ensure that the interview in the written format is a success?
7. What must you avoid?

Career Activity

Career Activity 5-1 Using Innovative Media Choices and Timing Options to Land a Job

Suppose that you are beginning a job search and have identified three companies you might like to work for. Brainstorm ideas for usi ng innovative media choices to approach each of these companies. (Your ideas may be different for each company.) The overall purpose of your communication activities will be to get a good job. Your immediate objective is to get an interview.

Pay attention to details as you evaluate your options. What media may constructively exceed the company's expectations? What media give you the best opportunity to present yourself? What media may be deemed inappropriate and should be avoided? Why?

Also, consider the timing of your message. Is the company facing special situations that may influence your timing decisions? (Consider the company's current situation, need for special skills, competitive environment, end of fiscal year, etc.) When will you follow up, for example? How can you mix media to make the most of your chances to be noticed and hired?

Write your plan of action, including media choices and details of timing.

myPHLIP Companion Web Site

Learning Interactively
Visit the myPHLIP Web site at www.prenhall.com/timm. For Chapter 5, take advantage of the interactive "Study Guide" to test your chapter knowledge. Get instant feedback on whether you need additional studying. Read the "Current Events" articles to get the latest on chapter topics, and complete the exercises as specified by your instructor. Expand your learning with a visit to the "Research Area." There you will find a wealth of information you can use to complete your course assignments.

Notes

1. Adapted from a discussion by Saul W. Gellerman in *The Management of Human Resources* (Hinsdale, IL: Dryden Press, 1976), p. 61.
2. Ibid., p. 62.
3. Richard Hatch, *Communication in Business* (Chicago: Science Research Associates, 1977), p. 96.
4. Paul R. Timm and James A. Stead, *Communication Skills for Business and Professions* (Upper Saddle River, NJ: Prentice-Hall, 1996), p. 142.
5. This classic early study was found in T. L. Dahle, "An Objective and Comparative Study of Five Methods of Transmitting Information to Business and Industrial Employees," *Speech Monographs*, 21 (1954), pp. 21–28.
6. D. A. Level, "Communication Effectiveness: Method and Situation," *Journal of Business Communication* (Fall 1972), pp. 19–25.

Step 2. Consider
Your Media and
Timing Options

Step 1. Define
the Context

SKILL OBJECTIVES

After you have studied this chapter, you should be able to:

- Choose an overall select-and-organize approach for your messages.
- Apply "big-idea-first" (BIF) and big-idea-a-little-later (BILL) as overall approaches to organizing a message.
- Explain under what circumstances BIF or BILL approaches are likely to work best.
- Explain when BIF or BILL approaches are inappropriate.
- Identify the key ingredients in effective routine-informative, persuasive, and bad-news messages.
- Justify different patterns of arrangement for various types of messages.
- Identify key factors that may damage goodwill in bad-news messages.
- Explain how the principles of organization covered in this chapter can be applied to long documents or presentations.

Step 3. Select
and Organize
Your Information

Step 5. Evaluate
Feedback for
Continued Success

Step 4.
Deliver
Your
Message

Select and Organize Your Information: Building Effective Message Content

CHAPTER 6
SKILL
FOCUS:

Applying In-Depth Message

Organization Skills

COMMUNICATING WITHOUT A STRATEGY

The Complicated Story of Wilde Mats and Matting

Erika and Ryan Wilde, like so many other 20-somethings, dreamed of owning their own business. They looked at dozens of opportunities and carefully weighed the options they could afford. After months of searching for the right opportunity, they settled on a business they would have never predicted: a floor mats company.

"High tech it's not," Erika jokes, "but the profits are looking very good." To put it simply, they sell industrial-quality floor mats and mat "subscription services." Wilde Mats and Matting's subscription service picks up and replaces leased floor mats each week, laundering the soiled mats in a large industrial washer. It also sells specialized "logo" mats on which companies can imprint their logo or slogan. Stores, restaurants, factories, and banks are among the company's many customers.

Wilde Mats and Matting's communication challenges are not unlike those facing many small businesses. The owners must constantly get the word out on their business and services, talking to customers every day. They repeatedly explain how floor mats keep dirt out, help maintain the appearance of businesses, and even reduce worker fatigue by providing a softer floor surface. They persistently recruit commissioned salespeople and train them. Recently, they stepped into cyberspace with a Web page—StopDirt.com—to broaden their market.

When you've got a thing to say, Say it! Don't take half a day . . . Boil her down until she simmers, Polish her until she glimmers.

—Joel Chandler Harris

When the Wildes decided to create a Web page for their company, they knew they would have to organize and present a great deal of information. As Ryan says, "We have dozens of products, all available in different sizes. We have outright sales of mats plus our mat subscription service, but we can only provide subscription services in certain geographic locations." They also realized that their Web site would have several audiences. People who need floor mats—potential customers—would be their primary audience, but they would also have hidden audiences. For example, they would need to project positive messages to sales reps who may work for them, to venture capitalists who may provide funding for business expansion, and to people or other companies who may eventually buy their company. "How will we ever organize this information to make our site's messages readable, effective, and appealing? This seems overwhelming," said Ryan.

In this chapter, we focus on the third step in the Strategic Communication Model—selecting and organizing information. After reading this chapter, like the Wildes, you will be better equipped to systematically attack your communication tasks. You will be able to choose between different patterns of arrangement for various types of messages—from short to long documents or presentations.

Review Your Decisions About Context, Media, and Timing

This chapter focuses on Step 3 of our Strategic Communication Model: select and organize your information. As you face the task of selecting and organizing ideas for your message, take time to review the context of your message. Specifically, jot down relevant facts about the situation, your audiences, and your objectives with those audiences. Your Context Analysis Worksheet will remind you of all the questions you need to ask yourself. Failing to have a clear picture of this context makes it nearly impossible to succeed as a communicator. Remember that the most successful communicators spend considerable time thinking about their audiences. Erika and Ryan Wilde, in our opening story, would be foolish to jump into simply

FOCUS ON

Malcolm Forbes on Purpose[1]

Well-known writer and publisher Malcolm Forbes stresses that a good message begins with good planning: "If you plan to ask for something, write one sentence that says what you want." Example: I want to meet with George within two weeks to discuss the computer proposal. Once you know what you want, says Forbes, list the points you need to include.

You also might try the question approach. Pose questions and make sure you have the answers before you prepare your message. Examples of such questions include:

- *If you want something:* What do I want? What details must I include so the person will know what I want?
- *If you have a complaint:* What's my complaint? What evidence do I have to support it? What do I expect or want to happen?
- *If you have a proposal:* What am I proposing? What is the audience's likely reaction? How should I anticipate and handle resistance to my idea?

Malcolm Forbes stresses that a good message begins with good planning.

listing their products and services without first carefully defining the context. Failing to define the context risks making their messages unfocused and confusing to the receiver. They may also miss opportunities to hit important hidden audiences. With a clear understanding of the context, you can construct high-impact, problem-solving messages.

As we discussed in Chapter 1, the "default" position for any message is that it must have an effective introduction, body, and conclusion that are appropriate for the situation, audience, and objectives. Even the briefest messages need these key elements. To produce these elements, you must first be clear about your main objective, or what we also call the *big idea*. In functional business communication, the big idea can be defined as what you want your reader or listener to *do, think,* or *feel* as a result of getting your message.

If you don't have a clear, hoped-for outcome, or if you don't take the time to consider your audience, the big idea of your message will be unclear and your message won't be functional. If you don't know what you are trying to accomplish, your reader or listener won't either.

Select and organize information in light of the message context and your media and timing options.

The big idea of any message is what you want receivers to do, think, or feel.

Be sure that you have a clear picture of exactly what you want to accomplish with your message.

Choose Your Overall Select-and-Organize Approach

Selecting information to put in a message is a natural outgrowth of defining the context. In other words, you will discover questions that need to be answered as you apply the Strategic Communication Model and gain a clear picture of the situation, audiences, and your objectives. These questions—resulting in answers about what your message receiver needs or wants to know—determine the information you

When organizing your information, assume the perspectives of your various audiences.

Consider your overall approach before choosing a specific pattern of organization.

Messages conveying routine information, making simple requests, or relaying information that will be seen as good news are most efficient using a BIF approach.

need for your message to succeed. Try to assume the perspective of your various audiences, and anticipate the questions they would likely ask. A complete and effective message answers all the receivers' potential questions. In the example of Wilde Mats and Matting, Ryan and Erika need to look at their messages from the viewpoints of customers, potential salespeople, and possible investors. Each of these audiences will have different questions.

Before choosing a specific pattern of organization—a specific way to arrange the information you have selected—consider your overall *approach*. Your approach is determined by whether you want to be *direct* or *indirect* with your particular message. This degree of directness is dictated by the context, your media and timing options, and your personal preferences. Let's look at the two possible approaches we call BIF and BILL.

The BIF Approach

BIF is an acronym that stands for *big idea first*. It is the direct approach to organizing a message. This pattern of arrangement starts with the major premise—the big idea—and then adds details that explain the major points as needed. These explanatory details should answer any questions you might anticipate from your audiences. Messages conveying routine information, making simple requests, or relaying information that will be seen as good news by receivers are most efficient using a BIF approach. Figure 6-1 shows an example of a congratulatory e-mail using the BIF approach. In it, the writer places her big idea first and follows up with supporting points.

Big idea: The writer wants him to feel recognized or appreciated

Answers the potential question, "How did she know about this?"

Supporting detail further reinforces big idea

Friendly close

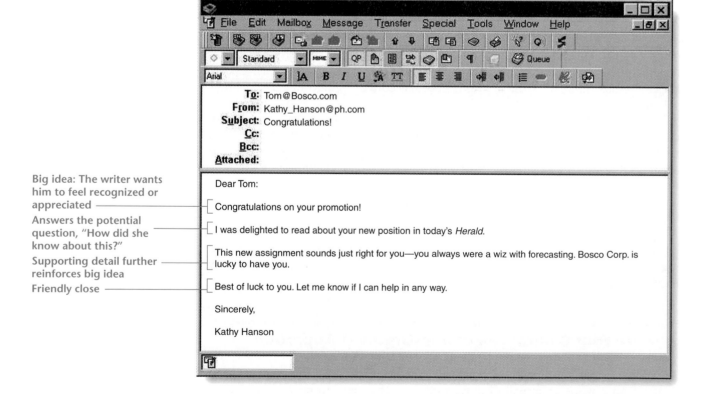

Figure 6-1
A BIF Good-News Message

Another BIF letter, this one making a direct request, might look something like Figure 6-2. In situations such as these, there is no reason to hold back or bury your main point. Tell your readers the big idea—what you want them to do or think—directly. Your reader will either be glad to get your message or will have no strong resistance to it. You can add clarifying details that may be useful or that help your message avoid sounding too abrupt.

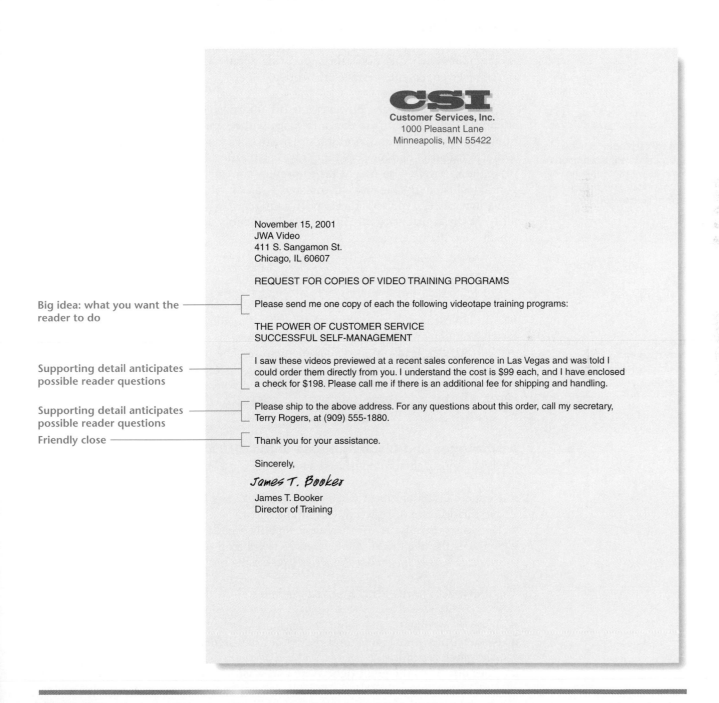

Big idea: what you want the reader to do

Supporting detail anticipates possible reader questions

Supporting detail anticipates possible reader questions

Friendly close

> **CSI**
> **Customer Services, Inc.**
> 1000 Pleasant Lane
> Minneapolis, MN 55422
>
> November 15, 2001
> JWA Video
> 411 S. Sangamon St.
> Chicago, IL 60607
>
> REQUEST FOR COPIES OF VIDEO TRAINING PROGRAMS
>
> Please send me one copy of each the following videotape training programs:
>
> THE POWER OF CUSTOMER SERVICE
> SUCCESSFUL SELF-MANAGEMENT
>
> I saw these videos previewed at a recent sales conference in Las Vegas and was told I could order them directly from you. I understand the cost is $99 each, and I have enclosed a check for $198. Please call me if there is an additional fee for shipping and handling.
>
> Please ship to the above address. For any questions about this order, call my secretary, Terry Rogers, at (909) 555-1880.
>
> Thank you for your assistance.
>
> Sincerely,
>
> *James T. Booker*
>
> James T. Booker
> Director of Training

Figure 6-2
A BIF Direct-Request Message

Advantages and Disadvantages of the BIF Approach   The BIF pattern offers several advantages. When used appropriately, it accomplishes the following:

- Saves valuable time because the reader or listener is tipped off right away to your purpose.
- Attracts attention with its direct beginning. For example, it is easy to keep reading when the first words in the message are "Congratulations," or "Thank you," or "Please send."
- Promotes efficiency. Once you know what the big idea is, you can create a message with little hesitation. As you think about probable reader reactions and anticipate likely questions, the supporting details will follow naturally. Likewise, the receiver gets the message efficiently.

The BIF approach can be inappropriate in some situations, such as with sales pitches or emotionally damaging or disappointing messages.

For all its advantages, however, the BIF approach can be inappropriate in some situations. If you anticipate that a message will be emotionally damaging or disappointing to receivers and you don't want to risk hurting them, you may want to avoid putting the bad news (the big idea) in the first line. Similarly, if you want to persuade receivers, you may want to present convincing evidence before you state your conclusion (the big idea). If you start a sales pitch by saying, "I want to sell you some insurance," you risk turning off your receivers before you can present your ideas. In these instances, the BIF approach probably won't work. Instead, try BILL, which we will discuss next.

The BILL Approach

BILL is an acronym that stands for *big idea a little later*. The effect of positioning the big idea a little later in the message is to prepare readers or listeners for the action or conclusion you are requesting. The BILL approach is indirect. It provides reasoning or evidence that leads up to the major premise—the big idea. In emotionally sensitive or some persuasive situations, presenting your reasoning before you get to the big idea is often good. The BILL approach often works best, for example, if you are telling Jeff that he is doing a poor job as a group member, or if you are attempting to persuade Andrea to do some additional work.

The BILL approach is indirect, providing reasoning or evidence that leads up to the big idea.

Advantages and Disadvantages of the BILL Approach   When used well, the BILL approach accomplishes the following:

- Reduces disappointment when delivering bad news by providing reasons that justify the decision or soften the disappointment.
- Demonstrates a writer or speaker's empathy and desire to maintain goodwill.
- Reduces the likelihood that the receiver will stop reading or listening before the message sender has had a chance to present the big idea.

The drawbacks to the BILL approach include:

- Takes more time to create and deliver.
- Is sometimes predictable, and the reader or listener knows that bad news or a sales pitch is coming.
- Does not get to the point right away and wastes time.

In the remainder of this chapter, you will learn three sets of general patterns for selecting and organizing message content that build on the BIF or BILL distinction.

The first set of patterns is best used for positive or routine requests and informative messages. The second set is used for persuasive messages, and the third set of patterns is used when you must convey bad news.

Select and Organize Information for Positive, Routine-Request, and Informative Messages

Positive and routine messages provide information or answer simple questions for the message receiver. Typical examples are simple requests, brief progress reports, and product orders. They convey information, update people, and/or provide good news. As we mentioned earlier, receivers of such messages are likely to be happy—or at least not unhappy—to get them. These messages almost always use a BIF approach.

Positive or routine-informative messages may contain opening lines such as the following:

> *The Company is pleased to announce the opening of our new Pleasant Grove location and invites you to attend the Grand Opening.*
>
> *In the next few minutes I will bring you up-to-date on the schedule for the introduction of our new fall line of merchandise.*
>
> *Sales results for May are very strong, reflecting our best month in over a year.*

Criteria to Apply to Positive, Routine-Request, and Informative Messages

Successful positive, routine-request, and informative messages should include information that is complete and direct. The selected information should be organized to get directly to the main point and then follow with clarifying details and a friendly close. Applying the following criteria to your messages will greatly improve your chances for success.

Be Complete   Make sure you provide the receivers with enough information to accomplish what you want them to do, think, or feel. If you are inviting people to an activity, for example, be sure to include its location, time, date, and what to bring or wear. If your message conveys a change in a procedure, be certain to tell the receivers exactly how to make the change. If your message reports information, be certain that you include all the relevant information. Remember to anticipate any questions the receivers may have, and then answer those questions.

Figure 6-3 shows an example of a business invitation that anticipates reader questions and uses the BIF approach.

Be Direct   As we have mentioned, the intent of good-news or routine messages is to tell people something they are glad to hear, or, at worst, are neutral toward. Accordingly, you can put the big idea up front and not worry about getting a negative emotional reaction. Follow the big idea of the message with other relevant, subordinate information that clarifies details.

Provide the receivers with enough information to accomplish what you want them to do, think, or feel.

FAST FACTS

RSVP

RSVP is an abbreviation for the French phrase, "repondez s'il vous plait," which means "respond, if you please," or simply, "please reply." It asks that the message receiver respond to the invitation by letting the sender know if he or she is planning to attend. Good etiquette calls for a prompt response (within a week of receiving the invitation) *whether you plan to attend or not.* If, after accepting an invitation, you cannot attend, good manners demand that you call and explain why you are unable to attend. Never be an unexplained no-show. That would display a serious breach of business manners.

Figure 6-3
A Business Invitation

> *Dear Sarina Lambard,*
> *You are invited to attend the New Employee Orientation Social on Saturday,*
> *September 19, 2002, 6 to 7:30 p.m., in the boardroom. Spouses or partners are*
> *also invited. A light buffet will be served. Dress is business attire.*
> *Please RSVP to Sandra Hopkins, the CEO's assistant, at extension 344.*
> *We look forward to seeing you there.*
> *Sincerely,*
> *Pat Portman*

FOCUS ON

Goodwill Messages

A goodwill message, such as the one shown in Figure 6-1, is one you convey even though you don't have to. Examples are greeting cards, notes, calls to congratulate or express appreciation, and sympathy messages. Many people fail to take advantage of goodwill opportunities. Few things make an employee, coworker, fellow student, or friend feel better than to receive a brief message of appreciation, congratulations, sympathy, or concern. Communicating such messages takes only a few minutes, yet these simple acts can do much to develop strong relationships. Additionally, customers who receive sincere, personal messages from people they do business with will likely harbor more favorable feelings toward that person and organization.

A manager of a busy office where clerical staff work very hard makes it a point to send short thank-you letters to the homes of employees whose work is exemplary. The payoff for such a simple action is that:

- Employees know their manager recognizes and appreciates their good work.
- By sending it home, the manager allows the employees' families to share in the praise.
- The letter becomes a part of the employees' personnel files and can be used when preparing performance reviews.
- By noting that copies have been sent to higher levels of management, the employees know they are getting additional attention.

Opportunities for goodwill notes come up almost daily. A significant accomplishment, a promotion or job change, and recognition for community service can all be opportunities to show you care.

Patterns of Arrangement to Apply to Positive, Routine-Request, and Informative Messages

If your BIF message calls for elaboration—is more than a brief thank you or routine request—help your receiver digest the details of your message by organizing supporting points using the patterns we discussed in Chapter 3. Start with the big idea and then elaborate with one or more of these patterns:

- **Chronological order.** Organize supporting information items as they occurred in time.
- **Problem-solution.** Tell your audience about problems faced and how you have fixed or propose to resolve them.

- **Topical or spatial order.** Progress systematically from one topic or place to another.
- **Cause-effect.** Tell your audience what happened and what caused it to happen.
- **STAR(R).** This acronym stands for situation, task, action, and result. (You may choose to add a second *R* that stands for recommendation.) Apply this pattern for a progress report by describing a *situation* you or the company faced, what *task* this situation required or what your specific task was, what *action* you took, and what finally happened as a *result*. Here is an example:

Situation: The department's sales results were dropping for three consecutive months.
Task: My assignment was to find a new incentive program that would motivate salespeople.
Action: I offered special cash bonuses for selling selected products.
Result: Sales increased.
(Recommendation): Other departments should use similar cash bonuses to boost productivity.

An example of a routine, positive message using an effective BIF pattern with appropriate support may sound like the following example, in which a team leader is speaking to fellow team members.

> *I want to congratulate the team on our outstanding case presentation in class this morning.* [BIG IDEA IS PRESENTED FIRST] *Each of you did a great job of finding just the right pictures for our PowerPoint slides, and the professor was very happy with our professionalism.* [CAUSE-EFFECT ORGANIZATION OF SUPPORTING DETAILS] *She told me that no other team had been able to solve the company's problems and that we took a difficult case and did a very thorough analysis. She especially liked the fact that we went beyond Internet research and got authentic information from interviews with company executives.* [PROBLEM-SOLUTION ORGANIZATION OF SUPPORTING DETAILS]

Select and Organize Information for Persuasive Messages

Persuasive business messages are *action* oriented. They seek to get readers or listeners to *do* something they normally would not do without some prodding. We judge the message's effectiveness by the action that results. The effective sales message sells. The effective collection message collects. The persuasive presentation sways opinion. The persuasive interview lands an internship or job. The communicator's job is to motivate readers and listeners to expend the effort to change in the desired direction. Thus, the more you know about the audience's needs, wants, and motives, the more likely you are to create such motivation.

Persuasive messages call on receivers to change or exert some effort. To make this happen, you need to appeal to their needs, wants, and motives.

Criteria to Apply to Persuasive Messages

Because your persuasive message will need to involve audience motivation, be certain to appeal to their wants or needs and to relate the features of your product, idea, or proposal to their specific benefits. Applying the following criteria to your messages will greatly improve your chances for success.

Use Information That Appeals to the Audience
Overcome resistance to your solution by selecting information that addresses anticipated objections your audience may have. For example, suppose you wanted to propose that your department

Overcome resistance to persuasion by using information that addresses audience objections.

upgrade its computer system. An obvious objection that comes to mind is the cost. Another objection might be the time the company needs to train department personnel on the new system. Now that you have anticipated these objections (and as many other possible objections as you can discover from your audience analysis) you can address them in your message. You might overcome these objections by showing how the cost and time will be offset by increased worker efficiency, for example.

As another example, suppose that you want to persuade your instructor to allow an open-book exam rather than a typical test. What objections would you anticipate, based on analyzing your instructor's wants and needs? Perhaps the instructor is concerned about students cheating or failing to apply original thinking. Anticipating these objections, you may try to convince the instructor that the subject matter being tested goes well beyond what is in the book and that use of a reference book would be perfectly appropriate in a real-world work environment. Will these arguments work? We can't say, but your likelihood of convincing the instructor would be greatly increased if you carefully consider his or her motives, and answer any anticipated objections. (Good luck. We never said communication is easy!)

Show your audience the personal benefit they will gain by doing what you want them to do. We have made this point, but it bears repeating. Many persuasive requests fail when the communicator forgets to phrase ideas in terms of the audience. The letter in Figure 6-4 illustrates what we mean. It was actually used by a political candidate to raise money for his campaign.

Would you be motivated by the message in Figure 6-4? Most receivers were not. Among the more obvious problems is that the writer phrased the letter in terms of what the writer wanted, not what the reader could gain. The use of the dollar figure as an attention-grabber may spark some mild curiosity in the reader, but the use of exclamation points and underlining for emphasis does nothing to increase the effec-

Figure 6-4
A Poor Application of the
Persuasive Pattern

ALAN JONES for STATE HOUSE

$37,279.47

The figure above is the amount that I must raise in order to win election to the North Carolina House of Representatives.

You are one of 700 friends I feel that I can count on. I'm asking for your financial support in the amount of $53.26!!!

July 25th is the date we must have all money on hand!!!

Please make checks payable to: Alan Jones for NC House and forward to: John S. Smith, Treasurer, 2000 Darwin Road, Pine Hill, NC 28207.

Thank you for your consideration.

Sincerely,

Alan

Alan Jones

tiveness of the appeal. Saying something louder does not make it more persuasive. Targeting the needs and motives of the receiver does.

Suppose you were working on this candidate's campaign. How could you rewrite this message to appeal to the reader? First, consider what the reader potentially has to gain by doing the desired action (that is, sending you $53.26). You may want to appeal to the reader's need or desire to have good people elected to public office, assuming, of course, that they perceive this candidate to be a good person. But, more specifically, people may feel a sense of status enhancement in having a friend they supported get elected to office. A positive appeal may imply that their contribution will result in the candidate's election and that his election will give them some special influence in the legislature. Thinking along these lines, you might rework this message, phrasing it in terms of the reader's interests, as shown in Figure 6-5. As you can see, the message in Figure 6-5 is likely to be far more appealing to readers because it considers their motivations. Thus, it will go further in getting Alan Jones elected than his original message did.

Use Information That Links Features to Benefits   As we have mentioned, the appeals you use in a persuasive message will work best when the benefits of what you are offering relate closely to audience needs. If you have carefully analyzed the context of your message (and, hopefully, completed a Context Analysis Worksheet), you should have a good picture of the nature of your audience.

Effective salespeople help their customers distinguish between features and benefits. A *feature* is simply some aspect or characteristic of your product, service, or idea. A vehicle may have a powerful engine; a vacuum cleaner may come with clever attachments; a package delivery service may guarantee against breakage at no cost.

Saying something louder does not make it more persuasive.

Persuasive messages work best when the benefits you are offering relate closely to audience needs.

ALAN JONES for STATE HOUSE

$37,279.47

The figure above is what it will cost to put *your* representative in the North Carolina House.

You are one of 700 friends I value deeply. Your past friendship and support have led me to believe that we share similar concerns for our state government and that I can effectively represent your interests in Raleigh. To bring this about, I'm asking for your financial help. Your contribution of only $53.26 puts us in a position where we can, and will, win the election on November 7.

To meet our campaign expenses, the money needs to be in the hands of John S. Smith, my campaign treasurer, by July 25. Please send your check to John at 2000 Darwin Road, Pine Hill, NC 28207.

With your help, your voice will be heard in the upcoming legislative session.

Cordially,

Alan

Alan Jones

Figure 6-5
A Better Application of the Persuasive Patterns

Refer to product features only as they relate to audience benefits.

These are features. A *benefit* is a "what-this-means-to-you" (the customer, reader, or listener) statement. To maximize the persuasive impact of features, they should be phrased in terms of the benefit your audience will get from them. For example, the truck can take you up the steepest gravel road; the vacuum can get disease-carrying dirt out of hard-to-reach places; intact delivery of your products will eliminate customer complaints and help your company be more profitable. You sell ideas and products with audience benefits. The skillful persuader alludes to the product's features only as they relate to audience benefits.

In our opening story, Erika and Ryan Wilde tell people how their floor mats catch incoming dirt (feature) so that the business looks more attractive and cleaning is easier (benefits). They tell other customers how their mats are padded (feature) to reduce worker fatigue and boost morale (benefits). We will discuss persuasive appeals more later in the chapter.

Patterns of Arrangement to Apply to Persuasive Messages

Because persuasion, by definition, seeks to get people to do something they otherwise would not do, many communicators prefer the BILL approach. The BILL approach leads up to the requested action and, thus, reduces the likelihood of turning the receiver off before you present the big idea. A BIF approach would state, "I want to sell you some insurance," whereas the BILL approach establishes some need before getting to the point. However, the direct BIF approach may be effective when your audience is predisposed to listen objectively to your proposal, when your proposal does not require strong persuasion, or when the audience prefers that you get to the point.

If you elect to use a BILL approach to persuade, the following ANSA pattern can be a useful guideline. We'll show you a direct BIF approach alternative later.

The ANSA pattern can work in many persuasive messages.

ANSA   In theory, successful persuasion is simple. All you have to do is help your readers or listeners get an answer to their questions or problems. The key word is *answer*. With a little New England accent, answer becomes ANSA, which stands for:

Attention

Need

Solution

Action

Admittedly, this is a bit corny, but corny can be memorable (like those awful commercials that you can't get out of your head). We want you to remember not only the four parts to the approach but also the key to successful persuasion—providing *answers*.

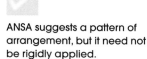

ANSA suggests a pattern of arrangement, but it need not be rigidly applied.

The ANSA pattern can work in almost any persuasive message. We will discuss each part as an isolated step in a four-step sequence, but these parts often overlap. Sometimes, the middle two parts are presented in a different order with the solution coming before the need development. Sometimes, when the need is obvious, more emphasis is placed on getting attention and reinforcing a proposed solution. With this understanding clearly in mind, let's look at each part of the ANSA approach separately.

Step 1: Gain audience attention.   We all get persuasive messages in the mail. Most are what we call direct mail—mass-mailed persuasive messages that some people refer to as junk mail. Only about 30 percent of the people who receive such sales let-

PICKLES   BY BRIAN CRANE

ters read them. Another 45 percent open and glance at the message, but the rest of us throw away direct mail, unread. Granted, many of your persuasive messages will not be direct mail but, from our experience with persuasive communication, the point is still valid: You don't have much time to get your audience into your message.

In Chapter 3 we cited general techniques for grabbing audience attention. These included the use of a statement of the topic or reference to the occasion, a startling statement or statistic, a rhetorical question, a quotation, a definition or narrative, and audience participation. To work best, these techniques need to appeal to specific audience needs by implying or offering some benefit to your audience. Such benefits are *persuasive appeals*. Business communicators use four categories of persuasive appeals to gain audience's attention. These are appeals to the audience's needs for

Appeal to specific audience needs by implying or offering some benefit to them.

- Success
- Power and status enhancement
- Self-satisfaction
- Curiosity

These attention-getting appeals may be phrased positively or negatively. Positive appeals focus on what the reader stands to gain; negative appeals accentuate what the audience might lose if they do not pay attention to your message. Examples of such appeals are presented in Figure 6-6.

Positive appeals focus on what the reader stands to gain; negative appeals accentuate what the audience might lose.

Step 2: Develop the need.   Often the attention-grabber combines interest-creating information with a description of a problem. As we have discussed, television commercials often follow this pattern. They present an unpleasant situation in such a way that we can identify with the victim of, say, embarrassment, discomfort, disappointment, or failure. Our reaction may be to empathize and share some of the need.

Why does need-agitation move the reader to action? Psychologists explain this in terms of *balance theory*. People prefer to be in a state of psychological balance or equilibrium; they want perceptions to fit together, to make sense, to seem rational, to be comfortable. When you expose a problem that your reader can identify with, you create a feeling of tension and imbalance in the reader or listener. If strongly felt, this is agitating. To reduce this agitation or tension, the audience will try to restore psychological balance. That balance comes about by doing what the persuader suggests.

Vividly presenting a need upsets the audience's sense of psychological balance, motivating them to seek a solution.

Step 3: Offer a solution to the problem.   Once you have your audience's attention and have helped them identify a personal need, your job is to explain to them how to satisfy that need. You can best do this by giving the reader or listener a *solution*. To convince your audience that you really do have the solution, you'll need to select

	Success	Power and Status Enhancement	Self-Satisfaction	Curiosity
Positive Appeals	Acting will lead to the audience's success in accomplishing goals. *Example:* "You can break into the million-dollar sales club . . ."	Acting will improve the audience's power and status. *Example:* "Do you want to master the art of negotiation?"	Acting will lead to a sense of satisfaction for the audience. *Example:* "I can show you how to achieve your goals of becoming your own boss."	Acting will answer questions the audience would like answered. *Example:* "How would you like to know your competitor's exact sales strategy?"
Negative Appeals	**Not** acting will lead to the audience's failure to accomplish goals. *Example:* "Can you be satisfied with another average sales year?"	**Not** acting will cost the audience loss of power of status. *Example:* "Are you coming up short in negotiations?"	**Not** acting will lead to dissatisfaction or missed opportunity for the audience. *Example:* "How much longer will you work to make someone else wealthy?"	**Not** acting will leave important questions unanswered. *Example:* "Is what you don't know about the competition killing you?"

Figure 6-6
Positive and Negative Attention-Getting Appeals

Once you have your audience's attention and have helped them identify a personal need, your job is to explain how to satisfy that need.

believable evidence—information that supports and clarifies your big idea. Such evidence can take the form of:

- Descriptions of benefits your product or idea has to offer
- Statistics and related facts
- Quotes or testimonials (perhaps from others who have tried your solution)
- Product samples
- Answers to possible objections about your product or idea

Step 4: Close with a call for action.   An action close makes the difference between a passive, informative message and one that gets results:
   The action close seeks to do two things:

The action close concludes the message. It should remind your audience of the benefits of your product or proposal.

1. Persuades your readers or listeners to do something specific.
2. Summarizes the benefit they can expect from taking this action. This becomes the conclusion of the message.

The action close should tell the receivers exactly what to do and should also make it easy for them to comply. The tone of the action step should be assumptive—it should convey that you assume the receivers will do what you ask. You should be moving from the conditional phrasing, such as "If you do it," which you used at the beginning of your message, to the more definitive "Here's how you do it." Assume that your audience has understood and agrees with your reasoning. They now simply need to be pushed a bit to obtain the benefits you promise.
   The following are two examples of action closes:

- *Drop the enclosed card in the mail—today, while you're thinking about it—and I'll send you a free examination copy of the Executive Planner. You'll be sur-*

prised how much time this modern management tool will save you. The impact on your productivity will be substantial!

■ *Authorize two additional employees to work on the task force, and I will pay to send them to the software training classes out of my departmental budget. The classes start in two weeks, so I need your approval right away.*

BIF Alternative   Although persuasive writing frequently uses a BILL approach such as the ANSA pattern just described, in some cases communicators elect to be more direct and state the big idea first. A BIF pattern for persuasion may:

Sometimes persuaders elect to be more direct and state the big idea first.

1. Begin with a recommendation and a brief rationale.
2. Present a smooth transition to the reasoning or necessary background information.
3. Support the big idea with testimonials, statistics, or other evidence.
4. Repeat the recommendation after presenting the supporting data.
5. Close on a positive, confident note that motivates prompt action.

Figure 6-7, on page 134, shows an example of a persuasive letter that uses a BIF approach. As you can see, this letter is both direct *and* persuasive. The writer gets to the point immediately and backs it up with supporting information.

Select and Organize Information for Bad-News Messages

Sometimes you need to convey information your audience does not want to receive. When this is the case, you need to make a cost decision. Is maintaining goodwill with your audience important enough that you are willing to expend some *extra* effort and cost in communicating with them? The alternative is to simply blurt out the bad news and let the public relations chips fall where they may. A tactful, carefully arranged bad-news message often costs more to produce but is likely to at least soften any negative impression your receivers have of you or your organization. The payoff in maintaining goodwill may be worth the effort.

Criteria to Apply to Bad-News Messages

The bad-news message gives audiences a message they probably would rather not get. These messages may refuse requests or convey information the receivers would see as detrimental to them. Although conveying such information is necessary in business, the way you communicate it can make a difference in how you are perceived. If overly blunt or insensitive, you may be perceived by your audiences as a poor communicator, and your relationships can be damaged. If you are too vague and tentative, people may see you as indecisive. Your credibility can be damaged.

Although conveying bad news is necessary in business, the way you communicate it can make a difference in how your audiences perceive you.

The ideal situation is for the receiver of your message to say, "I am disappointed (or upset, or even angry) about the message, but if I were in the sender's position, I would probably make the same decision." If you communicate effectively, receivers will understand why the bad news needed to be given and will respect you for making the tough call.

Be Empathic   Before preparing bad-news messages, you need to consider, once again, your audiences. Being empathic means putting yourself into the shoes of your message receiver and applying sensitivity in selecting the information you deliver.

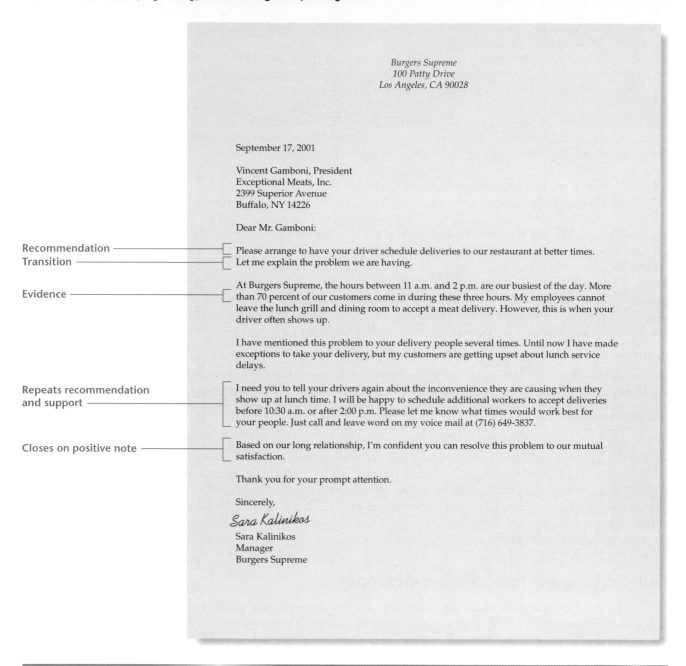

Burgers Supreme
100 Patty Drive
Los Angeles, CA 90028

September 17, 2001

Vincent Gamboni, President
Exceptional Meats, Inc.
2399 Superior Avenue
Buffalo, NY 14226

Dear Mr. Gamboni:

Recommendation — Please arrange to have your driver schedule deliveries to our restaurant at better times.
Transition — Let me explain the problem we are having.

Evidence — At Burgers Supreme, the hours between 11 a.m. and 2 p.m. are our busiest of the day. More than 70 percent of our customers come in during these three hours. My employees cannot leave the lunch grill and dining room to accept a meat delivery. However, this is when your driver often shows up.

I have mentioned this problem to your delivery people several times. Until now I have made exceptions to take your delivery, but my customers are getting upset about lunch service delays.

Repeats recommendation and support — I need you to tell your drivers again about the inconvenience they are causing when they show up at lunch time. I will be happy to schedule additional workers to accept deliveries before 10:30 a.m. or after 2:00 p.m. Please let me know what times would work best for your people. Just call and leave word on my voice mail at (716) 649-3837.

Closes on positive note — Based on our long relationship, I'm confident you can resolve this problem to our mutual satisfaction.

Thank you for your prompt attention.

Sincerely,

Sara Kalinikos

Sara Kalinikos
Manager
Burgers Supreme

Figure 6-7
A BIF Approach Persuasive Message

Empathize with your audience. Based on your context analysis, appeal to their needs, desires, and values.

Based on your analysis of the context, you should have some sense of what kinds of information will work best. If, for example, you are communicating with another businessperson and must refuse a request because it would cost too much, use an appeal to the value of maintaining a profitable company. The receiver should understand that line of reasoning. On the other hand, if you are communicating with someone who may not understand basic business needs (e.g., to be profitable), you may refuse a request on the grounds that it would be unfair to others. Most people understand the value of fairness and will accept that as a reasonable rationale for a decision.

Be Clear   Although conveying bad news is seldom pleasant, you need to be clear. Some people try to be so sensitive to their receiver's reactions that they never really get to the point—they never actually tell the bad news. Sometimes they try to sugarcoat the negative information so much that the receiver doesn't "get it." For example, a letter sent to tell job applicants that they did not get the job should be clear about that point. Saying "the position has been offered to another applicant" may seem clear to the writer but could leave doubt in the mind of some readers who may be unaware that you had only one position available. They may think they are still candidates for other openings. If you fail to make the bad news clear, you run the risk of leading people on. When the finality of the bad news eventually hits them, they will be more disappointed than ever.

Although conveying bad news is seldom pleasant, you need to be clear.

An example of lack of message clarity posed a problem in a small training company owned by Brian and Glenn. When people applied for jobs as trainers, Brian was constantly optimistic, implying that the company would hire the applicant. He did this because he hated being direct in telling people possible bad news. Glenn then found himself having to play the role of the "bad guy." His job was to be frank when applicants were not going to be hired. The outgrowth of this is that Glenn—the one who was candid with applicants—had far stronger credibility than Brian, who told people what they wanted to hear. The moral of the story: Bending over backward to "save" individuals from receiving bad news damages your credibility. Be clear in all your business communications—even the bad news.

Bending over backward to "save" people from bad news damages your credibility.

Patterns of Arrangement to Apply to Bad-News Messages

When faced with the task of organizing a bad-news message, these are your options:

1. Be straightforward and organize your bad-news message in the same direct manner as a routine letter. Tell your audience what you need to say and let the chips fall where they may.
2. Apply a pattern of organization that attempts to psychologically soothe your audience, or at least help them understand your reasons for conveying the bad news.

The Indirect Approach   If your context analysis tells you that option 2 makes sense, the BILL pattern of organization will help. Let's look at this indirect pattern first. This application of a BILL pattern of organization includes six key elements:

1. Buffer
2. Transition
3. Reasoning
4. Refusal or bad news
5. Alternative
6. Optimistic close

Some communication professionals argue that an indirect pattern is less effective than straight talk.

Be aware that, as we alluded to earlier, some communication professionals do not agree with this indirect pattern. They argue that this pattern is needlessly oblique and that message receivers see it as "beating around the bush" when straight talk would be more efficient. We will stay neutral on that debate and present this indirect

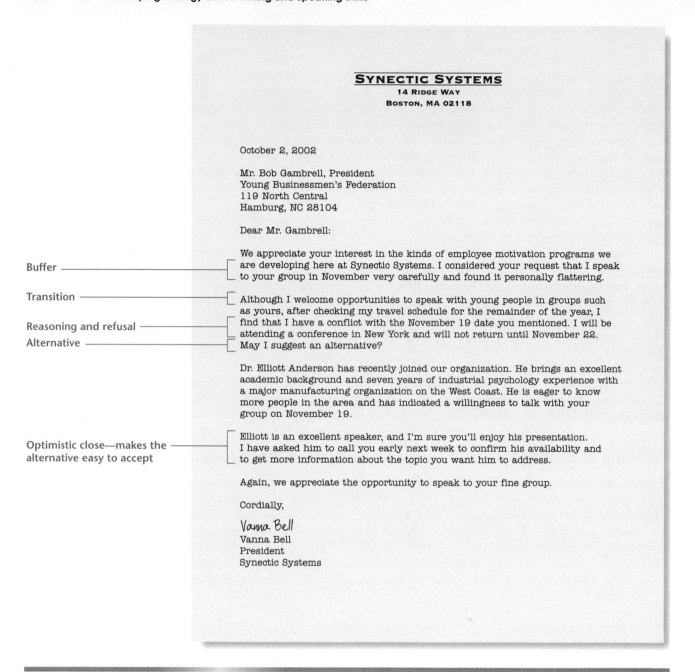

Buffer

Transition

Reasoning and refusal

Alternative

Optimistic close—makes the alternative easy to accept

SYNECTIC SYSTEMS
14 RIDGE WAY
BOSTON, MA 02118

October 2, 2002

Mr. Bob Gambrell, President
Young Businessmen's Federation
119 North Central
Hamburg, NC 28104

Dear Mr. Gambrell:

We appreciate your interest in the kinds of employee motivation programs we are developing here at Synectic Systems. I considered your request that I speak to your group in November very carefully and found it personally flattering.

Although I welcome opportunities to speak with young people in groups such as yours, after checking my travel schedule for the remainder of the year, I find that I have a conflict with the November 19 date you mentioned. I will be attending a conference in New York and will not return until November 22. May I suggest an alternative?

Dr. Elliott Anderson has recently joined our organization. He brings an excellent academic background and seven years of industrial psychology experience with a major manufacturing organization on the West Coast. He is eager to know more people in the area and has indicated a willingness to talk with your group on November 19.

Elliott is an excellent speaker, and I'm sure you'll enjoy his presentation. I have asked him to call you early next week to confirm his availability and to get more information about the topic you want him to address.

Again, we appreciate the opportunity to speak to your fine group.

Cordially,

Vanna Bell

Vanna Bell
President
Synectic Systems

Figure 6-8
A Bad-News Message

pattern as a possible tool for your use. Whether you use this pattern or not should depend on the analysis of your communication context.

Now, let's look at the parts of the indirect BILL approach pattern for presenting bad news. Each step in the approach is highlighted in the letter shown in Figure 6-8 and is discussed in detail in the following sections.

Step 1: Use a neutral or mildly positive buffer. The buffer sentences present neutral or positive information the reader is not likely to disagree with. Vanna Bell's comments in Figure 6-8 about "appreciating [his] interest" and finding the request "personally flattering" are examples of such comments. Often such buffers thank the audience for their interest or make other general statements with which anyone would be likely to agree. This buffer is designed to get the reader into the rest of the letter—to avoid a premature turnoff before you've had a chance to explain the reasoning behind your refusal. One caution: The buffer should not sound so encouraging that the reader is led to expect a favorable message. Keep it neutral or mildly positive.

Step 2: Make the transition. Once you have offered a buffer, step 2 is to transition carefully into your reasoning. A transition may be as short as a few words or as long as a full sentence. (Example: "Although I enjoy the opportunity to speak with young people. . ." or "Please let me explain the problem.") Its purpose is to connect thoughts and prepare the receiver for what is to follow. Some experts recommend that you avoid using "but" or "however," especially if these may sound like an abrupt shift in tone. Other experts argue that a direct-sounding "but" or "however" is a useful way to get into the reasoning step. A transition that still sounds too abrupt is a good indication that your buffer is misleading to the receiver.

Begin a bad-news message with a neutral or mildly positive buffer.

Be careful that your transition is not overly abrupt.

Step 3: Present your reasoning. When you deliver a refusal or other bad news, you should base it on your best reasoning—reasoning that makes sense to your audience. The task is to convey that reasoning in such a way that your audience will either agree with the bad news or at least understand *why* you decided as you did. Remember the ideal: The receiver will think, "I'm disappointed, but I would probably make the same decision if I were in his or her shoes." The information you select to present should be logical and clear. If your decision is based on prudent reasoning, you should have no reason to sound apologetic.

In Figure 6-8, the reasoning is simple—Vanna Bell will be out of town. In other cases, you may need to convey more detailed reasoning. For example, an employer refusing a job applicant may want to explain more detail about the job requirements and the fact that the candidate does not meet the specifications for that position.

Ideally, your audience will understand your reasons even though they may be disappointed.

Step 4: Give the actual refusal or bad news. Be tactful but conclusive. In Figure 6-8, the fact that Vanna Bell will be in another city clearly implies that she cannot speak to that group. In some cases, the finality of the refusal may not be quite so clear. As we have mentioned, the actual refusal or bit of bad news should be carefully worded and clear so that there is no misunderstanding on the part of the audience. Some people feel that they soften the blow by phrasing the bad news in the passive voice ("your request must be denied") versus active voice ("I must deny your request"). This passive phrasing, however, runs the risk of sounding evasive or indecisive. The decision to use passive voice should be based on how you think your audience is likely to react. (See Reference Tool A, "Avoiding Common Grammar, Punctuation, and Usage Mistakes," if you are unclear about passive versus active wording.)

Passive voice can be useful to soften the blow when conveying bad news.

Also consider positioning the actual refusal so that it naturally receives less emphasis. The positions of strongest emphasis (which should normally be avoided for bad news) are at the very beginning and the very end of each paragraph you write or speak. The top positions are emphasized because they are the first words the receiver reads or hears. The end positions are phrases that tend to linger in the receiver's mind and are thus emphasized. Your refusal or bad-news phrase would be best positioned toward the *middle* of the message for deemphasis. Don't de-emphasize it to the point where it is ambiguous; just soften it slightly.

Position your refusal or bad-news phrase toward the *middle* of the message for de-emphasis.

Step 5. Offer an alternative.   If at all possible, look for a way to give the bad-news recipient some alternative to his or her original request. Vanna Bell's letter in Figure 6-8 does this very effectively and sends a powerful message about her willingness to make the message less painful. The alternative should be explained in a positive tone conveying the assumption that it will be accepted.

When offering an alternative, make it easy for the reader or listener to accept. In some cases, letter writers simply toss the ball back to the reader. Notice that our example in Figure 6-8 did not say something such as, "If some other date would be acceptable or if another person from our company could be of help, please write to me again." That would fail to achieve closure—the problem remains unresolved. If you offer an alternative, follow through on the new idea. Don't just give the problem back to the reader and start the whole letter-response cycle over again. Offering a lesser alternative should not be used as a way to avoid saying no. Use it only when you genuinely want to offer an option to the reader.

Step 6. Use an optimistic close.   Once the refusal or bad news has been clearly and tactfully conveyed, deliver an *optimistic close*. The intent of such closing remarks is to further repair any damage to goodwill that may have occurred. Use this as an opportunity to express confidence that a good business relationship will continue. Vanna Bell's letter in Figure 6-8 expresses appreciation for being invited to speak.

Do not apologize. Since your decision has been based on sound, business reasoning, there is no need to apologize. In fact, the effusive apology may cause your audience to question the reasoning, wondering if you feel guilty for some misdeed. Instead, confidently express a desire to maintain a favorable relationship with the reader.

As you can see, the bad-news message requires more thought and effort than the routine informational message. Its payoff lies in projecting a favorable, caring image to the reader.

The Direct Approach   As we mentioned earlier, some communication experts advocate communicating more directly, even for bad-news messages. For example, when refusing job applicants, they recommend directness in a refusal letter—not rude bluntness but getting straight to the point. They reason that the BILL approach may patronize unsuccessful applicants when, from whatever motivation, you lead them through a circuitous route to the core of your message.

A direct approach presentation to employees may convey a disappointing message with key points such as these:

- *I learned that we are experiencing significant delays in shipping to our international customers.*
- *Our most important task now is to create a solution to this immediate problem and get back on track.*
- *Mandatory overtime is the only short-term solution. We will work on other systems improvements, but for now, I need to have your cooperation in spending some additional hours on the job until the backlog is handled.*
- *You will, of course, be paid the overtime rate.*
- *Over the years, we've built this company on a commitment to give our customers better products and service than they can get anywhere else.*
- *I expect the overtime to last no more than two weeks if we all pitch in and get our orders caught up.*

This direct approach is likely to be effective when the audience shares the value of good customer service and understands the importance of solving the problem

---

When offering an alternative, make it easy to accept.

Don't overapologize. Let your reasoning reflect sound decision making.

quickly. Although they may not like the idea of having to put in additional hours, they would probably accept the message without being offended.

Organize the Longer Message

The ideas for selecting and organizing information presented in this chapter will help you develop effective messages. You can readily apply these to letters, interoffice memos, e-mail, or brief presentations. But what about longer business communications such as major reports or multipart presentations? The answer is that the same principles of selecting and organizing information apply to the long document or presentation.

These ideas for selecting and organizing information can apply to longer messages as well.

Patterns for Longer Messages

For longer messages, simply break the overall message into smaller units of information and tie each section together with internal summaries and content preview. Follow these steps:

1. Be clear in your own mind about the purpose (big idea) of *each section* of the overall message. Example: The introduction section should make my audience familiar with the problem we are facing.
2. Determine if the section would best be presented using a BIF or BILL approach. Example: My audience is likely to resist my overall assessment in this report, so I should present reasoning before getting to my recommendation—use a BILL approach.
3. Organize each section of the report using the appropriate pattern (routine, persuasive, or bad news).
4. Link parts of the larger message with summaries and content preview. Example: "I have just introduced you to the problem we are facing. In the next section of this report, I will show what effect a continuation of the problem will have on our company." Another example: "We have just reviewed three possible alternatives. Next we will look more closely at the cost of each alternative."

Longer messages should tie each section together with internal summaries and content preview.

Select and organize information for long documents or presentations in the same way as for simpler business messages. Link a series of single-issue messages into the larger fabric of an extended document or presentation. In Chapter 8, you will learn additional details on organizing longer reports.

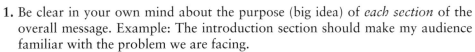

APPLYING THE STRATEGIC COMMUNICATION MODEL

Let's go back to Ryan and Erika Wilde and their need to communicate effectively in their mats business. One major need is to deliver effective sales messages. The following information appears on their Web site, Stopdirt.com. The arrows identify some of the ways they have applied the ideas in this chapter. As you read this, think about additional ways you could coach them in the use of the Strategic Communication Model based on what you have learned.

Our floor mats save your floors! Great selection with discount prices! FREE shipping on floor mats and FREE mat use bulletin. Best prices on name-brand floor mats. Stop dirt at the door with our beautiful, effective floor mats. (PUTS THE BIG IDEA FIRST BEFORE CREATING A NEED. WOULD A BILL APPROACH USING THE ANSA FORMAT BE MORE EFFECTIVE?)

We sell only name-brand, top-quality floor mats that are guaranteed to trap water and dirt and give you long-lasting performance. (RELATES FEATURES TO BENEFITS) *Our mats are beautiful and fashionable—making a great first impression on your customers. Looking for a mat that won't curl on the edges, won't stain your hard floor or carpet, and won't crawl?* (MORE FEATURES AND BENEFITS) *You're in the right place.*

Research proves that 90% of the dirt in offices and businesses is tracked in from the outside. (GOOD, CLEAR DETAIL; SHOULD IT BE USED EARLIER IN THE NEED DEVELOPMENT SECTION OF THE ANSA APPROACH?) *Dirt and moisture come in on shoes, clothing, wheels, and packages, destroying hard floors and carpets. Dirt and dust affect computers and any sensitive equipment. Slippery floors create safety hazards.* (MORE NEED DEVELOPMENT) *Our floor mats keep the outside out!* (SOLUTION STEP)

FREE MAT USE BULLETIN. Simply type in your e-mail address and press Submit. Your Free Mat Use Bulletin will be delivered to the e-mail address shown below. (CLEAR ACTION STEP AND INCENTIVE TO ACT NOW)

You could, undoubtedly, find additional critique points for Erika and Ryan's message, but these Web site samples illustrate the way they have applied some (and failed to take advantage of some) aspects of the Strategic Communication Model.

Summary of Key Ideas

- The default position for any message is that it must have an effective introduction, body, and conclusion. These elements are basic to almost any message.
- Be clear about your big idea: What do you want your reader or listener to *do, think,* or *feel* as a result of getting this message?
- Before choosing a specific pattern of organization—a specific way to arrange the information you have selected—decide on your overall *approach:* BIF or BILL. BIF is direct and puts the big idea first, whereas BILL is indirect and puts the big idea a little later. BIF is appropriate for most business communication. BILL is used when the receiver's emotions may come into play, such as in persuasive or bad-news messages.
- Positive and routine messages answer simple questions. They convey information, update people, and/or provide good news. These should use a BIF approach.
- Persuasive business messages seek to get readers or listeners to *do* something they normally would not do without some prodding. They stir up people's emotions and often use a BILL approach.
- The ANSA pattern of arrangement is a persuasive tool. ANSA stands for attention, need, solution, and action.
- Four kinds of persuasive appeals are widely used in business communication to gain the audience's attention. These are appeals to the audience's needs for success, power and status enhancement, self-satisfaction, and curiosity.
- Some persuasive messages use BIF if the audience is not expected to be too resistant.
- The bad-news message often uses a BILL pattern of arrangement, which includes these steps: buffer, transition, reasoning, refusal or bad news, alternative, and optimistic close.
- The decision to use a bad-news pattern depends on your desire to soften the blow and your willingness to spend more time and effort in preparing the message. Direct messages are easier to prepare but may risk offending or hurting the recipient, thus damaging goodwill.
- Some people prefer to receive direct messages (BIF), even when the news is unfavorable or disappointing.
- For long messages, organize information by breaking the overall message into smaller units and tying each section together with internal summaries and content preview.

Application Activities

Activity 6-1 Writing a Goodwill Letter

Write a goodwill letter to express appreciation to a teacher, fellow student, work associate, or friend. (You may want to review the sample letter in Figure 6-1.) Be specific and complete about what it is that makes you feel appreciation for him or her. Mail the letter and see what kind of response you get.

Activity 6-2 Persuading a Speaker

Prepare an outline of a persuasive message asking a local business leader to speak to your student group. Write down the ideas you would use to persuade this person if you called him or her on the telephone. Assume that the person will need some persuading because you cannot pay for a speaker. Complete a Context Analysis Worksheet (found in Chapter 4) and give special thought to potential motivators that would cause the receiver to consider accepting your invitation. Anticipate objections and address them. Turn in your Context Analysis Worksheet with your outline.

Activity 6-3 Fixing an Insensitive Letter

Assume that you received the note in Figure 6-9 from your boss, Peter Sammon. He wrote the note on top of John Slager's original letter, shown in Figure 6-10. Rework the letter according to your boss's request.

Activity 6-4 Preparing a Current Event Informative Presentation

Prepare a 3-minute oral presentation to fulfill the following situation:

Topic: A local current event. Identify a current business event reported in local publications that has an impact on you. (Check your local newspaper or its online version.)

You, the speaker: You are a consumer or a community member who is being affected by the event in some way.

Your audience: Students like yourself and their families.

Objective: To inform your audience of three things:

1. The summary of the article describing the event.
2. How the event will affect or has affected your audience(s).
3. What they (your audience) should do as a result of this event.

Time: 3 minutes, maximum.

Dress: Business casual.

Preparation: Prepare and turn in an Outline Worksheet (as shown in Figure 6-11).

Interactive CD-ROM Exercises

Figure 6-9
Peter Sammon's Note

Can you believe this guy? Slager has all the sensitivity of a dump truck. I intercepted this letter before it was mailed. This may be the last straw—Slager is on his way out.

Meanwhile, we need to let George Archer know we can't use him in corporate sales. But let's do it with some sensitivity. George has been with the company for a long time but we really can't transfer him as requested. He's a data input clerk in shipping right now. He seems to have little background for sales—other than a sincere desire.

Rework this letter for my signature, okay?
—Pete

Figure 6-10
John Slager's Original
Letter

Mr. George Archer
1334 Maison Rd.
Cincinnati, OH 32001

Dear Mr. Archer:

I received your recent letter requesting a transfer to corporate sales. Unfortunately, we cannot make that transfer at this time. Your work records show no selling skill whatsoever, and we can't imagine why you'd think you are qualified for an important sales position in corporate.

Selling is a very demanding position, one that requires stamina, independent thinking, perseverance, good judgment, etc. We've found that guys as old as you (51) can't make the adjustment from working inside to outside sales.

Your interest in ABCM is appreciated. If I can be of any further service, please do not hesitate to call upon me.

Sincerely,

John T. Slager

John T. Slager
Personnel Administrator

Career Activity

Career Activity 6-1 Identifying Your Features and Benefits

Consider yourself to be a professional self-owned business. We'll call you, "Me, Inc." What features (skills, abilities, attributes, etc.) can you offer to a potential employer? What benefits would an employer receive from hiring you for an internship or full-time job? Be specific in listing as many features as you can and be explicit in linking each to an employer's benefit. (Example 1. *Feature:* Eagle Scout; *Benefit:* Have demonstrated ability to accomplish many tasks and stick with a challenge until I reach the highest achievement. Example 2. *Feature:* Fluent in

Figure 6-11
Outline Worksheet

OUTLINE WORKSHEET

INTRODUCTION
• **Attention-grabber.** Based on what I know about my primary audience, what will get their attention (and also relate to topic and situation)?

_____

• **Purpose.** As a result of this message, what do I want my audience _to do_?

_____

• Are there any reasons I should be _indirect_ with the purpose of this message (including cultural considerations)? If so, how should I temper my expressed goals?

_____

• **Agenda.** How am I going to accomplish my objectives; that is, what is my _agenda_ for delivering the message?

_____

• **Benefit for audience.** What's in it for them, _specifically and personally_?

_____

CONCLUSION
• **Summary.** Exactly what do I want my audience _to remember_ (the essence of my main points)?

_____

• **Specific action.** Exactly what do I want my audience _to do_?

_____

• **Strong final statement.** What is the _last thought_ I want to leave with them?

_____

BODY
Choose from these common options:

1. Chronological order for simple, ordered instructions or reports
2. Problem-solution to explain a problem and your proposed solutions
3. Topical or spatial for related parts of one issue
4. Cause and effect to describe an event and what caused it
5. Pros and cons (or compare and contrast) for simple analyses or evaluations
6. STAR(R) to explain situation, task, action, result, and recommendations
7. ANSA to grab attention, establish need, offer a solution, and call for action
8. Bad-news format for information your audience does not want to hear

Point One: _____
Support Material (such as statistics or examples): _____
Point Two: _____
Support Material: _____
Point Three: _____
Support Material: _____
Point Four: _____
Support Material: _____

PowerPoint software; _Benefit:_ Can produce excellent visuals for presentations or documents. Example 3. _Feature:_ Years of dance or sports; _Benefit:_ Teamwork, consistent skill building, and stamina all are transferable to the workplace.)

Features of Me, Inc.   _Benefits to a Potential Employer_

1.

2.

3.

4.

myPHLIP Companion Web Site

Learning Interactively

Visit the myPHLIP Web site at www.prenhall.com/timm. For Chapter 6, take advantage of the interactive "Study Guide" to test your chapter knowledge. Get instant feedback on whether you need additional studying. Read the "Current Events" articles to get the latest on chapter topics, and complete the exercises as specified by your instructor. Expand your learning with a visit to the "Research Area." There you will find a wealth of information you can use to complete your course assignments.

Notes

1. Adapted from *Power-Packed Writing That Works* (Pitman, NJ: Communication Briefings, 1989), p. 31.

Step 2. Consider
Your Media and
Timing Options

Step 1. Define
the Context

SKILL OBJECTIVES

After you have studied this chapter, you should be able to:

- Recognize the importance of using visual information to improve both oral and written communication.
- Identify the functions that visuals fulfill for writers and speakers, as well as for readers and listeners.
- Describe the most commonly used visual formats and understand the use of each.
- Identify six consistency elements to be applied to visuals.
- Select appropriate design elements based on your context analysis.
- Avoid overcomplicating your visuals and overwhelming your message.
- Explain at least seven ways to make the most of projected visuals in oral presentations.
- Evaluate feedback on your visuals to continually improve your design and delivery.

Step 3. Select
and Organize
Your Information

Step 5. Evaluate
Feedback for
Continued Success

Step 4.
Deliver
Your
Message

Create Effective Visual Support Materials: Help Your Receivers Get the Picture

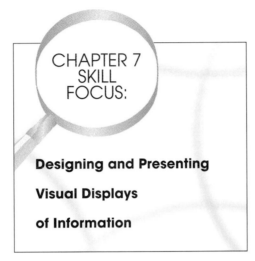

CHAPTER 7
SKILL
FOCUS:

Designing and Presenting

Visual Displays

of Information

Visual aids can make you

appear more confident,

more professional, and

more of an expert. They

can add color, humor, and

images that you could

never convey in words.

—Tony Alessandra

(Communicating at Work)

COMMUNICATING WITHOUT A STRATEGY

Danielle Botches a Briefing

Danielle Steenburg's boss asked her to give a 10-minute briefing on her department's activities at the weekly management meeting. She came to the front of the room with an ominously large stack of overhead transparencies. After fumbling for the on/off switch, she turned on the projector. All eyes in the room shifted to the glaring blank screen, but Danielle hadn't yet put up a transparency. She just felt she would be more comfortable with the projector switched on. As she presented her briefing, she covered more than 20 transparencies, often seeming to talk to the projector rather than to her audience.

She produced her visuals on the office copier from pages of a written report. Because her copier hadn't been well maintained, the print quality was fuzzy and, in spots, the clear plastic transparencies were smudgy. They averaged 18 to 25 lines of information per page. Some included charts and graphs, but many were just text and numbers. None had any clip art or pictures. The type was so small that the people in the front had to squint to read it. She hadn't bothered to put frames on her transparencies, so some of them stuck together and others floated in static electricity and refused to sit straight on the projector. Danielle knew that these black-and-white transparencies weren't exactly state-of-the-art visuals, so she told her audience, "You probably can't read this, but. . ." several times during the presentation. She then read what was on the visuals word for word.

If Danielle is lucky, her visual aids and the way she uses them are not significantly worse than what her organization expects. Hopefully (for her), everybody uses quick-and-dirty transparencies. If that's the case, all she's accomplished is to look average in front of her management. Even if others in her company are satisfied with shoddy visuals, she missed a great opportunity to project professionalism and build her credibility. And if her company culture expects well-prepared visuals used skillfully, her professional image just took a dive.

Preparing and using good visuals has never been easier, and the effect on a presentation of well-prepared visuals can be dramatic. In this chapter, we will show you how to create and use effective visuals for both oral presentations and written documents based on applications of the Strategic Communication Model. The guidelines for creating and using effective visuals are based on your analysis of your communication situation (with a particular emphasis on organizational culture), your audiences, and your objectives with those audiences, and are grounded in common sense. In addition, they are easy to remember and apply.

Use Visual Displays to Enhance Message Comprehension

Showing and telling greatly improve information recall.

This chapter continues our discussion of Step 3 of our Strategic Communication Model by showing additional ways to select and organize a message using visual media. The principles for effective visuals apply to both oral presentations and written documents. Oral presentations almost always need visuals to succeed, and you can make virtually any document better with graphic displays of information. For the purposes of this text, the term *visuals* refers to any information presented in forms other than text. Pictures, models, charts, tables, cartoons, artwork, and icons are all examples of visuals.

Why use visuals? People you communicate with today were raised with much visual stimulation: television, movies, video games, and computer graphics. As we mentioned in Chapter 2, about 70 percent of people prefer to receive information visually (as compared to hearing or feeling). They are not accustomed to processing words alone—they want to see something presented graphically. In addition, studies of listener comprehension over the years have repeatedly come to the same conclusion: Visuals help receivers get the message. Studies confirm that audiences remember up to twice the amount of information when they see it in addition to hearing it. In fact, Kodak estimates that any given audience remembers 20 percent of what they hear and 80 percent of what they see. (Of course, Kodak *is* in the visuals business.) The case for using visuals is solid. Any oral presentation and most documents will benefit from visual displays of information.

Visuals Help Both the Message Receiver and the Sender

Visuals are vital to you as a communicator because they help fulfill at least five important functions. Visuals help *writers and speakers* to:

- Develop the content of their message.
- Organize ideas and create continuity of thought.

- Strengthen the impact of their message.
- Clarify important concepts or associations.
- Provide variety.

In addition, visuals help speakers stay on track because they guide the speaker and can double as notes.

Visuals help *listeners and readers* to:

- Clarify and digest abstract ideas.
- Retain information.
- Avoid boredom, daydreaming, confusion, and apathy.

To make the most of these functions, you, as a communicator, should look at visuals as an internal part of your presentation or document, not as an afterthought. Plan your visuals as you draft your message.

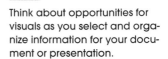

Think about opportunities for visuals as you select and organize information for your document or presentation.

FOCUS ON

Reasons to Use Visuals[1]

Two recent studies (3M/Wharton School and the University of Minnesota/3M) have clearly demonstrated the positive effects of using visuals in presentations. Both conclude that there are three areas in which the use of visuals can improve presentations:

1. **Communication effectiveness.** Visuals add another sensory channel to the oral communication process. Visuals utilize right-brain visual and spatial processing to complement the left-brain processing used in listening. Synergism between left- and right-brain processes create better "whole picture" communication.
2. **Audience's perceptions of presenter.** Audiences perceive presenters using visuals as significantly more prepared, professional, persuasive, credible, and interesting. Also, audiences perceive presenters using slides as more professional than those using overhead transparencies. Animated movements and transitions (as with presentation packages such as PowerPoint) raise the perception of professionalism even more.
3. **Speaker's confidence.** Visualization encourages better organization and planning, which

boosts a speaker's confidence. Poor presenters using good visuals can be as effective as good presenters not using visuals. A typical presenter using presentation support can be as effective as a better presenter using no visuals. The better a presenter is, the more he or she needs to use high-quality visual support.

In addition, the use of visuals results in improved efficiencies. Groups reached faster decisions (12 percent improvement with use of visuals), spent less time in meetings (average 18 minutes with visuals versus 26 minutes without visuals), and saw highly significant improvements in audience action.

The University of Minnesota/3M study showed the following improvements when visuals were used:

- The audience's likelihood to take action improved 43 percent.
- The perceptions of the presenter were 11 percent higher.
- Information retention, comprehension, attention, and agreement improved by 10, 8.5, 7.5, and 5.5 percent, respectively.

Make the Most of Your Visuals

Today, anyone can create professional-quality visuals quickly and easily with computer software programs. The most common software for creating visuals are spreadsheet programs such as Excel, which produce charts and graphs, and presentation programs such as Microsoft's PowerPoint and WordPerfect's Presentations. Once designed, visuals can be printed on paper (or on transparencies) or they can be shown on a screen via a computer projector.

If created properly, visual materials will reinforce your message. However, if poorly designed, visuals can act as a serious distraction from any message. Thus, as you create your visual material, keep in mind the guidelines we discuss in the following sections.

> If created properly, visual materials reinforce messages.

Use Individual Visuals for Major Points

Plan each visual so that it drives home a single point. The quickest way to lose the effectiveness of a visual aid is to overcomplicate it or try to convey too much information. This is especially true with charts or illustrations. Keep them simple and concise. Never display a chart or graph that your audience cannot comprehend in 30 seconds. You can accomplish this by sticking to one key point and removing any superfluous materials. Danielle, in our opening story, violated this rule by showing unreadable, "busy" data on her transparencies.

> Every visual should support one specific idea. Keep visuals simple and concise.

Be sure to know exactly when to present your illustration (or where to place it in a document) so it coincides with your message. Reveal the chart, graph, or illustration only when you are ready to reinforce a particular point. Otherwise, it will distract or confuse your reader or listener. If you are using the visual in a written document, consider placing the visual in the text and labeling it so the readers know what they are looking at. An example of this would be to write, "Figure 1 shows a graph of the cost-benefit ratio as it applies to our company" before the placement of the figure.

Use an Appropriate Type and Overall Design Concept

Use visuals that are appropriate in terms of type and overall design concept. To select the appropriate type of visual aids, pay attention to the expectations about

> Your visuals require the same context analysis as the rest of the message.

DILBERT © UFS

visual aids in your school, organization, or company. Carefully observe what other successful people are doing with visuals and then meet or exceed these expectations.

Knowing the appropriate design concept involves reviewing the first step of the Strategic Communication Model—defining your context. You should do so by analyzing the situation, your audience, and your purpose. Use the details you gathered to make your basic choices for templates, colors, fonts, clip art styles or pictures, charts, and especially words. We will discuss each of these elements later in this chapter.

Apply Common Visual Formats

Several tried-and-true formats work well for business visuals. Among these are word charts, pie charts, line charts, and bar charts. Additionally, reports and presentations often require the discussion of processes or organizational hierarchy, which suggests the use of tables, flowcharts, and organizational charts. Props or models can also enhance a presentation. In the next few sections, we will look at each of these useful formats.

Word Charts   A *word chart* states key ideas concisely and directly. It is probably your simplest visual and certainly the one you will use most often in oral presentations. In preparing word charts, economy of language is crucial. The sample chart illustrated in Figure 7-1 shows some rules for making word charts. Note that the five lines of body copy are parallel (each line begins with a verb) and that the clipboard template and pencil clip art are consistent with the message. The light yellow background offers contrast for the large black letters.

The word chart is a simple way of stating key ideas concisely and directly.

Pie Charts   A pie chart is a simple, circular illustration that is divided into segments to show part-to-whole comparison. It can effectively show only a few broad divisions. When creating pie charts, cut segments of the pie accurately, beginning at

A pie chart is a simple, circular illustration that is divided into segments to show part-to-whole comparison.

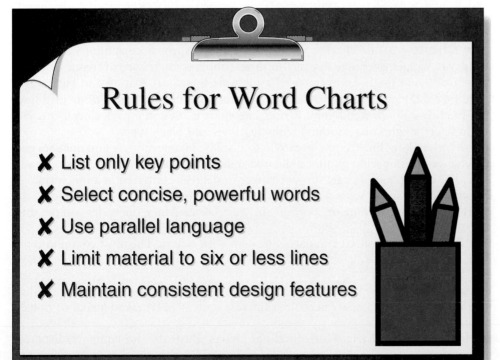

Figure 7-1
Sample Word Chart.

Use a word chart to help both you and your audience keep track of your key points.

Rules for Word Charts

- ✘ List only key points
- ✘ Select concise, powerful words
- ✘ Use parallel language
- ✘ Limit material to six or less lines
- ✘ Maintain consistent design features

Figure 7-2
Sample Pie Chart.

Use a pie chart to compare a part to the whole.

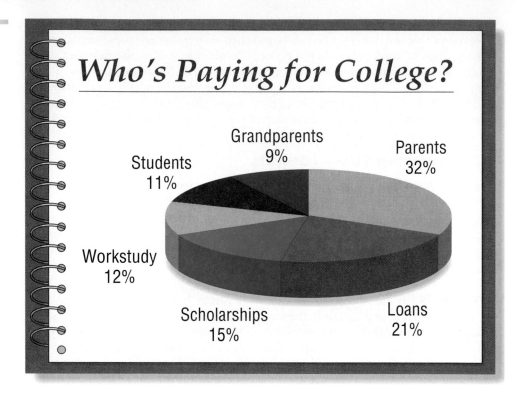

Who's Paying for College?

- Grandparents 9%
- Parents 32%
- Students 11%
- Workstudy 12%
- Scholarships 15%
- Loans 21%

the top and moving clockwise for each new segment. Label each slice, showing what it illustrates and the percentage it represents. Use large, clear lettering for the chart.

Graphics software packages such as Excel or PowerPoint will automatically slice the pie correctly for you. You can also select a three-dimensional design, as shown in Figure 7-2.

A line chart is a way to show a continuous picture of trends or changes over time.

Line Charts   A line chart is a "trendy" way to show a continuous picture of trends or changes over time. It can also show simple comparisons of trends by color-coding different lines. An example of a multiple line chart is shown in Figure 7-3. Note that the black background offers a dramatic contrast for the white grid lines and brightly colored trend lines. If your line chart is used in a print document, you might select a lighter background with gray lines and black type.

When making line charts, be careful to display data accurately and not exaggerate changes. Comparing graphical data with different scales can mislead your audience. For example, if a chart shows changes in degrees conferred at a much smaller school and the scales were 0 to 1,000 instead of 0 to 12,000 as in Figure 7-3, the chart might be misleading or confusing to the receiver. Make the scales comparable.

A bar chart compares one item with others.

Bar Charts   A bar chart compares one item with others. The most common types of bar charts are

- **Vertical bar charts.** Vertical bar charts are especially effective if you want to illustrate height and compare accomplishments, such as nearness to a goal or dollars of profit.
- **Horizontal bar charts.** Horizontal bar charts illustrate and compare distances over time.

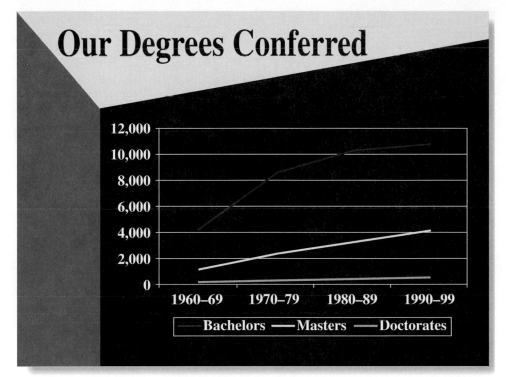

Figure 7-3
Sample Line Chart.

Use a line chart to show or compare changes over time.

- **Segmented bar charts.** Segmented bar charts clearly visualize how different parts contribute to a whole over time.
- **Grouped bar charts.** Grouped bar charts dramatically compare groups in specific times or areas, as shown in Figure 7-4.

Tables, Flowcharts, and Organizational Charts   Tables, flowcharts, and organizational charts usually require significant detail, so use them for oral presentation visuals only when you can make them very simply. In written documents, use a table to show exact numbers or to contrast and compare information. Flowcharts show step-by-step progression of processes or procedures to simplify the receiver's understanding. They are particularly helpful in giving instructions or explaining the solution to a problem. In many cases, you can use word charts to convey the same information.

Organizational charts illustrate the structure of a company, such as who works for whom and how many departments are in each division. Since many companies are complex, organizational charts are useful because they show lines of authority (chain of command) and job responsibilities. Software packages often have templates for building organizational charts.

Props and Models   When giving an oral presentation to a fairly small audience, you may want to use props or models. Motivational speakers often use one prop as a symbol of their messages, such as a glass of water ("your choice: half empty or half full") or a tennis ball ("it's in your court"). Sales representatives often bring a model or sample of their products for the customer to touch or hold, and they often leave something behind to remind the customer of the visit and the product. When giving a talk to explain the workings of a new machine or to sell a product, it obviously

Tables show exact numbers and contrast and compare information. Flowcharts show the step-by-step progression of processes or procedures.

Organizational charts illustrate the structure of a company.

Motivational speakers often use one prop as a symbol of their messages.

Figure 7-4
Sample Bar Chart.

Use a bar chart to compare one item with another.

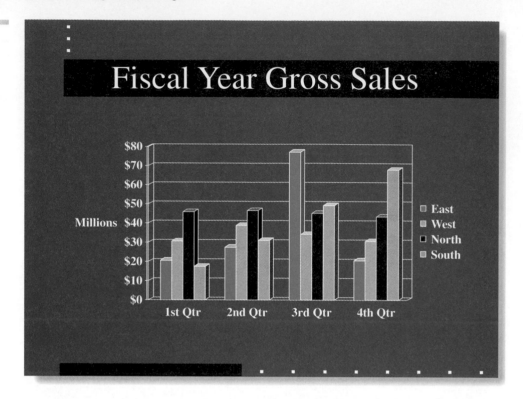

makes sense to have the machine or product there as a prop. In a written document, you can use pictures or cutaway views of items in place of props. (Cutaways are designer drawings that show the internal parts of a product. Articles and advertisements in automobile magazines often include them to show the internal design of cars.)

Check Visuals for Design Consistency

Your visuals should be consistent in terms of background, font, structure, capitalization, spacing, and illustrations. In the next few sections, we will look at each of these areas.

Background (Templates)   Presentation software such as PowerPoint allows you to select a template for your entire set of visuals. A *template* is a consistent design background for your visual materials. In selecting a template, choose only one and then stick with it for the entire presentation. Do not mix different templates because this will cause your message to look inconsistent and unprofessional. Keep in mind also that the more illustrations you plan to use, the simpler your template should be.

Choose a template style that symbolizes your message and shows respect for your target audience.

When deciding on a template, choose a style that symbolizes your message and shows respect for your target audience. For example, avoid overly cute templates if you are doing a serious business presentation or document. If the context of your message is somber, select a conservative style. If your purpose is motivational, consider a template with a border of stars, flags, or other icons associated with success. Be creative, but be certain that your overall design is suitable for the occasion, your audience, and your purpose.

When choosing color, keep in mind that high contrast between background and text on slides provides excellent visibility in a lighted room. The traditional standard is a dark background (often blue) with white or yellow text. You are not restricted to this combination, but remember that cool, dark colors (such as blue) appear to move away from the audience and warm, light colors (such as yellow) appear to move toward the audience. You might try colors that complement your company logo or that symbolize your message. Finally, consider colors that might be particularly appropriate for the country or culture of your audience. Most important, however, is that you have contrast so that your audience can easily read your slides.

For written documents, dark backgrounds are less appropriate because they do not reproduce well and make the message hard to read. Stick with lighter backgrounds and contrasting text and graphics.

Figures 7-5, 7-6, 7-7, and 7-8 show some sample templates that work for business presentations. Notice that these illustrations suggest different selections based on the situation, the audience, or the objective.

Fonts   Your fonts (also called typefaces) should be consistent throughout your presentation or document in terms of size and type. All titles should be the same size and the same font from slide to slide, as should all body copy. (If the font is larger on one visual and smaller on the next, your audience will feel like the screen is moving toward and away from them, which is most disconcerting.) However, title copy and body copy may be different from each other.

Two basic types of fonts are serif fonts (in which the letters sit on small platforms) and sans serif fonts (with no platforms). Serif fonts are traditional and easier to read. Sans serif fonts look contemporary and may be more dramatic. Figure 7-9 shows examples of some common serif and sans serif fonts.

For computer-generated transparencies and slides used in oral presentations, we suggest a minimum size of 28 point for body copy and 36 point for titles in

High contrast between background and text on slides provides excellent visibility in a lighted room.

Fonts should be consistent in size and type throughout your presentation or document.

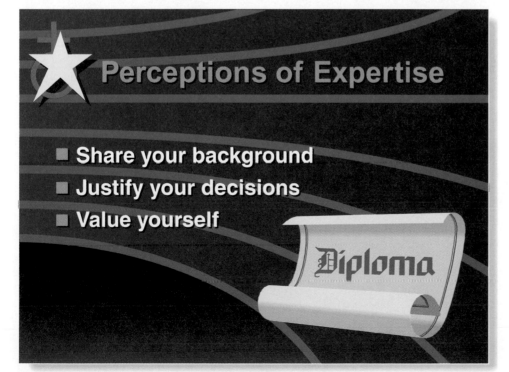

Figure 7-5
Sample PowerPoint Template for Business Presentations.

Subtle lines make this traditional dark blue template more interesting. Also note the traditional yellow and white lettering and the complementary colors of the clip art.

Figure 7-6
Sample PowerPoint Template for Business Presentations.

Warm, dark letters on a light background that looks like textured cloth set the mood for a presentation on multicultural communication.

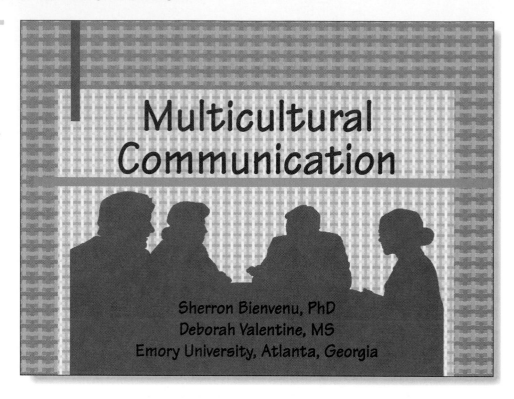

Figure 7-7
Sample PowerPoint Template for Business Presentations.

This template design features a lock on the title slide and a key on the following slide. The green and gold background suggests money and success and provides excellent contrast for the white and gold lettering.

Figure 7-8
Sample PowerPoint Template for Business Presentations.

Note how the key continues the message from the lock on the title slide. Also note that the clip art is appropriate for the message.

Examples of serif fonts:
Bookman Old Style   ***Bookman Old Style Bold and Italic***
Goudy   *Goudy Bold and Italic*
Times New Roman   *Times New Roman Bold and Italic*

Examples of sans serif fonts:
Arial   ***Arial Bold and Italic***
Universe   ***Universe Bold and Italic***
Legacy Sans   ***Legacy Sans Bold and Italic***

Figure 7-9
Examples of Serif and Sans Serif Fonts.

Notice the small ridges extending from the main strokes in the serif fonts.

most standard fonts. In many cases, 32 point for body copy and 40–44 point for titles works even better for easy reading. On written documents, major heads can be 18-point type or even larger; body copy should be 12 points. Title fonts or major headings should be easily distinguished from text or less important material by being bolded, italicized, or significantly larger. Figure 7-10 shows some contrasting font sizes.

Avoid the temptation to use many different fonts or many different sizes. You may mix a sans serif font for your titles with a serif font for body copy (or vice versa), but be certain they look sufficiently different from each other. Don't select similar fonts for titles and text copy; make them either exactly alike or very different. You might add an additional font somewhere for effect, but

Points

The term *points* refers to a sizing method for measuring typefaces. The term comes from the traditional printing industry in which 1 point equals 1/72 of an inch. This was a measure of how much lead to place in the molds used in old-fashioned printing presses. This form of measuring type sizes has carried over, although most printing processes no longer use lead type.

FAST FACTS

Figure 7-10
Font Sizes for Written Documents.

Notice the difference in contrast between the insufficient size contrast column on the left and the effective contrast column on the right.

Insufficient size contrast

Heading (14-pt. type)
Subordinate points

Heading (14-pt. type)
Subordinate points

Effective contrast

Heading (18-pt. type)
Subordinate points

Heading (18-pt. type)
Subordinate points

be careful. More than that creates a busy look that can be distracting. Be aware, also, that when producing PowerPoint slides some fonts do not show up as you expect. Stick with the common, traditional fonts (such as those listed in Figure 7-9) or, if you elect to use more unusual ones, be sure to check what they look like when projected—*before* your presentation (a good idea anyway). Remember that the fonts you choose will make an impression on your audience, just like the templates and colors you use.

Now, look back at Figures 7-5, 7-6, 7-7, and 7-8. In Figure 7-5, the title copy is Arial 22 point, and the body copy is Arial 16 point. This modern sans serif font works well with the lined background and the motivational topic. In Figure 7-6, the title font is called "Tekton." This font displays smaller than most fonts and, thus, had to be enlarged to 36 point for this slide. The title copy in Figure 7-7 and 7-8 is Impact, a dramatic, bold font. The title slide shows Impact in all capital letters at 54 point, and the title of the following slide is 44 point. The body copy is a more traditional, easy-to-read Times New Roman, 32 point.

Use common fonts that project clearly.

Structure   Bullet points and enumeration on visuals are a good way to break up the text and to provide information that is easy to digest. *Bullet points* refer to listed items that are preceded by a bullet (•) or small symbol. *Enumeration* refers to such a list when each item is numbered. Use enumeration when a list is sequential (e.g., step 1, step 2, etc.), or when you may need to refer back to the list of items.

When using bullets or enumeration on visuals, the points should be parallel— the grammar should be the same. For example, notice the parallel construction in Figures 7-1 and 7-5 and in the following sets of points:

Bullet points and enumeration break up the text and provide clear information.

The consistency provided by parallel structure is important when using bullet points or enumeration.

- "Analyze the environment, Consider the options, Select information" (EACH CLAUSE BEGINS WITH A VERB)
- "Cost of doing business, Return on investment, Comparison with competition" (EACH PHRASE BEGINS WITH A NOUN)
- "Overall goal, Specific purpose, Hidden agenda" (EACH PHRASE BEGINS WITH AN ADJECTIVE)

Making each point parallel makes the message clearer for your audience.

Capitalization   Use capital letters sparingly in visuals. You may print your titles in all capital letters, but a mixture of uppercase and lowercase letters is more natural and easy to read. Note that the titles of Figure 7-7and 7-8 are all capital letters, but the titles of the other figures are a combination of uppercase and lowercase.

Use capital letters sparingly in visuals.

Capitalize only proper nouns (names) and the first letter of the first word in each bullet point of body copy, as you see in the figures used in this chapter so far. Don't capitalize the first letter of each word because then everything will look like a title.

Spacing   Your titles or headings should begin on the same spot on each visual (such as centered, flush left, or flush right). Also start your body copy on the same line on each visual. The space between bullets should be consistent as well. Avoid the urge to spread bullets out if you only have two or three. Use that extra space for a picture or piece of clip art instead. If you don't have an appropriate illustration, white space (the portion of the visual with nothing on it) is perfectly fine and is preferable to spacing that varies. Imagine how distracting it would be to read a book that is single-spaced on one page and triple-spaced on the next!

The space between bullets should be about one-and-a-half times the size of the bullet font. So, if your bullet is 36 point (about half an inch), the space between items should be about three-quarters of an inch. This is not an exact rule, but remember to be consistent with your spacing, even when you have only a few bullet points.

Your titles or headings should begin on the same spot on each visual.

Illustrations (Clip Art)   *Clip art* is an assortment of pictures, cartoons, illustrations, and icons (symbols) available in computer graphic programs. The term comes from the old days when graphic designers would physically cut and paste pieces of art onto documents or layouts. Clip art helps to illustrate your points and creates visual access in your documents or slides. It can also help your audience to focus on the words on your slides if you choose illustrations that "point." Figures 7-11, 7-12, and 7-13 show samples of clip art and review other design elements.

The most realistic illustrations are photographs, which you can scan directly into your presentation or download from the Internet. You should be aware of copyright restrictions, however, and get permission when required. Figure 7-14 shows an example of a slide illustrated with a picture downloaded from the Web.

Graphs and clip art should be similar in size and type throughout your presentation. Their purpose is to enhance your message, not distract from it, so be sure the illustrations match the message. For example, don't mix cartoon-character clip art with realistic-looking photo art. If you choose photographs, try to use them throughout your presentation. Mixing art types, like mixing too many fonts and sizes, looks haphazard. Consistency looks more professional.

> **PowerPoint's Consistency Features**
>
> If you are using PowerPoint, you can check for consistency in spacing, type style, sizing, and bulleting by looking at your work on the Slide Sorter. Spacing standards can be set up using the Slide Master function. By taking time to get familiar with your software, you can save a great deal of time in the long run.

Consistency and attention to detail will make your visuals look professional.

Avoid the Misuse of Visuals

Although we are obviously enthusiastic about the value of good visuals, they can be misused. Communicators misuse visuals when they:

Don't let your visuals overwhelm the verbal message you are communicating.

- **Make them too complicated.** Probably the single most important thing to remember about visuals is to keep them simple and concise. A simple design lingers in the mind of the receiver very effectively. Your receiver should be able to look at a visual and "get it" within a few seconds.
- **Overwhelm the message.** Remember that the visual presentation of information is a way of supporting the speaker or writer and his or her message; it is rarely the message itself. Your business document or presentation will be primarily words; the visuals support and reinforce these words but do not typically replace them.

Figure 7-11
Sample of Clip Art and
Review of Design Elements.

Designed for a large
monitor in a college food
court, this slide features
an eye-catching dog and
a stack of coins, both of
which represent the
message. The title font is
Bernhard Mod 66 point,
selected to be seen
across the room. The text
is Arial 36 and 28 point.
The pale yellow
background provides
high contrast for the
dark letters and clip art.

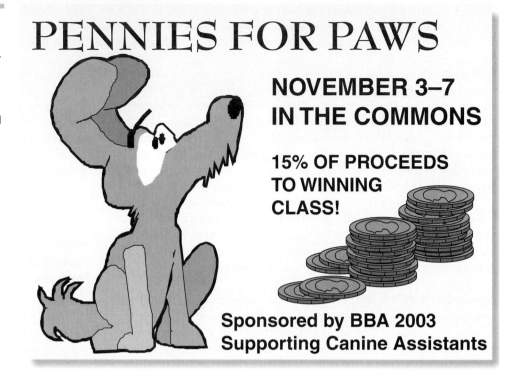

Figure 7-12
Sample of Clip Art and
Review of Design Elements.

The clip art in the
background of this slide
has been darkened (using
the Format Picture function
in PowerPoint) to illustrate
the message and provide
contrast for the white
letters. The title font is Book
Antiqua 60 point, a serif
font, and the body copy is
Arial 32 point, a sans serif
font. Also note that the
body copy is parallel—
each bullet begins with a
verb.

Figure 7-13
Sample of Clip Art and Review of Design Elements.

This clip art (called "human beans" or "screen beans") is laughing at the pun in the body copy of the slide about using calls and puts (stock broker terms) to trade options on the stock market. Also note that he is facing into the slide and is, thus, directing attention toward the body copy. The dark figure and lettering (title, 44 point, and body copy, 32 point; both in Arial Black) work well against the light background.

Figure 7-14
Sample of a Slide with a Photograph[2.]

If you have dramatic photos, select a simple template such as this one. Also note that the title font (22 point) and the body copy (16 point) are both Stone Sans. The white copy also appears dramatic on the black background. The bullets are parallel, all beginning with an adjective, and they are spaced in the same way on other slides in the presentation. White space (which is actually black in this slide) is also dramatic.

Don't get lost in your visual aids.

Try Advanced Visuals or Go Back to the Basics

When giving an oral presentation, you may want to try some visual support that goes beyond what we have already discussed, such as video or movie clips. You might also want to supplement your prepared visuals by using an old-school interactive medium: the flip chart. The next sections discuss the use of these forms of visual support.

Use Video or Audio Clips

Video or audio clips can add impact to oral presentations by using motion and sound.

Video or audio clips (short segments) can add impact to oral presentations by using motion and sound. Produce these using a tape recorder or camcorder and then download them into a computer presentation if your computer has sufficient memory and speed. When shooting video, be careful of random movement that can make your viewers dizzy. Use a tripod to steady the camera whenever possible. Videocassettes are easy to store and play back, and the cost of equipment is getting lower all the time. Technology is also making the use of CD and DVD systems more widespread. This trend will continue, we believe, because this newer technology is less cumbersome than video.

Video and audio clips can be especially useful when training people. Participants in role-plays, for example, can benefit from an objective view of themselves in action. In addition, video clips may be cost-effective for presentations that have to be given more than once. Commercial videotapes and CDs are also widely available, and you may find prerecorded tapes that fit in nicely with your presentation. If so, don't reinvent the wheel—use segments or the whole tape. The quality of such tapes usually exceeds home videos because of the professional lighting, sound recording, and content preparation. Get permission from the video producer if using them for commercial purposes.

Use Flip Charts, White Boards, and Chalkboards

Flip charts use large tablets of paper on an easel. They are inexpensive and can be especially useful in problem-solving meetings. Their major advantage is that they can record ideas shared by others and allow the group to react to input. Then you can remove pages and tape them on the walls around the room for easy reference. Flip charts are usually informal and work best with small- to medium-sized groups.

Classrooms and meeting rooms often contain white boards or chalkboards, which can serve the same purpose as flip charts. Although they can't be spread around the room like flip chart pages, white boards and chalkboards often give you more room to write. Again, select this form of visual aid only for very informal presentations or problem-solving meetings.

The major advantage of flip charts is that they can record ideas and allow the group to react to input.

Deliver Your Visual Aids with Confidence and Style

The following are some suggestions for boosting your effectiveness with visuals when delivering an oral presentation:

■ **Leave the lights on while you show slides.** This is probably the easiest remedy for the worst drawback to the use of slides. Your audience will be able to see properly prepared slides with normal projection equipment if the lights in the room remain on—especially if you use dark backgrounds. By keeping the room lighted, you avoid the problem of losing listeners who tend to doze off in the darkness. You

Use a flip chart to take notes or record ideas in a problem-solving meeting.

also maintain eye contact with them more effectively. Remember that the audience should focus on you first and then on your visual aid.

When changing slides or transparencies, be as unobtrusive as possible.

- **Use a remote control device that allows you to change the slide without physically touching the projector.** Similarly, if showing transparencies, be as unobtrusive as possible. Don't stop in the middle of a thought to abruptly change the visual. When preparing for your presentation, stack your transparencies in the correct order, and then move from one to the next smoothly and with minimal distraction to your audience. Set aside the used transparencies when finished with each.
- **Avoid turning away from your audience and talking to the image on the screen.** Glance at the visual but maintain eye contact with your audience.
- **Turn the transparency or slide projector off when not in use.** If you leave the light on a blank screen, or a slide already covered, it will distract your audience.
- **Keep your slides to a reasonable number.** Don't overload your audience, and don't expect the slide show to be a substitute for a good presentation.

Using too many gimmicks in a slide presentation is distracting.

- **Minimize the number of transition types you use with presentation software.** PowerPoint and similar software allow you to do a variety of actions when switching from one slide to the next. Options for screen changes include a simulated curtain coming down and slides dissolving from one to the next. Some novice users want to try every bell and whistle and gimmick in the software; however, too much gimmickry is distracting. If your audience is more curious about what your next slide change will look like than what your next idea will be, you're in trouble.
- **Check your visuals out in advance.** We've all seen presentations in which the gremlins inside the microphone, projector, or computer caused something to look different, burn out, or just die. It is crucial for you as a speaker to be as well prepared as possible for such problems. Be sure to arrive early enough to test equipment. Bring spare projector bulbs. Check out the videotape player, slide projector, and computer hookup. Make sure your videotape is set to the right place before you begin. Don't rewind or advance a tape while your audience waits. Know your equipment and use it smoothly.

Be prepared for all potential equipment problems.

Get Feedback on Your Visuals

In this chapter, we have focused on using visuals to deliver effective business communications. Just as in other forms of communication, however, your learning process does not stop with the actual delivery of your message. Step 5 of the Strategic Communication Model reminds us of the importance of evaluating feedback for ongoing improvement. In visuals, as in any other form of communication, reactions of your audiences can be valuable.

While you are designing your visuals, solicit feedback from trusted colleagues. Often another person will see gaps, missing data, confusing layout, or other problems that you miss. Ask them to react to the template or the colors. Use open-ended questions and listen carefully to their responses. Also be sure to have someone proofread your visuals. Typos, misspellings, or missing words can quickly undermine the effectiveness of your visuals and your credibility.

During the delivery of an oral presentation, note your listeners' reactions to the visuals. If they seem to be squinting at them, they are probably too hard to read. If your listeners are frowning or look puzzled, the slides may be too confusing or busy. Adjust your presentation accordingly.

Be willing to give others your feedback about their visuals. If they are good and helpful, let them know; if not, suggest why they were not helpful. Share the guidelines in this chapter with your associates, and you will all produce better visuals for better communication.

Solicit feedback from colleagues and proofread your visuals.

APPLYING THE STRATEGIC COMMUNICATION MODEL

Let's look back at our opening story of Danielle Steenburg and her presentation visuals. In her case, the visuals complicated the communication rather than reinforcing it. If she worked for a typical, progressive company today, she would lose credibility because of the lack of professionalism in delivering her message.

Danielle's use of transparencies—especially hastily prepared ones made from photocopies—is a throwback to another time and reflects poorly on her. Also, the way she selected and organized her information and then designed and used her transparencies violates many of the rules discussed in this chapter. She tried to show too much information crowded into visuals that were hard to read. Telling the audience "you probably can't read this. . ." does not excuse poor-quality visuals. She further compounded the problem by misusing the equipment—leaving the projector on when not showing a transparency and thereby blinding her audience.

Today's employees would be wise to assume that their company is more sophisticated than was Danielle's. Slides should accompany almost any formal presentation. Similarly, graphics of some sort should be a part of many written documents. Being unaware of this or being incapable of producing acceptable visuals will be a significant disadvantage to today's business communicator.

Summary of Key Ideas

- Using visual information improves both oral and written communication.
- Visuals used in both written documents and oral presentations help writers and speakers develop, clarify, and enhance their messages and help readers and listeners understand and remember.
- Review your analysis of your situation, audiences, and objectives with your audiences, and then plan the appropriate visual displays of information as you develop your document or talk.
- Common visual formats include word charts, pie charts, line charts, bar charts, tables, flowcharts, organizational charts, and props or models.

- Consistency elements to apply to visuals include background (template), font, structure, capitalization, spacing, and illustrations.
- Avoid overcomplicating your visuals; don't allow your visuals to overwhelm your message.
- Always check out your presentation visuals *before* your presentation. Surprises are never fun!
- Solicit feedback about your visuals from your peers and pay attention to the responses of your audience. Your visuals should clarify and enhance your message.

Application Activities

Activity 7-1 Preparing a Bar Chart

Using the following hypothetical information, prepare a bar chart showing the top 5 occupations in ascending order by percentage of growth. Use a presentation software package such as PowerPoint and select the style of bar chart that best expresses your message.

According to a survey by the U.S. Department of Labor (March 2001), the five most rapidly growing occupations are as follows. The number following each reflects the percentage of growth in employment between 1990 and 2002.

Paralegal personnel	132.4
Office machine and cash register servicers	80.8
Computer systems analysts	107.8
Data processing machine mechanics	147.6
Computer operators	87.9

Activity 7-2 Recognizing Design Mistakes

Based on what you have learned in this chapter, identify the design issues that should be corrected in the slide in Figure 7-15. The audience is advertising agency employees, and the presentation is about time management. The speaker is highly enthusiastic and funny, and the purpose is to motivate.

Look for changes in:

- *Template.* Is it appropriate for the situation? What kind of template would be better?
- *Color.* Are the colors appropriate and is there enough contrast? What colors would be better?
- *Font choice and size in the title and body.* Is the title larger than the body copy? Can you easily read both? Are the title fonts either alike or very different? What kind of fonts would you choose?
- *Construction.* Are there too many bullets? Are the bullets parallel? How would you simplify the wording in the body copy?
- *Capitalization.* Is only the first word capitalized in the bullet points? Is the title easy to read?
- *Illustrations.* Is the clip art appropriate, large enough, and focusing toward the words? What type of illustration would you choose?

Activity 7-3 Selling a New Taxi Service

Betting that corporate customers who visit Denver will support an upscale taxi service, Centennial Sedans launched its company with a fleet of 11 new Cadillac Fleetwoods shortly after Denver's new airport opened in the mid-1990s.

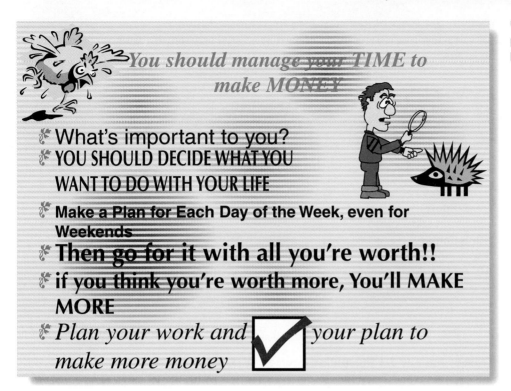

Figure 7-15
Poorly Designed Slide

"We are not a limo company," said Karrie Howard, Centennial's sales director. "We have upscale taxis, charge flat rates, and offer impeccable service without the ostentation of the limo." The company studied the market in Denver and identified a niche to serve customers who wanted a luxury car service that was dependable and available by reservation up to six months in advance.

Howard says that a major share of its business is done with customers who fly into Denver International Airport and then go to major corporate offices in the metro area. Each sedan is driven by a chauffeur in a black suit, and the vehicles are equipped with such conveniences as cellular phones, wireless Internet connections, and special reading lights.

Howard stresses that the convenience of a simple telephone call to make a reservation for a sedan appeals to many customers. And she adds that the flat rate cost, which is quoted when the reservation is made and can be paid with a credit card, is an added feature. The flat rate is for the service of the sedan; up to four persons may ride at no additional cost. "We only charge for pickup and delivery. If we get slowed down by traffic or a snowstorm, that is our loss," Howard says.

Cost comparison shows that Centennial's charge from Denver International Airport to downtown is $55, whereas Yellow Cab fares average $36 to $42, depending on traffic and weather conditions.

Optimistic about the future of Centennial's service, Howard said the company is adding more Fleetwoods, Cadillac's largest sedan, to its fleet each month. No vehicle remains in the fleet longer than three years, and each is inspected weekly. Howard also said each vehicle carries $1 million in liability insurance.

Using PowerPoint or similar software, prepare at least four visuals you could use to deliver Centennial's message to business organizations in Denver. Be prepared to explain what you did in each visual. Be sure to apply the ideas discussed in this chapter.

Interactive CD-ROM Exercises

Activity 7-4 Preparing Visual Aids for a Presentation

After reviewing Activity 6-4, "Preparing a Current Event Informative Presentation" in Chapter 6, prepare a computer-generated slide show (using PowerPoint or similar software) for your presentation. Create one good slide for each of the following:

1. Attention-grabber
2. Agenda/purpose
3. Benefit to the audience
4. Point 1
5. Support for point 1
6. Point 2
7. Support for point 2
8. Point 3
9. Support for point 3
10. Summary
11. Action step
12. Strong final statement (visualized)

Career Activity

Career Activity 7-1 Presenting Yourself to a Potential Employer

Select a company or profession in which you would like to eventually work. Then imagine that you will be making a presentation to a potential employer in this field for an entry-level position. Brainstorm some visuals, props, or work samples you could take with you to best present your abilities and skills. Be creative. Sketch out what these visuals might look like.

Using PowerPoint or a similar software package, prepare a slide show that highlights your experiences, talents, or abilities. Work to project something about your personality through the creative use of visuals, information, and design.

myPHLIP Companion Web Site

Learning Interactively

Visit the myPHLIP Web site at www.prenhall.com/timm. For Chapter 7, take advantage of the interactive "Study Guide" to test your chapter knowledge. Get instant feedback on whether you need additional studying. Read the "Current Events" articles to get the latest on chapter topics, and complete the exercises as specified by your instructor. Expand your learning with a visit to the "Research Area." There you will find a wealth of information you can use to complete your course assignments.

Notes

1. University of Minnesota/3M Study reported online at www.plu.edu/%7elibr/workshops/multimedia/why.html. Accessed November 20, 2000.
2. The photo in this slide is by Amy Sancetta, AP. Found at www.usatoday.com/olympics/sydney/gallery/gymnastics/content_template31.htm. Accessed October 10, 2000.

Delivering Powerful Messages and Evaluating Feedback

Part 3

Step 1. Define the Context

A. Define the situation.
  1. Limit the problem.
  2. Evaluate the problem within the external climate.
  3. Evaluate the corporate culture that impacts the problem.
B. Define your audience.
  1. Identify all potential audiences (distinct or overlapping).
  2. Learn about each audience.
C. Define your objectives with each audience.
  1. Define your overall goal.
  2. Identify the specific purpose of the communication.
  3. Acknowledge your hidden agenda.

Step 2. Consider Your Media and Timing Options

A. Select media options that are most appropriate for your message.
B. Evaluate your timing options.

Step 3. Select and Organize Your Information

A. Review your analysis of your situation, audiences, and objectives.
B. Compare key organizational patterns and select the most effective one.
C. Limit your main points.
D. Enhance your message with powerful support material (visual aids, numbers, and examples).

Step 5. Evaluate Feedback for Continued Success

A. Give feedback.
B. Solicit feedback.
C. Receive feedback.
D. Evaluate yourself with the Credibility Checklist:
  1. Goodwill: your focus on and concern for your audience
  2. Expertise: your education, knowledge, and experience
  3. Power: your status, prestige, and success
  4. Confidence: the way in which you present yourself and your message

Step 4. Deliver Your Message

A. Develop your writing, speaking, interpersonal, and group skills.
B. Prepare thoroughly (rehearse your presentations and edit your writing).
C. Express confidence in your topic and in yourself.
D. Be yourself (but adapt your style to your audience and situation).

SKILL OBJECTIVES

After you have studied this chapter, you should be able to:

- Identify the different types of business correspondence and reports.
- Describe the importance of accuracy and tone in effective business writing.
- Explain how tone problems can create psychological stress and friction between communicators and their audiences.
- Describe various ways writers can use principles of good human relationships in their written correspondence.
- Explain how reader self-interest can be better met by using reader-viewpoint wording.
- Contrast and provide examples of blanket tone versus personal tone.
- Contrast and provide examples of positive wording versus negative wording.
- Explain how to avoid tone problems such as abrasiveness, preaching, false sincerity, and sexist language.
- Break through writer's block using raw writing.
- Apply the concepts of sound writing to longer messages.

Deliver Your Message with Effective Business Writing: Writing with Class

CHAPTER 8
SKILL
FOCUS:

Building on the Foundation Skills to Write with Accuracy and Professionalism

COMMUNICATING WITHOUT A STRATEGY

Community Bank's Not-So-Friendly Messages

Tara is an intern at Community Bank. Her boss, Georgia Wilson, asked her to look at the letters the bank sends to its customers. "We need to be careful about how we communicate with our customers. We are supposed to be the friendly alternative to the big banks, so let's make sure we are projecting that folksy, local image." Georgia handed Tara a letter. "I don't like the way this one sounds. If I were the customer, I wouldn't feel warm toward Community Bank after reading it. Do you think you can fix this? Or better yet, can you develop guidelines we could use to write better?"

She then handed Tara the following letter written by Albert Hart and explained its background. The customer, Mr. Hocking, wanted to make no payment on his account this month but pay extra next month. He had been laid off from his job and needed a brief extension on the payment date. Mr. Hocking's credit history had not been outstanding in the past. He had been out of work several times and was, therefore, late in paying twice in the past seven months. However, it looked as if his work situation would be more stable in the future.

Tara shook her head slowly as she read the letter. "What was Albert Hart thinking?" she asked herself.

Dear Mr. Hocking:

It is impossible for us to extend you another month before your next payment on your auto loan. Already you have been late twice this year. Such behavior shall have serious detrimental effects on your credit rating.

I sympathize with your problem. We all have problems. I find myself short of cash every now and then, too. But I always—*always*—pay my debts first, before spending money on luxuries. Your auto loan is a special obligation, one that should not be taken lightly. If we let you off the hook this month, we'd have to do the same for all our other thousands of customers. I'm sure you see that would be out of the question, since we are in this business to make a profit. My suggestion to you (the same suggestion I've made to other young men who seem to have such problems) is to forgo some other spending urge and, instead, make your car payment on time, as agreed upon.

Thank you for doing business with Community Bank and have a nice day.

Yours sincerely,

Albert Hart
Albert Hart

The lack of professionalism in delivering written messages can have devastating effects on a business. Poorly written letters and memos can send all the wrong signals to customers, employees, and others involved in the organization's activities.

This chapter provides some useful guidelines on writing professional and effective business correspondence. Armed with the Strategic Communication Model, you have already defined the context of your message and considered your media and timing options. You have also decided that your message requires a hard copy or a degree of formality, that the cost of writing is justified, and that a written document is the medium most likely to succeed. You have selected and organized the information you want to convey to your readers. Now it's time to focus on delivering your message. Here we build on the information presented in Chapter 2, which stressed the importance of previewing, accessing, and using efficient, vigorous, and economical language appropriate for your audiences.

Write with a Careful Blend of Accuracy and Tone

This chapter focuses on Step 4 of the Strategic Communication Model: Deliver your message. Here we concentrate on written media. In Chapter 9 we look at oral communication.

Written business communication typically takes the form of *correspondence* and *reports*. Some of these documents are form letters, memos, and routine, computer-generated reports. We will focus on the more personalized, individual documents—the ones that address specific needs or problems in a systematic manner specific to the issue. E-mail is, of course, a form of written correspondence, although a hard copy is not automatically produced. What we say about letters and memos generally applies to e-mail messages as well.

Written business communication typically takes the form of correspondence and reports.

As we discussed in Chapter 6, correspondence typically can be classified as primarily:

■ Positive or routine information or goodwill messages
■ Persuasive/sales messages
■ Bad-news/refusal messages

Written business reports are documents prepared to meet three general purposes:

■ To *inform* readers by supplying necessary data and information
■ To *interpret* information by analyzing or integrating data
■ To *recommend* action based on analytical decision making

Regardless of the type of document, two elements of any written communication will have a powerful effect on the delivery of the message: accuracy and tone. Accuracy determines how clearly the writing explains the ideas it intends to convey. Tone reveals the writer's attitudes toward his or her subject and readers. Attention to these two elements allows you to project true professionalism and produce successful documents. In the next few sections, we will discuss ways in which you can create messages that are both accurate and that convey an appropriate tone.

Memos

A memorandum (often called simply a *memo*) is a concise, written message used for internal correspondence within an organization. It should deal with only one topic. Memo format is not used when writing to audiences outside the organization.

FASTFACTS

Professionalism in business writing requires attention to accuracy and tone.

FOCUS ON

Grammar Tongue-in-Cheek[1]

In the following rules for writers, author Paul Lima has fun with some common language-use errors. See how often you are "guilty" of committing such mistakes yourself. (If you don't recognize what's wrong with these sentences, spend some time reviewing Reference Tool A, "Avoiding Common Grammar, Punctuation, and Usage Mistakes.")

■ Verbs HAS to agree with their subjects.
■ Prepositions are not words to end sentences with.
■ Avoid clichés like the plague. (They're old hat.)
■ Also, always avoid annoying alliteration.
■ Be more or less specific.
■ Parenthetical remarks (however relevant) are (usually) unnecessary.
■ Also, too, never, ever use repetitive redundancies.
■ No sentence fragments.

■ Foreign words and phrases are not apropos.
■ Do not be redundant; do not use more words than necessary; it's highly superfluous.
■ One should NEVER generalize.
■ Don't use no double negatives.
■ Eschew ampersands & abbreviations, etc.
■ Analogies in writing are like feathers on a snake.
■ The passive voice is to be ignored.
■ Eliminate commas, that are, not necessary. Parenthetical words however should be enclosed in commas.
■ Never use a big word when a diminutive one would suffice.
■ Use words correctly, irregardless of how others use them.
■ Understatement is always the absolute best way to put forth earth shaking ideas like this.
■ Use the apostrophe in it's proper place and omit it when its not needed.

Continued

- If you've heard it once, you've heard it a thousand times: Resist hyperbole; not one writer in a million can use it correctly.
- Puns are for children, not groan readers.
- Go around the barn at high noon to avoid colloquialisms.
- Even IF a mixed metaphor sings, it should be derailed.

- Exaggeration is a billion times worse than understatement.

And finally . . .

- Proofread carefully to see if you any words out.

Strive for Message Accuracy

Failure to be accurate can lead to all kinds of unwanted consequences.

Failure to be accurate can lead to all kinds of unwanted consequences, ranging from a loss of credibility to downright embarrassment. Many communicators have put messages in writing that they would love to be able to retract. Consider how the writers of the following simple messages must have felt:

> "Buy one hot dog for the price of two and receive a second hot dog *absolutely free!*"
> —*Restaurant coupon*

> "Our February 9 issue reported our earnings per share as $1.88 billion. The addition of 'billion' was a typesetter's error, and we apologize for any ecstasy the error may have caused."
> —*AT&T employee magazine*

> "There was a typo in lawyer Ed Morrison's ad. His logo is: 'Your case is no *stronger* than your attorney,' not 'stranger.' "
> —*The Tulsa, Oklahoma, Gusher*

Obviously, these messages have not accurately conveyed what they were meant to convey. The following sections present some guidelines in forming accurate messages.

Choose Words That Communicate Accurately

Delivering a message with accuracy is largely a matter of careful word choices and attention to details. Attention to detail is a matter of polishing a document to be certain no glaring errors slip through.

Always consider your first draft just that—a draft, not the final product.

Virtually no one produces flawless writing on the first take. Always consider the first draft just that: a draft. Take the time to edit and polish your writing. Set aside your "pride in authorship" (just because you wrote it does not mean it is perfect) and ask difficult questions about the document. Some key questions might be:

- Will this message make sense to someone who knows less about the subject than I do?
- Are my readers likely to have unanswered questions?
- Am I presenting all the necessary information?
- Have I worded the information as clearly as possible?

Put yourself in the position of your audience and write so that you can answer each of the questions with a "yes." Then proofread for polish errors. Typos, mis-

INSTRUCTIONS FROM THE BOSS

Accurate wording can make all the difference.

DILBERT © UFS

spellings, grammar mistakes, and awkward wording can cloud your meaning and damage your credibility. Don't rely solely on your computer's spell- or grammar-checking software. Such software can be helpful to catch polish errors, but it cannot identify all problems and may offer incorrect solutions. (See "Focus On" at the bottom of this page.)

In short, seek to say what needs to be said with accuracy and professionalism. Write with your readers in mind and anticipate their questions, concerns, and possible confusion. Your goal is to be so clear that you deny the reader the opportunity to misunderstand.

Write in such a way that the reader cannot possibly misunderstand.

FOCUS ON

Complete Trust in the Spell Checker[2]

Although you may be tempted to rely on the electronic wizard to bail you out of the problem of being a poor speller, you still must check your work to find mistakes that no computer program will find or correct. The following are four good reasons why you shouldn't entrust your documents solely to the computer spell checker.

- If the word you've used isn't the right word but it is spelled correctly, the spell checker will let it pass. If you wrote your address as Bacon Street instead of Beacon Street, for example, the computer will think this is just fine. If you wrote *stranger* when you meant *stronger* (as in the earlier ad), the spell checker will see no problem.

Continued

- The spell checker will not flag incorrect homonyms (words that sound alike but have different meanings). Words such as *meet* and *meat, they're* and *their,* or *to, too,* and *two* all look equally correct to the spell checker.
- The spell checker won't flag sentences with words left out. One communication consultant writes, "I once had a sentence in a press release that read: 'We will share strategies for making conversational English standard of the business world.' Of course, there was a *the* missing before the word *standard,* but the only way I caught the gap was to read the sentence aloud." That's an excellent way to check your writing—read it aloud.

- The spell checker doesn't necessarily give the correct advice about hyphenated words. Some spell checkers allow both *data-base* and *data-base, on-line* and *online,* and don't offer any suggestions for whether the term *businesspeople* should be one word or two. In other words, you have to use your own judgment or defer to the most currently accepted usage.

Spell checkers and other tools offered by most computer programs are certainly helpful, and people should take full advantage of them. But whatever "ewe dew," please make sure you use the best tool: your own judgment.

Polish Your Message for Accuracy and Credibility

The layout of a letter or a report is an important aspect of its polish.

One aspect of polish unique to written documents is the layout of a letter or report. The business world has developed certain conventions about how business correspondence should look, and letters or memos that violate these conventions may be regarded as inappropriate, thus damaging the writer's credibility. Reference Tool D, "Formatting Written Documents," shows some currently acceptable letter and memo formats. If you are not familiar with what elements need to be in a letter or memo, take a look at this reference.

Also, as we discussed in Chapter 7, you have more flexibility than ever to use graphics, illustrations, charts, and tables, thanks to the capabilities of word processing and presentation software. Invest some time to learn these features and use them appropriately.

FOCUS ON

The Typo Debate

Writing teachers have an ongoing debate about the importance of checking for typos, spelling, and grammar—what many writers call polish. Some seem to think that a document with no polish errors is a good document. We disagree with that for the same reason we disagree that a smoothly delivered speech is necessarily a good speech. Polish errors in writing and platform speaking skills are relatively easy to evaluate, but the *content* of the message is critical to good communication.

This is not to say that polish is unimportant. Writing without errors is important, not so much because the message may be confused, but because a document with obvious or careless errors damages the writer's credibility. It sends the message that the writer doesn't care about detail. Such errors could cost someone a job, a customer, or a prized project assignment. So pay attention to both content *and* polish when writing messages.

E-mail documents should have most of the same elements found in written correspondence, although they tend to be less formal. Use the following guidelines to be certain that your e-mail will be polished and effective.

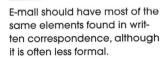

E-mail should have most of the same elements found in written correspondence, although it is often less formal.

1. Provide your audience with adequate context by:
   - Using informative subject lines to preview the upcoming message
   - Quoting the e-mail to which you are responding (you can cut and paste excerpts from the incoming e-mail and respond to each)
2. Be aware of page layout issues. Stick with:
   - Short paragraphs with adequate white space
   - Lines under 75 characters long
   - Messages under 25 lines long
   - Plain text
3. Find replacements for gestures and intonation (but don't overuse these):
   - Smiley faces :-)
   - Capital letters (use sparingly—they come across to the reader as SHOUTING)
   - Occasional use of different typefaces (but be sure the receiver's computer can reproduce these)
4. Be aware of what cues people will use to form impressions of you:
   - Name and domain name (Don't get too cute with funny names or use suggestive or obscene domain names.)
   - Grammar, punctuation, and spelling (It's still important, even in the relative informality of e-mail.)
5. Perhaps most important: Be sure your message has something worthwhile to say.

A typical e-mail message is typed onto a form such as the one shown in Figure 8-1.

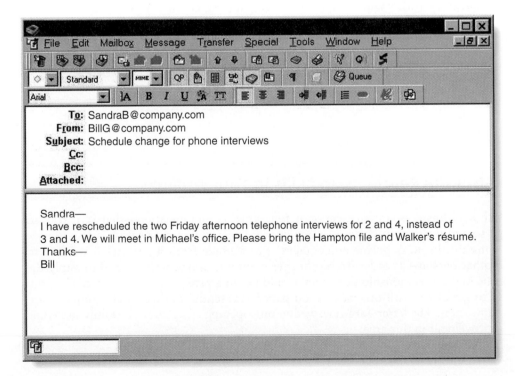

Figure 8-1
E-Mail Using a Standard Memo Format

E-Mail Full of Mistakes[3]

if you've received an e-mail that loks like this . . . you'r NOT alone !!!!!!!!! :)

Experts say people who communicate via computer are becoming increasingly informal—and sloppy. E-mail is routinely strewn with typos, grammatical errors, and various shortcuts, such as no capital letters.

The trend—as relaxed as the Silicon Valley dress code—really annoys some grammar purists. "A student wouldn't walk into a professor's office asking a question using bad English. Why would they send me that kind of mistake in an e-mail?" gripes Kenneth Brown, an assistant professor at the University of Iowa business school. An avid tracker of e-mail etiquette, Brown said he regularly chides students for sending sloppy e-mail to him and even to prospective employers.

Some faculty members have also gotten an admonishment. Shonquis Moreno, a 28-year-old writer from New York with a penchant for the lowercase, said she likes the "more intimate, casual, off-the-cuff tenor" her e-mails have. In many cases, she has even stopped fixing jumbled letters. "Maybe it's because I know that typos are recognizable as typos and not spelling errors," said Moreno, who works for an Internet start-up and finds herself scurrying to answer more than 30 e-mails a day.

By the end of last year, there were 335 million e-mailboxes—more than one per person—in the United States, according to the trade publication *Messaging Online*. That represents a 73 percent leap in just one year. Internet experts say the advent of instant messages—real-time conversations—has only heightened the casual, abbreviated nature of online "chatting." But they warn against misspellings and grammatical goofs.

On the Web, "you won't be judged by the color of your skin, eyes, or hair, your weight, your age, or your clothing," author Virginia Shea says in her rules of Netiquette, which are posted online. "You will, however, be judged by the quality of your writing." Asked via an online mailing list what they thought about e-mail's informality, everyday computer users replied in droves.

Jeff Rubin, a newsletter publisher in Pinole, California, said computer communication has become a "forum for people who cannot spell or string 10 words together." Sometimes, he said, "it's embarrassing." Still others raved about the ease e-mail has brought to communication. Now a student getting her master's degree in Internet strategy, Cincinnati resident Carol Boyd was relieved to escape the "legendary one-page memo" she spent years perfecting during her nearly 30 years at Procter & Gamble.

"Communication is less discipline, but oh!—what a timesaver!" Boyd wrote. "It's amazing what my teacher can convey in a one-word e-mail that simply says. 'Cool.' "

Apply Psychology and Human Relationship Skills to Your Writing

Although business communication is functional communication—that is, it tries to get something done—we must recognize that business communication is also *human* communication. A business document is a message from a person—a writer—to another person—a reader. To be effective communicators, writers need to apply the same human relationship skills they would use in a face-to-face encounter. The ability to get along with others, even on paper, is essential in successful business communication. The letter Tara reviewed in our opening story could certainly use some improvement in this area.

In the following sections, we will consider some specific principles of psychology and human relationships that apply in written communication. These principles are rooted in the need to write with an appropriate tone, to consider reader emotions, to satisfy self-interest, to be treated as individuals, to receive positive information, and to avoid being offended.

Write with an Appropriate Tone

As damaging as accuracy errors are, even greater problems can arise from inappropriate tone. Business writing should be courteous and polite. An otherwise accurate message can lose its effectiveness if the tone is offensive. For example, suppose you are chairperson of a student volunteer committee and you want to invite members to attend the next meeting. Which of these sentences conveys the best tone?

The psychological content of a message is conveyed by its tone.

1. The next planning meeting will be held on May 13.
2. We look forward to working with you again at our next planning meeting on May 13.
3. You are expected to attend our next planning meeting on May 13.

Each of these sentences conveys the same essential information, but each projects a different tone. The tone is partly conveyed by what the sentence implies about the reader's relationship to the writer. The first statement is strictly informational—it conveys neutral feelings and implies no differences in status between the writer and reader. The second statement seems more positive—it conveys a pleasant, collegial tone and an implication that working together in the past has been a pleasant experience. The third statement sounds almost dictatorial and demanding. It seems to indicate a boss-subordinate relationship that is probably inappropriate, especially in a volunteer organization.

Simple changes in phrasing can alter the tone of a written message.

Albert Hart's tone when trying to collect past dues for Community Bank leaves much to be desired. Look back at his letter at the beginning of this chapter and you'll see a preachy, condescending tone.

Consider Reader Emotions

Tone problems can create psychological stress and friction between communicators and their audiences. Figure 8-2 is an excerpt from a memo to the manager of a training and development department. The company president, Butch Rocco, isn't too happy about a recent training program and is quite clear about his feelings. How do you like the tone of his message? How would you feel if you were Chris Gardner, the recipient of this memo? Would the writer be likely to speak face-to-face with the reader using the same tone?

When message tone is bad, readers feel psychological stress.

What do you think of the accuracy and tone of that message? Accuracy may be fine. Perhaps everything Butch Rocco says is true. He does say what he wants to say, and he goes on to support his ideas with specific examples. (This support was not included in the excerpt we showed you.) But the most significant problem with Butch Rocco's memo is that his tone is likely to be offensive to the reader. If his goal is to improve future training, he may have so intimidated the reader that such improvement will be difficult. Let's look at a way he could have conveyed his message with a more diplomatic tone, as shown in Figure 8-3.

Figure 8-2
Memo Excerpt with
Inappropriate Tone

MEMORANDUM

TO: Training and Development
         c/o Chris Gardner, Manager
FROM: Butch Rocco, President
DATE: February 16, 2001

MY REACTIONS TO YOUR DEPARTMENT PRESENTATION ON TEAM BUILDING

Chris, as department leader, I want you to convey my message to the other members of the group. Whenever I say "you" in this memo, I am talking to all department members unless otherwise noted. Tell them that.

Overall, I was disappointed in the latest training sessions. They were lousy.

You gave a lot of information but few specifics on how to build and utilize team efforts. Training sessions like these need to focus more on specific behaviors. It is not important that the little people understand concepts so much. You got into your touchy-feely mode of teaching abstract ideas rather than actions because this is what you people are taught in college. Corporate training follows a different model.

You should have done a better job of identifying what you want us to do before charging forth with the presentation. What is it our guys can DO now that they couldn't do before your little show? I'd be hard pressed to answer that question.

Appeal to the Reader's Self-Interest

Our audience's primary motivation is self-interest.

People are egocentric; that is, they are strongly interested in themselves. It is human nature to be concerned with and motivated by one's own personal needs, wants, and interests. This self-centeredness is normal and not particularly harmful unless carried to extremes where there is *no* caring about others.

When people speak or write, they reflect this egocentricity in their language. Studies have shown that as much as every fifth word written or spoken is *I* or one of its derivations—*me, mine, my, we, ours, us.*[4] Even though we are all self-centered to some degree, most of us learn to temper the tendency to focus on and talk about ourselves exclusively. Indeed, the extremely egocentric person is avoided like some-

Figure 8-3
More Diplomatically
Worded Memo Excerpt

MEMORANDUM

TO: Training and Development
           c/o Chris Gardner, Manager
FROM: Butch Rocco, President
DATE: February 16, 2001

MY REACTIONS TO YOUR DEPARTMENT PRESENTATION ON TEAM BUILDING

Chris, because you are department leader, I would appreciate it if you would convey my message to the other members of the group. Please advise them that whenever I say "you" in this memo, I am referring to all department members unless otherwise noted.

Overall, I was disappointed in the latest training sessions. I don't feel that they were very successful in moving our company toward our goals.

I felt that you presented a lot of information but offered few specifics on how to build and utilize team efforts. I believe that training sessions like the one you did need to focus more on specific behaviors. To me, it is less important that the employees understand *concepts* so long as they can apply the kinds of *behaviors* that will improve performance. The training seemed to focus more on teaching abstract ideas rather than specific actions. Perhaps this model is appropriate for college classes, but in corporate training, I think we need to follow a different model.

Corporate training requires that we identify specifically what we want employees to be able to do. An evaluation of the training should answer the question, "What is it our people can DO now that they couldn't do before the training session?"

one with a contagious disease. The point here is that business writers can turn this egocentricity into an advantage if they recognize the reader's needs. Effective communicators learn to express concern and appreciation for the views of others in letters, memos, reports, and other documents. This, of course, assumes that they have done their homework and carefully defined the context of their message.

One important way to reflect consideration for your reader is by phrasing your message in terms of reader viewpoint. Expressing appropriate reader viewpoint involves much more than just selecting certain key words. Genuine reader viewpoint causes a document's tone to reflect a sincere interest in the reader. Self-centered writers think of themselves first. Reader-oriented writers think of and convey their messages in terms of what the reader wants or needs to know.

The reader-oriented writer thinks of the reader first.

As this ad indicates, appealing to the interests of your audience is important.

One "red flag" that the writer should look for is use of the words *I, me, my,* and so forth found in abundance in written messages. Second-person phrasing (using *you*) often conveys more interest in the reader. Third-person phrasing (using *the data show* or *the results indicate*) can convey greater objectivity.

However, don't conclude that you should try to *eliminate* the use of *I* and its variations from your business writing. To do so may be impossible in many cases, and trying to do so may result in rather tortured syntax and excessive wordiness. Besides, the use of *I, we,* or *me* does not always indicate a lack of reader viewpoint. For example, the person who says, "*I* hope you will be happy with this purchase," is not really violating a reader viewpoint, even though the sentence begins with the word *I.* The overall tone and sense of caring for the reader are far more important than simply avoiding the use of first-person pronouns. Also, if a supervisor says, "I enjoyed your talk," the meaning is just as welcome as, "You did a good job with your talk."

Look at the following sample sentences and see the difference in the tone of the I-centered versions compared to the reader-oriented ones.

I Centered	*Reader Viewpoint*
I am applying for this job because it would give me some great business experience.	I am applying for this job because I feel that my qualifications could benefit your company.
We require that you sign the sales slip before we charge this purchase to your account.	For your protection, your account will be charged only after you have signed the sales slip.
I have been a social studies teacher for 22 years.	Your training department can benefit from my 22 years of experience in teaching social studies.
I think you'll be interested in my young investor's program.	As a business student, you will see some real benefits in this young investor's program.
We are happy to announce that we now offer a 24-hour drive-through service.	Now you can shop with us conveniently with a 24-hour drive-through service.

Write to People as Individuals

Your written documents have a more appealing tone when you phrase information as though you are talking to individuals rather than to groups. A personally addressed business letter singles out a reader for individual attention. Such a letter conveys a more sincere regard for the specific person than one addressed to "Dear Customer" or "Dear Fellow Employee."

Names or other information can be easily inserted while most of the letter remains the same for all readers. Explore these possibilities when you consider a mailing. If using e-mail, consider techniques that will make each message look individual as opposed to a long list of addresses in the "To:" box.

The sweetest sound to most people is the sound of their own names. Personally address your reader when appropriate.

Avoid Blanket Tone   When a document makes the reader feel anonymous, the "blanket tone" may be responsible. Blanket tone uses the same message for all readers and, thus, lacks any personalization, any sense of individual communication. Contrast the blanket tone versus personal tone in the excerpts from the following letters.

Blanket Tone	*Personal Tone*
When a thousand requests are received from prospective customers, we feel pleased. These requests show that our product is well received.	A copy of the booklet you requested is being sent to you today. Thank you for requesting it.
The cooperation of our charge customers in paying their accounts is appreciated. By paying on time, they allow us to give better service.	We certainly appreciate your paying the account. Your prompt payment allows us to give you better service.

The blanket tone makes the reader feel anonymous.

Address Your Reader Directly   Appeal to individual reader's benefits by using direct address. Direct address uses "this means you"–type statements. Each day we see examples of this approach in television and radio commercials. The announcer "personally" addresses each of the several million people who may be listening and attempts to make them feel that they are spoken to as individuals.

Direct address shows your readers how your message applies to them and how it can meet their individual needs. One way to show this application is to clarify *features* and *benefits* as we discussed in Chapter 6. Tell readers how your ideas or the product's features can be of benefit to them with "what-this-means-to-you" statements.

Communicate with Positive Wording

People appreciate messages with positive wording because they sound more upbeat and because they actually convey more information than do messages with negative wording. Rather than telling a person what is *not* or what you *cannot* do, focus on the positive—what *is* or what you *can* do. For example, if you say, "I do *not* live on 14th Street," it conveys very little information—it only rules out one possibility. On the other hand, the positive statement, "I live on 20th Street," conveys a great deal more specific information. Positive language also has a more pleasant ring to the ear. Work to reduce the use of negative phrases in your business writing.

Positive wording conveys more information and projects a more upbeat tone than negative language.

To illustrate the difference in tone between positive and negative word choices, here are two responses to a civic group's request to use a company meeting room. The first response uses many negative words (which are in italics) and has an unnecessarily negative tone.

We *regret* to inform you that we *cannot* permit you to use our large meeting room for your function because the Little Town Book Club asked for it first. We can, however, let you use our conference room, but it seats *only* 25.

The use of negative wording in this response undermines the actual good news of the message, which is that the reader *can* use the conference room. "We regret to inform you" is an unmistakable sign of bad news, and "cannot permit" contains an unnecessarily harsh meaning. Furthermore, the one good-news part of the message is handicapped by the limiting word "only." A more positive response to the request might be written like this:

Since the Little Town Book Club has reserved our large meeting room for Saturday, we can offer you the use of our conference room, which seats 25.

This version avoids the use of negative words. Both approaches yield the letter's primary objective of denying the request and offering an alternative, but the positive wording in the second response does a better job of building and holding goodwill for the company.

Let's look at a few more examples of sentences with negative and positive wording. Listen to the tone of each. (The negative words are in italics.)

Negative Wording	*Positive Wording*
You *failed* to give us the part number of the muffler you ordered.	So that we may get you the muffler you want, will you please check your part number on the enclosed card?
You were *wrong* in your conclusion because paragraph three of our agreement clearly states . . .	You will agree after reading paragraph three of our agreement that . . .
We *regret* to inform you that we must *deny* your request for credit.	For the time being, we can serve you only on a cash basis.
We *cannot* deliver your order until Wednesday.	We can deliver your order on Wednesday.

Be Sensitive to Potentially Offensive Wording

Message tone can be offensive when the writer sounds abrasive, preachy, insincere, or exclusionary. The following sections discuss various ways in which you can avoid offensive wording.

An abrasive personality can come across in your writing and hurt the tone of your message.

Beware of Abrasive Tone   Abrasiveness refers to an irritating manner or tone, the kind of writing or speaking that sounds demanding or critical. If you tend to have a somewhat abrasive personality, this will come across in your writing and can hurt the tone of your message. To determine if you tend to have an abrasive personality, you might ask yourself questions such as these:

- Are you often critical of others? When you supervise others, do you speak of "straightening them out" or "whipping them into shape"?
- Do you have a strong need to be in control? Must you have almost everything cleared with you?
- Are you quick to rise to the attack or to challenge?

- Do you have a strong need to debate with others? Do your discussions often become arguments?
- Do you regard yourself as more competent than your peers? Does your behavior let others know that?

The abrasive personality will tend to communicate in a manner that can be irritating to others. Try to recognize in yourself the degree to which you have a strong need to control or dominate other people. If you suspect that you do have this need, make an extra effort to soften the tone of your written communications.

Replace Abrasiveness with Assertiveness   Assertiveness can project a productive tone whereas abrasiveness is generally damaging. Assertiveness simply means that you express your feelings and observations in a manner that is non-threatening to other people. For example, instead of saying to someone, "You don't make any sense," the assertive person would say, "I am having a difficult time understanding what you are saying." Or rather than saying, "Deadbeats like you burn me up," the assertive person might say, "People who consistently make late payments cause us extra work and lost revenue." Few people get offended by the assertive individual. Indeed, one definition of assertiveness is being pleasantly direct.

Assertive means being pleasantly direct in your messages.

Avoid a Condescending or Preaching Tone   People tend to be independent creatures and like to be treated as equals, not talked down to. Thus, writing that suggests that the writer and reader are not equal is apt to make the reader unhappy. Preaching, in the context of this discussion, refers to a tone that talks down to the reader or otherwise emphasizes status differences. Again, we encourage you to review Albert Hart's letter in our opening story. Usually, preaching in documents is not intended; it occurs when the writer is trying to convince the reader of something, as in this example:

Preaching, or talking down to the reader, is usually not intentional.

> You must take advantage of savings like this if you are to be successful. The pennies you save pile up. In time you will have dollars.

In this case, the point may be accurate, but saying something so elementary, as if the reader did not know it, is insulting. Likewise, messages that "remind" the reader of obligations may irritate. Here are some examples of condescending "reminders":

> When you agreed to serve on this committee, you knew that you had a responsibility to meet each week.

> The extension of credit is a privilege we give to those who have shown trustworthiness. Along with this privilege goes the obligation to make prompt, regular payments on your account.

Better phrasing might be:

> Committee membership calls for weekly meetings so that we can get the needed work accomplished.

> The continued extension of credit requires that regular, prompt payments be made.

Avoid False Sincerity   An overall impression of sincerity—an expression of caring—is a composite of much of what we have discussed in this chapter. Don't overdo the

Avoid terms that suggest an exaggerated sense of sincerity.

goodwill techniques (such as referring too often to your reader by name in the message), but do have a sincere desire to convey the best possible image of your company. Avoid terms that suggest an exaggerated sense of sincerity. One example of such exaggeration showed up in a form letter from a company president that was sent out to each person who signed up for a new charge account. It sounds artificial and lacks believability:

> I was delighted today to see your application for a Belko's charge account.

Or consider this one, taken from an adjustment letter of a large department store, which also overstates the "sincerity":

> We are extremely pleased to be able to be of service to you and want you to know that your satisfaction means more than anything in the world to us.

Avoid the use of superlatives and overly enthusiastic phrases such as *delighted* and *extremely pleased* unless you really mean it.

Avoid Sexist or Exclusionary Language   Language can offend or even perpetuate discriminatory behavior by emphasizing the differences between people, by implying that one group is superior to another, or by excluding some people. The most common business mistakes regarding biased language are:

- Choosing the word *he* as a generic pronoun
- Including unnecessary qualifiers
- Selecting gender-specific titles

Avoid *he* as a generic pronoun.   In general, avoid *he/she* and *s/he* entirely. Use *he or she* and *her or him* only when absolutely necessary. Try one of these replacements in a sentence such as *Each worker must wear his or her hard hat*:

- Convert to plural. *All workers must wear their hard hats.*
- Use second person. *Wear your hard hat.*
- Replace the pronoun (*his* or *her*) with an article (*a, an,* or *the*). *Each worker must wear a hard hat.*

Avoid unnecessary qualifiers.   Omit words that call inappropriate attention or offer irrelevant identification, such as *Hispanic lawyer, female construction supervisor, elderly stockroom worker, handicapped receptionist,* or *male nurse.* In addition, avoid descriptions for one gender and not the other. If you wouldn't describe the suit the male keynote speaker was wearing, don't describe the woman's clothing either. Too often we read, "Molly Hill, an attractive 35-year-old lawyer, and her husband, Jon Hill, a noted scholar." Instead, write equitably: "Molly Hill, a lawyer, and her husband, Jon Hill, a scholar."

Avoid gender-specific titles.   Replacing the generic *man* is not always easy. For example, changing *manhole cover* to *personhole cover* is ridiculous. However, follow these tips whenever you can:

- Avoid words that exclude women, such as *chairman* and *policeman.* (Instead, use words such as *leader* and *police officer.*)
- Avoid words that exclude men, such as *stewardess* and *actress.* (Instead, use words such as *flight attendant* and *actor.*)

■ Replace words that collectively include men and women but imply only men, such as *manpower* and *forefathers*. (Instead, use words such as *staff* or *human resources* and *ancestors*.)

Make titles, names of positions or occupations, and common references gender inclusive. The following are some additional examples of gender-inclusive positions, occupations, and common references:

Many readers are offended by language that seems to exclude one of the sexes.

Avoid:	*Prefer:*
businessman	worker, manager, executive, retailer
chairman	chair, chairperson
coed	student
congressman	member of Congress, representative, legislator
delivery man	delivery driver
draftsman	drafter
fireman	firefighter
foreman	supervisor
housewife	homemaker
husband, wife	spouse
mailman	mail carrier, letter carrier
man-hours	staff-hours
mankind	human beings, humanity, people
man-made	manufactured, artificial, synthetic
newsman	reporter
repairman	service technician
saleslady, salesman	sales associate, clerk, salesperson, sales representative
spokesman	representative, advocate, spokesperson
waiter, waitress	server
watchman	guard, security officer
workman	laborer, worker

You run the risk of demeaning at least half your readers by using sexist language. Whether you are offended by such language or not is irrelevant. Someone you write or speak to could be. Even if unintentional, your language can offend or even perpetuate discriminatory behavior by emphasizing differences between people or by implying that one group should be excluded.

Sensitivity to message tone helps a writer sound like a concerned, thoughtful, caring person.

Applying good principles of human relationships and avoiding the common pitfalls described in this chapter can do much to create appropriate tone in your messages. Business communication is functional in nature, but it need not lack human qualities. Sensitivity to tone helps a writer sound like a concerned, thoughtful, caring person. The positive overall impression created in the minds of your readers will be worth the slight extra effort expended.

Deliver a Professional Longer Document

A long report is a series of shorter messages.

Much of what we have discussed in this chapter clearly applies to memos, letters, and correspondence. If you are working on longer documents such as business reports, the writing principles are basically the same. A long report is just a series of shorter sections, each of which can be treated using the principles we've discussed in this chapter. In the next few sections we will outline the elements of a business report and will discuss how you can break through writer's block, which is a common problem experienced by writers of longer reports.

Understand the Three Key Elements in a Business Report

A business report can be defined as an orderly and objective communication of factual information that serves some business purpose. A report should describe findings and analysis, not express undocumented opinions. It should use facts, hard data, and documentation. When opinions, guesses, hunches, or predictions are presented, they should be clearly labeled as such so the reader will not mistakenly assume they are facts. And, of course, the report should be functional, offering specific recommendations. Three key elements of the typical report include:

- Defining the report's problem
- Stating the goal of the report
- Detailing the research procedures

We will discuss each of these elements in the following sections.

Define the Report's Problem   Clearly, defining the report's problem or topic is crucial to its ultimate success. Remember that your reader may view the nature of any given problem differently than you do. By stating the nature of the problem—even when it seems obvious—you can validate that the reader is working from the same information and definitions as you are.

An objective, unemotional statement of the problem should be your goal. Avoid emotional language that may be overly judgmental or convey biases. The following examples illustrate this:

[EMOTIONAL/JUDGMENTAL]: Supervisors are incapable of writing good performance reviews.

[MORE OBJECTIVE]: Most first-line supervisors are writing performance reviews that do not meet company standards.

Also avoid stating the problem in terms that are too broad or vague. When the problem is too grandiose or unusually wide in scope, the report loses focus. The following examples illustrate this:

[TOO BROAD]: This report will study the effects of foreign competition on our business.

[MORE OBJECTIVE]: This report will study the marketing strategy of the three foreign competitors that are having the most impact on our share of the market in cable television: Sony, Panasonic, and Mitsubishi.

[TOO VAGUE OR ILL-DEFINED]: This report will examine safety problems in our manufacturing operations.

[MORE SPECIFIC]: This report reviews lost-time accidents reported in the past 12 months and corrective actions taken to prevent recurrence.

State the Goal of the Report State the goal or objective of the report in concrete, specific language so that readers will understand exactly what they will be reading. Avoid being overly vague in this statement. The following examples illustrate this:

[TOO VAGUE]: This report will suggest some ideas for changes to cope with rising labor costs.

[MORE SPECIFIC]: This report will recommend a three-step approach to cutting labor costs in the assembly plant.

Detail the Research Procedures Relate the specific methods used for gathering and processing information. For example, "This report reflects results of interviews with 200 students at four major universities along with an extensive Internet search of comparable schools," or "The findings are based on a review of more than 20 organizations facing similar problems in the past two years."

Break Through Writer's Block

A long report can look like a huge mountain to climb. Some people, when facing such a task, get writer's block—the inability to get started on a writing project. We recommend using *raw writing* as a way to break through writer's block. Raw writing is a simple, three-step process for managing the task of writing long documents. The steps are:

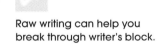

Raw writing can help you break through writer's block.

1. **Set a deadline.** Determine a realistic amount of time you'll need to convey your message. After collecting the raw data, you may decide to set aside two or three hours to write the finished report. Set your alarm clock for one-half of that time.
2. **Use half your time for outlining and fast writing.** Use the first half of your allotted time to sketch out an outline of the key ideas and to get something down on paper (or on the computer). Write fast. Capture any ideas you think may be relevant in light of the context (your audience and objectives). Don't be overly concerned about exactly the right wording, spelling, grammar, or any other details of presentation. Just capture your ideas and arrange them under a rough outline covering your main points. If you can't think of the right word, just leave a blank. If you can't write it the way you want to, don't worry. At this point in the process, dumping relevant data into your draft document is the most important activity.

In raw writing, the important thing is to get your ideas down on paper—fast!

   When the allotted time is up, stop writing and look at where you are. Even if you feel frustrated at not having written enough or you haven't figured out exactly where each idea goes, stop. (If composing on a computer, print a copy.)
3. **Use the second half of your time for fixing and polishing.** The second half of your allotted time should be used to be sure ideas are in the right places and to

Writer's block can be a major obstacle in communication efforts.

revise, move text around, edit, and polish the draft you made in the first half. Shift your mental gears from composing to being a ruthless, skeptical, rigorously logical *editor*. Polish the document by reading and asking others to review the draft document. The key to breaking through writer's block is to separate the writing from the editing processes.

Every writer experiences a mental block at some point. In addition to raw writing, professional authors recommend stopping in midsentence when you are finished for the day or are taking a break. Leave the document up on your computer screen. Then, when you return to work, the first thing you will see is the unfinished sentence on the screen, which you can then finish. With your fingers (and mind) moving, you will be more likely to continue writing, thus avoiding writer's block.

Get Feedback on Your Writing

Feedback does not come automatically with written media. You need to reach out for it.

The last step in the Strategic Communication Model is to evaluate feedback for continued success. We will talk in more detail about feedback in Chapter 12. For now, here are a few thoughts about feedback and written communication.

If you have chosen writing as the medium for delivering your message, you are aware that writing, by its nature, does not give immediate feedback. Using written media precludes getting nonverbal reactions, for example, from your audience. Because of the nature of the medium, you need to make a special effort to get feedback.

Several ways to get feedback on your writing include efforts made while in the draft stages as well as reactions made to the finished message. Ultimately, the most valuable feedback is to get people to do what you want them to do with the information you deliver. If Butch Rocco, the writer of the poorly worded memo earlier in the chapter, gets better training programs in the future, his memo will have been successful, and he is likely to continue to write as he did. If, however, the training manager quits the company as a reaction to Butch's sledgehammer tone, Butch will be getting some useful feedback.

Thus, the best time to get feedback is while your document is in draft form. Ask trusted colleagues to read your message to get their reactions to its content and tone. Read the message aloud yourself to see how it sounds and to catch typos. Also consider inviting readers to respond to your message, and make it easy for them to do so. Phrase this request for feedback in conversational, sincere words. Avoid the cliché, "If you have any questions do not hesitate to call upon me." Instead say something more conversational, such as "I'd appreciate any comments you have about this idea," or "Please give me a call at extension 664 if you need any clarification or additional information."

No writer produces perfect writing. You are likely to look back at documents you wrote yesterday and think of a dozen ways to improve them today. Getting feedback is an important part of the strategic business communication approach we have been following throughout this book. Reach out for it. Be open to it. And learn from it.

Ultimately, the most valuable feedback is to get people to do what you want them to do.

Get feedback on your draft writing if possible.

APPLYING THE STRATEGIC COMMUNICATION MODEL

Written messages reflect the culture of a company. If the messages are inappropriate or poorly worded, they speak volumes about the company's courtesy, refinement, and concern for others. Let's take a few moments to look back at our opening story.

Community Bank is trying to project an image as the friendly alternative to its big-bank competitors. To do so, it needs to communicate in a personal and sensitive manner. The tone of the letter written by Albert Hart doesn't support the objectives of friendliness and caring. His blunt, direct communication is conversational but not friendly or courteous. Saying "thank you" and "have a nice day" do not make up for his abrasive and condescending tone.

Albert would be wise to apply the ideas in this chapter as he delivers his messages, being direct yet much more sensitive to his audience. In making recommendations for guidelines for company writing, Tara should encourage her colleagues to strive for accuracy in their messages and to apply human relationship skills to their writing. This includes writing with an appropriate tone, considering the reader's emotions and needs, and being sensitive to offensive wording. Making such changes will allow Community Bank to project the warm and friendly image it values.

Summary of Key Ideas

- Effective writing calls for message appropriateness (use of the right medium), accuracy (of content correctly presented), and tone (application of psychology to meet reader needs).
- Polish is achieved through careful editing to check for typos, misspellings, grammar errors, and violation of document format conventions. The writer's credibility can be damaged by excessive polish errors.
- To create appropriate tone in a message, recognize that business communication is human communication. Consider people's feelings.
- Writers achieve effective tone by appealing to reader interests, addressing readers as individuals (avoiding blanket tone, using direct address), and using positive rather than negative wording whenever possible.
- People prefer to be treated like individuals. Good writers personalize their messages whenever possible.
- Positive wording tends to convey more information than does negative wording. It also tends to sound more pleasant.
- Assertiveness is not the same as abrasiveness. Use assertiveness by being pleasantly direct.
- Lecturing or preaching at people damages the tone of a message, as does exaggerated sincerity.
- Sexist or exclusionary language can demean some people and seriously affect the tone of a message. Avoid using *he* as a generic pronoun, adding unnecessary qualifiers, and selecting gender-specific titles.
- Longer writing projects such as business reports use the same techniques as shorter correspondence. A report can be seen as a series of shorter segments.
- Long document writers may face writer's block but can break through it by using raw writing—forcing themselves to limit the time they use to produce rough drafts and use additional time for editing and polishing.
- Effective writers seek feedback on their writing by having people review draft writing and by asking for responses from readers.

Application Activities

Grammar Assessment

Interactive CD-ROM Exercises

Activity 8-1 Rewriting Sentences to Improve Tone

Please visit the interactive CD-ROM included with your text to take advantage of the grammar assessment tool. Not only will you identify the areas within grammar and punctuation where you need work, you will also be given an opportunity to do several exercises to improve your skill in that area.

Rewrite the following sentences to improve the tone. Then briefly explain what tone problems you saw in the original version.

1. I am returning the unused portion of the enclosed Choco-crunchy candy bar because it tasted like garbage. I want my money back.
2. I am doing a report on the global strategies multinational corporations use to monopolize and exploit other countries. Please send me information on everything your company does internationally.
3. If you do not pay your overdue account immediately, your credit rating will be destroyed.

4. Why don't you answer my application letter for a trainee job with your company? I know I'm the best-qualified applicant you've seen.

5. Remember that it is better to give than receive. For this reason we want you to give to the annual Clarksville Freedom Festival with all your might, mind, and strength.

6. Like most people, you are probably aware of the great money that salesmen in the insurance industry make. For this reason, we want you to come on in for an interview in what may be the greatest career on earth.

7. I'm Ted Simmons, and I want to sell you a car.

8. Since you claim that the package was never received, I'll have my girl deliver a replacement right away.

9. Every salesman in this store is thoroughly trained in providing exceptional customer service. Therefore, it is obvious to me that you must have said something to set off the fistfight.

10. Your damage claim, like all such claims received, will be processed through our normal channels.

11. Obviously your qualifications are significantly less than what we are looking for in this position.

12. You failed to fill out the necessary paperwork for the loan.

13. Women typically have poorer repayment records than men. Therefore, I am rejecting your application for the loan.

14. Since virtually everyone wants to purchase season tickets for the upcoming games, I am sure you can see that we must be very selective about which fans are permitted this privilege.

15. We have had all kinds of people apply for the job: a fireman, a mailman, a busboy, even a stewardess! We cannot, of course, consider any more people.

Activity 8-2 Fixing Butch Rocco's Tone

Let's take another look at Butch Rocco's original memo to his training manager (page 180). Consider the tone of his message. What possible problems are likely to arise from this document?

Identify examples of

1. I-centered phrases
2. Blanket tone
3. Negative wording
4. Abrasiveness
5. Preachiness
6. Sexist language

Activity 8-3 Distinguishing Between Abrasiveness and Assertiveness

How can we be assertive without being abrasive? Rewrite the following five sentences that are clearly abrasive to make them assertive instead.

1. You have been one of the worst interns we have ever had at this company.
2. Chevrolets are any salesperson's best car because they last a long time.
3. Everyone is pretty sick of your goofing off on the job.
4. Customers always ask for me; I'm far and away the best sales rep in the store.
5. You have had your chance. Now I'm in charge, and things are going to be different.

Activity 8-4 Avoiding Sexist or Exclusionary Language

Replace the following terms with ones that are not sexist or exclusionary:

mailman	stewardess	fireman
coed	male nurse	chairwoman
salesman	the black actor	the gay manager

Activity 8-5 Overcoming Writer's Block

Many people face the problem of writer's block. Interview three people who write as part of their job responsibilities and ask about their experiences with this problem. How do they overcome it? Then prepare a one-page memo to your instructor describing specific tips you could use to overcome writer's block.

Career Activity

Career Activity 8-1 Writing a Letter of Application

Write a letter of application to a company for which you would like to work. Explain that you are enclosing your résumé (although résumé writing is not part of this assignment). The big idea of your letter is to get the reader to review your résumé and call you for an interview. Pay special attention to describing your skills and attributes using reader viewpoint—not being "I oriented." Provide positive information in an appropriate way. Avoid sounding boastful but do be assertive about your skills and abilities.

myPHLIP Companion Web Site

Learning Interactively

Visit the myPHLIP Web site at www.prenhall.com/timm. For Chapter 8, take advantage of the interactive "Study Guide" to test your chapter knowledge. Get instant feedback on whether you need additional studying. Read the "Current Events" articles to get the latest on chapter topics, and complete the exercises as specified by your instructor. Expand your learning with a visit to the "Research Area." There you will find a wealth of information you can use to complete your course assignments.

Notes

1. Adapted from Paul Lima, "34 Important Rules for Writers," www.wordarchive.com/articles/Culture/1/paullima942181518. (November 21, 2000)
2. Some of these ideas are adapted from an online business advice column (July 22, 2000) by Gary Blake, communication consultant and director of *The Communication Workshop.*
3. *The Oregonian,* April 3, 2000, p. 1A. Reprinted with permission of Associated Press.
4. Daniel Starch, *How to Develop Your Executive Ability* (New York: Harper & Row, 1943), p. 154.

SKILL OBJECTIVES

After you have studied this chapter, you should be able to:

- Maximize the skills necessary to give oral presentations for business.
- Describe several types of oral presentations frequently used in business.
- Polish your delivery using appropriate verbal, nonverbal, and platform management skills.
- Speak clearly and expressively, pay attention to timing, avoid distracting vocal patterns, and minimize verbalized pauses.
- Manage notes and visual aids comfortably and handle audience questions succinctly.
- Maintain eye contact, dress professionally, exhibit physical control, and project enthusiasm.
- Control speaker anxiety by reducing the number of unknowns you face.
- Express confidence through an understanding of your material and your audience's needs.
- Appreciate the importance of being yourself and continuing to improve your delivery skills.

Deliver Your Message with Effective Oral Presentations: Speaking with Confidence and Impact

CHAPTER 9
SKILL
FOCUS:

Building on the Foundation

Skills to Develop

Professionalism in Business

Speaking

There are four things

people you communicate

with won't forgive you for:

not being prepared,

comfortable, committed,

and interesting.

—Roger Ailes

(You Are the Message)

COMMUNICATING WITHOUT A STRATEGY

Uncertainty in a New Job

Brenda Flores was excited about her new internship with a high-tech company that recently moved into town. She smiled to herself as she thought of the interview last week. She scored near the top on the aptitude test, and the interview went just fine. After years of preparation, Brenda was now launching a career in a field she enjoyed. Only one thing worried her a bit.

Ms. Cheney, the woman who hired Brenda, kept talking about the importance of communication skills on the job. She said that she expected Brenda to participate in group decisions, greet visitors to the company, network with other corporate employees, and even lead tours of the company. One of Brenda's first jobs, she said, would be to teach other employees how to use the latest version of the WordGood idea-processing software.

"I've never done those kind of things," thought Brenda with some concern. In fact, Brenda saw herself as a fairly quiet person. She generally avoided getting in front of people and seldom took the lead in introducing people. She had served as a tutor for grade-school kids who had trouble reading, but other than that, she'd never really taught anything. The thought of teaching adults or, even worse, of "giving a speech" terrified her. The more she thought about this idea of communicating on the job, the more nervous she became. The more she thought about standing in front of people and speaking, the more she entertained the idea of quitting before she started the new job. "Maybe I'll stay in school a few more years," she said to herself.

Everybody worries a bit about communicating in front of others. Many people are concerned because they want others to think well of them; they care about how effective they are and sincerely want others to get their messages. They want to effectively participate in group decisions and offer suggestions and ideas. And employers want people who do exactly those kinds of things. A company's most valuable people are those who communicate well.

This chapter will provide some useful guidelines on giving successful presentations. Armed with the Strategic Communication Model, you have already defined the context for your message and have considered your media and timing options. You have decided that an oral presentation makes sense and have selected and organized the information you want to convey. You now have a well-organized outline of audience-focused information. This chapter discusses the fourth step in the Strategic Communication Model: delivering your message. Specifically in this chapter, we will build on the material presented in Chapter 3 by concentrating on five key factors necessary to deliver effective oral messages:

- Polishing your verbal delivery skills
- Polishing your platform management skills
- Polishing your nonverbal delivery skills
- Expressing confidence
- Being yourself and becoming your better self

The Widespread Use of Oral Presentations in Business

This chapter focuses on Step 4 of the Strategic Communication Model: deliver your message. Here we concentrate on oral presentations.

Oral communication in business often takes the form of *presentations*. These are not speeches, although a speech can be one form of presentation. Whenever you plan, prepare, and create a message to deliver to others, you make a presentation. Presentations vary in their degree of formality, but all are purposeful communication aimed at achieving a specific result. The following are some examples of presentations common in businesses:

- Alan Harris explains service department bills to his auto repair customers. He communicates what work was done, why it was done, and how much it cost. Alan makes presentations.
- Marilyn Pickard works as a receptionist at Frugal Farr's corporate headquarters where she greets visitors, invites them to wait in the reception area, offers them coffee, and introduces them to Farr's executives. Marilyn makes presentations.
- Heidi Ast sells clothing at the Sunshine Boutique. She greets customers, asks how she can help, suggests matching clothing, and rings up sales. Heidi makes presentations.
- Michelle Harker serves on a quality committee for her company. The committee needs her advice on purchasing cleaning supplies. As a custodial crew member, Michelle shares her expertise and recommends the best supplies for the company's needs. Michelle makes presentations.

Performance appraisals can be seen as a form of business presentation.

- Carol Tanaka is searching for a new job. She has interviews almost every day and works hard to sell her talents and skills to prospective employers. Carol makes presentations.
- Carl Steinburg is having a performance appraisal with his boss today. He feels good about his work accomplishments and hopes to be considered for a promotion. Carl will make a presentation.
- Eric Jessop represents his company in community service efforts that teach young people how to avoid drugs, alcohol, and relationship problems. Eric makes presentations.

"Hold it a second," you may be saying. "It's beginning to sound like *everything* people do is some form of presentation." Well, that's about right. We all spend a large portion of our lives making presentations—offering information and ideas to others. That is a reality of the business world.

Performance Appraisals

Performance appraisals are personal evaluations that measure the work effectiveness of employees. These take the form of one-to-one interviews between employee and manager and are used to review job expectations, productivity, work behaviors, and goals. Both the manager and the employee have opportunities to present information to each other.

FAST FACTS

Polish Your Verbal Delivery Skills

Your specific audiences and the culture of your business will help shape the decisions you make about your communication style over the course of your career. As you speak and observe the reactions to your speaking, you will learn appropriate responses and make adjustments that become your personalized style. Some generic guidelines for success—some tricks and some common mistakes to avoid—can also be helpful in polishing your delivery skills.

Your verbal delivery skills go beyond the words you choose. They also include the way you use your voice—pronunciation, articulation, volume, and pitch—and the dramatic aspects of emphasis, pace, and timing. In other words, verbal delivery skills include how you use words to speak clearly and expressively. In the following sections we will look at ways in which you can improve your message delivery.

Verbal skills go beyond the words of a message to include *how* you say those words.

Speak Clearly

Concentrate on improving your pronunciation, articulation, volume, and pitch so that your audience can easily and comfortably hear and understand your words.

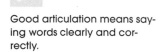

Good articulation means saying words clearly and correctly.

Pronounce words correctly. Replace just one "pitcher" for "picture," and you will lose credibility with your audience. Articulate your words. Say all the letters in all the syllables of every word. Don't relax into "lemme" for "let me" or "gonna" for "going to."

Adjust the volume of your voice to your audience. Don't speak so loudly that you sound like an orator—like an old-fashioned pitchman on a soapbox. But don't speak so softly that you sound insecure or lacking in enthusiasm either. One myth is that if you speak quietly, an audience will lean in to hear you. The truth is that if you speak too softly, your audience is likely to go to sleep. Instead, simply direct your talk toward the people farthest from you. This focus will help you increase your volume.

Vary voice volume, pitch, and rate to hold your audience's attention and interest.

Use variation in volume as well as in other vocal qualities. Sameness becomes monotonous; variation attracts and holds people's attention and interest. Psychologists say that no one can pay attention to an unchanging stimulus for very long. We can't watch grass grow or paint dry. It's just too boring. Unfortunately, speakers who insist on using never-changing vocal patterns sound just about as boring.

FOCUS ON

Speaking at a Lower Pitch

In many cultures, adults sound more credible when they speak using a lower pitch. To find the lowest pitch that is comfortable for you, try this: Lie flat on your back and relax. Breath from your diaphragm without moving your shoulders (this is easier to learn while lying down than while standing up).

Then read out loud. The pitch you hear is your natural pitch. Try to maintain the same sound when you are standing up by simply relaxing and breathing from your diaphragm. Do not, however, maintain this pitch monotonously. The idea is to speak naturally, just a little lower, and with more resonance.

Speak Expressively

Different emphasis changes a sentence's implications and meaning, so be sensitive to your inflections.

Work to perfect your emphasis and pace so that your audience can easily understand the meaning of your words. When you outline your presentations and practice your delivery, determine which words are the most important and then underline or highlight those words in your notes. The words you emphasize can change the meaning of your sentences. Think of the different inflections you could give the question "What do you mean by that?"

- *What* do you mean by that?
- What *do* you mean by that?
- What do *you* mean by that?
- What do you *mean* by that?
- What do you mean by *that*?

You can hear how different emphasis changes the sentence's implications and meaning. Be sensitive to implications of various inflections. The preceding examples can sound inquisitive or accusatory, depending on the emphasis.

Many speakers get feedback that indicates that they talk too fast. But trying to slow down may seem awkward. A better alternative is to identify material that is new, difficult, unusual, or particularly important for the audience and focus on presenting that information at a slower pace. Then return to your comfortable, normal, faster pace. Again, you may want to highlight this important information on your outline.

Adjust the pace of your remarks; slow down a bit when you deliver new or complex information.

Pay Attention to Timing

One of the most dramatic effects a speaker can learn to use is timing. The pause can be a powerful emphasis tool. There are many places a pause can enhance your presentation:

Pauses help refocus the audience's attention, so learn to use them wisely.

- After you walk to the front of the room but before you begin speaking
- Before you make an important point ("This is the bottom line:" . . . pause. . .)
- After you make an important point ("Our profits would be in the millions. . ." . . .pause. . . "if we. . .")
- When you ask a question (Pausing may feel awkward; however, most speakers don't wait long enough.)
- As a transition between main points ("That sums up the problem." . . .pause. . . "We are looking at several solutions.")
- After your final statement and before "thank you."

Avoid Distracting Vocal Patterns

Some speakers get into voice patterns that undermine their professionalism. Speakers who let the end of sentences trail off into a soft mumble are one such example. Another distracting vocal pattern is what is called "up-speak." Here the speaker raises intonation at the end of a statement to make it sound like a question. Say the following sentences aloud using up-speak—raising intonation on the italicized word—and you'll hear how this can undermine a message.

Up-speak can be annoying and makes assertions sound like questions.

- She's very good at everything she *does*. (The listener will ask: Is she?)
- The management is concerned about the *costs*. (The listener will ask: Are they?)
- My name is John *Mansfield*. (The listener will ask: Are you sure?)

Notice how up-speak creates a note of uncertainty. Unfortunately, some people habitually use up-speak without noticing how it can undermine their assertiveness and make them consistently sound tentative.

Minimize Verbalized Pauses

Few things can drive an audience crazy like the liberal use of verbalized fillers, such as *ah, um, uh,* and (the popular favorite) *ya know.* Some intelligent and apparently rational men and women salt their every utterance with these expressions until their listeners want to scream at them, *ya know?*

Try to eliminate your own filler words.

The human talker abhors a vacuum. When the detested monster, silence, raises its ugly head, some beat it to death with *ah, uh, um,* or *ya know.* Do yourself a favor: Ask someone you trust to point out when you are drifting into this habit. Commit yourself to listening for and eliminating your own filler words. Rid yourself of the fear of silence.

Filler Word Use[1]

Why do some people fill the air with nonwords and sounds? For some it is a sign of nervousness; they fear silence and experience speaker anxiety. Recent research at Columbia University suggests another reason. Columbia psychologists speculated that speakers fill pauses when searching for the next word. To investigate this idea, they counted the use of filler words used by lecturers in biology, chemistry, and mathematics, where the subject matter uses scientific definitions that limit the variety of word choices available to the speaker. They then compared the number of filler words used by teachers in English, art history, and philosophy, in which the subject matter is less well defined and more open to word choices.

Twenty science lecturers used an average of 1.39 *uh*'s a minute, compared with 4.85 *uh*'s a minute by 13 humanities teachers. Their conclusion: Subject matter and breadth of vocabulary may determine the use of filler words more than habit or anxiety.

Whatever the reason, the cure for filler words is preparation. You reduce nervousness and preselect the right ways to say ideas through preparation and practice.

Polish Your Platform Management Skills

As a speaker, one of your tasks is to manage the communication process. Two aspects of platform management include the careful use of notes and visual aids and the handling of audience interaction, especially question-and-answer (Q&A) opportunities. Work to achieve professionalism in these tasks, which we will discuss in the following sections.

Use Your Notes Carefully

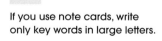

Be familiar enough with your topic to rely almost entirely on the outline on your slides.

If possible, avoid using notes altogether during your presentation and just use your visuals. Well-prepared visual aids provide a useful set of notes for your presentation. You should be familiar enough with your topic to rely almost entirely on the outline on your visual aids. However, you may need notes when:

- Your material is new or too complex to show using just visual aids.
- Visual aids are not appropriate, such as a speaker introduction or a less formal presentation.
- You need to emphasize certain, specific words or concepts, and precise wording is imperative.

If you use note cards, write only key words in large letters.

In such cases, we suggest writing key words or phrases on note cards that you can carry easily and unobtrusively. If you use note cards, be sure to write only key words (the fewer the better!) in large letters on the cards. Also use cards that are at least 5" × 8"; don't try to hide them from your audience.

As we have said, a big preparation mistake speakers make is to write a presentation word for word. If you write it, chances are you will read it. Reading a manuscript, no matter how well written, will negate the positive effects of all your other work on your presentation. You will appear unprepared and unprofessional, and you will greatly diminish your chances for success. The only exceptions to this may be in high-level negotiations or when presenting a carefully worded public announcement in which a misstatement could create legal difficulties.

If you choose to use handouts, determine if you want the audience to follow along with you as you speak, or if your handouts are for later reference. If the handouts cover additional material or follow a different order than your presentation, distribute them afterward.

Manage Your Visual Aids

When using visual aids, convince your audience that you are the one in control. Your visual aids should not appear to be managing you (like the dog who "walks" the owner). First, learn to work your equipment. Know, for example, how to return to your previous slide. Be prepared to use either a keyboard or a mouse. Check that bulbs are bright enough in your overhead projector and that markers are fresh for your flip chart.

Always practice using audiovisual equipment before making a presentation.

When you are presenting, focus on your audience, not on your visual aids. Avoid facing the screen, either reading the slides or talking to them. You may turn and gesture toward the screen to draw your audience's attention to a bullet point or illustration, but immediately turn your face and body back toward your audience.

Stand to the audience's left of your visual aids so their focus is first on you and then on your visual aids.

Almost every culture reads from left to right, and after we blink or look down, we automatically look to the left first. Therefore, you should stand to the audience's left of your visual aids so their focus is first on you and then on your visual aids. Remember, you are most important; your visual aids are just that—aids to support you and your message.

Handle Questions Constructively

You should consider two platform management issues regarding questions: when to take them and how to answer them. Planning the "when" part makes the "how" part easier. We will discuss these issues in the following sections.

Know how to manage your visual aids.

Let your audience know when you will be taking questions.

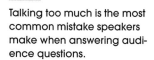

Always have the last word. Don't end your presentation with an awkward answer to a difficult question.

Know When to Answer Questions   Some speakers feel that they lose control of the situation when the Q&A section starts, so they avoid it as long as possible in hopes that time will run out. We advise a different strategy. First, tell your audience when you are going to take questions during your presentation. If you are comfortable with interruptions, encourage them, but be aware that you are likely to be interrupted with a question about something that you are planning to cover later in the presentation. When that happens, you either have to jump ahead in your organization (not the best solution) or tell the questioner that you will address the material soon. Most speakers are better off announcing that they will take questions at the end of each section or at the end of their presentation. This avoids the problem of having the presentation organization thrown off and gives you the opportunity to answer most of the questions that would have come up.

Second, decide exactly when you will ask for questions at the end. You have two choices: before your summary or after your summary. Either time is fine, based on your personal preference and style. However, do not wait until after your final statement to ask for questions. If you do, you run the risk that the last question asked will be the one that is awkward for you to answer, and that will leave a lingering impression on your audience. Instead, tell your audience something such as this: "I'll take one last question, and then I have a final thought to leave with you."

If you take questions after your summary, you might want to briefly summarize again, perhaps enhancing that summary with issues you addressed in your Q&A. But always leave the audience with a strong, carefully rehearsed final word.

Know How to Answer Questions   Entire books have been written on strategies for answering questions. The basic format, however, is comprised of three simple steps:

1. Answer the question directly.
2. Offer one piece of support or elaboration.
3. Stop.

You don't need to go on and on, which is the most common mistake that speakers make when answering questions. Make your point and *stop* talking.

Don't try to bluff if you are asked a question to which you don't know the answer. It's perfectly fine—actually, it's preferred—to just say, "I don't know." Then follow up with a comment about finding the answer and getting back to the person who asked the question, if you really intend to do so.

Talking too much is the most common mistake speakers make when answering audience questions.

Polish Your Nonverbal Delivery Skills

Your nonverbal skills include how you look and how you move. Obviously, you should take your cues from your target audience and your organization, but some fundamental nonverbal abilities are essential. Among these are eye contact, professional appearance, physical control, and enthusiasm, which we will discuss in the following sections.

Establish and Maintain Eye Contact

In business situations in western cultures, we expect speakers to look at us when delivering a message. Speakers who do not look us in the eyes are regarded as insecure or untrustworthy. When addressing groups, the best way to maintain eye contact is to look at one individual for a few seconds and then move on to another person. Don't just scan over the audience—really *look* at individuals. Try to get to everyone in the room, and be aware of tendencies to look too much at some people and not enough at others. (Some speakers tend to look to one side of a room more than another. Avoid this tendency.)

Don't just scan over the audience—*look* at individuals.

Dress and Groom Yourself Professionally

Appearance, dress, and grooming communicate powerful messages. Your audience will make some assumptions about you and your message based on how you look. If you aren't sure how to dress for a particular presentation, you are better off being dressed too formally than too informally. Success experts encourage people to dress like the kind of person they want to be. If you want to be an executive, dress like executives do. If you want to be perceived as having credibility, dress appropriately.

Dress like the person you aspire to become.

Most importantly, don't wear anything that is distracting. In business contexts, men should not wear ties with odd patterns or belt buckles with unusual designs. If they are short, stout, or gesture broadly, they should not wear a double-breasted jacket that makes them look wider and constricts arm movement. Women should not wear anything that moves or makes noise (such as dangling earrings or charm bracelets). They should not select bright nail polish or unusual makeup colors that distract their audience. If you ever find yourself tugging at anything, then you know what to fix next time. (For example, if your hair falls in your face, either cut it or fasten it back.) Many excellent books and magazine articles can provide dress and grooming tips. Stay current with what is acceptable for the business environment in which you work.

Generally avoid dress styles that draw attention to your clothing rather than to you as a speaker.

Exhibit Physical Control

Your sense of personal dynamism or self-confidence comes across via such body language as gestures, posture, and mannerisms. Gestures can be useful to punctuate what is being said. Your body movements should be spontaneous and natural, yet purposeful.

Dress appropriately when you give a presentation, avoiding any loud or distracting clothing.

Contrived movements can look silly; inappropriate hand placements create distractions.

Gesture Spontaneously and Naturally Everyone has different tendencies to use or avoid gestures. For some, it feels uncomfortable to point or raise hands in exclamation. For others, it may be said that if you tied their hands, they'd be speechless. Common mistakes people make with gestures include:

- Failing to use gestures when they can help emphasize.
- Repeating the same gesture to the point that it becomes monotonous, distracting, or annoying.
- Using contrived hand movements that look artificial or overly dramatic.
- Choosing gestures that cannot be seen clearly (a hand motion hidden from audience view by a podium is of no value).
- Leaving their hands in the wrong place for too long.

Your audience should believe that everything you are doing with your face, your hands, your feet, and the space around you is purposeful, yet not forced.

The rules for where you should put your hands have relaxed somewhat. Speech teachers used to have clear lists of "do" and "don't" positions. Now, for example, it may be acceptable to put a hand in your pocket in some speaking environments—but not at the moment when you are making your most serious point. The following are some hand movements you should still avoid:

- Crossing your arms (this may convey defensiveness) or putting your hands on your hips (this can look angry or aggressive).
- Placing your hands in front of you in the "fig leaf" position (especially for male speakers).
- Hooking your fingers together at your rib cage in the "opera singer" pose.
- Gripping the podium (the "white knuckle" syndrome) or clasping your hands behind your back (for more than a moment or two).

Make body movement purposeful, not just random.

Use Appropriate Body Movement Body movement is another important way to bring life to a presentation. Pausing between key points and physically moving to another place in the room helps your listeners know that you have completed one point and are now ready to address another. This pause and motion helps your listeners follow your logical development. If you cannot freely move around, you may still use the pause with a shift in position or a change in the direction you're looking to indicate the same things. Whenever possible, avoid the speaker-behind-the-podium format. If you need a microphone, a cordless, clip-on mike is best for freedom of movement.

A smile communicates warmth and sincerity and relaxes your audience.

Smile Start your presentation with a smile. It relaxes both you and your audience. Look for other places in your speech when a smile would be appropriate as well. The rest of the time use facial expressions to enhance the emotions you are communicating with your message.

We once worked with a young man who was building his career as a platform salesperson. He regularly stood before large audiences and sold business opportunities. To develop his skills, he videotaped his performance. Upon watching the video with us, he was shocked at how stern and intense he looked. He learned to lighten up and smile, and it made a dramatic difference in his sales success.

Keep your weight evenly on the balls of both feet.

Keep Your Weight on Both Feet Speakers tend to forget that the audience can see their feet. They will cross them, bounce, and rock back and forth, all of which can be terribly distracting. To avoid this, concentrate on keeping the weight on the balls of your feet and you will be balanced and ready to move when you want to.

Smile when you begin your presentation.

Use Physical Space Wisely   In many speaking situations the space at the front of your room is yours, so use it to enhance your presentation. The rule about moving around is: Either walk or stand still. When you are standing still, stand *completely* still. Do not dance with your feet, your knees, or your shoulders. When you walk, do it for a reason. As we mentioned earlier, changing your position in the room can show a natural break or emphasize a point in the content of your talk. It can also refocus the audience's attention, allow them to adjust their own physical positions, and give them a chance to think about what you are saying.

Either walk or stand still. Don't sway, dance, or bob.

Be Enthusiastic

Remember one overriding delivery skill that will enable you to be effective with your target audiences: enthusiasm. Your audience may forgive you if you walk too much or not enough, if you sometimes talk too fast, if you look down more than you should, or if you forget to smile. They will be much less likely to forgive you—and to agree to your objectives—if you are not enthusiastic. You must project sincere enthusiasm for them, for their needs, and for your objectives.

Project sincere enthusiasm for your audience, their needs, and your objectives.

Conveying enthusiasm does not mean you need to be loud or fast-talking. A quiet enthusiasm is conveyed by careful word choices, good eye contact, and vocal variation. The obnoxious used-car commercial model is not what you normally want to emulate. If you have done your homework and have really sought to understand your communication context, you will know how to deliver an enthusiastic, sincere presentation with impact.

Express Confidence

Some degree of speaking anxiety is useful in keeping you mentally alert.

By reducing the number of unknowns you face, you will become a more confident speaker.

Don't write a presentation word for word. If you do, it will sound like you are reading or reciting, not giving a presentation.

Videotape your practice if possible. If not, watch yourself in a mirror.

Brenda, in our opening story, is worried about giving a speech, and that is perfectly normal behavior. Do you feel that flush of nervousness when asked to introduce yourself to your class or committee members? Do you have nightmares about being forced to give a speech in front of a crowd? Have you bottled up a good idea rather than risk speaking up in a meeting?

If you answered yes to any of these questions, you are not unusual. Everyone feels some degree of these emotions. Fortunately, you can apply some proven ways to reduce discomfort—but don't expect it to go away totally. That really isn't even desirable. Anxiety plays an important role in keeping you mentally alert. Yes, nervousness can be your friend.

You can best cope with anxiety and improve confidence by reducing the number of unknowns you face. Fear is almost always rooted in uncertainty. As you become more certain about some facts, you reduce the worry about standing up and talking loud enough (you learned how to do that as a child), about remembering your co-workers' names (you learned them), or about organizing your thoughts (you learned some tips for this in Chapter 6). The following sections discuss ways in which you can further build your confidence in giving presentations.

Prepare Thoroughly

Nothing reduces anxiety like being well prepared, even to the point of being over-prepared—totally confident of your grasp of the subject matter. And nothing improves the likelihood of speaking success like thorough preparation of the content and delivery of the presentation as well as practice in handling anticipated questions that may arise.

When preparing, put special emphasis on the opening remarks and the conclusion. If the opener goes well (because you've practiced it repeatedly), you'll gain confidence for the rest of the presentation. The best way to practice is to work on one section at a time, such as the introduction or the transition from your introduction to your first main point. As we mentioned earlier, don't write your talk word for word. If you memorize it, you will sound like you are reciting to the audience rather than having a conversation with them. Instead, practice each section until you are comfortable and fluent. Even if it comes out a little different during the actual presentation, it will still sound natural and spontaneous.

You should also time the presentation to make sure it fits the time allotment or is simply not too long. Audiences are almost always pleasantly surprised when a speech is shorter than expected; they are almost always disappointed when it runs longer than anticipated.

Ideally, you should have someone videotape you practicing. We highly recommend this for important, formal presentations, especially if you are inexperienced. If video is not possible, the second best place to work is in front of a large mirror so you can see your nonverbal behavior while you are going over the words. In either case, you can see and hear what works and what you want to improve. Do not practice with *only* an audio tape recorder. A flat verbal recording without the enhancement of your nonverbal skills is not sufficient feedback.

Watching yourself on video *can* be difficult, but it will help you improve your presentation skills.

For Better or Worse © UFS

Be Idea Conscious, Not Self-Conscious

Keeping your specific purpose at the top of your mind helps reduce overconcern for irrelevant details. Let your "unconscious success mechanism" work for you. This mechanism is the part of your brain that focuses on the desired goal and allows the unconscious mind to get you there. It works best when you don't think of each step needed to complete a task but instead focus on the desired result and *let* your mind get you there.

Focus on your goals and let your unconscious success mechanism get you there.

For example, baseball outfielders going after a high fly ball don't consciously think, "I'll take six steps to my left, two steps forward, raise my glove with my left hand, and shield my eyes from the sun with my right hand." Instead they fix their eyes on the ball and visualize the desired result of catching it. Their unconscious success mechanism handles the details so they don't need to think about the little things such as tripping over a shoelace, taking the wrong size steps, or raising their glove too late. They let success happen.

The same principle applies in any planned oral communication. Overconcern with mechanics once you've reached the point of giving the presentation can only distract and create anxiety. The following is some good advice we have paraphrased from speech experts:[2]

> Self-consciousness tends to be self-destructive. If you are overly worried about the way you look, you often overcompensate, and this draws attention to yourself that would not ordinarily be centered on you. It's when you are trying to walk nonchalantly that you walk stiffly or affectedly. It is when you are trying to smile naturally (say "cheese") that your smile tends to look artificial. If you are caught up in conversation or telling a story and the conversation or the story causes you to smile, you are usually unaware of the smile itself, and it is at that point that the smile is, and appears, most natural. So, when you are speaking and get caught up in the message—when you are interested in communicating the ideas to the listeners—you are not usually uncomfortable or noticeably concerned with how you look or how you sound. It's the idea that is at center stage, not the self. Simple remedies: Be listener centered; be message centered; do not be self-centered.

Relax

Relaxing is easier said than done, you may say. However, if you are well prepared and idea conscious instead of self-conscious, you should be able to relax to a degree where anxiety should not be a problem. You may still feel that flush of nervousness just as you are being introduced or beginning your talk, but it will soon leave because you are prepared. Such nervousness is perfectly natural and is seldom visible to your listeners.

Speaking anxiety (stage fright) is perfectly normal and can be useful.

Remember that "stage fright" is normal; it's your body's adrenaline kicking in, which provides extra energy. In fact, speakers who say that they are not nervous at all may face a greater challenge because an audience might perceive their relaxed attitude as apathy or a lack of enthusiasm.

Overcome Anxiety Symptoms

Try exercises to reduce symptoms of anxiety.

Everyone's nerves show in a different place. Here are some tricks for common complaints:

- **Racing heart.** If you have time before your presentation, plan a workout or a run. If your time is limited, find some way to get your heart rate up with some form of exercise such as sit-ups, push-ups, squats, or a quick walk to burn off excess energy and take advantage of the extra oxygen.
- **Dry mouth.** Chew your tongue. We know this sounds disgusting, but chewing your tongue creates saliva and helps dry mouth. Don't do it where people can see you; you'll look like a cow.
- **High or weak voice.** If you would like your voice to sound stronger or lower, try exercises to improve your voice.
- **Shaky hands.** While you are waiting to speak (and while no one is looking), make hard fists and then stretch out your hands several times to increase blood flow and control. However, if you still have the shakes, don't show the audience! Avoid holding up your hands. In most cases, your hands will stop shaking when you get involved with your presentation.

FOCUS ON

Exercises for Voice Improvement

Try the following simple exercises to build better vocal tone and a stronger-sounding voice:

1. As you are waiting to speak, concentrate on deep breathing. Your lowest natural pitch is supported by good breath control from your diaphragm.
2. Concentrate on moving your belt buckle in and out when you inhale and exhale. Don't move your shoulders when you breathe deeply. This heaving motion tightens the muscles around the throat and makes a tight voice problem worse.

3. Borrow a relaxation strategy from yoga: Inhale on two counts, hold for two counts, then exhale for four counts.
4. If you have a table in front of you, lean forward and put your elbows on the table and breathe deeply, counting your breaths. This will help you relax because you are concentrating on counting your breathing rather than stressing about your speech. Your pitch will drop because you have relaxed the muscles in your neck and chest and you are supporting your voice from your diaphragm.

■ **General insecurity.** This is our best all-purpose solution: Stand up straight. Nothing conveys personal confidence better than good posture. The extra benefits are that you look more attractive and you can breathe better. Lift your chest, pull your shoulders back and down, and raise your head. Face your audience squarely with your body and look them in the eyes. Smile. You're ready to go.

Stand up straight and you will convey personal confidence.

Know That Your Audience Wants You to Succeed

Your audience doesn't want your presentation to fail. When people have taken the time to hear what you have to say, they don't want to feel their time has been wasted. Even listeners who strongly disagree with you—what we call "hostile listeners"—want you to explain yourself clearly if for no other reason than that they can then attempt to shoot down your ideas.

Your listeners want you to succeed.

A poor presentation can be just as embarrassing and uncomfortable for the audience as it is for the speaker. Think of times that you've seen people do a poor job of expressing an idea. What has your reaction been? You probably felt some embarrassment for those persons and may have found yourself trying to rephrase their ideas for them. Remember that no one is out to get you. Just as you want speakers to succeed, your listeners want you to succeed.

Know That You and Your Audience Need Each Other

Every presentation begins with the listener needing something. By coming to your presentation or inviting you to talk, listeners are expressing a need for information, friendship, help, approval, clarification—maybe even inspiration. They hope that something you say will improve their lives.

You as a presenter have needs, too. Probably the strongest need is for approval. Only your listeners can give you this, but they can give you this in many forms from a simple vote (a raising of hands) to a signature on a document (a sales agreement) to an outburst of applause or a hearty thank you. Ron Hoff teaches that "without some indication of approval, response, endorsement, confirmation—*something*!— the presenter is lost at sea, adrift, seeking a signal. This can be tough on the ego. (*No response is in many ways worse than outright rejection.*)"[3]

Your audience can give you much need satisfaction via positive reactions and feedback.

Because listeners need what you have to offer—information, suggestions, instructions, a welcome, or even a little entertainment—and you need what they offer—approval, appreciation, or applause—work together to create a circle of rapport. A good presenter is like a duck—calm and serene on the surface and paddling like crazy underneath. Remember these pointers, and you can look and sound confident about your message content, your organization, yourself, and about handling unforeseen objections or other surprises.

A good presenter is like a duck—calm and serene on the surface and paddling like crazy underneath.

Have Confidence in Your Ideas

If you have completed your homework, including thoroughly analyzing your audience and selecting material based on the needs of that audience, you should have confidence in your point of view. The time you invest in the first four steps of the Strategic Communication Model always pays off. Avoid the temptation to skip a step. Develop the habit of being thorough and professional in developing your messages. A little extra effort and thought can pay huge dividends in your professionalism.

Be Yourself and Become Your Better Self

Let your personality shine in all your communication.

Some people who are perfectly comfortable communicating one-on-one believe that they must become someone different when they address a group. They may have seen effective speakers and try to mimic their excellent platform skills. Such emulation can be valuable as you learn delivery techniques from other people, but you should not try to become someone else. Allow your personality to be reflected in all your communication. In brief, be comfortable as yourself. You are as good as anyone, and, because you have prepared your topic, you are likely to be perceived by your audience as the expert on that topic.

Adapt your style for the corporate or social culture of your audience.

Being yourself does not mean that you should disregard the corporate culture of the organization where you are speaking or the social cultures of your audience. You may need to adapt your style. If in doubt, for example, about your casual, energetic style with an unfamiliar audience—particularly an international audience or one made up of individuals considerably older or higher in status than you are—don't try to change your style. Instead, temper your exuberance and try to be a bit more formal in your delivery. As your audience becomes comfortable with you and you build credibility with your excellent material, you can share your personality with them.

Remember Feedback and Constant Improvement

In Chapter 12, we will talk more about specific guidelines for giving, soliciting, and receiving feedback. This is a critical part of the Strategic Communication Model and is the key to becoming your better self. For now, keep in mind that improvement of delivery skills is a lifelong project, and the guidelines we have discussed in this chapter are just ways to get you moving toward improvement.

Continue to polish your verbal and nonverbal skills to develop a style that meets your audience's expectations.

It is important that you continue to polish your verbal and nonverbal skills to develop a style that meets your audience's expectations and is comfortable in their corporate culture. Speak clearly and expressively. Dress professionally. Exhibit control with appropriate facial expressions, hand gestures, and body movement. Prove that you know your material by thoroughly rehearsing in advance. Be comfortable with your notes and your visual aids. Be prepared to answer questions. Express confidence in your material based on your preparation. Display confidence in yourself through your professionalism and enthusiasm. Most of all, be yourself. That's who the audience came to see. You are the most important part of your message, and your unique personality is your most valuable platform skill.

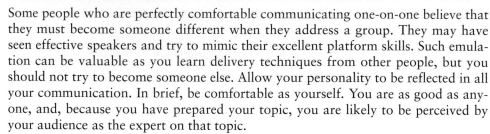

As Brenda in our opening story discovered, oral communication skills are very much at the core of many jobs. She did fine in her interview for the job but suddenly found herself outside her comfort zone when required to make presentations. As she shifted to a different media option (from interview to presentation), her confidence initially left her. This need not be the case.

The major difference between interviews and presentations lies in message delivery. On the positive side, delivering a message in an oral presentation allows communicators some real advantages over a typical interview. Once you gain control over your anxiety, you, like Brenda, have the opportunity to dazzle your audience with good platform skills, visuals, and a projection of confidence that is the hallmark of professionalism. By applying each step of the Strategic Communication Model, you can achieve considerable success in that all-important part of almost any job: delivering oral presentations.

Summary of Key Ideas

- Oral presentations of many types are frequently used in business. Effective employees learn the skills necessary to maximize this medium.
- Thorough preparation for an effective business presentation includes complete context analysis and the selection and organization of material based on your analysis.
- Delivering effective oral messages depends on your ability to polish your verbal and nonverbal delivery skills, develop your platform management skills, express confidence, and be yourself.
- Polishing your verbal delivery skills includes speaking clearly and expressively, paying attention to timing, avoiding distracting vocal patterns, and minimizing verbalized pauses.
- Polishing your platform management skills includes using notes and visuals effectively and handling audience questions constructively.
- Polishing your nonverbal delivery skills includes maintaining eye contact, dressing professionally, exhibiting physical control, and projecting enthusiasm.
- Expressing confidence is accomplished by practicing your material, being idea conscious, and knowing that you and your audience meet needs for each other.
- Being yourself and becoming your better self are functions of your sensitivity to the speaking context (especially the culture) and of feedback you receive.

Application Activities

Activity 9-1 Evaluating a Successful Speaker

Attend a live presentation or view one on TV or a video. (The speaker may be someone you know personally, a business or political leader, a sales person, a television show host, or anyone who makes a living doing oral presentations.) Take notes during the presentation. Look for applications (or misapplications) of the ideas in this chapter. Then write a brief description of the speaker, commenting on this person's delivery style. Suggest ways he or she could improve.

Activity 9-2 Preparing a Team Presentation

1. As a class, select a company that is internationally known and that is currently managing multiple issues. (For example: In 2000, Coca-Cola was managing issues such as contaminated product in Europe, discrimination suits from employees, executive personnel changes, and erratic stock prices.)
2. Working in teams of three or four, select a target audience—any person or group inside or outside the company.
3. Determine a specific purpose for your presentation: You want to persuade your target audience to do something specific. Your team will have 10 minutes to present and 2 minutes to answer questions from your audience.
4. Complete the Context Worksheet found in Chapter 4.
5. Complete the Outline Worksheet found in Chapter 6.

6. Prepare computer-generated visual aids for your presentation.
7. Practice your presentation based on the information in this chapter.
8. Double-check your preparation using the Presentation Evaluation Worksheet in Figure 9-1. Your class and your instructor may use the same evaluation sheet to give you feedback on your presentation.
9. Before you present, be prepared to tell the class about your target audience so they can role-play and ask you questions as if they were that audience.

Figure 9-1
Presentation Evaluation Worksheet

PRESENTATION EVALUATION WORKSHEET

SPEAKER: _____

TOPIC: _____

SPEAKER'S TARGET AUDIENCE: _____

EVALUATOR: _____

Directions for speaker: Evaluate yourself on each point before you present.
Directions for evaluator: Evaluate the speaker on each point.

	Good!	Needs work
CONTENT		
Uses relevant material for audience's knowledge level		
Acknowledges audience's wants and concerns		
Has sufficient depth in support material		
Uses interesting examples for audience and situation		
Uses appropriate visual aids		
ORGANIZATION		
Grabs audience's attention		
States clear agenda		
Includes benefit in introduction		
Follows clear organizational plan		
Summarizes essence of main points		
Asks for clear action in conclusion		
Closes with strong final statement		
DELIVERY		
Moves comfortably and gestures naturally		
Looks at each member of the audience		
Speaks conversationally and enthusiastically		
Handles visual aids effectively		

Overall comments: _____
_____

Finally, would you hire this person, buy this product, or support this proposal? _____
Why or why not? _____

Activity 9-3 Preparing a "How-To" Presentation

Prepare a 4- to 6-minute "how-to" presentation to deliver to your class. To get double benefit from this presentation, select a topic that teaches how to improve speaking effectiveness. Some examples are:

- How to use gestures for greater communication effectiveness
- How to use vocal variation
- How to reduce speaker anxiety
- How to dress for a business presentation
- How to create and use humor in a presentation
- How to create an effective introduction (or conclusion)
- How to handle questions and answers after a presentation

You are not limited to these topics, but your presentation must be communication related. Apply the ideas discussed in this chapter. Practice in front of a mirror.

Activity 9-4 Selling a Product

Develop and deliver an effective 7- to 8-minute sales pitch. Select a product or service that would be appropriate to sell to a person who is just completing college and beginning a business career. This should be a real product (or service) and should sell for not more than $300.

Apply a persuasive pattern of arrangement and be prepared to explain why you structured the presentation as you did. If possible, videotape your delivery and review it with your instructor or a fellow student or colleague. Ask for concrete feedback.

Career Activity

Career Activity 9-1 Taking a Self-Inventory

a. Oral communication skills and attitudes improve through evaluation—by others and by you. This self-inventory identifies your starting point. It will be useful to you only to the degree to which you are totally honest in your answers. You need not show this to others. Use it as an honest look within yourself. You may want to retake it after you have finished this course or have developed your communication skills further.

Interactive CD-ROM Exercises

The following checklist shows how you see yourself as an oral communicator. Read each statement and circle yes or no. After answering yes or no, review each answer and circle the (+) or (−) to indicate how you feel about your answer. A plus means you are satisfied; a minus means you wish you could have answered otherwise.

Answer honestly based on how you actually feel or act, not how you wish you would.

1. Before I enter into an important communication event, I often consider what I can do to ensure a positive outcome.

           YES   NO   (+)   (−)

2. I often have great ideas I'd like to share with other people.

           YES   NO   (+)   (−)

3. I enjoy trying to explain my ideas to others.

           YES   NO   (+)   (−)

4. I often get the conversation going among my friends and even with people I don't know.

YES   **NO**   **(+)**   **(−)**

5. When I stand up to speak in any group, I feel a great deal of stage fright.

YES   **NO**   **(+)**   **(−)**

6. Before trying to influence others, I make it a point to be certain that I know as much as possible about my audience(s).

YES   **NO**   **(+)**   **(−)**

7. When I disagree with others, I often become too heated and afterward regret what I've said.

YES   **NO**   **(+)**   **(−)**

8. I usually keep calm and poised even in discussions when I disagree.

YES   **NO**   **(+)**   **(−)**

9. I am good at persuading others to my views.

YES   **NO**   **(+)**   **(−)**

10. I am comfortable and efficient in preparing visual aids (PowerPoint slides, etc.).

YES   **NO**   **(+)**   **(−)**

11. I would have more influence in my job and in social settings if I could better communicate my feelings and ideas.

YES   **NO**   **(+)**   **(−)**

12. I like to teach groups of people new things.

YES   **NO**   **(+)**   **(−)**

13. I regularly clip and save ideas from articles I read.

YES   **NO**   **(+)**   **(−)**

14. When I know something that could be helpful to others, I like to tell them this information and encourage them to change.

YES   **NO**   **(+)**   **(−)**

15. I enjoy planning ways to simplify and present ideas so others will understand them.

YES   **NO**   **(+)**   **(−)**

16. While listening to others, I try to identify and organize the main ideas being spoken.

YES   **NO**   **(+)**   **(−)**

17. When communicating, I consider audience feelings and attitudes to be at least as important as facts and ideas.

YES   **NO**   **(+)**   **(−)**

18. In comparison with my friends, I think I speak more clearly and carefully than they do.

    YES   NO   (+)   (−)

19. In comparison to my peers, I think I persuade better than they do.

    YES   NO   (+)   (−)

20. I have a good vocabulary.

    YES   NO   (+)   (−)

21. My physical delivery (use of hands, posture, expressiveness) is one of my strongest communication skills.

    YES   NO   (+)   (−)

22. My voice is pleasant and conveys enthusiasm well.

    YES   NO   (+)   (−)

23. I am eager to hear helpful criticism from others after I speak up.

    YES   NO   (+)   (−)

24. Improving my oral communication skills is one of my highest priorities.

    YES   NO   (+)   (−)

25. I have the basic qualities needed to be an excellent oral communicator.

    YES   NO   (+)   (−)

26. I speak clearly and pronounce words correctly.

    YES   NO   (+)   (−)

27. People seem to enjoy what I say; I hold their interest.

    YES   NO   (+)   (−)

28. I use humor effectively.

    YES   NO   (+)   (−)

29. I am a good storyteller.

    YES   NO   (+)   (−)

30. I handle audience questions very well.

    YES   NO   (+)   (−)

31. I feel that I am getting better and better in my communication skills.

    YES   NO   (+)   (−)

32. After a communication experience, I often think of what I should have done differently to create a positive outcome.

    YES   NO   (+)   (−)

b. Now review your self-inventory. For each item in which you circled a minus sign (indicating that you don't feel good about your answer), write a goal for personal improvement. Your goal should be specific and clear. For example, if you write a goal for statement 4, you might say, "I will start conversations with one person I don't know each day this week." For statement 18, you might say, "I will learn to listen more carefully." For statement 26 you might say, "I will make a list and learn the pronunciation of one difficult word each day."

Write your goals in the spaces that follow. If you have more than five areas to work on, put them in order of importance. Then write your top five goals here:

Goal 1:

Goal 2:

Goal 3:

Goal 4:

Goal 5:

c. For each goal you have set, sketch out an action plan and time line for its accomplishment. Be specific about the activities needed to achieve the goal. Where will you get the knowledge you need? How will you gain the experiences needed for growth? Be specific about what you will do.

myPHLIP Companion Web Site

Learning Interactively

Visit the myPHLIP Web site at www.prenhall.com/timm. For Chapter 9, take advantage of the interactive "Study Guide" to test your chapter knowledge. Get instant feedback on whether you need additional studying. Read the "Current Events" articles to get the latest on chapter topics, and complete the exercises as specified by your instructor. Expand your learning with a visit to the "Research Area." There you will find a wealth of information you can use to complete your course assignments.

Notes

1. Michael Waldhold, "Here's One Reason, Uh, Smart People Say 'Uh', " *Wall Street Journal,* March 19, 1991, p. B1.
2. This discussion was adapted from Harold P. Zelko and Frank E. X. Dance, *Business and Professional Speech Communication,* 2nd ed. (New York: Holt, Rhinehart and Winston, 1978), pp. 77–79.
3. Adapted from Ron Hoff, *I Can See You Naked, A Fearless Guide to Making Great Presentations* (New York: Andrew and McMeel, 1988), p. 10.

SKILL OBJECTIVES

After you have studied this chapter, you should be able to:

- Apply the Strategic Communication Model to your role as a leader of a meeting.
- Consider the advantages and disadvantages of meetings when selecting communication media options.
- Define *synergy* and describe how effective groups can achieve it.
- Know how to invite the appropriate mix and number of people to a meeting.
- Prepare an effective agenda.
- Use brainstorming, criteria setting, and the nominal group process (NGP) to help the group select and process information and achieve viable solutions.
- Recognize and deal with individual dominance and groupthink to make better group decisions.
- Apply the Strategic Communication Model to your role as a participant in meetings and group decision making.
- Describe the rules of effective meeting participation.

Contribute to Effective Meetings: Applying Communication Strategy and Skills to Group Activities

CHAPTER 10
SKILL
FOCUS:

Developing Listening, Team, and Group Communication Skills

 OMMUNICATING WITHOUT A STRATEGY

The High Cost of Fruitless Meetings

Shawn Hughes was delighted to get a job as an intern at Moose Lips Corporation, a midsized manufacturer of camping and recreational gear in the Pacific Northwest. When his supervisor saw that Shawn had studied business communication, she asked him to look at the problems the company was having with their meetings. Shawn's first step was to gather some background information about previous meetings from the company president, Matt Bayless.

Matt had built Moose Lips from a one-person operation to a substantial company. Despite rapid financial growth, Matt was worried about increasing production costs and competitor activity. He didn't see any specific problem, but he was uneasy about the future. Then he had an idea: "We'll have a big meeting and get some new ideas."

Matt sent a memo to all employees "inviting" them to an all-day retreat at the Homestead Conference Center about 20 miles out of town. The agenda was set: All employees would get together to "share their ideas" on how to retain market share and "any other topics relevant to the success of the business." The entire company would be shut down all day Friday while the employees met.

A few days before the big meeting, word filtered back to Matt that a number of the Moose Lips employees had been complaining about having to spend a whole day at Homestead. They were feeling pressure to keep up with their work and were coming up on the busiest time of the year. Besides, no one clearly understood what they were supposed to accomplish at the meeting.

Matt was upset by the grumbling. He sent another memo explaining that, although no specific proposals would be voted on at this meeting, the opportunity to "share input" was very important, and he expected everyone to be there.

The big day came, and 115 people showed up. In the opening session, Matt said he was concerned about the company's market share and production costs. He explained that the morning would be spent in 12-member "buzz groups" dealing with market share issues. Each group would report back to the whole assembly just before lunch. The afternoon would follow the same format but would deal with production cost issues.

The groups were assigned randomly, and everyone from Matt down to the lowest-level employee participated. By five o'clock when the meeting broke up, it was clear that most people were frustrated by the process. No one could clearly describe what had been accomplished. And the cost to the company went far beyond the rental cost of the facilities and the catered coffee breaks and lunch. The cost included well over a thousand personnel hours.

Shawn took careful notes while Matt admitted that the meeting was a disaster. "And a lot of other meetings are almost as bad," he told Shawn.

Meetings are a fact of life in every organization. Unfortunately, many meetings are not productive. Nevertheless, group communication can be valuable if those participating learn when and how to make the most of meetings. This chapter discusses that challenge from two points of view. First, we will consider how you, when called on to a lead a meeting, can maximize results. Second, we will discuss ways you can be a productive participant in meetings.

Apply the Strategic Communication Model When You Lead a Meeting

This chapter focuses on Step 4 of the Strategic Communication Model: deliver your message. Here we concentrate on meetings and small group communication skills.

The first decision a leader must make is whether to have the meeting in the first place. This decision will be largely influenced by the first step in the Strategic Communication Model in which you define the communication context.

Define the Context from a Leader's Perspective

To define the context of a meeting from a leader's perspective, you must take into account the meeting's situation, audiences, and objectives with each audience, which we will discuss in the following sections.

Define the Meeting's Situation   The leader's first task is to assess the situation that calls for a meeting. For example, a sudden drop in sales of a particular product or a sharp increase in customer complaints may pose problems that the organization needs to address. Another example may be a conflict between employees who need to work together. Although employees may see such conflicts as merely good-natured competition, the leader may see the situation as potentially damaging to the organization—a situation that calls for a meeting.

Define the Meeting's Audiences The decision to hold a meeting is often driven by the vested interest of certain people. In the sales or customer service problems mentioned earlier, sales managers would be likely to have a major interest. The example of departmental conflict would be something company supervisors would want to address. If the situation requires that only two or three people make a decision, a face-to-face conversation or a conference call may be preferable to a formal meeting. If the situation involves the interests of more than a few people, and a meeting looks like the best way to resolve the issues, the leader must next decide who should be invited to attend. People invited to a meeting should meet the following criteria:

Invite the right people representing a variety of opinions.

1. **They have some expertise about the issue being discussed.** When people in the group don't know enough to deal with the problem (such as when all the employees of Moose Lips were asked to work on complex productivity issues), the solution will reflect pooled ignorance. The group process simply won't help.
2. **They have some involvement or vested interest in the outcome of the discussion.** Make sure that departments or people who will be affected by the solution are represented in its discussion. If such key people are excluded from the decision-making process, they are unlikely to be committed to implementing a solution—even a good one.
3. **They are reasonably skilled in the group decision-making process.** Invite people who express themselves well and who appreciate that differences of opinion can be useful. Avoid narrow-minded, inflexible, or dogmatic people.
4. **They share the overall values of the organization.** If participants are antagonistic or in disagreement with the company's goals, it makes no sense to have them participate in decisions affecting those goals.
5. **They hold similar organizational rank or level.** Participation by top executives in a company may inhibit free discussion from lower-level workers or supervisors. People feel more comfortable to open up with others of similar organizational rank.

People who will be affected by a meeting's solution should be represented in its discussion.

Be sure, too, to invite the right *number* of people. Groups should have enough people to represent a variety of opinions but not so many that the process bogs down. Ideally, for problem solving, groups of four to 12 participants work best. Many fast-moving companies prefer action teams of four or five members for most situations.

Define the Objectives with Each Audience Although participants may be encouraged to concentrate on the topic dictated by the situation, meetings seldom have just one goal. People will have other secondary or unspoken objectives even when the task seems clear. These subsidiary objectives, or hidden agenda items, real though they may be, are implied but never stated. As long as participants' hidden agendas do not take away from the effectiveness of the group, leaders should not worry about these subobjectives. If the ulterior motives of the hidden agendas deter the group from accomplishing its work, leaders should talk with participants candidly (in private) and solicit their cooperation in putting the group's needs above their own.

If hidden agendas do not hamper the purpose of the meeting, leaders should simply acknowledge them and go on with the group's work.

Consider Your Media and Timing Options as a Leader

Group decision making can be a very expensive medium. As illustrated in our opening story, people costs can add up quickly, especially when too many people are involved or the meeting is poorly managed. To determine whether a meeting makes

sense for a particular communication situation, the leader should consider the advantages and disadvantages of meetings as a medium. When the disadvantages outweigh the advantages, *do not have a meeting*. Use another medium instead.

Determine the Advantages of Meetings   An obvious advantage of group decision making is that a variety of points of view can be brought to bear on the problem. This can be useful if the group has developed ways of processing the ideas that come up. To be successful, the group must develop ways of:

- *Sharing ideas* so participants can build on one another's insights.
- *Resolving differences* among group members that, if left unattended, would lead to excessive conflict and prevent eventual agreement.
- *Drawing out* useful information from all participants while toning down those who tend to dominate.

When groups succeed at doing these things, synergy and high commitment can result. *Synergy* is a frequent outcome of the combined efforts of people. Synergy happens when the group's solution or output is greater than the sum of the input from all the participants individually. For example, a synergistic result happens when three workers who can each produce 200 gizmos per hour when working alone increase their combined output to 800 gizmos per hour when working together.

The likelihood that synergy will result from a meeting is largely determined by the nature of the problem and by the way the group processes information and builds consensus. Studies show that groups are better at solving problems that require the making of *relative* rather than *absolute* judgments. That is, groups can better solve problems for which there are many potential solutions. Problems having only one correct answer can often be better solved by a motivated individual—or, in some cases, by a computer.

The first question a leader should ask is, "Is this meeting likely to be useful?"

Synergy

Synergy is sometimes described as a 1 + 1 = 3 (or more) phenomenon. Management expert Stephen R. Covey calls this "the creation of third alternatives that are genuinely better than solutions individuals could ever come up with on their own."[1]

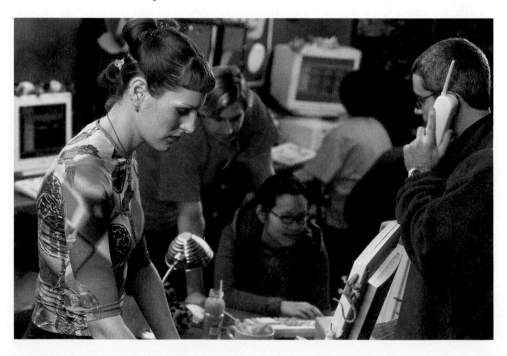

Problem-solving groups work best when people share ideas, resolve differences, and draw out all participants.

The group process can be more successful than people working alone when the problem is complex, has many parts, or requires that a number of steps be followed. Groups also seem better at dealing with controversial or emotionally charged problems. A problem is emotionally charged when people have taken strong moral or ethical points of view and cannot feel good about a compromise or another viewpoint. Their strong feelings make them less flexible.

Another important advantage of group decision making is that participants are likely to feel a stronger commitment—or, at least, less resistance—to a group solution they've helped make. Similarly, when those participating are commissioned to execute the decision, they will do so more faithfully because they understand how the decision was reached. This level of commitment is tough to achieve when someone else makes the decision without consulting others.

People are likely to be more committed to the implementation of a decision they helped make.

Determine the Disadvantages of Meetings When leaders opt for group problem solving, they give up some control over the decision process; they give the group some power that was theirs. Although giving up control can result in more useful decisions, the decisions may not be what the leader would like to see happen. When leaders give power to a group, they must be willing to accept the group's decision. If the group's work is overturned by a leader who wanted a different result, the entire process is a sham, and people may not be willing to participate in the future. The leader's credibility will be damaged as well.

Unfortunately, some leaders use meetings as a way to pass responsibility to others instead of having to make a difficult or painful decision. They use meetings as a substitute for action. Consciously or unconsciously, they hope that by "talking it out," they can avoid the unpleasant necessity of acting.

Another disadvantage of group decision making is, as we mentioned earlier, that meetings cost much time and money. A group decision takes more time than a leader's decision, and the costs of such time can really add up. If it takes a 12-member committee three hours to make a decision, and the average committee member's salary is $35,000 a year, the decision costs over $600. And this estimate includes only direct labor costs.

You also need to consider the ripples of psychological costs to the individual and the organization, which can be staggering. For example, subordinates may do monotonous busywork while awaiting direction from their boss who is in conference. Customers may be annoyed that they cannot talk with someone tied up in a meeting. The meeting participants' work piles up, so that they are faced with a stack of phone messages, a pile of papers in the in-basket, and half a dozen people who just have to talk about some pressing matter when the meeting ends.

Groups Versus Teams[2]

Organizations place a lot of emphasis on working in teams. Do work *teams* differ from *groups*? Organizational behavior experts do see a distinction: A work *group* interacts and shares information primarily to make decisions and to help one another perform within each member's area of responsibility. Groups create no positive synergy that would result in a performance level higher than the sum of the individual efforts. *Teams,* however, generate positive synergy through coordinated effort. The sum of the team's output is something greater than the sum of the individual inputs. The implication for business communication is that teams require meetings and group interaction, whereas work groups could use other media, such as instructions given to individuals.

A "when in doubt, call a meeting" mind-set wastes a lot of time and money.

Help the Group Select and Organize Its Information

Groups work with two types of information: that brought by the individual participants and that generated during discussion. Leaders can get the process of selecting and organizing information off to a good start by assigning advance preparation and by using a written agenda.

Tell people the objectives of the meeting so they can prepare.

Assign Advance Preparation   The meeting's objectives should not be a mystery. If people are invited to work together, they should know what the meeting is about and what kinds of information and/or ideas they may need to gather and bring with them. Examples of needed data might be sales results, personnel records, copies of competitors' publications, or creative ideas being used by other companies. Effective leaders get people thinking on the right wavelength even before the meeting begins.

Distribute an Agenda   Give each participant a written agenda (or a draft agenda) in advance of the meeting. Include the following elements in your written agenda:

- Items to be handled (presented in proper sequence). Be sure to distinguish between *informational items* (for which little discussion will be needed) and *discussion items* (in which participants will be actively involved in information sharing and problem solving).
- The starting time and anticipated ending time.
- Time for scheduled breaks (if any).
- The name of the person responsible for leading the discussion of each agenda item.

E-mail is often an excellent medium for advance preparation and agenda distribution. Using e-mail, people can respond and make suggestions more easily than with a paper copy. These suggestions or adjustments can then be easily distributed to others. This is also an efficient means of distributing minutes of a meeting.

Keep in mind also that most word processing programs provide templates that can be helpful in organizing an agenda. Check your software documentation to see how to access and use these templates.

Leaders should direct their meetings to systematically generate and process information.

Apply Systematic Idea Processing   Leaders need to direct their meetings to systematically generate and process information. Three approaches to doing this are brainstorming, criteria setting, and the nominal group process.

Brainstorming.   The term *brainstorming* is often used loosely to describe the process of generating creative ideas in a free-flowing environment. Actually, the term refers to a specific process, requiring adherence to clear rules. The rules for effective brainstorming are:

1. Participants must withhold criticism (verbal or nonverbal) of any ideas.
2. The group must avoid judging any idea as being too "wild."
3. The *quantity* of ideas generated is most important.
4. Participants should seize opportunities to "hitchhike" on or add to ideas suggested by others.

Brainstorming is a specific idea-generating process. For it to succeed, all participants must adhere to the rules.

Brainstorming requires an open climate in which participants can toss out highly creative ideas without being subject to criticism. As such, it is a process for producing *tentative* ideas that can later be refined to solve specific problems. Once the group has generated ideas, the next step is to see whether these ideas are viable for solving the problem or dealing with the issue on which the group is focusing.

Criteria setting.   The process of setting decision criteria is used to answer the question, "What would the ideal solution to the problem be like?" or "What specific

standards or measurements (such as cost, time, availability, and so forth) must be met to make this an optimal solution?" The criteria spell out a picture of such an optimum or ideal answer—in detail. For example, if a company selling consumer electronic products were dealing with a problem of deciding what new products or services to offer for sale on its Web site, it might establish the following criteria for the ideal product or service:

- Appeal to a typical family-oriented customer
- Be of high quality or rugged durability
- Sell for less than $500
- Be unique and not available in other stores
- Produce profit margins of at least 30 percent

After clearly stating criteria, the group can compare each recommended product or service idea against the criteria to narrow the field and result in a decision. Taking time to specify the criteria of an ideal solution is an important step in the group process.

Decision criteria should answer the question, "What would the ideal solution to the problem be like?" or "What specific standards must be met to make this an optimal solution?"

The nominal group process.   Both brainstorming and criteria setting are effective techniques for identifying potential problem-solving ideas. Once these potential solutions are generated, however, groups must process the data and determine which can best meet the group's objectives. The group can boil down input into the best possible solution by listing and ranking ideas as a group, by voting on proposals, or by using what is called the *nominal group process (NGP)*. The NGP is an idea-processing approach that combines individual work with the group process. Rather than having group members immediately speak up with their point of view (a process that may *commit* them to that view since they've voiced it "publicly"), the NGP has participants write down ideas privately. Following a clear definition of the problem or issues, group members spend 10 to 20 minutes writing their ideas about possible solutions. Then each participant provides one idea from his or her list, and

The nominal group process provides a way of processing tentative ideas and determining the group's best solution.

A flip chart is a good place to record ideas in a brainstorming session.

a facilitator writes the idea on a flip chart in full view of the group. Ideas are not discussed at this point, although people may clarify or explain the concept. This round-robin listing of ideas continues until the members have no further ideas. Then a silent vote is taken in which participants rank order the ideas.

The steps of the process, once again, are:

1. Individuals write their solution ideas.
2. The group moderator records ideas from each person, one at a time, usually on flip charts.
3. Participants clarify ideas if necessary.
4. Participants silently vote to rank the ideas (several votes may be needed before a final solution is accepted).

Monitor the Delivery of Information in the Group

The leader must constantly monitor the flow of ideas in a group. The two most common problems to avoid are individual dominance and groupthink.

Avoid Individual Dominance   In many groups, certain individuals (or small subgroups) can dominate a discussion by virtue of their personality, organizational position, or personal status. These people may range from being particularly charming (and, thus, disproportionately influential because everybody likes them) to being highly autocratic or stubborn. The problem is compounded when status differences are involved. A military general working in a small group with low-ranking personnel will have more influence, even if the general knows less about the topic. In our opening story, Matt Bayless, the president of Moose Lips, should not have placed himself in one of the buzz groups. He would naturally dominate the group because he's the boss. A leader should also take care to handle conflict directly. If participants disagree, it is up to the leader to ensure that each person gets his or her say.

Avoid Groupthink   The term *groupthink* describes a condition of like-mindedness that can arise in groups that are particularly cohesive. Under groupthink, people in the group will exert pressure against any dissenting viewpoints. Such thinking deters creativity and fresh approaches to problems or issues. Although cohesiveness is normally a desirable condition in groups, it can be carried so far that it becomes counterproductive. This is especially likely when the group has high enthusiasm and when members' desire for consensus or harmony becomes stronger than their desire for the best possible decision. Under such conditions, critical thinking and the independent and objective analysis of ideas become less important than keeping everyone in the group happy and friendly.

Groupthink is a condition in which no one wants to rock the boat with new thinking.

FOCUS ON

Symptoms of Groupthink

Some monumentally poor decisions can arise when everyone in a group thinks alike and the group culture pressures people toward conformity and cohesiveness. The following are key symptoms of groupthink:

1. An *over*emphasis on team play, unanimity, and getting along harmoniously.
2. A "shared stereotype" view that sees competitors or those in opposition to the group as inept, incompetent, and incapable of doing anything to thwart the group's efforts.
3. Self-censorship by group members; individuals are suppressed to avoid rocking the boat.
4. Rationalization to comfort one another and reduce any doubts regarding the group's agreed-upon plan.
5. Self-appointed "mind-guards" who function to prevent anyone from undermining the

group's apparent unanimity and "protect" the group from information that differs from their beliefs.
6. Direct pressure on those who express disagreement.
7. Expressions of self-righteousness that leads members to believe their actions are moral or ethical, thus letting them disregard objections to their behavior.
8. A strong feeling of esprit de corps, faith in the wisdom of the group, and a tendency to take risks.

Each of these symptoms of groupthink can damage realistic thinking and effective decisions. A combination of several or all of these can be devastating to group effectiveness.

Evaluate Feedback for Continued Success: Following Up After the Meeting

The last step in the Strategic Communication Model reminds you to evaluate feedback for continued success. Meeting follow-up largely determines whether the time spent was worthwhile. Leaders can help to ensure that meetings are successful by following up on assignments, reviewing meeting minutes or notes, and sharing feedback.

Follow Up Promptly on Assignments   Be sure to know what follow-up is expected of each group member and review this information at the end of the meeting. Make notes of what people agreed to do. Then follow up to be certain that the work is completed. Don't let group decisions drop through the cracks. If you do, people will see the time spent on the meeting as a waste.

Review the Minutes   Good meetings usually include minutes, a written record of major ideas, solutions, and actions agreed upon by the participants. Typically, the leader asks one person to take the minutes, then type, copy, and distribute them for group members to review later. Be certain that these minutes are accurate and complete.

Follow-up actions after a meeting can help improve future meetings.

Give, Solicit, and Receive Feedback   Write a note, send an e-mail, or call the group members to provide feedback. Tell them what you liked about the process or suggest ideas on how they and the group might be more effective. Be tactful and constructive. Likewise, compliment participants who have made good contributions. Let them know that you respect their communication skills and enjoy working with them. This can help build future rapport, making your next group meeting more comfortable. If you disagree with group members, reassure them that you respect their opinion or still value them as friends or colleagues but have a different point of view. Respect differences. (See Chapter 12 for more tips on giving feedback.)

Test Solutions   The ultimate feedback about a solution, of course, is whether it works or not. Do follow-up systematic observation to determine whether the decision produced the desired results. If not, reopen discussion of the problem and try again. No one or no group makes the perfect decision every time. Group problem solving, like all forms of communication, requires constant monitoring and continuous improvement. To accomplish this, remember that feedback is your friend.

The ultimate form of feedback is to see if an idea works as planned.

Apply the Strategic Communication Model When You Participate in Meetings

As with leaders, each participant plays a role in determining the success of a meeting. Attention to the Strategic Communication Model will improve your effectiveness when participating in meetings or group problem solving, which we will discuss in the following sections.

Define the Context as a Participant

Just as when you lead a meeting, the first step in applying the Strategic Communication Model to communication when you participate in meetings is to define the context. The context of the meeting is defined by the situation, the audiences, and the objectives with those audiences.

Define the Meeting's Situation   Understanding the situation includes limiting or focusing on the meeting's central issues, evaluating the external climate, and evaluating corporate culture. To the extent possible, clarify the purpose for the meeting. Ask the person who called the meeting what the meeting is about. Then think about the external climate and corporate culture as they relate to the situation. For example, if the meeting is going to deal with a sharp drop in sales, learn what you can about current market factors that may be causing this decline. Search publications or the Web about the product and competitors.

Understanding the situation includes focusing on the meeting's central issues, evaluating the external climate, and evaluating corporate culture.

Define the Meeting's Audiences   Find out who else will be attending the meeting so that you can plan ways to meet their needs and expectations. The other participants are the primary audience for your meeting. (But don't forget the hidden audience or the decision maker who may not be present at the meeting.) Then take some time to view the situation through the eyes of the other participants. Could the drop in sales be a result of high turnover of salespeople? Are the manufacturing people feeling a lot of pressure to meet demand? How are these people likely to react in the meeting?

Take some time to view the situation through the eyes of the other participants.

Define the Objectives with Each Audience   Next, think carefully about what you want to accomplish with each of these audiences. Hopefully, you will want to work to solve the problem, but you will also face opportunities to make an impression on other people who may be useful to you in your career. Plan your objectives with each audience.

Once you have a clearer picture of the context of the meeting and have researched the meeting's topic, make notes of ideas you may want to offer. Having these ideas already thought through will help you present them more clearly. However, don't come to the meeting intent on selling your predetermined idea. Plan to first listen to the give and take of others.

Don't come to the meeting determined to sell your idea. Plan to listen first.

As you define your objectives with each audience, be aware of hidden agendas—yours and theirs. For individual participants, hidden agendas may include:

- Getting some exposure (that is, to favorably impress others)
- Providing a status arena in which they can assert their power or ability
- Filling some perceived quota for going to meetings
- Socializing with others
- Asserting dominance of one group or department over another (or breaking that dominance)
- Working on communication skills
- Diffusing decision responsibility so that one person won't have to take all the heat if a decision fails
- Avoiding unpleasant work duties

Understanding these unspoken objectives can help you recognize people's motives and better understand their participation.

FOCUS ON

Selling Versus Participating

As a participant, avoid the temptation to force or intimidate people into accepting your preconceived ideas. Selling your point of view, while supposedly being open to participation, is one kind of a hidden agenda. It implies that you really just want the group members to *think* they are participating. Don't try to manipulate the group into ratifying an idea you have already selected as the best option. Be prepared to share your thoughts, but use the group process to generate and test other ideas as well.

Present your ideas when the group is ready to deal with them.

Consider Your Media and Timing Options as a Participant

Communication media options for participants in a meeting are somewhat limited. You, as a participant, will normally be limited to oral media with the possible use of visuals. Meanwhile, timing can be important in meetings. Be careful to present your ideas when the group is ready to deal with them. Don't jump the gun and offer your solution before there has been appropriate discussion or before the issues have been clearly delineated. This can be a real temptation when your preparation has unearthed a great solution. Jot down your ideas, but hold back until the group is ready to consider solutions before offering your input.

Select and Organize Information as You Prepare for a Meeting

To understand how you can best select and organize your thoughts for a meeting, you should be aware of the different types of meetings. Companies use meetings for two general reasons:

Informative meetings are mostly presentations with question-and-answer sessions. Decision-making meetings involve much more give-and-take.

- **To inform** (**advise, update, sell**). Informative meetings use primarily one-way communication from leader to participants. As such, the participant's job in an informative meeting is to listen and assimilate the information. In many cases, an informative meeting is really a presentation to a group with some question-and-answer interaction. Reaching group consensus is not a top priority.
- **To make decisions** (**solve problems, set goals**). Decision-making meetings involve much more give-and-take. They succeed or fail in large part based on the climate created. If the group creates a climate of openness and free expression, the likelihood of success improves. In decision-making meetings, you will combine the ideas and information you bring to the meeting with those of other participants. Through discussion, these ideas are refined and combined with other participants' information, resulting in group-generated information. Ideally, the group's ideas, generated through group discussion, will be greater than the sum of the individual inputs (synergy will occur).

As we mentioned previously, two common ways of producing group-generated information are through brainstorming and criteria setting. These should be used only after the group has clearly defined the purpose and objectives of the meeting.

Deliver Your Ideas by Participating Actively

Your effectiveness in meetings will call on the entire range of communication techniques and skills discussed in this book. Your participation affords opportunities for listening actively, delivering mini-presentations, and participating within the rules or guidelines that make meetings effective.

The group's success often arises from the participants' feelings about being at the meeting. Be open-minded and optimistic that the meeting will accomplish its goals. Arrive at the meeting a few minutes early. Be fresh and organized. Greet others cheerfully and contribute to a friendly, positive climate.

Be open-minded and optimistic that the meeting will accomplish its goals.

Listen Actively   In Chapter 4, we discussed listening as a way to define the context of your communication activity. In meetings, it is especially important to use retention listening—the kind of listening that helps you remember and use information being offered by others. To do this, it is important to concentrate on the group member who is speaking. Force yourself to keep your mind on that person and avoid doing other things such as daydreaming or doodling.

Do your best to find areas of interest between the group member who is speaking and yourself. Focus on what you can get out of what the person is saying. Listen for central themes rather than for isolated facts. For example, you may find that many of the arguments from one person are focused on costs, whereas another person may talk more about creativity. Too often, listeners get hopelessly lost because they focus on unimportant facts and details and miss the speaker's main point. Ask questions when you don't understand a topic.

Perhaps the best advice is to listen as if you will be required to report the content of a message to someone within eight hours. Take notes of what others are saying. Don't try to get their ideas word for word, but jot down key points. The simple process of writing key ideas as you hear them helps you retain information. Learn ways to do this efficiently.

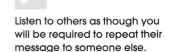

Listen to others as though you will be required to repeat their message to someone else.

Deliver Effective Mini-Presentations   Present your ideas in clear, organized ways with support for your key ideas. Use the delivery techniques discussed in Chapter 9 to convey enthusiasm and sincerity. In particular, speak clearly and expressively. Avoid rambling. Instead, contribute your ideas directly and concisely, usually using a BIF (big idea first) approach. Remember to focus on a specific benefit for your listeners. Pay attention to timing so that you do not monopolize the meeting or present an idea before the group is ready to deal with it. Use visuals if appropriate. For example, feel free to sketch out a concept you are trying to explain if that would help people understand.

Deliver your ideas freely. That's why you were invited to the meeting. Likewise, listen to other participants. Consider their ideas carefully. Add your thinking by hitchhiking on the ideas of others. That is how groups can make better decisions than individuals.

Hitchhiking on ideas of others can lead to better group decisions.

FOCUS ON

Participating Within the Rules

Many meetings fall apart because people are unwilling to play by the rules. Participants may jump ahead to present their solution ideas before the problem has been clarified or other ideas have been collected. They may fail to support the climate of openness by putting down other people's ideas. Avoid those behaviors. Instead, apply the following ideas for participating within the rules of group communication:

- Help the leader stay focused on the topic; avoid going off on a tangent with unrelated talk.
- Avoid getting into side conversations, dominating the discussion, interrupting the meeting, or getting overly emotional.
- Be open and supportive of the ideas of others. Ask clarifying questions in nonthreatening ways. Express approval when appropriate.

- Help the leader control the meeting. If arguments break out, try to clarify both points of view objectively. If participants wander off the topic, suggest that they refocus on the key question.
- If the group selects brainstorming or criteria setting, stick to the guidelines. If the group wants to define certain decision criteria, don't jump ahead to proposing a solution before the criteria are clearly established.
- Pay attention. Make notes.
- Remember that much of your value to your organization comes from your ideas and contributions to the group. Give them the benefit of your experience and point of view.

Evaluate Feedback for Continued Success

Improvement in communication skills is based on realistically evaluating feedback from others. As we discussed in Chapter 1, giving, soliciting, and receiving feedback are important to your growth as a communicator. The key to succeeding is to determine when your communication is working and when it is not, so that you can modify the areas that are less effective. Chapter 12 provides a great deal more information about how to give, get, and use feedback—a crucial aspect of the Strategic Communication Model.

In meetings, pay special attention to nonverbal messages from other participants that may indicate that you are dominating the conversation, talking about things that are unrelated to the group's focus, or failing to draw in other people. If nonverbal cues indicate that you may be doing these things, simply ask the group, "Am I going down the wrong road here?" or "Have I been talking too much?" People will respect your openness and willingness to accept feedback. In addition, be willing to offer feedback to others and to the leader about the meeting. If you are tactful, everyone will benefit from your thoughtful suggestions.

If nonverbal cues indicate that you may be communicating ineffectively, simply ask the group, "Am I going down the wrong road here?"

APPLYING THE STRATEGIC COMMUNICATION MODEL

Let's revisit the meeting at Moose Lips Corporation described at the beginning of the chapter. As you think about the Strategic Communication Model, consider the context. The president, Matt Bayless, had built the company from a tiny one-man operation to a 100-plus-member company. As a company grows, the complexity of communicating increases. While leaders of a small organization can sit down and chat about ideas, things get more complicated (the context changes) when more employees participate. Each employee brings his or her agenda to a discussion, and, although multiple inputs can be useful, processing these ideas can be a challenge.

At the heart of Moose Lips' problem is the inappropriate choice of medium (Step 2 in the Strategic Communication Model). A large-scale meeting involving all employees simply doesn't work. The discussion topics themselves are vaguely worded with no clear objectives, and the participants don't have the appropriate background information to address the topics. The typical outcome in such a situation is pooled ignorance rather than useful ideas. Matt further damages the likelihood of a successful meeting by participating as an equal with the group. His formal power as president of the company will undoubtedly stifle discussion or cause participants in his buzz group to work toward a hidden agenda of impressing the boss.

Summary of Key Ideas

- You can apply the Strategic Communication Model to your role as a leader of a meeting.
- The first decision leaders must make is whether to have a meeting in the first place. To do so, they should consider the situation in light of the advantages and disadvantages of meetings as a media option.
- Synergy is a major objective of problem-solving meetings. You will achieve synergy when groups work effectively and avoid the pitfalls of the group process.
- Invite the right people to a meeting and keep the number workable.

- An effective agenda can streamline a meeting by helping participants prepare in advance.
- Leaders help their groups select and process information by using techniques such as brainstorming, criteria setting, and the nominal group process (NGP).
- The Strategic Communication Model can be applied to your role as a participant in meetings and group decision making.
- Brainstorming and criteria setting are two ways to generate and process useful information from meeting participants.
- You can be an effective meeting participant by using retention listening techniques, by offering clear, direct mini-presentations, and by participating within the rules or guidelines that make meetings effective.
- Individual dominance and groupthink can damage a meeting and result in poor group decisions.

Application Activities

Activity 10-1 Knowing the Advantages and Disadvantages of Meetings

Summarize in your own words the two major advantages of meetings:

1.
2.

Summarize in your own words the two major disadvantages of meetings.

1.
2.

Now summarize in your own words the ways in which meetings can lead to poor decisions.

1.
2.
3.
4.

Activity 10-2 Filling out a Meeting Evaluation Checklist[3]

Consider a typical meeting you have recently attended (at school, in a club, at work, or in a church or civic organization). Compare your meeting to the following characteristics of an effective meeting. Check only those statements that applied to the meetings you attended.

_____ 1. The leader prepared an agenda prior to the meeting.
_____ 2. Meeting participants had an opportunity to contribute to the agenda.
_____ 3. Participants received advance notice of the meeting time and place.
_____ 4. The meeting's facilities were comfortable and adequate for the number of participants.
_____ 5. The meeting began on time.
_____ 6. The meeting had a scheduled ending time.
_____ 7. Participants monitored the use of time throughout the meeting.
_____ 8. Everyone had an opportunity to present his or her point of view.
_____ 9. Participants listened attentively to each other.
_____ 10. The leader paused for periodic summaries as the meeting progressed.
_____ 11. No one person or subgroup dominated the discussion.

_____ 12. Everyone had a voice in decisions made at the meeting.

_____ 13. The meeting ended with a summary of accomplishments.

_____ 14. The meeting was evaluated by participants.

_____ 15. People carried out any action agreed to during the meeting.

_____ 16. The leader distributed a summary memo or minutes of the meeting to each participant following the meeting.

_____ 17. The meeting leader followed up with participants on action agreed to during the meeting.

_____ 18. The appropriate and necessary people attended.

_____ 19. The decision process used was appropriate for the size of the group.

_____ 20. When used, audiovisual equipment was in good working condition and did not detract from the meeting.

Score the meeting's effectiveness

Number of Statements Checked × 5 = Meeting Score

A score of 80 or more indicates you attend a high percentage of quality meetings. A score below 60 suggests that your organization has many opportunities to improve the quality of its meetings.

In a memo to your instructor, discuss the results of this checklist and what actions could be taken to improve the meeting.

Activity 10-3 Brainstorming

Working in groups of five to seven people, practice the process of brainstorming. Select one of the following problems and, carefully applying the rules of brainstorming discussed in this chapter, generate as many ideas as possible for solving the problem. Set a time limit of 10 minutes. Encourage creativity and innovation. Be especially careful to avoid judging ideas. Record all ideas on a chalkboard or flip chart. From your brainstorming process, identify five ideas that have the best potential for solving the problem or achieving the goal.

Use one of these topics (or select your own problem):

- Overcoming student parking problems on campus
- Developing an advertising program for _____ (a product or service)
- Living on an extremely limited income (determine a dollar figure)
- Restructuring your school or company
- Getting people to use mass transit, one-dollar coins, valet parking, online courses (or similar topics)

Be prepared to discuss the effectiveness of your brainstorming session.

Activity 10-4 Using the Nominal Group Process

Apply the nominal group process to the problem dealt with in Activity 10-3. After brainstorming, dedicate a fixed amount of time to working individually to list and prioritize the best ideas. Then go through the process of recording and narrowing the ideas as described in this chapter. Select your best alternative based on group input.

Career Activity

Career Activity 10-1 Rating Yourself as a Meeting Participant

Because meeting participation can be an important part of many careers, take a few moments to review your attitudes toward meetings. Answer yes or no to each of the following questions based on how you tend to react to and participate in meetings. Be honest.

Interactive CD-ROM Exercises

1. Do you enjoy most meetings?
2. Do you understand the specific purpose of the meetings you attend?
3. Do you understand your roles in meetings you attend?
4. Do you hold back on judging the ideas of other people until they've been fully explained?
5. Do you complete your "homework" such as looking up information or studying proposals before meetings?
6. Do you arrive at meetings a few minutes before they are scheduled to begin?
7. Do you engage in side conversations while the meeting is in progress?
8. Do you look for excuses to leave meetings for reasons such as nonemergency telephone calls?
9. Do you ask clarifying questions when you are not sure about something?
10. Do you use both support and retention listening techniques?
11. Do you actively participate in discussions when you have something worthwhile to contribute?
12. Do you suggest ways to stay on the subject or move the group process along toward a conclusion?
13. Following meetings, do you follow up with agreed-upon action?
14. Do you contribute to improving meetings by giving feedback to the people who conduct them by a note, phone call, or visit?

Except for questions 4, 7, and 8, a yes response is preferred. If you answered no to these and yes to questions 4, 7, and 8, your contribution to meetings is less than it can be. Your career progress may depend on your developing different attitudes and skills with regard to meetings.

myPHLIP Companion Web Site

Learning Interactively
Visit the myPHLIP Web site at www.prenhall.com/timm. For Chapter 10, take advantage of the interactive "Study Guide" to test your chapter knowledge. Get instant feedback on whether you need additional studying. Read the "Current Events" articles to get the latest on chapter topics, and complete the exercises as specified by your instructor. Expand your learning with a visit to the "Research Area." There you will find a wealth of information you can use to complete your course assignments.

Notes

1. Stephen R. Covey, A. Roger Merrill, and Rebecca R. Merrill, *First Things First* (New York: Fireside, 1994), p. 215.
2. Adapted from Stephen P. Robbins, *Essentials of Organizational Behavior,* 6th ed. (Upper Saddle River, NJ: Prentice-Hall, Inc., 2000), p. 105.
3. This sample evaluation form is reprinted from Marion E. Haynes, *Effective Meeting Skills* (Menlo Park, CA: Crisp Publications, Inc., 1988), p. 3. Used with permission of the publisher.

SKILL OBJECTIVES

After you have studied this chapter, you should be able to:

- Identify key characteristics of conversations and interviews.
- Apply interviewing skills and, in doing so, feel greater confidence and comfort with people, display increased professionalism, create healthier relationships with others, and display your intelligence and good judgment.
- Recognize the three key ingredients of the successful interview: (1) a clear purpose for having the interview, (2) ample opportunities for interaction between participants, and (3) effective listening.
- Understand that conversations have many of the same characteristics as interviews, although they are generally less structured.
- Identify some generalizations about the communicative culture found in most American businesses.
- Apply some basic conversation skills including (1) having things to talk about (being well read and informed), (2) finding your conversation partner's interests, (3) practicing conversation starters, sustainers, and closers, and (4) being willing to take time for conversation.
- Utilize the three key ingredients (clear purpose, interaction, and effective listening) of the successful interview.
- Apply the five-step Strategic Communication Model to interviews as an interviewer or interviewee.

Participate in Effective Conversations and Interviews: Applying Communication Strategy and Skills

CHAPTER 11
SKILL
FOCUS:

Developing Conversation

and Interviewing Skills

Questions have the power

to turn confusion into clarity,

resistance into acceptance,

division into consensus, and

the frustration of not

knowing what to say into

the satisfaction of having

said it.

—Sam Deep

and Lyle Sussman

(What to Ask When You

Don't Know What to Say)

COMMUNICATING WITHOUT A STRATEGY

Luca Gets Tongue-Tied

Luca was attending his first company conference. The whole office staff was at the hotel training room, and the morning session had just ended. For the first three hours, he had listened to reports given by various leaders in the company. The new product introduced was particularly interesting. Even to a new employee like Luca, the company's future looked rosy.

At lunchtime, the employees went to the room next door where tables for six were set for the meal. Luca didn't know many company people and wasn't sure where to sit. After stalling a few minutes, he selected an empty chair at one of the tables. It wasn't until after he'd sat down that he discovered that one of the company vice presidents was also seated at his table. "Oh, no," Luca thought. "What am I going to talk about with this guy? I'm sure I'll make some stupid remarks—after all, I haven't been speaking English all my life. Maybe I should move to another table."

It was too late. John Bannister, the vice president of marketing, warmly introduced himself to Luca. He knew Luca was new with the company and cheerfully welcomed him aboard. Then the conversation went something like this.

Mr. Bannister: "So what do you think of the company so far?"
Luca: "It's fine."
Mr. Bannister: "Are you originally from around here?"

> Luca: "No."
>
> Mr. Bannister: "Then what brings you to the city?"
>
> Luca: "My girlfriend."
>
> Mr. Bannister: "Oh, what does she do?"
>
> Luca: "She's looking for work. She wants to be a model, or maybe an actress."
>
> Mr. Bannister: "I see."
>
> Luca: "Yes, sir."

Can you feel the tension between Luca and Mr. Bannister? In all likelihood, the lunch conversation will now turn to others at the table. Luca's lack of conversational skills may prove to be a serious problem for his career and his relationships.

Effective interviewing goes beyond conversation in that it is *planned* and has specific *purposes*. Although we often associate interviewing with the job-seeking process, it has many other equally important functions in business communication. Interviews actually take many forms, ranging from informal social conversations to highly structured interrogations. This chapter looks at a broad range of conversation and interview skills needed in the business world. We will use the term *interview* throughout, but the principles apply to less formal, one-to-one conversations as well. The advantages to learning such skills include:

- Greater confidence and comfort with people
- Increased professionalism and image
- Healthier relationships with others
- Greater ability to display your intelligence and good judgment

Understand the Characteristics of Conversations and Interviews

Interviews are one-to-one communications that allow two-way sharing of information in a somewhat structured manner.

This chapter focuses on Step 4 of the Strategic Communication Model: deliver your message. Here we concentrate on conversation and interview skills. Interviews are one-to-one communications that allow two-way sharing of information in a somewhat structured manner. Interviews are a form of conversation and, like good conversations, all participants in the interview will give and get information, and all will hopefully think they benefited in some respect from the exchange. But there are some differences between conversations and interviews as well.[1]

Unlike casual conversations, interviews have a purpose other than, or in addition to, affording the participants enjoyment. In truly productive interviews, both parties share a sense of purpose. In addition, interviews have time limits, and participants should bring their remarks to a close by a time that is agreed on near the start of the interview.

Both conversations and interviews can be highly effective ways to gather ideas, build relationships, and solve problems. In many situations, no medium is as effective as the interview. For example, when sensitive or highly personal information is being shared, the interview provides for opportunities to give and take, verbally and nonverbally, as no other medium does. In the next sections we will show some key factors necessary for interview effectiveness.

Have a Clear Purpose

The key question for both the interviewer and person being interviewed must always be: "What am I attempting to accomplish in this communication situation?" Sometimes the intentions differ between the participants. Differing intentions can become barriers to effective interviews, although such differences are normal. For example, in a job interview, applicants want to reveal information about themselves that makes them look good and avoid revealing anything that reflects negatively on themselves. The interviewer wants to discover the candidate's strengths and weaknesses. The greater the gap between participants' intentions, the more likely communication barriers will arise.

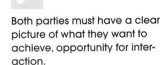

Rule 1: Keep the interview's purpose clearly in mind.

In the business world, interviews are commonly used for hiring, gathering information, reviewing performance, counseling, reprimanding, expressing grievances, and getting feedback when an employee is leaving the organization. To be successful, both parties in each of these kinds of interviews should be well prepared and clear about their objectives. Defining the context (Step 1 of the Strategic Communication Model) is as critical in this form of communication as in any other. We will talk more about this later in the chapter.

Both parties must have a clear picture of what they want to achieve, opportunity for interaction.

In addition to both parties having a clear picture of what they want to achieve, two other key ingredients must be present for a successful interview:

- Ample opportunities for interaction between participants
- Effective listening

Create Opportunities for Interaction

Effective interaction means that both parties have ample *opportunity* to participate. If interviewers find themselves talking uninterruptedly for two or three minutes, they are probably failing to maximize this communication medium. Any interview should include a good deal of give-and-take. Thus, creating an environment that is "safe" for interaction is an important task for the interviewer. This is accomplished largely by not monopolizing the conversation and by soliciting and encouraging feedback with good listening skills.

Create a "safe" environment for interaction by allowing others to say what they want without fear of being criticized or judged.

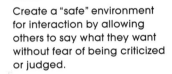

Apply active listening skills to gather important, relevant information.

Apply Active Listening

We talked about listening as an information-gathering technique in Chapter 4. In this chapter, we want to review a few ideas about applying both support and retention listening to the interviewing process.

Excellent conversation and interviewing skills arise from *sharing* information, not from *telling*. To share effectively, all parties need to listen. Unfortunately, really good listeners are scarce. For many people, listening means impatiently waiting for a place to jump in with their ideas. As we discussed in Chapter 4, far too many people think of listening as something passive—something they *sit back and do* while they wait for their turn to talk. Effective listening requires active mental effort. People who do learn to listen well tend to learn more and build stronger interpersonal relationships as well.

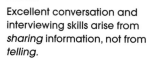

Excellent conversation and interviewing skills arise from *sharing* information, not from *telling*.

FOCUS ON

Improving Your Listening Skills

The following are some tips for improving your listening skills when you are engaged in conversations and interviews.

- **Look at those to whom you are listening and give them your undivided attention.** If you can't give them your attention, say so and arrange another time when you can. (For telephone interviews, resist the temptation to look around the room or play solitaire on the computer.) Stay focused.
- **Work at being an active listener.** Become deeply involved in what is said. Do not let your mind drift off or mentally rehearse what you plan to say in response.
- **Use supportive and clarifying comments.** We talked about some supportive behaviors in Chapter 4. One approach is called the "uh huh" response. As a person talks to you, periodically say "uh huh," "oh?," "umm," or similar phrases to let speakers know that you are "with them." This is particularly important when interviewing by telephone, since your caller can't see you. If you are silent, the speaker may wonder if you are still there.
- **Use open-ended questions to clarify the speaker's points.** Remember that an open-ended question is one that cannot be simply answered "yes" or "no" or with a one-word answer. For example, in the following exchange, Tony poses an open-ended question to encourage Tom to speak more.

Tom: I really don't think you've treated me fairly, Tony. You seem to give everyone else more opportunities, while I'm still stuck in the same old job.

Tony: I'd like to understand what you're saying. In what ways do you think I've given other people more opportunities?

- **Use thoughtful pauses.** When people ask your opinion, pause for a moment before responding. This suggests to them that you are thoughtful and that their question is worth pondering. And taking time to think before you speak may enable you to offer a helpful and wise response.
- **Imagine that you will be asked to report what you hear.** If you approach listening with the notion that you will be required to communicate what you hear to others, you will listen more carefully.
- **Repeat key ideas back to the speaker for clarification.** Repeating has several benefits. It lets speakers know that you are following their thoughts and that you consider it important to understand what they are saying. If you do not understand something, ask the speaker to clarify. Don't pretend to understand when you don't. It is better to admit a lack of understanding and receive clarification than to be left in the dark.

Understand the Nature and Functions of Conversation

Each culture has unique ways of conversing. One of the problems faced by Luca in our opening story may have resulted from his experience in talking with people whose "rules" are a bit different from his. Although he may have felt that his brief, direct responses showed respect to John Bannister, he missed the point. Bannister wanted him to open up and share more information.

When people from different cultures interact, they sometimes feel ill at ease, and they may misjudge or misunderstand each other. To reduce the communication problems that arise in multicultural organizations, it is helpful to know something about the communicative styles of the people with whom you work. (We are not talking just about national cultures but also about subcultures in which people from varying groups apply different communication styles.)

To reduce communication problems, learn about the communicative styles of the people with whom you work .

Recognize the Nature of Conversations, American Style

The following are some generalizations about the communicative culture found in most American businesses.[2] These are, of course, *generalizations*.

- **Preferred topics.** In casual conversation (what we call "small talk"), Americans prefer to talk about the weather, sports, jobs, mutual acquaintances, and past experiences, especially ones they have in common with their conversation partners. Most Americans are taught to avoid discussing politics and religion, especially with people they do not know well, because politics and religion are considered controversial topics. Sex, bodily functions, and emotional problems are considered very personal topics and are likely to be discussed only with close friends or professionals trained to help.

  By contrast, people in some other cultures are taught to believe that politics and religion are good conversation topics, and they may have different ideas about what topics are too personal to discuss with others.

Americans prefer to talk about the weather, sports, jobs, mutual acquaintances, and past experiences.

- **Favorite forms of verbal interaction.** In a typical conversation between Americans, no one talks for very long at a time. Participants in conversations take turns speaking frequently, usually after the speaker has spoken only a few sentences. In addition, Americans prefer to avoid arguments. If an argument is unavoidable, they prefer it to be restrained, carried on in a normal conversational tone and volume.

  Americans are generally impatient with ritual conversational exchanges that don't really convey much meaning. Nevertheless, a few expressions are common. For example, "How are you?" "Fine, thank you, how are you?" Or, "It was nice to meet you." "Same here." Or the cliché, "Have a nice day."

  People from other cultures may be more accustomed to speaking and listening for longer periods when they are in conversation, or they may be accustomed to more ritual interchanges (about the health of family members, for example) than Americans are. They may enjoy argument, even vigorous argument, of a kind that Americans are likely to find unsettling.

In the typical conversation between Americans, participants take turns frequently.

- **Preferred involvement.** Americans do not generally expect very much personal involvement from conversational partners. Small talk—without long silences that provoke uneasiness—is enough to keep matters going smoothly. In the workplace, Americans rarely discuss highly personal topics, which include financial matters. Many Americans are very uncomfortable if you ask how much money they make or the cost of something they own. Personal topics are reserved for conversations between very close friends or with professional counselors. However, American women tend to disclose more personal information to each other than do American men. (Please read more about the gender differences in workplace communication in Reference Tool C, "Recognizing Gender Differences in Workplace Communication.")

Some people from other cultures prefer even less personal involvement than Americans do and rely more on ritual interchanges. Others come from cultures in which individuals openly discuss personal information.[3]

Americans and people from other cultures may have different attitudes toward nonverbal behaviors.

- **Tone of voice and nonverbal behaviors.** Most American businesspeople are verbally adept—have a good vocabulary—speak in moderate tones, and use some gestures of the arms and hands. Touching behaviors in normal business communication are usually limited to a handshake or occasional pat on the back.

  By contrast, other cultures might be accustomed to louder voices or many people talking at once. Similarly, people from different cultures vary in such things as vigorous use of hands and arms to convey emphasis, more touching between conversation partners, and use of personal space (such as how far apart people stand or sit).

Apply Basic Conversation Skills

Conversing with all kinds of people can be a pleasant experience—and a valuable business skill. The following are some ideas on how to initiate and sustain effective conversations.

- **Have something to talk about.** Good conversation is a process of finding topics of common interest. It stands to reason that the more topics you know something about, the more comfortable you will be in talking with people.
- **Be well read.** Regularly read magazines and newspapers. Also, tune into *quality* broadcast programs. Good conversationalists pick up a lot of information from in-depth news shows, documentaries, and quality programming. Public radio and some talk shows can also stimulate thinking and keep us up-to-date. Make it a point to listen to people. Note what they talk about in conversations. Some typical topics you may hear include sports, TV news or current events, magazine reports, organizational changes or news, personal or family news, gossip, entertainment, or politics.

Use information about other people's interests to stimulate conversation with them.

- **Find your conversation partners' interests.** Think about the interests of people with whom you would like to converse. Identify one or two topics you know that person likes to talk about. You may find, for example, that Bob is a 49'ers football fan, Robin loves sports cars, Sharon is active in a support group for women, and Lynn plays drums in a band. Then try to learn something about the topics others are interested in. Once learned, mention this information when talking with them. Don't proclaim what you've learned as though you're a new expert, but use what you know to *ask* how they feel about the topic. Then be a good listener. You'll learn more and strengthen your relationship.

Practice conversation starters, sustainers, and closers for smoother conversations.

- **Practice conversation starters and sustainers.** Learn to make small talk, initiate conversations, and keep those conversations from dying. Use support listening techniques and open-ended questions such as "What do you think of the changes in the course requirements?" or "Where do you think tech stocks are headed?"

- **Practice conversation closers.** Don't get trapped in endless discussion. Learn ways to end a conversation without being abrupt or rude. Use nonverbal cues to indicate that you need to end the conversation (look at your watch; begin to move away from your partner). Also use subtle verbal cues that you want to end the conversation ("Well, it'll be interesting to see the effects on class enrollment" or "I'll get back to you if I hear anything new"). Sometimes, however, being direct is better ("Oops, I better get back to work").
- **Be willing to make time for conversation.** If you don't take time for some social conversation, you may send unspoken messages to others that you are aloof or not interested in them. You may find yourself isolated from the grapevine and out of touch.

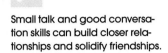

Small talk and good conversation skills can build closer relationships and solidify friendships.

Avoid Inappropriate Conversation

As we mentioned earlier, other than your closest friends, people don't normally want to hear about your personal problems. (One exception is your supervisor when the problem affects your work.) As a TV talk show host quipped: "Eighty percent of the people don't care, and the other 20 percent are *glad* you've got problems, too."

Complaints about your boss, co-workers, company, or school may come across as whining or inappropriate griping. Everybody has relationship problems at times. Unless you are seeking advice from a close friend or trusted advisor on how to improve the situation, keep your negative opinions to yourself. And when starting conversations with people you don't know well, avoid the more sensitive topics such as politics, gossip, and topics for which people may have strong or opposite feelings.

When starting conversations with people you don't know well, avoid sensitive topics.

The acceptability of topics changes from time to time. For example, years ago hunting would have been a safe topic among many people. Today, with increasing concern about animal rights, hunting talk can create serious controversy. By contrast, some subjects once considered very personal are now more openly discussed. So stay in tune with current issues and controversies.

As a general rule, *avoid*

- Criticizing or belittling others
- Griping about the company, department, or classroom
- Passing on gossip or hurtful comments about others
- Using excessive profanity
- Stirring up bad feelings among people
- Making racial, religious, or gender insults
- Flirting or using comments with unwanted sexual overtones

As a general rule, *do*

- Make your comments positive and upbeat
- Be supportive of other people
- Give others the benefit of the doubt
- Compliment freely and often
- Acknowledge peoples' accomplishments, birthdays, and religious holidays—respectfully

The remainder of this chapter looks at those specialized conversations called interviews.

Apply the Strategic Communication Model When You Are the Interviewer

The Strategic Communication Model discussed throughout this book is clearly applicable to interviewing. By now you are familiar with its steps and can probably see how each can apply. But for clarity, the following sections present ideas about the model's application.

Define the Context for the Interview

As we said earlier, interviews are commonly used in business for hiring, information gathering, reviewing performance, counseling or reprimanding, expressing grievances, and conducting an exit interview. Following is a brief description of the context (situation, audiences, and objectives with those audiences) for each of these types of interview.

Hiring interviews call for sharing information about the company and job position and the applicant's ability to fit the needs of the company.

- **Hiring interviews.** Hiring interviews call for sharing information about the employer's company and job position and the applicant's ability to fit the needs of the company. The primary audience is typically the interviewee, with hidden audiences potentially being customers, shareholders, or others who may apply for jobs with your company in the future. The objectives are to assess whether the applicant meets the needs of the company and vice versa.
- **Information-gathering interviews.** Information-gathering interviews call for systematically soliciting information from a number of respondents. The data are typically tabulated and used for making decisions. This is common practice in opinion polling, market analyses, and when trying to figure out causes of problems. The primary audience is the person being interviewed. However, when word gets around that you are interviewing people, others who may be polled in the future may be hidden audiences. How you handle today's interview could, for example, influence the responses of future interviewees. If people hear that you are argumentative or indiscrete, they may have little desire to participate or to be candid.

Market Analyses

Market analyses are systematic evaluations of a market for a particular product or service. A careful analysis of the potential market helps companies predict how well something may sell and helps them plan production and distribution activities.

- **Performance review interviews.** Performance reviews (or performance appraisals) are periodic evaluations of an employee's work and are common to virtually all organizations. The goal in a performance review is to evaluate employee job performance and agree upon behaviors or goals for future work. The primary audience is the employee being evaluated, with other organizational leaders being secondary audiences. The interviewer's objectives may include motivating the employee, while the employee will seek to present a positive picture of his or her work performance. When done well, this form of interview provides a forum for managers to give feedback to employees and for employees to explain past performance.
- **Counseling or reprimand interviews.** Counseling or reprimand interviews occur when a supervisor feels the need to address employee behavior problems. The audiences are similar to those in a performance review; however, the objectives may vary. Often, interviewers want to change employee behaviors; the employees may want to defend or explain their behavior and, perhaps, avoid punishment.
- **Grievance interviews.** Grievance interviews are reprimand interviews in reverse. In grievance interviews, the employee feels a need to complain or address a problem, and the supervisor may be defensive about the situation. Audiences will include

Performance review interviews provide important feedback to employees.

the supervisor; possible hidden audiences could be labor union leaders or other employees. The objective is to get some problematic situation changed.

■ **Exit interviews.** Exit interviews are conducted when an employee leaves the organization. Employees have already made a decision to go, so the objective of an exit interview is to gather honest information about why they are leaving—to perhaps change the conditions that made the employee leave.

Grievance interviews are reprimand interviews in reverse.

As you can see, the contexts for real-world interviewing in business are many and varied. Defining the context (situation, audiences, and objectives) as prescribed by the Strategic Communication Model is an important first step toward interviewing effectiveness.

Managers conduct an exit interview when an employee leaves the organization.

Consider Your Media and Timing Options When You Are the Interviewer

The most common medium for an interviewer is verbal, face-to-face communication, although sometimes interviews (especially information-gathering interviews) are conducted by telephone. Phone interviews forgo many nonverbal cues and must rely on especially careful listening. Of course, nothing precludes interviewers from using other media. For example, they may support or explain ideas expressed with print materials, tape recorded information, or even visual aids. However, the primary medium of most interviews is face-to-face oral communication.

Timing of an interview can impact its effectiveness. Often, later interviews are influenced by earlier ones. As an interviewer, you will often adjust the questions and base some observations on the earlier responses. Sometimes, you may want to go back to the earliest interviewees in light of ideas you got from later interviews. Also, schedule interviews such that you do not get overly tired or overloaded with too much information. Take breaks so that you remain fresh and focused.

Select and Organize Information as You Prepare to Interview

The quality of an interview is largely determined by the kinds of questions asked. Prepare key questions in advance that will help achieve the goal of the interview. As interviewers, you have several types of questions to choose from, each useful under certain conditions. (The term *question* refers to any comments made to elicit responses from the other party. Sometimes these take the form of statements or commands.) Let's look at some common types of questions.

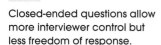

Closed-ended questions allow more interviewer control but less freedom of response.

- **Closed-ended questions.** This type of question allows the respondent little freedom in choosing a response; typically, only one or two possible answers exist. Examples: "Did your study group meet last Tuesday?" "Have you completed the Tompkins report yet?" "How long have you been on your present job assignment?"

   Use of closed-ended questions permits the interviewer to exercise close control over the exchange. This is, of course, the technique most frequently used by trial lawyers or police interrogators to elicit specific information. This technique's drawback is that it rigidly structures the interview and, although often efficient, may completely miss opportunities for exchanging other relevant information.

   Closed-ended questions can be manipulative. Respondents may feel frustrated when they must choose between one or two possible answers without an opportunity to clarify. Sometimes, however, these kinds of responses are the most useful to the questioner. But in most business interviews, other kinds of questions are more useful.

Open-ended questions allow the respondent maximum freedom in answering.

- **Open-ended questions.** Open-ended questions allow the respondent maximum freedom in answering because they impose no limitations on how the question may be answered. Examples: "How do you feel about working with your study group?" "What would be a better way to handle that job?" Often open-ended questions take the form of statements such as, "Tell me about your experiences with the new study group," or "Explain that procedure to me."

   The success of this questioning approach depends in large part on the interviewee's ability to express thoughts clearly. Often it is necessary for the interviewer to seek additional clarification by using probes when the respondent is talking in generalities or using unfamiliar language.

Probing questions ask the interviewee to clarify a response for better understanding.

- **Probing questions.** Probing questions ask the interviewee to clarify a response for better understanding. Examples: "Could you give me an example of something that happened in the study group that upset you?" "Can you clarify what you mean when you say she's ruthless?" "Can you give me more details about the problem from your perspective?"

   Probing questions serve to move the language level from the vague or general toward more concrete, specific, and descriptive terms. Probing questions can also determine the intensity of feelings. For example, if a person comments about a study group being disorganized, a probing question may be, "Can you give me an example of why you see the group as disorganized?" The interviewee then has the opportunity to unload some feelings about how frustrating working with the group has been.

- **Leading questions.** While probing questions lead respondents to elaborate on their own feelings, the leading question typically suggests the response desired. Occasionally this is helpful, but more often it is a block to the emergence of authentic information. Examples: "I'm interested in how well your study group is doing. Did you learn a lot while working with this group?" (Obviously, the interviewer wants the respondent to say yes.) "Don't you think it's important for our students to learn to work in teams as they will in business?" (Of course. What else could you say?) When the question is prefaced by a remark that suggests the kind of answer the interviewer would like to hear, the range of responses is reduced. The interviewee may feel too intimidated to offer useful and honest but conflicting information.

- **Loaded questions.** So-called loaded questions also suggest the desired response to the interviewee primarily through the use of highly emotional terms. Sometimes they are used to determine a respondent's reactions under stress and when a questioner seeks to "crack" a reluctant respondent. Interviewees who are wearing a mask or acting a role may become angry enough to let their true feelings or honest answers emerge.

   Examples: "How can you stand working in such a *mess?*" or "Everybody I've talked to says you are *a pain to work with*. How do you respond to that?" "I've heard reports that you are satisfied with *slipshod* quality. How would you respond to that?" The person hit with a loaded question may respond by attacking. The loaded question, like a loaded gun, occasionally goes off in the wrong direction. Avoid them under all but the most desperate circumstances.

- **Hypothetical questions.** Hypothetical questions can be used to learn how a respondent might handle a particular situation. They are helpful in identifying creativity, prejudices, the ability to conceptualize the big picture, and other respondent characteristics. Examples: "If you were asked to lead the study group, what would you do differently?" "Put yourself in the shoes of the sales manager and suggest some approaches she might take to make your internship more valuable." "Let's assume that you discovered one of your co-workers was intoxicated on the job. What would you do?"

Leading and loaded questions are often manipulative and should be used only sparingly, if at all.

Hypothetical questions require responding to some possible situation and reveal information about how people might act in a given circumstance.

In a well-executed interview, each question is asked for a particular reason. Participants should think through each question and response in light of the interview's purpose rather than babble on with ill-defined exchanges that do little to create understanding. Don't worry about pauses in the interview. It is not necessary to fill every moment with the sound of someone's voice.

When the interview is over, the interviewer should summarize briefly and be sure the respondent understands what to do next. There should be a clear agreement about the outcome of the discussion. Often, testing for such understanding is appropriate. You might ask, "Okay, Sarah, now what did we agree must be done next?" Each participant may explain the interview's outcome as he or she sees it. Then close on an upbeat comment and express gratitude for the person's participation in the interview.

You should close every interview with an upbeat comment.

Deliver Your Ideas Effectively When You Interview Others

An effective interviewer typically uses a variety of questioning formats to generate as much discussion as possible. Remember that leading an interview involves mostly information gathering. Therefore, we stress again the importance of listening.

Sometimes we need to deliver information in the context of an interview. For example, supervisors may need to describe how they gathered performance review data or an employee recruiter may need to explain something about the company. When doing so, apply the same principles as when delivering an oral presentation. (See especially Chapter 3.) Prepare in advance and organize the messages you need to convey to the interviewee. Pay attention to the delivery skills we have discussed throughout this book.

You can use visuals or props in interviews, just as in other forms of oral presentation.

As you interview others, be aware of the nonverbal messages you are sending.

As you interview others, be aware of the nonverbal messages you are sending. An effective interviewer should:

- Focus on the interviewee by maintaining eye contact.
- Avoid interruptions from others that may upset the flow of the interview.
- Create a comfortable physical environment for the interview.
- Set a tone for the interview (formal or informal) with such things as greeting the interviewee, making small talk, using humor, or by clarifying the format of the interview.
- Explain the ground rules for the interview. Example: "We'll take the first few minutes to get to know each other a little better, and then I'll ask you some more technical questions."

Evaluate Feedback for Continued Success

Building good interviewing skills requires getting constructive feedback. As in any other communication situation, having someone observe your techniques and critique you can be very valuable. Videotaping practice sessions can be very valuable as well. We will discuss feedback in more detail in Chapter 12, but for now, think about sources of feedback for your interviewing skills. Identify people who might provide constructive criticism. Also think about how you could provide such feedback to your associates.

Apply the Strategic Communication Model When You Are Being Interviewed

Having discussed ways of being effective when conducting an interview, let's now take a seat across the table and consider what we need to do when we are being interviewed. Again, the Strategic Communication Model gives us guidance.

Define the Context for the Interview

As the person being interviewed, you should strive to understand the context and purposes of the interview and anticipate possible questions. Then practice ways of responding to those questions. If you are unclear about the reason for the interview, look at the descriptions of common interview formats discussed earlier. As with any communication situation, it makes sense to put yourself in the shoes of the interviewer and anticipate what he or she wants to gain from the interview.

Also, don't forget your hidden audiences and the objectives you have with each audience. For example, if you participate in an information-gathering interview with someone in your company, your performance may be described to others—perhaps your supervisors. If you participate helpfully, they may notice your cooperation and appreciate your input.

Consider Your Media and Timing Options When You Are Interviewed

Although media options are often limited in interview situations, you may use illustrative materials. Prepare visual aids, supporting documents, samples of products or work you have done, or even a video clip if you feel these will help build understanding. Be creative about these possibilities. The interview need not be limited to just what you say. You may also want to *show*.

Some companies use a TV camera in connection with a computer for long-distance interviewing. This is like teleconferencing in which both parties have the advantage of oral and visual media. If you are interviewed in such a situation, apply many of the principles of the oral presentation. Be aware of your facial expression, dress and grooming, gestures, and other visual stimuli as well as your voice.

Consider timing as well. For example, determine when you would prefer to be interviewed. Are you fresher and more alert in the morning? Do you prefer doing mental work on Mondays and deferring information sharing until later in the week? Likewise, most people applying for a job prefer to *not* be the first one interviewed. Later candidates allow the interviewer to compare behaviors—often to the advantage of the more recent interview.

An interview need not be limited to just what you say. You may also want to *show*.

Select and Organize Information as You Prepare to Be Interviewed

Determine in advance what information you are willing to share and what you will not. You need not bear your soul or reveal damaging information if such data are irrelevant to the interview's purpose. Practice ways of phrasing your key ideas. Consider what supporting information or materials you may want to use.

In addition, when interviewing for a job, be thorough in researching the company and position in which you hope to work. Be prepared with questions you want to ask the interviewer. (Almost every job interview includes asking the candidates what questions they have about the company.) You can do much of this research on the Internet, although you may also get good insights from people at the company or in similar jobs.

Deliver Your Ideas Effectively When You Are Interviewed

When asked questions, answer clearly and decisively. Do not ramble or go on and on once you have answered the question. If you don't understand a question, ask for clarification. Always remember that an interview is a two-way communication

I WILL NOT ACCEPT ANY FOOD OR LIQUID. I WILL REMEMBER TO BLINK. I WILL SMILE WHEN TALKING ABOUT MY LAST JOB. I WILL NOT SLOUCH IN MY CHAIR. I WILL SHAKE HANDS FIRM AND BRIEF. I WILL NOT STARE AT ANY PECULIAR ANATOMICAL FEATURES ON THE INTERVIEWER. I WILL SMELL CLEAN.

JOB INTERVIEW exercise.

jantze 4.21   mjantze@aol.com   www.thenorm.com

©2000, Michael Jantze / Dist. by King Features Syndicate

Preparation makes for more effective interviews.

Reprinted with special permission of King Feature Syndicate.

process. As in any presentation, a good approach when answering most questions is to:

- Answer the question directly and honestly
- Provide one supporting example when necessary to clarify
- Stop talking

For example, if asked what you felt about working in your study group, you may answer this way:

> "My study group has not been very effective." [A DIRECT, HONEST ANSWER]
> "At last week's meeting, only three members had completed the workbook exercises, even though we were supposed to have done that." [ONE SUPPORTING EXAMPLE]
>   [STOP]

Be open and willing to discuss your ideas and feelings in an interview.

As a general rule, be open and willing to discuss your ideas and feelings in an interview. Deliver your point of view objectively, clearly, and honestly. In doing so, you maintain your credibility.

If you don't know the answer to a question, it's okay to say "I don't know, but I'll get back to you with that information." If you are asked a question that is unclear, you can often rephrase it so you can better answer it. For example,

Questioner: "How would you come into the department as a new employee and make everything more efficient?"

Respondent: "I think what you are interested in is what would be my first priority in implementing some of my ideas. Here is where I would begin . . ."

For further examples of rephrasing the question, just watch television interview shows. Politicians and other people in the public eye have often mastered this skill. They "adjust" many questions to give themselves an opportunity to say what they want to say. This is an appropriate technique, so long as it is not used to distort information or evade answering the real questions.

Evaluate Feedback for Continued Success

Practicing for interviews can be as important as practicing for giving an oral presentation. Write out possible questions you may be asked. Then practice appropriate responses out loud. If possible, get someone you know and trust to throw potentially difficult questions at you and respond to these. Some communication coaches use a process called "dirty Q" to throw all the tough and dirty questions at you and help you work out possible responses. You may never be able to anticipate every question you will receive, but you can guess many of them, especially if you focus on the interview's purpose from the other person's viewpoint.

After an interview, do a self-critique to assess how you did. If appropriate, ask the interviewer for pointers about how you could better maximize this medium of communication. As with any communication skill, feedback can be useful in improving your skills. In Chapter 12 we will talk at length about communication feedback.

In closing, interviews are a powerful medium for information sharing. They can provide exceptional opportunities for people to build strong work and personal relationships if participants define the context accurately, select and organize their information appropriately, and deliver that information honestly and openly.

You may never be able to anticipate every question you will receive, but you can guess many of them.

APPLYING THE STRATEGIC COMMUNICATION MODEL

How did our friend Luca, in the opening story, handle his conversation with his boss, Mr. Bannister? Not very well. He came across as insecure, tongue-tied, and perhaps, uninformed. This impression could not serve him well in his career with the company. Bannister asked him a series of open-ended questions—ones Luca could have answered with more than a simple yes, no, or one-word answer. But because Luca had not developed his conversational skills, he missed an opportunity to convey a constructive message to his boss or to project favorable credibility.

Although this encounter was not a formal interview, Luca could have utilized the ideas in this chapter to present himself with greater confidence and professionalism. From making small talk to handling formal interviews, to selecting and organizing ideas and delivering messages with professionalism and skill, one-to-one conversation and interviewing skills such as those discussed in this chapter will serve you well in any career. The Strategic Communication Model applies as well to one-to-one communication as it does to more formal writing or speaking. Every serious business communicator should seek to develop these skills.

Summary of Key Ideas

- Interviews are one-to-one communications that allow two-way sharing of information in a somewhat structured manner. Conversations are similar but are slightly less structured.
- A common problem with interviews is the lack of effective preparation by both parties. The best interviews happen when both people involved are fully prepared.
- The advantages of learning to interview well are that you will have greater confidence and comfort in communicating, healthier relationships with others, and greater ability to display your intelligence and good judgment.

- Three key ingredients for successful interviewing are (1) having a clear purpose for the interview, (2) providing ample opportunities for interaction between participants, and (3) listening effectively.
- Conversations have many of the same characteristics as interviews, although they are generally less structured. Some basic conversation skills include (1) having things to talk about (being well read and informed), (2) finding and addressing your conversation partner's interests, (3) practicing conversation starters, sustainers, and closers, and (4) being willing to take time for conversation.
- Business people use interviews for hiring, information gathering, reviewing performance, counseling or reprimanding, and expressing grievances.
- The five-step Strategic Communication Model can help you prepare for an interview when you are the interviewer or interviewee.
- The predominant media option for interviews is verbal, face-to-face, or telephone communication. This may, however, be supplemented with visuals, documentation, or other materials.
- The kinds of questions used will largely determine the quality of an interview. Both interviewer and interviewee should prepare in advance for key questions that will help achieve the goal of the interview.
- Common types of questions used in interviews include closed- and open-ended, probing, leading, loaded, and hypothetical.
- As a general rule, the best way to respond to questions is to answer them directly and honestly, provide one supporting example when necessary to clarify, and then stop talking.
- Interviews are a powerful medium for information sharing when each participant accurately defines the context, selects and organizes information, and delivers that information honestly and openly.

Application Activities

Activity 11-1 Determining Your Self-Confidence

The following self-evaluation looks at how comfortable you may be when it comes to making conversation with others. Take the quiz and then prepare a brief response to it. Does the instrument reveal any new information? In what areas might you improve or change your approach to conversations? Be specific.

Circle the number that best reflects your agreement with each statement. Use the following scale: 1 = Strongly Disagree, 2 = Disagree, 3 = Undecided, 4 = Agree, 5 = Strongly Agree.

1. I can approach strangers and make them into friends quickly and easily.   1   2   3   4   5
2. I can attract and hold the attention of others even when they haven't met me before.   1   2   3   4   5
3. I go out of my way to introduce myself to strangers.   1   2   3   4   5
4. I have many close friends and good acquaintances.   1   2   3   4   5
5. I enjoy making small talk with all kinds of people.   1   2   3   4   5
6. I am very comfortable in any social setting.   1   2   3   4   5
7. I welcome the opportunity to use the telephone to contact people I don't know.   1   2   3   4   5
8. I don't allow other people to intimidate me.   1   2   3   4   5
9. I can find some common area of interest with anyone.   1   2   3   4   5

10. I read a wide variety of publications and always keep   1   2   3   4   5
    up-to-date on current events.

    My Total: _____   Date: _____

Total your score, paying close attention to the items on which you scored the lowest. These will signal areas in which you could profit from some changes. Set goals to improve in weak areas as you develop your interviewing skills.

Activity 11-2 Checking Your Listening Attitudes and Behaviors

Circle the number that indicates how true each statement that follows is for you. Use this scale: 1 = Almost Never True, 2 = Seldom True, 3 = Sometimes True, 4 = Usually True, 5 = Almost Always True.

1. When listening, I concentrate carefully and never fake   1   2   3   4   5
   attention.
2. I am not easily distracted from what people are saying   1   2   3   4   5
   to me.
3. I mentally organize ideas as I hear them.   1   2   3   4   5
4. I give feedback by nodding, saying "uh huh," or in   1   2   3   4   5
   other ways encourage the speaker to go on.
5. I make it a point to ask for clarification when I don't   1   2   3   4   5
   understand someone.
6. I often take notes of what others are saying.   1   2   3   4   5
7. I don't let a person's speaking mannerisms interfere   1   2   3   4   5
   with my listening to his or her ideas.
8. Accents, voice quality, and the appearance of a speaker   1   2   3   4   5
   do not distract me from the message.
9. I never let my eyes glaze over and my attention drift   1   2   3   4   5
   when listening.
10. I am a very good listener.   1   2   3   4   5

    My Total: _____   Date: _____

If you scored between 40 and 50, your listening skills are better than most people's. Congratulations! Keep sharpening them. If you scored between 25 and 39, you are an average listener. If your score was below 25, you need to work to improve, otherwise, listening problems may prove to be a real stumbling block to your success.

Activity 11-3 Preparing for a Performance Review

Assume that a class instructor is going to review your performance in a course you have taken. He or she has scheduled 15 minutes for an interview with you. How would you prepare to meet with that instructor for your performance review?

Use the Strategic Communication Model to describe your preparation. Write a brief description of how you would define the context, consider your media and timing options, select and organize information to present, deliver your messages, and receive feedback. Then write three questions you would expect to get from your instructor and the responses you would give to each question.

Interactive CD-ROM Exercises

Activity 11-4 Being Luca

Go back to the opening story and put yourself in the position of Luca, the new employee. Imagine that you are being asked the same questions by your new boss in a similar situation. How would you respond?

Career Activity

Career Activity 11-1 Preparing for an Employment Interview

Although only one of the many types of business interviews, the job interview is an activity virtually everyone goes through and, of course, it is important. How can you best prepare for such an interview? The best advice we can give is to apply the Strategic Communication Model. Consider each step of the model that you have worked with throughout this book, and then focus on Step 4, delivering your message, and Step 5, getting feedback, as you practice your approach.

Identify a type of job position or career area for which you would like to interview in the future. List five of the most challenging questions you might face in an interview. (We have added a few such questions here but encourage you to check other sources to see what other questions are likely to be used. Also the Internet has a wealth of information about job search interviewing. Do a search using keywords such as "job interview questions." Look for sites that provide sample questions and suggested answers.)

Jot down a few notes for each question. Then ask a classmate or experienced friend to do a mock interview with you. Videotape or audiotape your responses and review how you did. Review your answers carefully to be sure you did not convey unintended messages. Make your responses positive and constructive.

Start with a few of these typical questions:

1. Tell me a bit about yourself.
2. In what school activities did you participate? Why? Which did you enjoy the most?
3. What jobs have you held? How did you get the job? Why did you leave?
4. How did you spend your vacations while in school?
5. If you were starting school all over, what courses would you take?
6. What are your weaknesses?
7. How do your former team members describe you?
8. Do you prefer working with others or by yourself? Why? Can you give me an example?
9. How did previous employers treat you?
10. What interests you about our company or products?
11. Tell me about a time that you had a conflict with a peer at school or work and how you resolved it.
12. What do you know about our company?

Now go online and search for Web sites that list interview questions to which you can practice responding. The popular job search site Monster.com, for example, offers interview tips. You can also use any search engine and look for "job interviews" or "interview questions." Pick 10 difficult questions and prepare answers to each.

myPHLIP Companion Web Site

Learning Interactively

Visit the myPHLIP Web site at www.prenhall.com/timm. For Chapter 11, take advantage of the interactive "Study Guide" to test your chapter knowledge. Get instant feedback on whether you need additional studying. Read the "Current Events" articles to get the latest on chapter topics, and complete the exercises as specified by your instructor. Expand your learning with a visit to the "Research Area." There you will find a wealth of information you can use to complete your course assignments.

Notes

1. Larry R. Smeltzer and Donald J. Leonard, *Managerial Communication* (Burr Ridge, IL: Irwin, 1994), p. 276.
2. For an excellent reference on how to do business in other countries, see T. Morrison, W. A. Conaway, and G. A. Borden, *Kiss, Bow, or Shake Hands* (Holbrook, MA: Adams Media, 1994). For basic information on communicating with individuals with roots in European, African, Asian, or Latino cultures, see S. Bienvenu Kenton and D. Valentine, *CrossTalk: Communicating in a Multicultural Workplace* (Upper Saddle River, NJ: Prentice Hall, Inc., 1997).
3. Some of the information in this section is adapted from a handout for foreign students found in Gary Allen, *The Handbook of Foreign Student Advising* (New York: Intercultural Press, Inc., 1983).

Step 1. Define the Context

A. Define the situation.
1. Limit the problem.
2. Evaluate the problem within the external climate.
3. Evaluate the corporate culture that impacts the problem.

B. Define your audience.
1. Identify all potential audiences (distinct or overlapping).
2. Learn about each audience.

C. Define your objectives with each audience.
1. Define your overall goal.
2. Identify the specific purpose of the communication.
3. Acknowledge your hidden agenda.

Step 2. Consider Your Media and Timing Options

A. Select media options that are most appropriate for your message.
B. Evaluate your timing options.

Step 3. Select and Organize Your Information

A. Review your analysis of your situation, audiences, and objectives.
B. Compare key organizational patterns and select the most effective one.
C. Limit your main points.
D. Enhance your message with powerful support material (visual aids, numbers, and examples).

Step 5. Evaluate Feedback for Continued Success

A. Give feedback.
B. Solicit feedback.
C. Receive feedback.
D. Evaluate yourself with the Credibility Checklist:
1. Goodwill: your focus on and concern for your audience
2. Expertise: your education, knowledge, and experience
3. Power: your status, prestige, and success
4. Confidence: the way in which you present yourself and your message

Step 4. Deliver Your Message

A. Develop your writing, speaking, interpersonal, and group skills.
B. Prepare thoroughly (rehearse your presentations and edit your writing).
C. Express confidence in your topic and in yourself.
D. Be yourself (but adapt your style to your audience and situation).

SKILL OBJECTIVES

After you have studied this chapter, you should be able to:

- Understand the crucial role of both giving and receiving feedback in the process of communication improvement.
- Apply effective techniques for giving communication feedback that acknowledge excellence, point out needed improvements, and offer suggestions for how to make those improvements.
- Give constructive feedback without demotivating the speaker or writer.
- Understand that closed-ended questions are rarely the best for getting people to express their true feelings; open-ended questions are more effective.
- Understand ways to solicit useful feedback about your own communication.
- Recognize how to receive and utilize useful feedback to improve your communication skills.
- Understand the role of sender credibility in any communication situation.
- Recognize the key elements of personal credibility.
- Evaluate your personal credibility using the Credibility Checklist.
- Apply the Credibility Checklist to ongoing improvement in communication effectiveness.

Evaluate Feedback for Continued Success: Using Internal and External Information for Ongoing Improvement

12

CHAPTER 12
SKILL
FOCUS:

Giving and Gathering

Feedback for Continuous

Communication Improvement

The trouble with most of us is that we would rather be ruined by praise than saved by criticism.

—Dr. Norman Vincent Peale

COMMUNICATING WITHOUT A STRATEGY

Rick's Job Search Strikes Out

Rick and Renee have done everything together as twins tend to do. Rick was born seven minutes before his sister and frequently reminds her that he is "older and wiser." But when it comes to landing a job, Renee seems to be the wiser one. Both graduated last month from the same college, but only Renee has landed a full-time job. In fact, she had three good offers from which to choose. Rick is continuing his job search but rarely gets beyond the first interview.

They met for coffee Saturday morning, and Renee asked how things were going. "I'm doing okay," Rick assured her. "I have two more interviews set up for next week, and both look good. I'd be a perfect fit for either job."

"How are you preparing for your interviews, Rick?" she asked. "And did you ever get the Career Center people to critique your résumé and cover letters?"

"I went by there a couple of times, and they were too busy. My résumé looks good. I've polished it a thousand times. I also got hold of a list of interview questions and have read them through and thought about my responses. I'm ready for any question. Come on, Mr. Recruiter, give me your best shot. I can take it. These people are nuts if they don't hire me."

Renee laughed at her brother's usual self-confidence, but she knew him well enough to know that he wasn't nearly as confident as he tried to appear. In fact, he was getting pretty discouraged with the rejections. Finally, he admitted it. "Renee, I'm getting worried. I get my foot in the door, but I can't seem to get to second base with these companies."

"Maybe it's your use of mixed metaphors," she joked. "Or maybe you're not targeting your message as well as you could. You're a good communicator, Rick, but sometimes you go off on tangents and talk about the wrong things at the wrong times. Have you considered asking the recruiters who turned you down for some feedback? For that matter, have you asked *anyone* for feedback?"

Rick looked into his coffee cup as his sister's words sunk in.

Effective communication is an ongoing process of practice and improvement. You won't improve on your communication skills if you keep interviewing, writing, or speaking the same way over and over. As we said in Chapter 1, if you always do what you've always done, you'll always get what you've always gotten. Feedback-based changes are crucial to the continuous growth needed to be an effective communicator.

This chapter shows you how to take advantage of the opportunities for continuous improvement by getting and using feedback to improve. We have intentionally talked about feedback in almost every chapter of this book because it is a crucial part of the Strategic Communication Model. In this chapter, we will build upon and reiterate our discussion of feedback in other chapters, discussing in detail the final step in the Strategic Communication Model. We do this for emphasis. The feedback process really is the key to ongoing growth and development of communication skills. Having a positive attitude toward feedback and applying some key behaviors to get and give such feedback can make all the difference in building excellent communication skills for yourself and others.

The Four Aspects of the Feedback Process

Develop and apply the ability to give, get, and use feedback—a crucial aspect of the Strategic Communication Model.

This chapter focuses on Step 5 of the Strategic Communication Model: Evaluate feedback for continued success. This last step in the model is critical to any learning about and improvement of our communication skills.

Feedback is the term we use to describe any response, critique, criticism, or comment about the way we communicate. Feedback may take the form of a direct criticism or complaint, but often it is subtler, such as nonverbal reactions (a listener dozing off), edited comments on a written document, rejection of an idea presented in a meeting, or, worst of all, simple failure to respond to our communication. Indeed, the worst feedback may be no feedback—when nothing happens after we attempt to communicate.

Feedback comes from two sources: external and internal. External feedback comes from your target audience—your readers and listeners—and trusted colleagues. Internal feedback comes from the process of self-evaluation. Both types of feedback form the basis for any improvement in communication skills.

You will develop your communication skills by applying four aspects of the feedback process—giving, soliciting, and receiving feedback, and evaluating yourself with the Credibility Checklist. The remainder of this chapter looks at these processes and shows how to make the most of each.

Give Constructive Feedback

Most people enjoy giving feedback if it's positive and complimentary. People like to get compliments, and you are probably glad to dispense positive comments that make others feel good. However, if you only offer positive feedback and ignore or dilute any negative comments, you are cheating everyone. The speaker or writer will miss the opportunity to learn something about the way the message came across to you. You, as an evaluator, will miss the opportunity to learn from recognizing your own shortcomings that you may see in someone else's work. Without this information, communicators will never know if what the receivers heard or read mirrors what they meant to say as speakers or writers.

You do people a disservice if you only give positive, complimentary feedback.

The most useful feedback points out a need for improvement and offers suggestions for how to make that improvement without discouraging the message sender. How this feedback is given will largely determine whether the receiver will use the feedback. Obviously, tact and clarity are helpful. Truly useful feedback is that which first acknowledges excellence, then points out a need for improvement, and finally offers a suggestion for how to make that improvement without demotivating the speaker or writer. In Chapter 1 we introduced some basic guidelines for giving good feedback. Let's review these guidelines:

Truly useful feedback acknowledges excellence, points out a need for improvement, and offers a suggestion for how to make that improvement.

- Describe something positive (such as, "Your letter made a lot of good points. . .").
- Express constructive criticism in terms of "I" (such as, "I got lost when you were talking about. . ." or "I had difficulty understanding your information about. . .").
- Give a specific example (such as, "For example, I couldn't see the connection between your description of the market and your solution. . ." or "I didn't understand what you meant by. . .").
- Offer an option for a solution (such as, "Perhaps if you could show me that information on a chart. . ." or "It would help me if you'd define some key terms. . .").
- Close with another positive statement (such as, "Your writing style is good, so I'm certain you can. . ." or "With a bit more clarification of the budget, I think we'll be ready to make a decision.").

Giving useful feedback need not be negative if you apply appropriate guidelines.

Applying these guidelines might sound something like this:

> "Julie, your attention grabber was really clever. That was a perfect story to introduce the need for improvement in the team. (POSITIVE OPENING) However (TRANSITION), I didn't understand the explanation of the change in the cost of raw materials. (CONSTRUCTIVE CRITICISM IN TERMS OF "I") Maybe a graph or an illustration of some kind would have made it clearer for me. (OPTION FOR SOLUTION) Since you tell such good stories, I know you can even make the numbers simple and interesting for us nonnumber types." (POSITIVE, MOTIVATING CLOSE)

Solicit Feedback from Others

To be an effective business communicator, you need to reach out for feedback. Feedback is your friend. Okay, sometimes it's a friend you would rather not hear from, but virtually any feedback can be useful. We will discuss ways to know whom, when, and how to ask for feedback in the next few sections.

Feedback is that friend you sometimes want to avoid.

Often feedback takes the form of one-to-one coaching.

Identify Whom and When to Ask

Choosing people to ask for feedback and knowing when to ask them are very important decisions. The following are two simple guidelines for soliciting the kind of feedback that will help you improve your communication:

Identify people you respect and trust and ask them *in advance* to evaluate your presentation, document, interview, or meeting participation.

- **Identify people you respect and trust who can provide you with the feedback you need.** Don't just ask friends you know will validate you. They may make you feel good but will be less likely to give you the beneficial information. Look for people who are experienced and effective communicators.
- **Ask people *in advance* to evaluate your presentation, document, interview, or meeting participation.** An example of a simple request may be: "Terri, I would sure appreciate it if you would. . . ("review this cover letter before I send it," or "look at the way I participate in our group meeting," or "ask me some interview questions and give me some pointers," or "let me run my presentation past you before I do it in class.").

FOCUS ON

Customer Feedback Builds Stronger Businesses

A complaining customer can be a company's best friend. Without complaints (feedback), organizations could never know how to improve. Without improvement, they would stagnate and eventually fail. Yet many companies make it hard for customers to complain—to give needed feedback.

The best ways to get feedback are to let customers know that you are receptive to it and provide ways for them to give it to you. Ask open-ended questions to give your customers opportunities to suggest ways they'd like to see you do business. Let them know that their input is really wanted.

Why do we want to give customers easy opportunities to complain? Because 63 percent of unhappy customers who do not complain will *not* buy from you again. But, of those who *do* complain and *have their problems resolved*, only 5 percent will not come back. Put another way, you have a 95 percent chance of saving unhappy customers if you hear their complaints.

Ask for feedback, take it seriously, don't be overly defensive about "the ways we've always done it," and express appreciation to customers for pointing out problems.[1]

Know How to Ask for Feedback

The way you ask for feedback ask will have a considerable impact on the quality of feedback you receive. As we discussed in Chapter 11 on interviews, closed-ended questions rarely get people to express their true feelings. If you ask a yes-no question such as, "So, how'd I do?" you may hear "great" or "fine" and feel better, but you won't get the information you need to learn and grow. Instead, ask open-ended questions that avoid single-word responses. The following are some possible open-ended questions you could use to get good feedback:

- Why do you think my material resonated with my audiences? Which examples seemed to keep the target listeners' (readers') attention?
- How did you interpret what I wanted my receiver to do at the end of my message? Could I phrase the action step better?
- How can I improve this message?
- How do you think I could better make sure the reader got the main objective of my message?
- What would you suggest for me to do to improve my interviewing (or meeting or presentation) skills?
- I'm concerned that my visuals aren't interesting enough. It seems like my slides are just lists of words. How could I improve them?

Consider asking people to look at specific areas in which you think you could improve.

Mayor Koch's Feedback

When legendary New York City Mayor Ed Koch was greeted by crowds of constituents, he would shout out "How'm I doing?" This became his tag line and endeared him to the people of New York. It suggested that he really wanted feedback from the people he served.

In addition to using open-ended questions, consider asking people to look at specific areas in which you think you could improve. For example, you may say, "Raul, I have been trying to cut back on filler words when I speak. Would you look for those and point out when I say 'ah,' 'um,' and 'ya know'?" Or, you may ask for feedback on your writing style. For example, you may say, 'Saleen, you're really good with layout ideas. Please look at this draft report and give me some ideas on how to use graphics or improve the access.' In some cases, you may ask people to complete a form such as the Presentation Feedback Form or the Writing Feedback Form found at the end of this chapter.

FOCUS ON

Eliminating Filler Words at Toastmasters

Toastmasters International, an organization dedicated to improving public speaking, has a common practice at its meetings. Speakers are required to deposit 25 cents in a jar for each "ah," "uh," "um," or other filler word they use. This can get expensive for people who slip into the distracting habit of verbalized pauses.

Toastmasters International is a not-for-profit group dedicated to helping people develop better listening, thinking, and speaking skills. The organization tends to focus more on delivery skills and less on context analysis and organization of messages. It has chapters throughout the world and can be contacted on the Web at www.toastmasters.org.

Receive and Process Feedback

How you respond to feedback will largely determine whether you will continue to get it. People will not continue to give you feedback if you overreact emotionally (display anger or hurt), disregard (express that the evaluator's idea is unimportant), or blame others. None of these reactions will help you improve as a communicator.

Remember that the people giving you feedback are doing you a favor. (Granted, it may not always feel that way, but they could easily avoid giving feedback and deny you its benefit.) Be appreciative, even when you may not agree with what they are saying.

As we have mentioned in earlier chapters, you can apply the following positive attitudes and behaviors to receiving feedback:

The person giving you feedback is doing you a favor.

Be open and listen carefully.

Ask for examples.

- Develop feedback-receptive attitudes—be open to, and appreciative of, good feedback.
- Listen carefully to comments, display nonverbal cues (eye contact, nodding, "uh huh") to indicate that you are listening, and take notes if appropriate. Let the person giving the feedback know that you are taking his or her input seriously.
- Ask for specific information and examples. Then repeat these back to the person giving the feedback for clarification.
- Notice nonverbal messages from your audience. For example, when giving a presentation, observe audience eye contact, nodding agreement, looks of confusion, or restlessness. These can tip you off as to how well you are *really* doing.

- Correct in the direction of the evaluation—don't overreact. A person's critique of your communication may be disconcerting or even hurtful. But within almost any feedback is at least a grain of truth. You need not accept all feedback as valid, but you will often find something of value in almost any feedback.
- Accept responsibility for any needs and changes. Ultimately, you will sort out the valid and valuable feedback from all you receive. When you identify the best insights, accept the responsibility for applying suggestions to your future communication.
- Recognize that whatever your audience perceives, real or not, is very real to them—show appreciation for their point of view.

Don't overreact to feedback. Accept responsibility for what needs to change.

Evaluate Yourself with the Credibility Checklist

Giving, soliciting, and receiving external feedback from other people is critical to communication improvement. Without knowledge of how our readers and listeners react to us, we would be unaware of ways to improve our communication. However, another source of feedback can be equally valuable: the internal feedback of honest self-evaluation. Self-evaluation looks inward at the most important element of your communication strategy: your ability to project *credibility*. Credibility is the quality of being worthy of belief. A so-called credibility gap exists when receivers see a message as lacking believability or as seemingly manipulative.

External feedback should be supplemented with internal feedback or self-evaluation.

Centuries ago, the Greek philosopher Aristotle taught that people use three kinds of persuasive appeals to successfully communicate. These persuasive appeals utilize our audience's emotions (*pathos*), our audience's recognition of logic (*logos*), and our audience's sense of ethics (*ethos*). Much of what Aristotle discussed is what we refer to as "credibility" today. In short, who you are speaks louder than what you say. No skillful argument can compensate for poor credibility—at least not in the long run.

The success of any communication attempt depends heavily on the message receiver's perception of the sender's credibility. Thus, if your audience perceives that you are credible—if they believe you, trust you, have confidence in you—you will be more effective and persuasive as a communicator. Your credibility is based on the way your message receivers perceive four key characteristics about you:

- Your goodwill
- Your expertise
- Your power
- Your confidence [2]

These four elements make up what we call the Credibility Checklist. This checklist, which you will find later in the chapter, is your way of producing internal feedback—of double-checking how you are coming across to your message receivers as you apply the Strategic Communication Model. Your goal is to carefully assess how you are being perceived and then to make the kinds of adjustments that help your audiences see you as being credible. Your assessment may not be 100 percent accurate, but it is a valuable exercise to put yourself into the shoes of your audience and anticipate how they perceive your credibility.

In any communication, the audience's perceptions of your credibility will have a dramatic impact on your effectiveness.

We discuss the four elements of credibility in more depth in the following pages. These provide the basis for self-evaluation that can provide internal feedback.

Consider each element honestly and openly. Objectively assess the degree to which you are likely to measure up in your receivers' minds, and then consider ways to build stronger credibility and, thus, better communication skills.

Establish Goodwill: Your Focus on and Concern for Your Audience

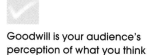

Goodwill is your audience's perception of what you think of them.

Goodwill, the first credibility element, is your audience's perception of what you think of them. If you don't convey to your audience that you are concerned about them, they will not believe in you as a communicator. Put another way, people won't care what you think unless they think you care (about them).

You will best project your goodwill by carefully selecting information based on your analysis of your audience, situation, and objectives. (If this sounds like Step 1 of the Strategic Communication Model, it's because it is.) If you haven't thought carefully about the people hearing your presentation, reading your e-mail, or participating in your meeting, they won't perceive you as having goodwill toward them (and, therefore, they won't perceive you as credible). Expressing your goodwill to your audience lets them know what you think about them—how unique they are, how special they are, and how important they are to you.

Demonstrate Expertise: Your Education, Knowledge, and Experience

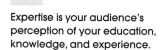

Expertise is your audience's perception of your education, knowledge, and experience.

Expertise, the second credibility element, is your audience's perceptions of your education, knowledge, and experience. This element evaluates how smart your listeners and readers think you are with regard to the topic of your message. To project strong expertise, let your audience know that you have it, but avoid appearing arrogant or bragging about what you know. This can be tricky. You want to be seen as smart, but you don't want to lose goodwill points by acting superior or cocky.

You can best project expertise through illustrative examples that demonstrate your knowledge without boasting. Share your experiences with your receivers but

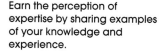

Earn the perception of expertise by sharing examples of your knowledge and experience.

be careful to not directly take full credit for something you did as a part of a team. For example, you might include phrases such as:

- "Last year I led a group of students in a project to collect food for the homeless, and we found that. . ." (IMPLIES EXPERIENCE)
- "The current research published in *Entrepreneur* magazine suggests. . ." (IMPLIES CURRENT KNOWLEDGE)
- "In last week's class we covered that process, and. . ." (IMPLIES RECENT EXPOSURE)
- Several laws have changed since I first learned about this in my college program. . ." (IMPLIES RELEVANT EDUCATION)

Look for ways to insert evidence of your credibility by projecting your expertise in appropriate ways.

Display Power: Your Status, Prestige, and Authority

Power, the third credibility element, is your audience's perception of what other people think about you—your status, prestige, and authority. Such power arises from six sources:

Power is your audience's perception of what other people think about you—your status, prestige, and authority.

- **Rank in your current organization (class) or formal positions.** Tell a story in the context of when you were president of an organization or leader of a team.
- **Awards or recognition you have received.** The recognition is best when it is relevant to the topic, of course. If the relevance is not obvious, you might have to make the connection for your audience. For example, being an award-winning swimmer demonstrates stamina and endurance, important characteristics in most business endeavors.
- **Personal power (your ability to control your own environment).** Illustrate this with examples of situations when you took charge of a situation at school or work and by comfortably taking charge of a communication situation, such as a presentation or a meeting.
- **Interpersonal power (your ability to influence other people).** Use an example that demonstrates your reputation as a successful sales representative or refer to an incident when you persuaded someone to change his or her mind.
- **Organizational power (your ability to mobilize resources).** Share examples of situations when you met deadlines or delivered on promises. This might be authority you have earned (e.g., you are a trained police officer, a licensed emergency medical technician, or an elected representative).
- **Power by association with others who have power.** Without bragging, tell stories that include your position near people in power (e.g., you are the administrative assistant to a company leader, or your father is the dean).

From the perspective of a college student, "power" may seem to be an attribute that you can only achieve when you are old or wealthy. However, the good news is that the power you achieve in other situations is often transferable. This means that, although your current communication situation may be different from one in which you were seen as having power in the past, you may still carry power credibility in the eyes of your audience. For example, the power of being an officer in a student organization illustrates leadership ability that you can apply on the job, such as being the project leader of a work team. Being involved with a decision made by your boss on a manufacturing problem (association power) may be transferable to a recommendation you make for a study group. Having authority as a squad leader

Power you have had in other situations is often transferable.

Display your power—but don't be intimidating.

THE BOONDOCKS by AARON MCGRUDER

Confidence is your audience's perception of the way you present yourself and your messages.

If your audience perceives you as confident, you will be more persuasive.

for a National Guard unit may demonstrate your ability to lead a student project. All this is, of course, perceptual—in the eyes of your audience.

Express Confidence: The Way You Present Yourself and Your Message

The fourth credibility element, confidence, has to do with your audience's perceptions of the way you present yourself and your messages. This element may be the most important credibility dimension and the one over which you may have the most control. Readers and listeners generally perceive confident writers and speakers as having more goodwill, more expertise, and more power.[3] Confidence arises especially from your success in applying the Strategic Communication Model's Step 3 (selecting and organizing information), Step 4 (delivering your message), and Step 5 (evaluating your feedback).

You will best project confidence through excellent message preparation and delivery skills. These skills, of course, require doing your homework and preparing messages tailored to your audiences' needs and concerns. Once your material is right, it will be easier for you to feel confident. When you feel confident, the audience sees that confidence and responds positively.

Get Internal Feedback

The remainder of this chapter deals with the Credibility Checklist—a way to gain feedback through introspection. Use of this checklist calls for being honest and candid as you consider how your message receivers are likely to perceive your credibility.

The Credibility Checklist may be completed before you communicate a message and again after you have completed a significant communication event (a written report, presentation, meeting, or interview). The first use can help you anticipate audience reactions and can provide ideas for strengthening your message before it is delivered. Insights you gain from reviewing what you did can provide a foundation for future improvement and continued success.

A sample, completed checklist is shown in Figure 12-1. In this example, we look at how one student—we'll call him Jack—might fill out the checklist for an oral presentation he would be giving in a class. Later in the chapter, a blank Credibility Checklist is provided for your use. We recommend that you complete this using your own best guesses as you apply it to specific communication situations.

The Credibility Checklist

Communication Situation:

Oral presentation to the class advocating that we perform a community service project instead of writing a final paper based on a written case.

Goodwill: The audience's perception of my focus on them and my concern for them.

What did I do to show my target audience that I care about them?

My target audience is my classmates, but the decision maker is the teacher. I stressed the benefits of hands-on learning to both. I tried to convey that doing community service gives hands-on experience and will be beneficial.

Expertise: The audience's perception of my knowledge, education, and experience.

What knowledge, education, and experience do I have that might impress my audience?

I told the group about my experience last year as a coordinator for a feed-the-homeless program that was very successful. I also explained that I knew how to get the necessary government permits for the proposed project.

What have I accomplished that I am really proud of?

Last year's efforts were very successful. More people than ever before were given a good meal. I also coordinated the efforts of health care providers who set up booths to do vaccinations and dental checks for kids.

Power: The audience's perception of my status, prestige, and power.

What is my rank in my current organization (class) and how might this impress my audience?

While I have no formal rank in the class, my classmates know that I have worked with community leaders in past projects, so I have some power from those associations.

What awards or recognition have I received that might impress my audience?

Last year's project received newspaper coverage and a story on the local TV news broadcast. I was interviewed briefly.

What is the source of my personal power (my ability to control my own environment)?

I can get the cooperation of several local clergy and civic leaders to arrange our event.

Figure 12-1
The Credibility Checklist: A Sample

The Credibility Checklist that Jack filled out provides internal feedback about how his audience is likely to perceive him and his ideas. Completing this checklist helps assess the realities of the communication situation. If he had not been able to answer the checklist questions fully, he would know that his persuasion attempts would be more of an uphill battle. He could also think about ways to improve his credibility by enhancing the audience's perception of his goodwill, expertise, power, and confidence.

Figure 12-1 (*continued*)
The Credibility Checklist: A Sample

The Credibility Checklist (continued)

What is the source of my interpersonal power (my ability to influence other people)?

I have been successful in persuading other classes to do a similar project in the past.

What are examples of my organizational power (my ability to mobilize resources)?

I can get the local TV station to help sponsor and cover the event if we organize it well.

What relationships give me "power by association"?

My work with clergy and civic leaders and the fact that I know the TV station manager—he's my uncle.

Confidence: The audience's perception of how I present myself—how sure I am of myself and my message.

What are some examples of how I exhibit confidence in my verbal and nonverbal behavior?

I feel comfortable pitching this idea to the class. I have spoken in front of audiences about such a project many times.

APPLYING THE STRATEGIC COMMUNICATION MODEL

Let's go back to our opening story of Rick's unhappy job search. His description of his preparation may provide the key to this problem. Remember what he said to Renee? "(My) résumé looks good. I've polished it a thousand times. I also got a hold of a list of interview questions and have read them through and thought about my responses."

Based on what you have read in this chapter, you know that Rick's use of feedback was inadequate. Rereading his résumé without getting an outside perspective and mentally answering sample questions in ways that sound good to only him are not effective ways to use feedback.

Renee's suggestion about having the Career Center look at his résumé is a good one. In fact, Rick could probably solve his problem if he would apply the ideas in this chapter and actively solicit and use feedback. We would suggest that Rick contact some of the recruiters who turned him down and ask some open-ended questions: "What would you suggest I do differently?" "How can I better present myself in the job interview?" "What were the key things that caused you to reject my application?" It isn't always pleasant to get negative feedback, but these are the kinds of questions Rick *must* get answers to. We would also suggest that Rick complete a Credibility Checklist to honestly assess his strengths and weaknesses.

If Rick fails to use feedback, he will continue doing what has not worked. He will miss an excellent opportunity for communication skill improvement.

Summary of Key Ideas

- People cannot improve on their communication skills if they continue writing and speaking the same way over and over.
- Communicators can take advantage of the opportunities for continuous improvement by applying four aspects of the feedback process—giving, soliciting, and receiving feedback, and evaluating themselves with the Credibility Checklist.
- The most useful feedback is that which first acknowledges what was done well, then points out a need for improvement, and finally offers a suggestion for how to make that improvement without demotivating the speaker.
- The way you ask for feedback will have considerable impact on the quality of the feedback you get. Open-ended, sincere questions generally elicit the most useful information.
- To improve communication, identify people you respect and trust who can provide you with the feedback you need.
- The internal feedback of honest self-evaluation can also be useful in improving communication skills.
- If your audience believes you, trusts you, and has confidence in you, you will be more effective and persuasive as a communicator. The success of any communication attempt depends heavily on the message receiver's perception of the sender's credibility.
- Goodwill is your audience's perception of what you think of them—of whether you really care about them.
- Expertise is your audience's perceptions of your education, knowledge, and experience as these relate to the topic of your message.
- Power is your audience's perception of what other people think about you—your rank, recognition earned, personal power to control the environment, organizational power to mobilize resources, and power of association with others.
- Confidence has to do with your audience's perceptions of the way you present yourself and your messages.
- Writing specific and full answers to each item on the Credibility Checklist can generate internal feedback and a realistic assessment of what your audience thinks of you and your message.

Application Activities

Activity 12-1 Using the Credibility Checklist

Consider a communication situation, such as a meeting with your adviser at school, your supervisor at work, a presentation to your class or Greek organization, or a

Interactive CD-ROM Exercises

proposal to a student government organization. Use the Credibility Checklist in Figure 12-2 to gain an assessment of how your audience is likely to perceive you. Write specific and full answers to each of the items on this Credibility Checklist to generate internal feedback. Then assess your current credibility perceptions and create a plan for bolstering your credibility.

Activity 12-2 Using the Presentation Evaluation Worksheet

A written feedback form can be invaluable for gaining feedback when you do an oral presentation. In Chapter 9 (Figure 9-1) we included a sample Presentation Evaluation Worksheet. (Other forms are, of course, available and may be more useful for certain situations. This one is generic and easy to apply to almost every oral

Figure 12-2
The Credibility Checklist
Form

The Credibility Checklist

Communication Situation:

Goodwill: The audience's perception of my focus on them and my concern for them.
What did I do to show my target audience that I care about them?

Expertise: The audience's perception of my knowledge, education, and experience.
What knowledge, education, and experience do I have that might impress my audience?

What have I accomplished that I am really proud of?

Power: The audience's perception of my status, prestige, and power.
What is my rank in my current organization (class) and how might this impress my audience?

What awards or recognition have I received that might impress my audience?

What is the source of my personal power (my ability to control my own environment)?

What is the source of my interpersonal power (my ability to influence other people)?

What are examples of my organizational power (my ability to mobilize resources)?

What relationships give me "power by association"?

Confidence: The audience's perception of how I present myself—how sure I am of myself and my message.
What are some examples of how I exhibit confidence in my verbal and nonverbal behavior?

presentation situation.) Make a copy of the Presentation Evaluation Worksheet. Then ask a colleague or fellow student to observe your presentation (a rehearsal or the real thing) and provide written feedback using this form. Then write a one-page memo discussing the feedback you received. Address your critiquer's assessment and describe ways you could improve.

Activity 12-3 Using the Written Document Feedback Form

Complete a feedback form such as the one shown in Figure 12-3 to a written report or document. This may be a finished document or one that is in the draft stage. Answer each question as fully as possible, being objective and complete. Compare your assessment with those of others to see if you missed anything.

Figure 12-3
Written Document
Feedback Form

Written Document Feedback Form

Document: _____

Author: _____ Date: _____

	Good	Needs Work
CONTENT		
Focuses content to meet the needs of the audience(s)		
Acknowledges audience wants and concerns		
Provides sufficient depth in support material		
Uses interesting support materials for reader		
Is written clearly, using concrete nouns and action verbs		
Presents attractive document: polished; free of grammatical errors, misspellings		
ORGANIZATION		
Includes appropriate content preview to prepare the reader for the material presented		
States clear agenda with good content set		
Answers all anticipated reader questions.		
Follows clear organizational plan		
Includes appropriate support for key ideas		
Asks for clear action in conclusion		
DELIVERY		
Written efficiently; avoids rambling		
Uses good access to help reader identify most important points		
Communicates a conversational tone		
Includes appropriate visuals, charts, tables, graphs, etc.		
Overall comments:		

Activity 12-4 Understanding Resistance to Feedback

On a sheet of paper, list some reasons people may resist soliciting feedback. Then list some major advantages of getting feedback. Describe a recent situation when you gave someone feedback. What was the outcome of that communication activity? Next describe a recent situation when you received feedback. What was the outcome of that activity?

Career Activity

Career Activity 12-1 Applying the Credibility Checklist to Your Job Search

Identify a career position and an organization in which you would like to work. Prepare a Credibility Checklist assuming that you have been invited to visit the organization and interview for an entry-level position. Be thorough, candid, and complete. Then invite a trusted colleague to critique your checklist. Solicit and process the feedback you receive. Write a brief summary memo addressed to your instructor identifying what you learned from this experience.

myPHLIP Companion Web Site

Learning Interactively

Visit the myPHLIP Web site at www.prenhall.com/timm. For Chapter 12, take advantage of the interactive "Study Guide" to test your chapter knowledge. Get instant feedback on whether you need additional studying. Read the "Current Events" articles to get the latest on chapter topics, and complete the exercises as specified by your instructor. Expand your learning with a visit to the "Research Area." There you will find a wealth of information you can use to complete your course assignments.

Notes

1. Adapted from Paul R. Timm, *50 Powerful Ideas You Can Use to Keep Your Customers,* 2nd ed. (Franklin Lakes, NJ: Career Press, 1995), p. 51.
2. Sherron Bienvenu introduced the first version of the four-dimensional credibility model in "Speaker Credibility in Persuasive Business Communication," *The Journal of Business Communication,* Spring 1989, pp. 143–158. A derivation appeared in *CrossTalk: Communicating in a Multicultural Workplace* (Upper Saddle River, NJ: Prentice Hall, 1997). Bienvenu introduced the current version in *The Presentation Skills Workshop* (New York: AMACOM, 2000).
3. D. K. Berlo, J. B. Lemert, and R. J. Mertz, "Dimensions for Evaluating the Acceptability of Message Sources," *Public Opinion Quarterly,* 33 (1969), pp. 563–575.

Avoiding Common Grammar, Punctuation, and Usage Mistakes[1]

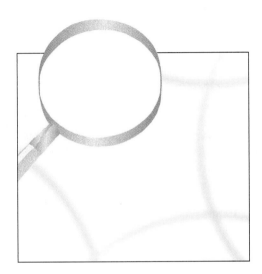

This reference tool shows you how to avoid common grammar and usage mistakes. Some of the issues refer primarily to writing, but many of these usage guidelines also apply to spoken messages. This reference tool is not intended to be a substitute for a good style guide or book that you can refer to for specific questions. We recommend that you keep a reference book handy or use an online guide for dealing with the less common rules and language conventions.

In our quick review of common language problems, we will focus on the following:

- Punctuation
- Agreement (subject–verb and pronoun–antecedent)
- Pronoun case
- Voice
- Prepositions and connectives
- Modifiers

Mastering the information in this reference tool will allow you to avoid the vast majority of common language use problems.

Common Punctuation Questions

The following sections present useful guides on using punctuation correctly.

Using Commas

1. Don't insert a comma in a sentence just because the sentence sounds like it needs a comma, and don't leave out commas just because you're afraid of using them incorrectly.
2. Learn the names or functions of the commas; then use the right commas to get your point across.

Following is a discussion of the names and functions of different types of commas.

The Conjunction Comma   The *conjunction comma* is used with a conjunction such as *and, but,* or *so* to separate two main clauses. The choice of either *and* or *but* or another conjunction depends on the relationship you want to convey between two main clauses. However, be sure to include a conjunction—a conjunction comma without a conjunction cannot do its job properly. Examples:

- The attorney filed the appeal today, <u>but</u> the judge will not make a decision on it until next week.
- The material used in our suit coats is the very best available, <u>and</u> we guarantee you will be satisfied with every coat you purchase from us.
- I scored 97 percent on my final exam, <u>so</u> I think I will probably get an A in the class.

The Series Comma   The *series comma* is used to separate items in a list of three or more items. Items in a list can be single words, phrases, or clauses. Examples:

- We purchased books, papers, pencils, and erasers. (words in a list)
- He studies for an hour in the morning, at noon, and in the evening. (prepositional phrases in a list)
- John typed the letter, Mary copied it, and I mailed it. (main clauses in a list)

The Introductory Comma   The *introductory comma* separates introductory words, phrases, and dependent clauses at the beginning of a sentence from the main clause. Examples:

- Therefore, we signed the papers as he requested. (introductory word)
- In addition, we agreed to rewrite the contract next week. (introductory phrase)
- When the check arrived, we were disappointed to learn that only $50 was being refunded to us. (introductory dependent clause)

The Explanation Comma   The *explanation comma* separates a clause or phrase of explanation or clarification at the end of a sentence from the main clause. The explanation comma is very much like the introductory comma, except that it *precedes* something that has been added to the *end* of a sentence whereas the introductory comma *follows* something added to the *front* of a sentence, as shown in the following examples:

- Hoping to be on time for the meeting, I ran up the stairs. (introductory phrase followed by an *introductory* comma)

■ I ran up the stairs, hoping to be on time for the meeting. (explanatory phrase preceded by an *explanation* comma)

The *And*-Omitted Comma   The *and-omitted comma* separates consecutive or independent adjectives that would otherwise be separated with the word *and*. Thus, if you can insert the word *and* between two adjectives, you can use an *and*-omitted comma instead. Examples:

■ The report had a long, wordy conclusion. (long *and* wordy)
■ The sharp-looking, expensive car was totally demolished in the accident. (sharp-looking *and* expensive)

The Parenthetical Comma   The *parenthetical comma*, as its name implies, is used to enclose thoughts that could be enclosed in parentheses. Such thoughts are usually interjections or interruptions to a sentence, as in these examples:

■ The man was, as you know, fired from his last four jobs.
■ The equipment, in the meantime, sat idle and became rusty.
■ We did not, however, forget that you were interested in taking over the project.

Notice that parenthetical commas can be used to enclose interruptions that are single words (such as *however*) and phrases (such as *in the meantime*).

The Renaming Comma   The *renaming comma* is used to enclose a word or group of words that renames a person or thing already named in the sentence. Examples:

■ Bill Jones, the president of Interwest Health Services, will speak at the luncheon. (*the president of Interwest Health Services* renames *Bill Jones*)
■ Pamela Adams, a business education teacher in the Manchester School District, has received the district's "Teacher of the Year" award again this year. (*a business education teacher in the Manchester School District* renames *Pamela Adams*)
■ We sent the checks to the president, Marlow Marchant, and to the vice president, Alan Kimball. (*Marlow Marchant* renames *the president*, and *Alan Kimball* renames *the vice president*)

The Dates and Addresses Comma   The *dates and addresses comma* is used to enclose information in dates and in addresses.
Examples:

■ On Friday, December 22, we will hold the department Christmas party.
■ On December 22, 2003, we will hold the department Christmas party.
■ The King visited Buffalo, New York.
■ Please send my package to 123 South Main, Denver, CO.

The "Hey You!" Comma   The *"hey, you!" comma* is more formally called the direct address comma. It is used in pairs to enclose interjections used to get the reader's attention—usually the person's name. Examples:

■ Thank you, Raul, for your time and effort on this project.
■ Stacy, can I take half a day off today?
■ I can understand your wanting the job, Kevin.

Using the Semicolon or "Super Comma"

The *semicolon* (;) is stronger or more powerful than a comma and can, therefore, be called a super comma. The *super comma* performs just two functions: that of joining (or separating) two independent clauses or that of clarifying items presented in a list (a series) when at least one of the items in the list has a comma in it. Example:

■ We presented the sales seminar in Houston, Texas; Salt Lake City, Utah; Denver, Colorado; Reno, Nevada; and Los Angeles, California.

Do not use the semicolon to separate dependent clauses, to follow introductory phrases, to enclose parenthetical information, or to introduce lists.

Using the Colon or "Super Period"

You can use the *colon* (:) to separate two main clauses in certain situations. When the second of two main clauses is the expected or natural explanation or result of the first clause, use a colon to introduce the second clause, as in this example.

■ His prediction came true: We never did finish the manuscript.

Use a colon *only* when you could use a period—after a *complete* thought (main clause); do not use a colon after only part of a sentence, as in these examples.

■ Please purchase the following items: a pen, a pencil, and an eraser.
■ His talents are many: He paints, he writes, he acts, and he sings.
■ His answer was simple: no.

One exception to the rule that a colon must come after a complete thought is this: When you use part of a sentence to introduce items that will be enumerated or listed beginning on a separate line from the introductory sentence fragment, you may use a colon to end the partial sentence.

■ He discussed several important principles in the communication seminar. They are:

　　1. Context
　　2. Options
　　3. Organization
　　4. Delivery

You should also use a colon in the salutation in business letters (e.g., Dear Sarah:).

Using the Dash

In most word processing programs, you form a *dash* (—) by typing two hyphens followed by a space. The software will automatically make it into a dash.

Use the dash—like the colon—to separate two main clauses when the second clause is the natural or expected result or explanation of the first clause. The dash acts somewhat as an arrow would—it alerts the reader to important or emphasized points of information. Examples:

■ He was right about one thing—we never did finish the manuscript.
■ His answer was very clear—no.

A dash can also be used in place of parenthetical, nonessential, or renaming commas as a way of emphasizing the enclosed part of the sentence. Example:

- His attempts to cover his error—attempts that were weak and poorly planned at best—were seen by us as being sufficient reason for his dismissal.
- We were—fortunately—able to finish the project before Christmas.

The difference in using dashes versus commas is that of emphasis—*dashes* tend to emphasize enclosed items, *commas* merely identify the enclosed items as being parenthetical or nonessential, and *parentheses* tend to deemphasize the importance of enclosed items.

Using the Hyphen

The hyphen (-) is used to join two or more words that act together as a compound adjective to provide a single description of a noun that follows. Examples:

- His low-scoring game was the cause of his depression on Monday.
- The small-computer industry is one of the largest in America today.

Hyphens are also used in some nouns and adverbs. Examples:

- mother-in-law or father-in-law
- commander-in-chief (also commander in chief)
- governor-elect
- co-worker
- full-time or part-time

Also, *self-* words are hyphenated (except *selfish, selfless,* etc.). Examples:

- self-service
- self-examination
- self-evaluation

Common Subject–Verb Agreement Questions

Subjects and verbs must agree (be consistent) in terms of *tense, number, person,* and *gender.*

Achieving Tense Agreement: Past, Present, and Future

Tense refers to *time,* be it past, present, or future. Examples:

- Yesterday, I *wrote* several e-mails to our customers. (past tense)
- I *write* to several customers each day. (present tense)
- Tomorrow, I *will* write to several customers. (future)

You must use the appropriate tense to reflect the correct time.

Using Progressive Forms of Verbs

In addition, each verb form has a perfect form meaning that the action expressed by the verb has been *completed* (perfected) at a particular point in time: past, present, or future. Thus, we can choose from *past perfect, present perfect,* or *future perfect.*

The perfect tenses are formed by using what is called the present participle form of the verb along with a helper—*have, has,* or *had.* Examples:

- At 4:00 yesterday afternoon, he *had written* four letters. (past perfect)
- Today he *has written* only two letters. (present perfect)
- By 2:00 tomorrow, he *will have written* all 15 letters. (future perfect)

Recognizing Other Changes in Verb Form

Whether the verb has a singular or a plural subject and whether the subject is in the first, second, or third person will usually affect the form of the verb. For example, notice the change in the verbs *do, am,* and *was* as the subject changes from first person to second person, from singular to plural, and so on:

Subject	*Do*	*Am*	*Was*
I	do	am	was
we	do	are	were
you	do	are	were
he/she/it	does	is	was
they	do	are	were

If you're a native English speaker, you've been using all these forms of verbs most of your life, and you use them correctly without much thought. The reason that this introduction to verbs is important to you is that it contains useful terms you should be familiar with before you study the guidelines that help you make proper choices of verb tense to fit each situation.

Following the Rules

In the next several pages we will describe some important rules for using verbs correctly.

Rule 1: Use the Correct Verb Form   Verbs have four basic forms:

1. Present (also called the *infinitive*)
2. Past
3. Past participle (the *have, has,* or *had* form)
4. Progressive or ongoing (*-ing* form)

We can put each verb on a chart such as the one that follows to show its present, past, past participle, and progressive forms.

Infinitive or Present	Past	Past Participle	Present Participle or Progressive
run	ran	run	running
think	thought	thought	thinking
go	went	gone	going
do	did	done	doing
lay	laid	laid	laying
lie	lay	lain	lying
sit	sat	sat	sitting
set	set	set	setting
watch	watched	watched	watching

We form present and past verbs by simply choosing the present or past forms. We form perfect tenses by choosing the past participle form and using it with *have, has,* or *had* (*have* run, *has* run, *had* run). Progressive verbs are formed by choosing the present participle form and using it with a being verb (*was* running, *is* running, *will be* running). We form perfect progressive verbs by combining *have, has,* or *had* with a being verb and the progressive form of the verb (*had been* running, *has been* running, *will have been* running).

Rule 2: Express True Statements in Present Tense   Statements that are *still true* must be expressed in the present tense. Statements that *used to be true* but that *are no longer true* because facts or circumstances have changed should be expressed in the past tense. Examples:

- Ancient people thought the world *was* flat. (not true)
- Columbus knew the world *is* round. (a truth)
- I noticed that the report *had* many typographical errors. (the errors have been corrected)
- I noticed that the report *introduces* many new ideas. (the report still does introduce many new ideas)

Rule 3: Use Present Tense Infinitives After Past Tense Verbs   Whenever a past tense verb is followed by another verb, that second verb must be an infinitive or present tense verb. Often the infinitive is accompanied by an "infinitive marker"—the word *to*. Examples:

- He didn't dare *to swim* after dark.
- I wanted him *to go* home early.
- I had hoped *to be* at the meeting.

When a past tense verb hasn't been used first, using *to have been* or a similar phrase is all right. Examples:

- By this time tomorrow, I *want to have finished* the report.
- By the end of my career, I *hope to have been* recognized as an authority on the subject.

Rule 4: Make Subjects and Verbs Agree   *Agreement* is simply a matter of deciding whether you're talking:

1. About one person (singular) or about more than one person (plural).
2. About ourselves (first person—*I, we,* etc.) or about the reader or listener (second person—*you, your,* etc.) or about someone else (third person—*he, she, they, it,* etc.).
3. About a woman, about a man, or about people or things in general, regardless of gender.

Once you've decided exactly whom or what you're talking about in relation to these three characteristics (*number, person,* and *gender*), you must make sure all parts of each sentence agree with (are consistent with) all other parts of the sentence.

A verb changes form to sound right with its subject, depending on whether the subject is singular or plural and on whether it is first person, second person, or third person. For example, notice how the verb *write* changes in these sentences, depending on the subject of each sentence:

- I *write* a department management report every week.
- She *writes* a department management report every week.
- They *write* a department management report every week.

Subject–verb agreement (or lack of agreement) is usually very easy to hear, although it is sometimes tricky with the same kinds of subjects. The following rules will help you handle some potentially confusing agreement situations.

Rule 5: Separate Subjects Joined with *and* Need a Plural Verb Unless the Two *Subjects* Are Not Really Separate Subjects   Subjects joined with *and* can be singular or plural. The word *and* means about the same thing as a "+" in math—it means "both." Whenever you join two subjects with *and,* you are obviously talking about more than one—about *both*—and have to use a plural verb. Examples:

- Understanding English grammar *and* knowing how to use grammar effectively *are* important to a good communicator.
- The investment broker *and* her assistant *were* at the meeting yesterday.

The two subjects in each sentence could be split and used in two separate sentences (this time with singular verbs, of course) without modifying the wording of the subjects themselves, as shown here:

- Understanding English grammar *is* important to a good writer.
  and
- Knowing how to use grammar effectively *is* important to a good writer.

Likewise:

- The investment broker *was* at the meeting yesterday.
  and
- Her assistant *was* at the meeting yesterday.

  Sometimes, a *single* subject happens to have the word *and* in it:

- My friend *and* associate (the same person)
- Ham *and* eggs (one menu item)

These are *singular* subjects (subjects that identify just one person or thing) that have the word *and* in them. Thus, we could construct the following sentences using singular verbs. Examples:

- My friend and associate *is* attending the meeting. (We could not separate *my friend* and *associate* into separate sentences without adding another *my* before *associate*.)
- Ham and eggs *is* my favorite breakfast. (*Ham and eggs* is one breakfast dish—one menu item. Thus, we would not communicate the same idea if we said *Ham is my favorite breakfast* and *eggs are my favorite breakfast*.)

Separate subjects joined with *and* need a plural verb. But if the two subjects are not really separate subjects, we use a singular verb.

Rule 6: When Two or More Subjects Are Joined with *or*, the Subject *Closest to the Verb* Determines Whether the Verb Should Be Singular or Plural

When we join two *plural* subjects with *or* (or *nor*), as in "the books *or* the tapes," the subject *closest to the verb* determines whether the verb should be singular or plural. For example,

- The *book* (singular) *or* the *tapes* (plural) *were* (plural) sent.
- The *books* (plural) *or* the *tapes* (plural) *were* (plural) sent.
- The *books* (plural) *or* the *tape* (singular) *was* (singular) sent.
- The *book* (singular) *or* the *tape* (singular) *was* (singular) sent.

When you join a singular subject and a plural subject with *or,* put the plural subject last so that the sentence will have a plural verb. Doing so will make the sentence sound more natural. Examples:

- The Smiths *or* John *is* coming. (sounds awkward)
- John *or* the Smiths *are* coming. (sounds more natural)

Rule 7: Prepositional Phrases Do Not Affect Agreement Between the Subject of the Sentence and the Verb

Often a singular subject will be followed by a prepositional phrase that contains a plural word as the object of the preposition.

Prepositional phrases *do not affect agreement between the subject of the sentence and the verb*. We can mentally "block out" the entire prepositional phrase from the sentence while we decide whether to use a singular or a plural verb.

For example, notice the plural words that are objects of the prepositions *of, in,* and *at* in the following sentence parts:

- An examination *of* the *records*. . .
- The spectator *in* the *bleachers*. . .
- The worker *at* the *controls*. . .

When a verb follows such plural words, many of us understandably (but mistakenly) make the verb plural (as in "the worker at the controls *are*. . ."). But the plural word (*controls*) that follows the preposition is *not* the subject of the verb that follows—the singular subject that precedes the prepositional phrase is the subject (*the worker* at the controls). Thus, the sentence should read: "The worker at the controls *is*. . .").

Rule 8: Singular Subjects Such as *Each* and *Either* Are Always Singular

Subjects such as *each, either, neither,* and *everyone,* followed by prepositional phrases containing plural words ("each of the men," "either of the children"), can be thought of as really meaning "each *one*" and "either *one*." These are *always singular.* Examples:

anybody	anything	every	every one
anyone	each	everybody	everything
any one	either	everyone	neither
nobody	nothing	somebody	some one
no one	one	someone	something

Thus, we use singular verbs with them:

- *Each* of the men *is* applying for the promotion.
- *Either* of the children *sings* well.
- *Neither* of the applicants *was* qualified for the position.
- *Something is* wrong here.

Rule 9: Collective Subjects Can Be Used with Either Singular Verbs or Plural Verbs Depending on the Meaning

Subjects that describe collections of people or things are called collective subjects. Examples:

committee	class	team
jury	group	staff
family	crowd	audience

Such collective subjects can be used with either singular verbs or plural verbs depending on whether we want to tell the receiver that only one thing (a single "unit") is involved in the action or that at least two persons or things (individuals) are involved in the action. For example, if we wish to make an announcement on behalf of all our family members and want to show our readers or listeners that our announcement is really being made by *all* family members, we would say:

- The family *are* happy to announce Mom and Dad's fiftieth wedding anniversary.

But if the family is being talked about as a *single unit* instead of as individual family members, we write:

- The family *is* living in Lockport, New York.

Some verbs name actions that *require* only one performer; other verbs name actions that *must* be performed by more than one. Example: The action named by the verb *argue* requires more than one performer because it takes two to argue. Thus, we write or say:

- The team *are* arguing about who will be chosen for the award. (Although this is correct, most people would probably say, "the team members. . ." because it sounds more natural.)

If the team members are united in arguing *with the coach*, we can talk about the team as a *single unit*:

■ The team *is* arguing with the coach about who will be chosen for the award.

Common Pronoun and Antecedent Agreement Questions

Pronouns are the generic words that are used to rename or replace other "brand-name" nouns. Common pronouns include:

I	me	my	you	your
we	us	our	he	him
his	she	her	hers	who
they	them	their	theirs	that
whom	whose	it	its	those
which	there	this	these	

Antecedents describe the word (or group of words) that a pronoun refers to, replaces, or renames. A pronoun has meaning to the reader or listener only if it has an antecedent—a noun that the pronoun is meant to replace—and only if it refers to the antecedent clearly. The underlying principles about the link between pronouns and their antecedents are these:

1. Every pronoun must refer clearly to one and only one specific noun in the same sentence or in a preceding sentence.
2. Every pronoun must agree with its antecedent in terms of number, person, and gender.

Following the Rules

The following section discusses rules for correct pronoun–antecedent reference and agreement.

Rule 1: Make Sure That The Antecedent Reference Is *Clear* and Cannot Refer to Something Else   Communicators have the responsibility of ensuring that the receiver cannot misunderstand pronoun–antecedent reference. To avoid misunderstandings, be wary of these kinds of reference problems:

■ Unclear reference
■ "Distant relatives" (relative pronouns like *who* and *which* that are placed too far from their antecedents)
■ Meaningless pronouns

Avoid unclear reference.   Sometimes we're not sure what word message senders are trying to replace or to refer to when they use a pronoun. Examples of unclear pronoun reference:

- When I received the letter and the check, I noticed that it did not have a signature on it.
- When the cheerleaders distribute copies of the school cheers, let's take a good look at them.
- If the printer doesn't make a clear impression on the paper, I'll be glad to check it for you.

If a pronoun can refer to more than one possible antecedent, you'd better rework the sentence. The examples we just gave you can be corrected as follows:

- When I received the letter and the check, I noticed that the check did not have a signature on it.
- Let's take a good look at the school cheers when the cheerleaders distribute them.
- If the printer doesn't make a clear impression on the paper, I'll be glad to check the printer for you.

Avoid "distant relatives."   A "distant relative" is a relative pronoun or a relative clause that has been placed too far from its antecedent. People often mistakenly put a verb or some other part of the sentence between the relative pronoun and its antecedent, as shown in the following examples:

- Take the report to John *that has February's sales figures* in it.
- Leave information off the résumé *that does not relate* to your qualifications for the job.

We improve the sentences by placing the relative clause immediately after the antecedent in each sentence, as shown in the following examples:

- Take the report that has February's sales figures in it to John.
- Leave information that does not relate to your qualifications for the job off the résumé.

Rule 2: Avoid Meaningless Pronouns (also Known as Expletives)

Pronouns without antecedents are also called *expletives*. The most common expletives are probably *it* and *there*, although other pronouns can also be expletives. For example, we often use *they* as a meaningless pronoun, as in "*they* say the grass is always greener on the other side." Examples (the italicized pronouns don't refer to an antecedent at all):

- He said that *it* is very important to listen carefully.
- *They* claimed that *there* was nothing wrong with the book.
- *It* is essential to our project to have you on the committee.

Notice the difference in the following examples, which have been rewritten without expletives.

- He said that listening carefully is very important.
- The critics claimed that nothing was wrong with the book.
- Having you on the committee is essential to our project.

Rule 3: Be Certain That Pronouns Agree with Their Antecedents in Number, Person, and Gender   Pronoun *agreement* refers to consistency between the pronoun and its antecedent in these areas:

- Number (singular or plural)
- Person (first, second, or third person)
- Gender (male, female, or neutral)

In addition, *relative* pronouns must agree with their antecedents in one other way: *human* or *person* pronouns must be used to refer to people, and *non-person* or *thing* pronouns must be used to refer to things other than people.

Check for agreement in number.   Certain words must always be referred to by singular or plural pronouns, as in the following examples:

- *Everybody* is invited to choose *his* or *her* own research topic. (singular)
- *Some* of the managers are being asked to bring *their* departmental reports to the meeting. (plural)
- *Much* of the work is finished, but *it* is in draft form. (singular)
- The *company* is selling *its* old equipment to interested employees. (singular)
- As the *workers* punched in, *they* learned about the strike plans. (plural)

The most common problem with pronoun–antecedent agreement in number is the use of *they* or *their* to refer to a singular pronoun. Examples of misuse: "*Everybody* is invited to choose *their* own research topic" or "The *company* is selling *their* old equipment."

Check for agreement in person (viewpoint).   Message receivers can be confused by illogical shifts within a sentence from one viewpoint (person) to another. Example: The following sentence begins in second person (referring directly to the reader) and then shifts to third person (referring to someone other than either the sender or the receiver):

- When *you* choose a long-distance telephone company, *one* should consider the company's billing practices.

Check for agreement in gender.   The most obvious gender-agreement error would be to refer to a man as "she" or to a woman as "he." But few people make such obvious errors. The more subtle gender-agreement errors have to do with using all masculine pronouns (*he, him, his*) or all feminine pronouns (*she, her*) to refer to antecedents such as *managers, secretaries, workers, one,* and so on—antecedents that are *neutral* in terms of gender.

Rule 4: Use *Who* to Refer to People, *That* to Introduce *Essential* Clauses, and *Which* to Introduce *Nonessential* Clauses   Pronouns and antecedents should agree in the proper use of the relative pronouns to:

- Refer either to persons or to things
- Introduce either essential or nonessential clauses (although not strictly an *agreement* problem)

The principles governing the use of relative pronouns are summarized as follows:

1. *Who, whom,* and *whose* refer to humans (although *whose* is also used to refer to things other than humans) and can introduce either essential or nonessential clauses.

2. *That* refers to things other than humans and is used to introduce *essential* clauses.
3. *Which* refers to things other than humans and is used to introduce *nonessential* clauses.

Examples: Instead of saying "The police officer *that* made the arrest," say "The police officer *who* made the arrest." Instead of saying "The company *who* bought the materials," say "The company *that* bought the materials."

The key to choosing between *that* and *which* is knowing whether the clause to be introduced is *essential* or *nonessential: Essential clauses* limit—or more narrowly define—the meaning of the antecedent and are necessary to the meaning of the sentence. Examples of essential clauses:

- The car *that I bought yesterday* is missing. (the receiver needs to know *which* car)
- The lake *that* we visited last year is now severely polluted. (identifies *which* lake is polluted)
- The teacher *who* wrote the textbook is Mr. Allen. (identifies *which* teacher)

Nonessential clauses give additional or supplementary information about the antecedent and could be removed from the sentence without changing the meaning of the sentence. Examples of nonessential clauses:

- My new car, *which I bought yesterday,* is missing. ("which I bought yesterday" could be eliminated from the sentence without changing the meaning of the sentence)
- Snowflake Lake, *which* we visited last year, is now severely polluted. (additional information only—is not needed to identify *which* Snowflake Lake)
- Our teacher, *who* wrote the textbook, is Mr. Allen. (additional information— "our teacher" is not identified or differentiated by "who wrote the textbook")

Common Pronoun Case Agreement Questions

Pronoun case tells the reader or listener whether the pronoun is naming:

- The *performer* or *subject* of an action (called *nominative* case)
- The *receiver* or *object* of an action (called *objective* case)
- The *owner* of something in the sentence (called *possessive* case)

Before studying the rules that help you to choose the correct form of a pronoun for particular sentences, take a minute to review Table A-1, which shows the various pronouns and their nominative, objective, and possessive forms. In reviewing Table A-1, remember these terms:

- *First person* refers to the person speaking.
- *Second person* refers to the person being spoken to by the first person.
- *Third person* refers to the person being spoken about by the first and second persons.
- *Singular* means that just one person is involved.
- *Plural* means that more than one person is involved.

Table A-1
Pronoun Forms

	Nominative (Names the Performer or Subject)	Objective (Names the Receiver or Object)	Possessive (Shows Ownership)
First person			
Singular			
	I	me	my
Plural			
	we	us	our
Second person			
Singular			
	you	you	your
Plural			
	you	you	your
Third person			
Singular			
	he	him	his
Singular			
	she	her	her
Plural			
	they	them	their
Third person/unknown			
Singular			
	who	whom	whose
Plural			
	who	whom	whose

(Continued)

Table A-1
Pronoun Forms

	Nominative (Names the Performer or Subject)	Objective (Names the Receiver or Object)	Possessive (Shows Ownership)
Third person/nonpersons			
Singular			
	it	it	its
Plural			
	they	them	their

Following the Rules

The following discussion explains the rules for the correct use of pronouns.

Rule 1: Use Nominative Pronouns (*I, we, you, he, she, they*, and *who*) to Complete the Meaning of Being Verbs (*is, am, was, were, be, been, are*)   The following are correct uses of nominative (naming) pronouns:

- This is *he*.
- The project chairmen are *they*.
- The accountant who made the mistake is *she*.
- *Who* did you say that man is? (In this sentence, the being verb comes at the end of the sentence, but it is still completed by the pronoun *who*.)

Rule 2: Use Nominative Pronouns as *Subjects* of Verbs   Examples of the correct use of nominative pronouns used as subjects:

- *He* and *I* are going to class. (*he* and *I* are subjects of the verb *are going*)
- *I* will give the assignment to *whoever* volunteers to work more hours this week. (*I* is the subject of the verb *will give*; *whoever* is the subject of the verb *volunteers*)

Rule 3: Use Objective Case to Name the Receiver of an Action (the *Object* of the Verb)   Examples of objective case pronoun use are:

- The manager agreed to show *us* the movie at no cost.
- Please introduce *him* to the group.
- I told *her* to be here at 8:00 this morning.

We can always locate the objective of the verb by saying the verb and then asking "who?" or "what?" Example: "Please introduce him to the group," we can read the verb *introduce* and ask "who?" The answer is "him"—so *him* is the object.

Rule 4: Use Objective Pronouns to Complete a Preposition (words such as *among*, *under*, *over*, *in*, *at*, *beneath*, *beside*, *between*, *around*, *toward*, *to*, *on*)   The following are examples of objective case pronouns:

- Send the book *to him* in the morning.
- The child stood *between him* and *her*.
- The secret must be kept *among us* workers.

Rule 5: To Use a Possessive *Pronoun*, Use the Possessive Form of the Pronoun—Don't Add an Apostrophe to the Pronoun   Possessive case pronouns show ownership such as this:

- The book had *its* cover torn off.
- Bob lost *his* report.
- Mary quit *her* job.

Important Note: A very common writing mistake is confusing *its* and *it's*. *It's* is never a possessive. *It's* (with the apostrophe) always means the contraction form of *it is*.

Rule 6: To Use a Possessive *Noun*, Add an Apostrophe and Sometimes an *s* to the Noun   If the noun ends in *s*, add just an apostrophe:

- The *boys'* bicycles were locked in the bicycle rack.

If the noun ends in *s* but the possessive form of the noun is pronounced with an extra *s* sound, add an apostrophe and an *s*:

- This is *Chris's* book.

If the noun does *not* end in *s*, add an apostrophe and an *s*:

- The *boy's* puppy was a Christmas gift.
- This is *Mary's* book.
- The *children's* department is on the fourth floor.

Rule 7: To Use the Possessive Form of a *Plural Noun*, Make the Noun Plural and Add the Apostrophe as with Singulars   First make the singular form of the noun into the plural form:

- *boy* is changed to *boys*
- *man* is changed to *men*
- *woman* is changed to *women*
- *Jones* is changed to *Joneses*

Then treat the plural noun as you would any other noun: If it ends in *s*, add just the apostrophe; if it does not end in *s*, add an apostrophe and an *s*:

- The *boys'* toys were shared between themselves.
- The *men's* jackets were left in the front room.
- We walked through the *women's* department.
- This is the *Joneses'* car.

Rule 8: When Objects Are *Separately* Owned by Two or More Owners, State the Name of *Each Owner*   Examples of this rule:

- These are Paul's and Ramon's books. (Paul owns some of the books, and Ramon owns some of them.)
- These are Bob's and her reports. (Bob owns some of the reports, and she owns some of the reports.)

Rule 9: When One or More Objects Are *Jointly* Owned, Use the Possessive on Only the Last Owner Named   Examples of this rule:

- These are Paul and Ramon's books. (Because only *Ramon* is possessive, we know that Paul and Ramon *share* ownership of the books.)
- Let's go to Grandma and Grandpa's house. (The possessive is formed only on *Grandpa,* so we know that Grandma and Grandpa *share* ownership of the house.)

Rule 10: Use Possessive Nouns and Pronouns as Subjects of *Gerunds* (Gerunds are *-ing* Words That Act as *Subjects* or *Objects* in a Sentence)   Examples of this rule:

- *His* coming to class late was very disruptive. (*He* or *him* was not disruptive—his *coming late* was disruptive.)
- I can understand *your* wanting the job. (I'm not saying I understand "you"—I understand your *wanting.*)

Some Tricky Situations in Correct Pronoun Case

Here are a few special pronoun usage situations, cases in which we can't always "hear" the correct way to use pronouns:

Using Pronouns After Being Verbs   Being verbs like *is, was,* and *are* can be seen as "equals" signs (=). Thus, saying:

- The company president is he.

means the same thing as saying:

- The company president = he.

Likewise, we should be able to reverse the parts of a sentence that appear on both sides of a being verb and not change the meaning or correctness of the sentence. Example:

- The company president is (=) he.

can be reversed without any problems:

- He is (=) the company president.

If you mistakenly use nominative pronouns after being verbs, the sentence may sound like this:

■ The company president is (=) him.

This would sound strange when reversed to

■ Him is (=) the company president.

So whenever you see a being verb that is completed by a pronoun (that usually means that the pronoun comes right after the being verb), write an equals sign above the being verb:

$$=$$

■ The keynote speaker was her.

Then read the sentence parts backward:

$$=$$

■ Her was the keynote speaker.

If the sentence sounds right, the pronoun is correct. If it doesn't, change the pronoun:

$$=$$

■ She was the keynote speaker

$$=$$

■ The keynote speaker was she.

Getting *Who* and *Whom* Choices Correct   For some reason, we often can't "hear" whether *who* or *whom* should be used in most situations. We can hear *he* and *him* and *I* and *me* and *they* and *them* quite easily, but *who* and *whom* are difficult. To solve the problem, rearrange a *who/whom* sentence and replace the *who* or *whom* with one of those words we *can* hear—*he/him, they/them, I/me.*

If we choose a word with an <u>m</u> in it (*hi<u>m</u>, the<u>m</u>, <u>m</u>e*), we know that *who<u>m</u>* is correct. If we choose a word without an <u>m</u> (*he, they, I*), we know that *who* is correct.

Here are the steps to this trick that we call the "M&M Rule" (because the <u>m</u> in the words we *can* hear tells us whether *who* or *who<u>m</u>* is correct):

1. Delete the part of the sentence that comes before the who or whom:
   ■ whoever/whomever asks for a copy of it.
2. Replace the *who/whom* or the *whoever/whomever* with *he or him*, with *they or them*, or with *I or me:*
   ■ . . . *he* asks for a copy of it.
3. Read the part of the sentence that you haven't deleted (sometimes you'll have to rearrange it a bit before it makes sense as a sentence) and see whether an <u>m</u> word or a non-<u>m</u> word sounds right. If an <u>m</u> word sounds right, use *whom* in your original sentence. If a non-<u>m</u> word sounds right, use *who* in your original sentence. For example, because:

   ■ . . . *he* asks for a copy of it.

Sounds good to us, we know our original sentence should say:

- Send the report to *whoever* asks for a copy of it.

Using pronouns joined with *and* correctly.   Correct case of a pronoun joined to another pronoun or to a noun is often difficult to hear, as in this sentence:

- Ted and *me* are going to the meeting.

The simple solution to this problem is to *separate the words that are joined with* and. Then read the two words alone in separate sentences:

- Ted and me are going . . .

Becomes:

- Ted is going . . .
- *Me* is going . . . (should be *I* am going. . .)

Therefore, the sentence should say:

- Ted and *I* are going to the meeting.

Our ears will tell us whether the pronoun has been used correctly.

Active and Passive Voice

Subjects that are *doing* are called active subjects—the subject and its verb are said to be in active voice. Subjects that are being *done unto* by others or are receiving the action are called passive subjects—the subject and its verb are said to be in passive voice. Examples of active voice:

- East Coast Services conducted the opinion poll to determine the public's views toward the upcoming election.
- The volunteers assigned to the project tabulated the survey results.

Examples of passive voice:

- The opinion poll was conducted by East Coast Services to determine the public's view toward the upcoming election.
- The survey results were tabulated by the volunteers assigned to the project.

Choosing Between Active and Passive

As we recommend in Chapter 2, minimize the use of passive voice in most business communication. This is because passive voice is usually:

- More wordy than active voice, because passive voice requires that a being verb be used with the verb itself.

- Less "lively" or vivid than active voice, because the subject of the sentence is not really doing anything.
- Less direct and sometimes less easily understandable than active voice.

Passive voice can be useful, however:

- When the performer of the action is unknown. *Example:* The report was lost yesterday.
- When the performer of the action is unimportant to the writer's message. *Example:* The scanner was repaired quickly.
- When you want to emphasize the receiver of the action instead of the performer of the action. *Example:* Jamie was fired immediately.
- When you want to be diplomatic and to avoid "pointing the guilty finger" at the performer. *Example:* If the sales receipt had been returned with the merchandise, a refund could have been made.

Conversely, active voice places the *performer* of the action in the subject position in the sentence and, thus, emphasizes the performer while deemphasizing the receiver of the action. *Example:* Terrance gave the customer a full refund.

Maintaining Voice Consistency

A sentence should not shift from one voice to another. And, when possible, entire paragraphs will usually read better if they contain sentences that are alike in voice. Examples of unnecessary changes in voice:

- When the meeting was adjourned (passive), the employee breathed a great sigh of relief (active).
- If the file has been misplaced by Wendy (passive), Chad will go to the main office for another copy (active).

Examples of all active voice:

- When the chairman adjourned the meeting, the employee breathed a great sigh of relief.
- If Wendy has misplaced a file, Chad will go to the main office for another copy.

Prepositions and Connectives: Putting Ideas Together

Prepositions and other connectives are the signals we use to show how parts of a sentence link together. *Connectives* in a sentence show whether we are stopping our discussion of one thought, turning to a new thought, or repeating or emphasizing thoughts we have already discussed. Connectives include *prepositions* (words such as *in, by, to, among,* and *between*); *conjunctions* (joining words) such as *and, but, so,* and *because; relative pronouns,* including *that, whether, whichever, whatever, whoever, who, whom,* and *which;* and *relative adverbs* such as *where, when,* and *while.*

Words, phrases, and clauses in a sentence can be joined:

- To show that one idea continues or adds to the thought expressed in another part of the sentence. *Example:* I learned the material, *and* I did well on the test.

- To show that one idea presents a new or separate thought from what is presented in another part of that sentence. *Example:* I learned the material *by* attending class and *by* taking notes in class.
- To show that one idea is really a subpart of another part of the sentence: *Example:* I learned the material *by* attending class and taking notes.

Maintaining Parallelism

Effective use of connectives often centers on making sure that connected ideas or sentence parts are parallel. *Parallelism* is often a matter of simple consistency. More exactly, though, parallelism is defined this way: *Equal grammatical structure* for items that are of *equal rank or importance.*

Example of a sentence lacking parallelism: "Please send $10 *to* Alex and me."

Example of a sentence with parallelism: "Please send $10 *to* Alex and *to* me."

In "send $10 *to* Alex and *to* me," *Alex* and *me* are treated as separate, equally important parts of the sentence. That is, they are expressed as *parallel* items in the sentence because they have the same grammatical structure—"*to* Alex and *to* me." This second example also clarifies the ambiguity of the first example in which it is unclear as to whether we *each* get $10 or just $10 to share. In the second example, we clearly each get $10.

Following the Rules

The following rules will guide you in the use of prepositions and other connectives.

Rule 1: Use Simple Prepositions Instead of Wordy Prepositional Phrases

The wordy prepositional phrases in the left-hand column of the following listing can usually be replaced by the simple prepositions shown in the right-hand column.

Wordy Prepositional Phrase	Simple Preposition
inasmuch as	because, since
for the purpose of	to
in the event that	if
in order to	to
prior to	before
subsequent to	after
in regard to	about

In the following sentences, notice the improvement in sentence readability that is brought about by the user of a simple preposition in place of a wordy prepositional phrase:

Wordy Prepositional Phrase	Simple Preposition
Inasmuch as we were late for the meeting, we missed the new product announcement.	*Because* we were late for the meeting. . .

In the event that he attends the meeting, ask him for a copy of the report.	*If* he attends the meeting. . .
Subsequent to receiving your request for information *with regard* to the new store, we called the New Haven office.	*After* receiving your request for information *about* the new store. . .

Make a conscious effort to improve the "receiver friendliness" of your writing and speaking by eliminating wordy prepositional phrases whenever possible.

Rule 2: Use a Preposition at the End of a Sentence If the Preposition Sounds Natural and Is Needed

Many an English teacher has taught that ending a sentence with a preposition is a situation "up with which we cannot put." But the fact is that when you force yourself to avoid ending a sentence with a preposition, you are often left with an awkward and unnatural-sounding sentence. On the other hand, some prepositions are not needed at the end of a sentence and can be omitted. Examples: "Where are you *at?*" or "I will type that *up.*" In deciding whether to end a sentence with a preposition, you should consider two important questions:

1. Does ending the sentence with a preposition sound natural—would rewriting the sentence to avoid ending it with a preposition make the sentence sound awkward or artificial?
2. Is the preposition necessary, or can the preposition be omitted without any loss of meaning? Examples: Where are you? I will type that.

Rule 3: Omit Unneeded Prepositions

People often use unnecessary prepositions. Eliminating the italicized pronouns in the following examples does not change the meaning of the sentence.

- Let's try *out* the new procedure.
- Where did you sit *at* when you saw the concert?
- Add *up* the sales figures.
- Let's start *in on* the report in the morning.

Rule 4: Include All Needed Prepositions

Two kinds of sentence structures require prepositions that we often leave out: sentences with connected parallel elements (elements of equal importance) and sentences that include split constructions.

Connecting parallel elements. As we mentioned earlier, because you should treat elements of equal rank or importance with equal grammatical structure, be sure to repeat the preposition before the second of two connected elements. For example,

- We told the job applicants *to* submit a completed application form and *to* call next week for an interview time. (Two elements of equal importance—"to submit" and "to call"—are separate actions.)
- The students prepared for the test *by* studying the textbook and *by* taking careful notes in class. (Two elements of equal importance—"studying the textbook" and "taking notes"—are separate actions.)

If two connected elements are *not* of equal rank, do not repeat the preposition before the second element. Examples:

- We told the job applicants *to* call next week and set an interview time with us. (Two elements but not of equal importance—"call and set an interview time" is essentially *one* action.)
- The students prepared for the test *by* attending class and taking notes. (two elements but not of equal importance—"attending class and taking notes" is essentially *one* action.)

Completing split constructions.   When you use two words that are completed by different prepositions in one sentence, be sure to include *both* prepositions:

- She was interested *in* and prepared *for* the new job in the accounting department.
- The mayor was involved *with* and committed *to* the conservation program.
- The students were active *in* and impressed *by* the social club's activities.
- I was aware *of* but not excited *about* the proposal to build a new school.

Rule 5: Use Connective Pairs to Show Parallelism   Some conjunctions work in pairs to connect elements and to show the relationships between the elements. These pairs are called connective pairs. Some connective pairs are:

- either–or
- neither–nor
- not–but
- both–and
- not only–but also

To use connective pairs correctly, follow these two guidelines:

1. Don't mix the first half of one pair with the second half of another pair. *Either* must be used with *or*—it cannot be used with *nor*. Likewise, *not only* must be used with *but also*—it cannot be used with *but*.
2. Use the same parts of speech after each half of a pair. If *both* is followed by a phrase, *and* must also be followed by a phrase. If *neither* is followed by a noun, *nor* must also be followed by a noun.

The following sentences show the correct parallel use of connective pairs:

- I said I would *either* go home *or* go to the office. (*either* verb *or* verb)
- *Neither* money *nor* fame could tempt him to sign the letter. (*neither* noun *nor* noun)
- The runner *not only* won the race *but also* broke the school record. (*not only* verb *but also* verb)
- We decided *not* to send a letter *but* to make a phone call instead. (*not* infinitive *but* infinitive)

Repeating the verb after each half of the connective pair will achieve greater emphasis. *Example:* "He *not only runs* fast *but also jumps* high."

Rule 6: Use Conjunctive Adverbs to Show Relationships Between Complete Thoughts   We use conjunctive adverbs to join two complete thoughts (two independent clauses or two separate sentences) and to show the relationship between them. Conjunctive adverbs include words such as *therefore, however,* *accordingly, consequently, nonetheless, moreover, furthermore, nevertheless, besides,* and *still.* In addition, phrases such as *on the contrary, on the other hand, in addition, for example,* and *at the same time* can be used to connect complete thoughts in the same way a conjunctive adverb is used.

Because a conjunctive adverb introduces a complete thought, it is followed by a comma. And because conjunctive adverbs have less "connecting power" than do conjunctions such as *and* and *but,* they must be preceded by either a period or a semicolon. *Examples:* "We tried to finish the project before 5 o'clock; *however,* we were unable to complete it." Or "The jail was built to hold only five prisoners. *Nevertheless,* it often holds as many as ten prisoners."

Rule 7: Repeat Relative Pronouns to Connect Parallel Clauses   Relative

pronouns such as *which, who,* and *that* can be used effectively to show parallelism between dependent clauses in a sentence. Just as we repeat a preposition such as *to* or *by* before the second of two connected elements to show parallelism, we repeat the relative pronoun before each clause in a list of parallel clauses. Examples:

■ The weather forecaster said *that* it will rain today but *that* it will snow tomorrow evening.
■ The laptop computer *that* was placed in Room 458 and *that* was stolen after only a week has been returned.
■ Hideo Tada, *who* attended school here for a year and *who* wrote this report for us, is now living in Tokyo.
■ We wanted to hire a secretary *whom* we could depend on and *whom* customers would feel comfortable working with.

Rule 8: Use the Connectives *Where* to Indicate Place, *When* to Indicate Time, and *While* to Indicate Duration   Commonly misused connectives are

where, when, and *while.* Here are some guidelines to help you use these connectives correctly:

Using *where*.   Use *where* to refer to a *place* or *location.* Do not use *where* to give a definition, as in "Communication is *where* encoding and decoding take place successfully." Instead, say something such as "Communication is the successful encoding and decoding of a message."

Where is used correctly to refer to a place or a location in the following sentences:

■ The New York Stock Exchange is *where* stock shares are bought and sold.
■ Las Vegas is *where* the largest gambling casinos in the world are located.
■ Southern Arizona is the only place *where* these early Native American ruins are found in such good condition.

Using *when*.   Use *when* to refer to a period of *time.* Do not use *when* to give a definition. Instead of saying "Free enterprise is *when* businesses are free to buy and sell in an unregulated market," say something such as "Free enterprise is the unregulated market in which businesses are free to buy and sell."

When is used correctly to refer to a period of time in these sentences:

■ This is the year *when* we are going to achieve our $10 million sales goal.
■ *When* he arrives with the pizza, pay him with cash from my desk.

Using *while*. Use *while* to indicate *duration of time.* Do not use *while* to indicate contrast or comparison; use words such as *although, but,* and *whereas* to show contrast or comparison. If you can replace *while* with a phrase such as *during the time that,* then *while* has been used correctly, as in these sentences:

■ *While* the speaker made his last remarks, I began distributing the study packet.
■ Alex operated the printing press *while* I stacked the printed copies on the paper cutter.

In the following sentences, *although, but,* and *whereas* have been used correctly instead of *while* to show contrast or comparison between two ideas:

■ *Although* (not *while*) I forgot to bring the graded papers to class, I did bring your new assignments.
■ I cleaned the windows in the office on Friday, *but* (not *while*) Bob cleaned the windows in the hallway on Saturday.

Modifiers: Saying It in Color with Adjectives and Adverbs

Adjectives and adverbs—the two kinds of modifiers or describing words—can be distinguished from each other by the kinds of things they describe. *Adjectives* describe *things,* and *adverbs* describe *action* or *other describing words.*

Using Adjectives

Adjectives are describing words that answer the questions "what kind of [thing]?" or "which [thing]?" Examples (the italicized words are adjectives):

> The *national* economy
> The *friendly* neighbor
> The *up-to-date* report

Not all adjectives are just one word. Notice the multiple-word adjectives in the following sentences:

■ The *half-done* report is on the desk.
■ He gave us a "*get-lost-before-I-get-mad*" look.
■ The man *who wanted the report* was referred to us.

Using Adverbs

Adverbs are words that describe verbs (action), or other describing words (generally adjectives, and other adverbs). Adverbs answer these questions: "Where?" "When?" "How?" "How much?" Examples (the italicized words are adverbs):

■ Do the job *quickly* (do the job *how?*)
■ It is good *enough* (*how* good?)
■ It was *very* expensive (*how* expensive?)
■ Read the letter *immediately* (*when?*)
■ Don't leave it *there* (*where?*)

Just as some adjectives are made from two or more words, many adverbs are *adverb phrases*. For example, in "he will work for an hour in the morning," the phrase "in the morning" answers the question "when?" And in "she works part-time for us," "part-time" answers the question "how?" or "how much?"

Following the Rules

The following are some key rules for using modifiers correctly.

Rule 1: Do Not Omit the —*ly* Ending from Adverbs

In conversation, many people drop the —*ly* ending from adverbs. For example, we incorrectly say things such as "I was sure lucky and "the work went real good" instead of "surely lucky" and "really well."

Especially in writing, the adverb form should be used to describe verbs and other describing words:

He *surely* is lucky to get the prize money.

I am *really* pleased to hear of your promotion.

I think you did *well* yesterday.

Rule 2: Keep Related Words Together

Adjectives should be placed next to the *things* they describe, and adverbs should be placed next to the *action* or the *other modifiers* they describe.

The most common problem with keeping related words together is the simple misplacement of an adjective—especially adjectives such as *only, just, about,* or *almost.* Examples of adjectives *not* placed next to the words they are meant to describe:

- I almost have enough money to start a new company.
- Please bring the speaker a cold glass of water.
- He only has $5 to spend at the store.

Notice how much more exact the sentences sound when the modifiers are placed close to the words they describe in these examples:

- I have almost enough money to start a new company.
- Please bring the speaker a glass of cold water.
- He has only $5 to spend at the store.

People often mistakenly place relative clauses too far from the words they are intended to describe. Remembering to keep related words together will help you to avoid mistakes such as these:

- The man is here *who quit.*
- The report is very good *that he wrote at home yesterday afternoon.*

These sentences would have a greater effect if they were rewritten like this:

- The man *who quit* is here.
- The report *that he wrote at home yesterday afternoon* is very good.

Rule 3: Avoid Dangling Modifiers   A *dangling modifier* is an adjective that does not refer clearly to a specific word or group of words in a sentence. In the following sentences, the adjective phrases dangle because they do not refer clearly to a particular word or group of words—or they are not next to the words they describe:

- *Having rotted in the cellar all winter,* my brother was unable to sell the apples.
- *To be sure the report would be delivered on time,* "URGENT" was written across the front of the envelope.

In the first sentence, the participle phrase *having rotted. . .* is supposed to describe *the apples,* but it is placed right in front of *my brother* instead. In the second sentence, the infinitive phrase *to be sure. . .* is supposed to describe *we* or *I* or someone else not named in the sentence, but it is placed in front of "URGENT" instead.

To correct these dangling modifiers, we could rewrite the sentences as shown here:

- Having rotted in the cellar all winter, *the apples* could not be sold by my brother.
- To be sure the report would be delivered on time, *we* wrote "URGENT" across the front of the envelope.

Rule 4: Avoid Overusing Modifiers   The use of too many modifiers detracts from the effect they are meant to have. Example:

- The lengthy, unorganized report describing last year's budgeted expenses in the personnel department was analyzed carefully and thoroughly by our very competent and willing auditors who work regularly in the accounting department.

The many modifiers make the sentence wordy and ineffective. Notice how the careful use of only two or three modifiers (and changing passive voice to active) makes the sentence much easier to read:

- The auditors carefully analyzed the personnel department's expense report for last year.

Rule 5: Use Comparative Modifiers to Compare Two Things and Superlative Modifiers to Compare More Than Two Things   We often use adjectives and adverbs to compare two or more things. When comparing only two things, the adjectives and adverbs should be *comparative* modifiers—modifiers used with words such as *more* and *less* and adjectives with *-er* added to them (such as *greater* and *smarter*). Examples:

- This half is *better* than that half.
- Of the two, John is the *smarter* student.
- Betty types *faster* than Elliott.
- Hal sells *more* than the rest of the team combined.

When more than two things are compared, the adjectives and adverbs should be *superlative* modifiers—modifiers used with words such as *most* and *least* and adjectives with *-est* added to them (such as *greatest* and *smartest*). For example:

- She is the *tallest* member of the team.

- He is the *smallest* quarterback to play in the NFL.
- She is the *most* qualified of all the applicants.

Rule 6: Make Complete, Logical Comparisons Incomplete comparisons often make the reader guess at what you are comparing. Examples:

- The Gilbreth diamond is far more beautiful—and costs less, too. (More beautiful that what?)
- You look much better today. (Better than when?)
- We have received more applications for technical positions this year. (Compared to another year or to nontechnical positions?)

Be sure that your comparisons are logical. That is, don't compare apples to oranges, as has been done in these sentences:

- My duties were much more difficult than my brother.
- The houses and shops I saw in Japan were just like any town in America.

The first sentence compares *my duties* to *my brother* and the second sentence compares houses and shops in Japan to *any town in America*. Restated to avoid the illogical comparisons, the sentences would say this:

- My duties were more difficult than *my brother's duties* were.
- The houses and shops I saw in Japan were just like *the houses and shops of any town in America*.

Rule 7: Use Hyphenated Compound Adjectives as Single Modifiers A *compound adjective* is a group of words that provides a single description of a noun that follows. Use hyphens between the words to make the words appear as a single unit. Thus, proper hyphenation of compound adjectives increases understanding and speeds the reader along. Notice the proper use of hyphens to form compound adjectives in the following sentences:

- The Small Business Administration approved a small-business loan for $2 million.
- He said that the large-appliance industry has been weakened by the recent economic depression.
- His "better-late-than-never" attitude kept him from hearing the opening remarks of many meetings.

Each compound adjective in these sentences provides a *single* description of the noun that follows it, regardless of whether the adjective has two, three, or more words in it.

The decision to place a hyphen between two words or to leave the hyphen out will often have a significant effect on the meaning of a sentence. Examples:

- We need more qualified workers. (We need what? Great numbers of qualified workers.)
- We need more-qualified workers. (We need what? Workers who are more qualified than the workers we have now.)
- The large appliance industry is suffering. (Which industry? The appliance industry, which is large.)
- The large-appliance industry is suffering. (Which industry? The industry that produces large appliances.)

Hyphenated compound adjectives are used only *before* nouns. When they come after nouns, they are not hyphenated:

- The up-to-date report was submitted on time. (comes before the noun)
- The report was up to date. (comes after the noun)
- It was a well-written report. (comes before the noun)
- The report was well written. (comes after the noun)

Rule 8: Never Hyphenate After an-*ly* Adverb   Although hyphens are often used after adverbs, as in *a well-written report,* they are never used after-*ly adverbs* such as *carefully* and *quickly.* Notice the absence of a hyphen after the-*ly* adverbs in the following sentences:

- He presented a *thoroughly* documented report to the city council members.
- The *easily* missed turnoff is just a mile from the main intersection.
- The *carelessly* typed report had to be returned to the word-processing center.

Rule 9: Separate Consecutive Adjectives with a Comma   As we mentioned earlier, if two or more adjectives provide *separate* descriptions of the noun or pronoun, they are called consecutive adjectives. Because they do not act as a single unit to provide just one description of the noun, they are not joined into a single unit with hyphens. Instead, they are separated with a comma. Examples:

- It was a clear, sunny day. (*two* descriptions of *day—clear* and *sunny*)
- He submitted a long, poorly written report. (*two* descriptions of *report—long* and *poorly written*)

As you learned earlier, an easy way to decide whether you should put a comma between two adjectives is to separate the adjectives with the word *and.* If the word *and* makes sense—and sounds right to you—put a comma between the adjectives. Of course, you can leave the *and* between them if you want; in that case, you should leave the comma out. Notice how we've used this trick to decide whether to put a comma between the adjectives in the following phrases:

- The new (,?) inexpensive information appliance. . .

"New *and* inexpensive information appliance" sounds right, so we should put a comma between *new* and *inexpensive:*
>The new, inexpensive information appliance. . .

- His adjusted gross income. . .

"Adjusted *and* gross income" does not sound right, so we should *not* put a comma between *adjusted* and *gross.*

As we said at the beginning of this reference tool, the grammar and usage issues covered here are certainly not exhaustive but, rather, focus on commonly experienced questions. Always consult a style guide or dictionary if in doubt about grammar or usage, especially when preparing written documents or text for visuals.

Note

[1]The authors express appreciation to Ray L. Young of Brigham Young University for his extensive help in developing this reference tool.

Researching Your Topic and Documenting Your Findings

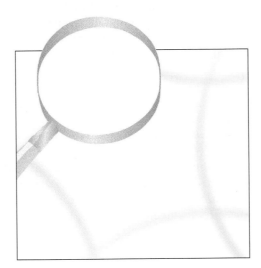

The world of business research has changed dramatically in the past decade with the widespread availability of the Internet. In the past, research often meant long hours sifting through endless documents in a library. Today, you can find answers to a huge array of questions by searching the Web.

This reference tool overviews some ways of gathering information for use in your messages and shows how to document those findings.

Primary and Secondary Research

Gathering information for business messages requires either *primary* or *secondary* research. Primary research involves gathering data that are not already available. Examples of such specific information are data about how well your company's customers like you, facts about how your products are used or how well they hold up, information about how vendors display what you sell, and many other kinds of information. You can't go to a published source to find these kind of data. Primary research information is generally gathered via such approaches as structured observations (e.g., watching the way customers use your product), surveys and interviews (either written or via telephone), or experiments (e.g., the famous taste tests to see what cola people like better). Gathering information in these ways can be expensive but is sometimes necessary.

Student research and most business issues will more often use what is called *secondary research.* You are doing secondary research when you search publications or documents (either printed matter or electronic documents) for information you need. Online files, books, magazines, newspapers, pamphlets, government documents, atlases, and encyclopedias are all examples of secondary sources. The use of secondary research techniques allows writers and speakers to save time and dollars by avoiding unnecessary duplication. You need not "reinvent the wheel" when someone else has already gathered the information you need.

Because most business communication uses secondary sources or information already gathered by individual companies, this reference tool will not go into techniques for gathering primary research. If your message requires primary research, we recommend reading a book on research design. One easy-to-use and inexpensive book is Paul R. Timm and Rick C. Farr's *Business Research: An Informal Guide* (Menlo Park, CA: Crisp Publications, Inc., 1994).

Use the Internet for Secondary Research

Never in history has so much information been so readily available to so many people. The Internet truly has revolutionized data collecting and should be your starting point for gathering information about virtually any topic. When you find the information you want, you need to document it—that is, let your receiver know where it came from.

How to Find the Right Search Engines

A *search engine* is an electronic system for sorting through and selecting information relevant to the topic or question presented. New search engines come online regularly and the techniques they use get increasingly sophisticated. Because of the constantly evolving nature of the Internet, take our recommendations about where to search as simply starting points. New sources become available every day.

Many magazines publish feature stories (or complete issues) on favorite Web sites. For business topics, we recommend you look at *Forbes, Fortune, Business Week, Fast Company,* and *The Wall Street Journal* for starters. Get in the habit of bookmarking sites that seem particularly useful to you. (Your Internet service provider will have ways of saving, or bookmarking, these for your individual use. Once bookmarked, you can go back to a Web site without having to type in the electronic address.) Many people find it useful to set their home page to a search engine site such as InfoSeek, AltaVista, Yahoo!, Excite, Google, or DogPile. These are only a few of the hundreds of search engines out there.

For business research, we recommend that you check out www.CEO Express.com. This site provides instant links to hundreds of other business-related Web sites providing a wide range of data. Developed to organize the best resources on the Web for busy businesspeople, CEOExpress.com registers over 1.7 million visits per month. The site provider recognizes that businesspeople have precious little time to obtain all the information they require to conduct business. CEOExpress.com takes information that executives need and pares it down to the 20 percent that is most critical and useful. That information is delivered to users in a clear, easy-to-use format.

Again, we stress that the Internet is constantly changing and new and better search engines as well as new sites are constantly coming online. For up-to-date information about search engine features and performance see www.Search Engines.com. Take some time to discover which sources will provide the kinds of information you most frequently need.

How to Write Citations for Online Materials

When you use secondary research sources, you must cite where the information came from. Failing to do so would constitute plagiarism—the illegal and unethical use of another's information without giving them credit for it. Citing is done with footnotes or endnotes. The difference between these is where they are placed in a document. Footnotes are at the bottom (the "foot") of the same page where the reference is. Endnotes are presented at the end of the document or chapter. Both types of notes are numbered in the order in which they appear in the document.

Be aware that notes are often, but not always, just a citation of sources. Some footnotes or endnotes may offer comments or give the reader additional information that is not important enough to put in the main document, but which may be of further interest. Example:

> [1]*Thompson does not agree with Simpson's pessimistic view, but he is equally cautious in his recommendations.*

Different style guides recommend slightly different formats for citations. Some popular guides are the Chicago Manual of Style, the American Psychological Association (APA) style guide, and the Modern Language Association (MLA) guide. Which style you select is, in our opinion, less important than being consistent. For other style guidelines, search the Web or purchase a print version.

- For questions about using *The Chicago Manual of Style*, see
  http://www.press.uchicago.edu/Misc/Chicago/cmosfaq.html
- For a guide to writing research papers using the APA-style documentation, see
  http://webster.commnet.edu/apa/apa_index.htm

The citation guidelines that follow are recommended by the MLA and are widely accepted.

Citation Format for Online Magazine Articles   Citations for online magazine articles should include:

- Author (last name, first name)
- Title of article (in quotation marks)
- Name of magazine (underlined or in italics)
- Date of publication (day, month, year)
- Date you read it (day, month, year)

Examples:

- Harmon, Debbie. "The Little-Known Tricks of Online Searching." *MultiMedia Schools,* November–December 2000. 31 January 2001
  <http://www.infotoday.com/MMSchools/nov00/story.htm>.
- Scott, Cintra. "What Yahoo! Has to Do." *Smart Money,* January 2001. 11 January 2001
  <http://www.smartmoney.com/stockwatch/index.cfm?story=200101112>.

Citation Format for E-Mail Messages   Citations for e-mail messages should include:

- Author of the message (last name, first name)
- Author's e-mail address (username@host)
- Subject line of the message

- Date it was written (day, month, year)
- Kind of communication (personal e-mail)

Examples:

- Farr, Cynthia.
  cfarr@yahoo.com "Latest Spin on Profits." 4 September 2001. Personal e-mail.
- Peterson, Brent.
  bdpete@franklincovey.com "Recommendation letter" 11 January 2001. Personal e-mail.

Citation Format for Online Newspaper Articles   Citations for online newspaper articles should include:

- Author (last name, first name)
- Title of article (in quotation marks)
- Name of newspaper (e.g., "*New York Times* on the Web")
- Date of publication (day, month, year)
- Name of section (e.g., Business News, Local News, LifeStyles)
- Date you read it (day, month, year)
- Address/URL

Examples:

- Stevens, William K. "Winter demand for gas increases." *New York Times* on the Web 4 November 2001. Business News. 31 December 2001
  <http://www.nytimes.com/library/businessnews/week/110401weather.html>.
- Collison, Kevin. "Trouble at Roswell." *Buffalo News* on the Web 12 January 2001. Front page. 13 January 2001
  <http://www.buffalonews.com/>.

How to Write Citations for Print Materials

You need to cite printed materials used or referred to in your writing or visuals using an accepted format. The key information provided in such citations allows the reader of your message to go to the original source to verify what you have said or to gain additional information.

Citation Format for Magazines, Newspapers, and Journal Articles
Citations for magazines, newspapers, and journal articles should include:

- Author (last name, first name)
- Title of article (in quotation marks)
- Name of magazine (underlined or in italics)
- Date of publication (day, month, year)
- Page number(s)

Examples:

- Brady, Diane. "Service Stinks," *Business Week,* 23 October 2000, pp. 118–128.
- Sterne, Jim. "Creating Your Own Online Customer Service Checklist," *Customer Service Management,* September–October 2000, pp. 57–59.

Citation Format for Books   Citations for books should include:

- Author(s) (last name, first name)
- Title of the book (underlined or in italics)
- Place of publication
- Name of publisher
- Copyright date (year)
- Page number(s)

Examples:

- Bienvenu, Sherron. *The Presentation Skills Workshop* (New York: AMACOM, 2000), pp. 201–2.
- Jones, Christopher, Terry Hanson, and Aaron Briston. *The Neuropsychology of Loafing* (New Haven, CT: Concerned Press, Inc., 2002), p. 43.

How to Write Citations for Other Materials

Again, bear in mind the reason for documenting sources: Your reader (or listener) should be able to go back to the source you cite and verify or get additional information. When in doubt about the "correctness" of a citation, simply provide enough information for such verification.

Citation Format for Interviews   Citations for interviews should include:

- Whether the interview was conducted face-to-face or on the telephone
- Name of the person interviewed (and his or her position, if applicable)
- Location of the interview
- Date

Examples:

- Telephone interview with James B. Steadman, President, Campus Credit Union, Pittsburgh, Pennsylvania, October 3, 2001.
- Personal interview with Marion G. Rooney, Dean of Students, Columbia Western College, Portland, Oregon, January 14, 2002.

Citation Format for Classes or Lectures   Citations for classes or lectures should include:

- Circumstances
- Name of source
- Name of course (if appropriate)
- Location
- Date

Examples:

- Executive lecture series, Professor Pete Clarke, Bannion College, January 23, 2002.
- Class lecture, Business Management 201, University of Iowa, Professor Danielle Meier, March 2, 2001.

Citation Format for Unpublished Documents   Citations for unpublished documents should include:

- Name of document's writer
- Title (if available)
- An indication that it is "unpublished"
- Organization name (if relevant and available)
- A date (if available)

Example:

- Rassney, Michael. "April Sales Results Summary." Unpublished report. ABC Corporation, Jacksonville Branch, May 2, 2001.

Why Go to All This Trouble?

As we have said, correct documentation enables your message receivers to get additional information. They can go to correctly cited references to validate or enlarge on the ideas presented. But two other reasons for documenting data are also important:

- **Doing so strengthens your credibility.** Good information from reputable sources helps convince your message receivers that what you say is logical and sound. This, of course, assumes that you use high-quality sources. (Be aware that much information—especially that found on the Internet—can be biased or unfounded opinions. Look for information from credible organizations or respected experts.)
- **Doing so protects you against charges of plagiarism.** It is unethical and illegal to use substantial amounts of other people's information without citing the source and, in commercial cases, without getting written permission.

Recognizing Gender Differences in Workplace Communication

Scientists, cultural anthropologists, social psychologists, and other researchers agree that the perceptions and realities of men and women constitute separate cultural awarenesses. When these different cultural awarenesses manifest themselves in workplace communication, we find two resulting behaviors:

1. Men and women communicate *differently.*
2. Men and women communicate the *same* way but are *perceived differently* by audiences of both genders.[1]

As you read this reference tool, note that we have based our application of the Strategic Communication Model on American men and women with roots in European cultures, which is where researchers have focused most of their work. However, much of the information is applicable to individuals with roots in African, Latino, and Asian cultures, as well. Also keep in mind that *everything* we say is based on *tendencies* of men and women as cultural groups. Individuals may exhibit *any combination of* male or female behaviors. In addition, many successful professionals have adopted situation-specific communication behaviors that we normally attribute to the opposite gender. We have designed suggestions and options for guidance rather than as absolute, definitive solutions.

Define the Context

As you now know, the context of your communication includes the existing situation, the target audiences, and your objectives with those audiences (Step 1 of the Strategic Communication Model). Your thorough understanding of all three always begins your communication process, regardless of the cultural background of your audience. However, the unique differences of your male and/or female target audience may determine how you analyze your situation and your objectives, so we will begin the application of the Strategic Communication Model with audience analysis.

Define Your Audience

Individual traits and behaviors vary greatly. As you identify your potential audiences and learn specific details about them, use the Context Analysis Worksheet (found in Chapter 4) to facilitate a thorough examination of each to help avoid making assumptions and the resulting miscommunications.

Identify Your Three Potential Audiences: Primary, Hidden, and Decision Makers   As we explained in Chapters 1 and 4, these audiences can overlap, and there may be no hidden audience at all. After you identify your audiences, investigate and learn about them. Be very careful to look beyond the obvious as you focus on facts, attitudes, wants, and concerns.

Facts. Researchers have identified hundreds of facts about potential differences between the male and female individuals who may comprise your multiple audiences. We are focusing on the information that impacts communication. Remember that this information is based on countless studies of the tendencies of men and women as groups. These are not absolutes, and every man or woman you know may not display these behaviors and characteristics. You might choose to add "probably" or "is likely to" in your head as your read.
   If your receiver is a *man:*

- He has been socialized to perform aggressively and to boast of his successes.
- His childhood games taught him that competition is fun and winning is good. He continues to be motivated by competition.
- He views conflict as impersonal, a necessary part of working relationships.
- He has traditionally been afforded attention-getting roles, as reflected in his interest in personal benefit and use of the word *I.*
- He is impressed by power, ability, and achievement.
- His left-brain orientation yields problem-solving skills that are logical, analytical, factual, and hierarchical.
- He focuses on one thing at a time.
- His friendships are built on mutual activities and goals. He builds trust on the basis of actions and accomplishments.
- He may only hear your literal words and miss your underlying emotion. He may not express his true feelings through facial expressions.
- His communication style tends to be direct.
- When he succeeds, he attributes it to his ability. When he fails, he attributes the failure to outside circumstances, or he blames someone else.

If your receiver is a *woman:*

- She has been socialized to work cooperatively and to be modest about her successes.
- Her childhood games taught her to compromise and collaborate, and she continues to be motivated by affiliation. She competes primarily with herself (that is, with her own expectations of what she should be able to accomplish).
- She takes conflict personally. (Note: Women with roots in East-European Jewish, Italian, and Greek cultures, however, tend to view conflict as a positive function of a close relationship.)
- She has traditionally been afforded attention-giving roles, as reflected in her interest in the wider needs of the corporate community and use of the word *we.*
- She is impressed by personal disclosure and professional courage.
- Her right-brain orientation yields problem-solving skills that are creative, sensitive, and nonhierarchical.
- She has the ability to focus on multiple projects simultaneously. She is probably accustomed to balancing the demands of work, family, home, school, and/or community issues and, thus, applies these skills to her job.
- Her friendships are based on personal closeness. She builds trust by sharing both secrets and herself.
- She is proficient at decoding your nonverbal meanings and displays her feelings through facial expression and/or body language.
- Her style will tend to be indirect, except with other women of equal rank.
- When she succeeds, she believes she was lucky. When she fails, she blames herself.

Attitudes. The gender of both the sender and the receiver affects your audience's attitudes about you, about your topic, and about their being there to receive your information. First, consider your receivers' attitudes about you. If you are communicating . . .

- Man to man, he may afford you instant credibility based on similarity.
- Man to either man or woman, you may start off with a higher perception of credibility than your female counterpart has, especially in terms of expertise, status, and power.
- Man to woman, she may expect that you will not really listen to her. She may also surmise that your idea or plan is based on your independent thinking and that it is an inflexible decision with little opportunity for compromise.
- Woman to woman, she may expect you to be friendly, nurturing, and concerned. She may afford you instant credibility based on similarity.
- Woman to either man or woman, you should expect to have to demonstrate better skills and more experience than your male counterpart does to be perceived as equal to him in credibility.
- Woman to man, there are two major issues to consider:
  1. He will expect you to be friendly and nurturing, even passive-dependent. Aggressive behavior and other deviation from his expectations can cause discomfort, confusion, and even negative responses.
  2. He may simply disregard you.

Men and women may have different initial reactions to and attitudes about your topic. Your female audience member's greater psychological resilience makes her more agreeable to change, which is, of course, an element in most persuasive messages. Your male receiver may only accept your message if he immediately perceives personal benefit.

Finally, men and women may respond differently to actually being your audience. That is, they may have different attitudes about being there to receive your memo, hear your presentation, or attend your meeting. Your male receiver is more likely to be an autocratic problem solver. He may resent interrupting his schedule to hear your message, unless the other audience members are hierarchically superior and, thus, inclusion is a compliment. He will assume that your presentation of a problem is a direct request for a solution. Your female receiver, often a team player who is motivated by acceptance and affiliation, is more likely to appreciate being included in your audience. She will respond to your presentation of a problem with support and reassurance, and she will offer to share experiences and jointly discuss the solution.

In analyzing attitudes, remember that your audience may prefer to be somewhere else, doing something else, with someone else. However, it is likely that the women to whom you write and speak will be more receptive to you, your topic, and being there than a male counterpart. Recognize that your audience might share these perceptions about you, your topic, and being there to receive your message. Plan strategies to establish a more accurate understanding of you and your intentions.

Wants. The next step in audience analysis involves your determination of what information your audience wants to know. Avoid confusing what they want to know with what you believe they "need to know." Until you tell them what they *want* to know, they may not be receptive to what they *need* to know.

A man is likely to want to know the benefit for himself and just what he has to do to win. He may be thinking, "What's in this for me?" and "What's the bottom line?" He will want to know how your plan will help him compete, both as an individual and as an organization. A woman is likely to want to know the benefit for the individuals in the organization and what she should do to facilitate the process. She may be thinking, "What will be the impact of this plan on the working relationships of the people involved?" She will want to know how your "winning" plan will allow her to provide a win-win situation for everyone, rather than a loss for someone else.

Concerns. Finally, your audience's fears—the consistent concerns that your male and female audience members express—exhibit a summary of gender differences. Again, a caveat: *Do not assume* that *every* man and woman will exhibit each gender-specific trait. In fact, many men and women have adopted situation-specific, successful behaviors of the opposite gender. You may expect, however, that a careful review of these traits will enhance the depth of your understanding about your audience and, therefore, increase the probability that you will select the appropriate persuasive information. Remember:

■ Men tend to be most concerned about *winning*. They will work as hard as necessary to win against their standard of comparison, which is usually other men. They fear defeat. They are interested in how the facts affect the bottom line.

■ Women tend to be most concerned with *relationships*. They work to do their best; their standard of comparison is their personal ideal of their abilities. They fear that their successes mean someone else's defeat. They are interested in how the process affects the organization as a whole.

Again, analyzing your audience may be the most important component of your entire communication process because every decision you make depends on your accuracy and detail at this point. Remember:

1. Identify your primary, hidden, and decision-making audiences.
2. Discover personal and professional facts, avoiding generalizations.
3. Be aware of their attitudes about you, your subject, and being there to receive your message.
4. Determine what they *want* to know over and above what they *need* to know.
5. Recognize consistent concerns.

Define Your Situation

The next part of defining context involves a close look at the problem that has created the need to communicate, the external environment in which that problem exists, and the corporate culture that influences the problem.

Identify and Limit the Problem   Isolate the decision that now requires you to communicate a message to a particular audience.

1. What is the distinct cause for the message you are preparing?
2. What are the specific parameters that reduce the situation to manageable proportions?

Both your gender and that of your audience can affect the definition of the problem. A man may define a problem in terms of outcome. A woman may define the same problem in terms of the people affected. Be certain that your definition of the problem is consistent with that of your male or female receiver and that you anticipate a mixed audience of both men and women.

Evaluate the External Climate   If your audience is male, they may tend to focus more on what is going on in the specific industry and in related industries than do female colleagues, who may focus more specifically on internal issues.

Evaluate the Corporate Culture That Impacts the Problem   A woman may be more sensitive to the nebulous attitudes and norms shared by members of an organization, even though men probably established those behaviors. Therefore, a female audience member will recognize if your plan or idea or even a potential employee's behavior is consistent with that of the corporate culture. Male audience members, while acutely recognizing the presence or absence of "fit," may not attribute the reason to the effects of corporate culture. In spite of their sensitivity to culture, however, women may not be as involved in office politics, which may reduce their comprehensive understanding of the *overall* culture.

Define Your Objectives

Most messages, no matter how simple or apparently insignificant, encompass three objectives: an overall goal, a specific purpose of the communication, and your hidden agenda. The overall goal, based on the mission statement of the organization, should be inherent in any corporate message and may appear to be an objective guideline. However, men may take the actual words of the mission statement literally, while women may broadly apply the intention and allow for a more liberal interpretation.

The specific purpose of the communication depends on your needs and on your analysis of the target audience. Also consider your own gender tendencies. Men tend to overestimate their potential for success, whereas women tend to underestimate it. As you assess your audience's level of knowledge about your topic, you may expect that your male audiences may allege more knowledge than they actually have, whereas your female audiences may be modest about their knowledge.

And finally, you have a hidden agenda, a personal objective to which you are aspiring. *Everybody* has one, including the members of your audience. Men's goals are likely to be competitive; women's goals may be affiliative. Men may even interrupt when they notice chances to offer information that fulfills their hidden agendas. Women may be more indirect and wait for an opening.

Choose Your Media and Timing Options

After evaluating your situation, audience, and objectives, you can explore the communication options available to you: how the message should be sent (medium) and when it should arrive (timing).

Define Which Medium Is Most Appropriate for Your Message

As you assess your options for how your message should be sent to your intended receiver, review Chapters 1 and 5. Base your choices on the wants and needs of your target audience rather than on your own. Table C-1 presents additional considerations.

Table C-1
Differences Between Male and Female Message Receivers

Male Receivers May:	Female Receivers May:
• Never hear a message circulating on the **grapevine**, particularly if there are women in this communication network.	• Receive your message from the **grapevine** quicker than you want her to, particularly if there are other women in the communication network. (Depending on the number of people who repeated the message on its way to her, what she hears may be distorted.)
• Expect to discuss important information in a casual **conversation**, especially if you are a man.	• Appreciate information received in informal **conversation**.
• Be defensive about being called to a formal **interview**, especially if you are a woman.	• Be intimidated by a formal **interview**, especially if she is a subordinate who is "summoned" to your office. She may expect that your purpose is negative, that is, that she has done something wrong.

Male Receivers May:

- Be annoyed by a **phone call** that interrupts him, particularly if the caller is a subordinate who does not make the benefit clear.

- Pay little attention in a **meeting** or **formal presentation,** unless he understands immediate personal benefit and recognizes that his superiors are included as well.

- Appreciate the technology involved in a **teleconference.**

- Not recognize the personal energy involved in a **personal note.**

- Prefer the brevity of a **memo** or **e-mail.**

- Appreciate a **letter** that he can read at a time of his own choosing.

- Read only the executive summary and selected sections of a **report.**

- Be impressed by your title on your **business card.**

Female Receivers May:

- Sound hesitant in response to your **phone call** that caught her off guard or unprepared.

- Appreciate being included in a problem-solving **meeting.** She may offer her attention and positive nonverbal feedback to your **formal presentation.** Do not overestimate her approval, however.

- Appear uncomfortable in a **teleconference** where nonverbal behaviors are altered by technology.

- Appreciate the thought and effort that went into a **personal note or a greeting card** that recognizes a special occasion.

- Feel short-changed by the brevity or terseness of a **memo** or **e-mail.**

- Try to read the hidden meaning in a **letter.**

- Be impressed by the detail you include in a **report.**

- Recognize the creative aspects of your **business card.**

Determine When the Message Should Arrive

Again, consider the needs of your audience in conjunction with your own communication objectives when deciding when the message should arrive. We too often communicate at our own convenience, which may not be consistent with the timing needs of our male or female audience.

Male receivers are more likely to be rigid about the deadline they have set for you, even though they may be more relaxed about their own deadlines. Female receivers are more likely to be considerate of your needs in adjusting a deadline, but they are probably very concerned about keeping theirs.

The complex messages that you send to multiple male and female audiences require analysis that includes information about gender and about the specific individuals involved. Review your Context Analysis Worksheet for all of your audiences when you consider the order of your messages and how much time there is between them.

Select and Organize Information

If you have done your homework to this point, you have defined the context (Step 1) and considered your options (Step 2). In other words, you understand your target audiences, your objectives with each of those audiences, the situation in which you are involved, and your choices in terms of media and timing. Select the appropriate information and the format will now fall into place more easily.

The organizational patterns in Chapters 3 and 6 are flexible, depending on your specific choices of material. Keep the following gender qualifiers in mind, however, when applying your information to these patterns.

Plan a Beginning, a Middle, and an End

For your male receivers:

- Emphasize *personal* benefit in the introduction.
- Be succinct with your introduction (but do not delete it!), so that you can quickly make your point.
- Reestablish personal benefit in the conclusion.

For your female receivers:

- Emphasize the benefits for her department or team in the introduction.
- State the organizational plan for your presentation and stick to it.
- Confirm a win-win situation in the conclusion.

Limit Your Information

Remember that most communication experts recommend no more than three main points. Then, for your male receivers:

- Be direct with your main points.
- Include issues concerning long-term impact on the organization's bottom line.

For your female receivers:

- Consider an indirect approach to your main points.
- Include issues concerning short-term impact on individuals and teams.

Enhance Your Message with Visual Aids, Numbers, and Examples

For your male receivers:

- Illustrate your points with numbers that impact the bottom line.
- Avoid personal disclosure to illustrate professional points, especially if you are a woman.
- Avoid attempting to impress your male audience with sports metaphors, especially if you don't fully understand them yourself.

For your female receivers:

- Employ personal anecdotes.
- Be careful about sports or war metaphors, especially if you are a man, unless you are certain that your audience will appreciate them.

Review Chapter 7 for more guidelines on creating visual aids.

Tailor Your Message for Each Individual Audience

Remember: These are guidelines, not absolutes! You can never assume that any individual is going to think or behave a certain way simply because of gender. However, allow this information to expand your thinking and broaden your considerations as you select the most appropriate and effective material for conveying each message to each audience.

Deliver Your Message (Oral or Written)

Now that you are armed with well-selected, well-organized, and well-supported information, you may confidently present that information by means of your chosen medium to your target audience.

Deliver Effective Oral Messages

Refer to the guidelines for speaking to individuals or groups in Chapters 3, 9, 10, and 11. Here are some additional suggestions based on both your gender and that of your audience. If you are a man speaking to men:

- Express your confidence through direct eye contact but do not expect them to reciprocate.
- Expect interruptions and appreciate them, since they indicate that your male audience is listening.
- Avoid being overenthusiastic about your topic.

If you are a man speaking to women:

- Warm up your facial muscles to enhance your ability to express yourself through facial expression.
- Make direct eye contact with each individual.
- Allow enough space for your female receivers to be comfortable. Watch for signs such as stepping away or sitting back in their seats that indicate you are too close.
- Encourage feedback during your presentation, since they may be hesitant to interrupt you.
- Develop and communicate a transition from their thought to yours, rather than ignoring their comments and just changing the subject.
- Show enthusiasm for your product or idea. Your female audience may interpret a relaxed style as uncaring.

If you are a woman speaking to men:

■ Warm up your voice to achieve the deepest, most well-projected sound that is possible for you. Your male audience will expect you to have excellent vocal skills.
■ Warm up your body so that you will be more comfortable using whatever space is available for you.
■ Express your confidence through direct eye contact. Do not look down or at the ceiling.
■ Avoid reading or even appearing to read, which reduces the perception of your confidence and, therefore, of your credibility.
■ Remove physical barriers that diminish your size, such as lecterns. Try to stand if your audience is sitting. If you must sit, try to use a seat that puts you at an equal or higher eye level than that of your male audience.
■ Employ natural, broad movements to convey confidence. Relax; a perception of nervousness will damage your credibility.
■ Avoid tag questions, that is, phrases attached to statements that change the statement to a question ("This is a great idea, don't you think?"). Your male receivers may perceive that you lack confidence about your statement.
■ Anticipate interruptions as normal male communication rather than personal attacks or even negative feedback.
■ Recognize that you may receive little if any active listening, such as smiles or head nodding. This does not mean they are not listening.
■ Control your energy and focus your enthusiasm. If you are too dramatic, your male audience may enjoy your performance but miss your message.

If you are a woman speaking to women:

■ Warm up your facial muscles so that the smile your female audience is expecting will look natural and so that you can freely express the emotional content of your message in your facial expression.
■ Reduce space barriers to a minimum by getting as close as you can to your large audience and by sitting on an equal level with an individual or small group.
■ Take advantage of your female audience's tendency to be able to read the true emotional context of your message by using your face, hands, and body to express yourself.
■ Understand that the active listening and nonverbal feedback you are likely to receive may be more polite than positive.
■ Express your enthusiasm sincerely and personally.

Finally, *be yourself*. Remember that most people are comfortable one-to-one but believe that they have to become someone different when they address a group. The preceding suggestions are designed to help you become more adaptable to multiple communication situations, not to change you into someone else.

Deliver Effective Written Messages

Consider these guidelines in addition to the ones in Chapters 2 and 8, based both on your gender and that of your audience:

If you are a man writing to a man, or a woman writing to a woman:

■ When writing to someone of your own gender, your task tends to be easy. Simply imagine yourself in a conversation and write accordingly.

If you are a man writing to a woman:

■ Temper a direct approach with polite buffers and qualifiers.

- Emphasize the positive points. Her cognitive filter may cause her to focus on your negative messages and miss your positive messages.
- Avoid exaggeration, particularly of your own accomplishments.
- Be careful with gender-specific metaphors, especially about war or sports.

If you are a woman writing to a man:

- Avoid qualifiers, disclaimers, fillers, and intensifiers, all of which reduce the impact of your message.
- Avoid excessive cushioning of negative information. His cognitive filter may cause him to focus on your positive messages and miss your negative messages.
- Curb your impulse to flaunt your vocabulary, especially if you perceive yours to be superior to his. He will not be impressed.
- Be careful with gender-specific metaphors, especially about homemaking, cooking, or childbirth.

Evaluate Feedback for Continued Success

The differences in the way men and women receive feedback tend to be so substantial and obvious that even cartoonists lampoon them. Differences regarding giving and receiving feedback center around the ways in which men and women:

- Listen
- Attribute success and failure
- Accept responsibility and blame
- Filter positive and negative information

Understand Listening Behavior

In general, a man who is actively listening is likely to look directly at the speaker without moving or speaking. A positive response from him indicates "yes," not just "I'm listening." When a woman listens, she usually offers an active response; that is, she nods her head or says "um-hum" to indicate her attention.

Understand Attribution of Success and Failure

When a man succeeds, he often believes it is because of his ability. When he fails, he may believe that the situation was simply beyond his control (that is, his assistant didn't prepare the correct report, the client wasn't ready to buy, or the deal wasn't meant to be). When a woman succeeds, she often believes that she was lucky, had an excellent support team, or was in the right place at the right time. When she fails, she may believe that she simply lacked ability.

Understand Accepting Responsibility and Blame

Men tend to have a difficult time understanding that assuming responsibility does not mean accepting blame. If a man does not disassociate responsibility and blame, he might refuse both. He additionally may allow the blame to fall on whoever is willing to accept it. A woman may be quick to say "I'm sorry," meaning that she regrets that something happened, not that she regrets she did it. However, she may find herself not only responsible, but at fault, by her own admission.

Understand Filtering Good and Bad News

Male defense mechanisms are usually better developed than those of women, which means that men tend to be better at shaping reality to their own advantage. As a result, men tend to focus on positive information and filter out the negative, which results in positive self-esteem but little improvement. Women, on the other hand, tend to focus on negative information and filter out the positive, which offers them greater potential for improvement but continues to challenge their self-esteem.

Apply the Guidelines for Soliciting and Evaluating Feedback

The following are some guidelines, in addition to those in Chapters 1 and 12, to facilitate your ability to solicit and evaluate feedback:

If you are a man *receiving* feedback:

- Avoid interrupting; this is your time to listen, not to talk.
- Write down negative comments with the same detail that you note positive comments.
- Ask for examples of negative comments, not just positive ones.
- Look for nonverbal messages along with literal ones.
- Avoid rejecting information with which you do not agree, recognizing that there is some truth in every perception.
- Accept responsibility. You are being held accountable, not being blamed.
- Plan some change in behavior as a result of this feedback.
- Express sincere appreciation for all the feedback, not just the *positive* part.
- Leave the evaluator with the perception that you understood all of the feedback, both positive and *negative*.

If you are a woman *receiving* feedback:

- Expect interruptions from the men to whom you are speaking.
- Write down positive comments with the same detail that you note negative comments.
- Ask for positive comments in writing.
- Avoid overinterpreting nonverbal information. Pay attention to the actual words, especially if the sender is a man. If the sender is a woman, her nonverbal cues are important, but they should not lead you to exaggerate their meaning.
- Avoid overreacting. Plan a minimum of correction in the direction of the evaluation (your minimum response will probably be perceived as a large behavioral change).
- Avoid apologizing, justifying, or giving reasons. Focus on solutions.
- Express appreciation for all the feedback, not just the *negative* part. Leave the evaluator with the perception that you understood all of it, both negative and *positive*.

Evaluate Yourself with the Credibility Checklist

As we discussed in Chapters 1 and 12, your effectiveness as a communicator depends on the target audience's perception of your credibility. But your goal here is not just achieving credibility, which you will accomplish by applying the Strategic

Communication Model. Rather, your concern is that men and women who exhibit the same behaviors and who are equal in terms of training, rank, and experience are often not *perceived* as equal. Reviewing the Credibility Checklist summarizes the important points about gender differences in workplace communication.

Establish Goodwill: Your Focus on and Concern for Your Audience

Women have traditionally been afforded attention-*giving* roles, and men have traditionally been afforded attention-*getting* roles. As a result, both male and female receivers expect that a woman will focus on them more than on herself. However, if a man offers the same kind of nurturing and attention that is expected of a woman, he receives "extra points." The woman who does not meet expectations loses credibility. Although women may benefit from initial expectations that they will show goodwill, if they do not behave accordingly, receivers will judge them more harshly than they would men who behave exactly the same way.

If you are a woman, you may want to meet expectations that you will nurture your subordinates and show concern for your many audiences. If you are a man, you should exceed expectations by expressing concern for your many audiences.

Demonstrate Expertise: Your Education, Knowledge, and Experience

Researchers have discovered that even when a man and woman possess equal expertise, both male and female receivers perceive the man as being the more qualified expert. If you are a man, do not exaggerate your knowledge and experience at the risk of becoming unbelievable. Receivers will perceive your modesty as charming and persuasive. If you are a woman, do not diminish your expertise. Receivers might perceive your humility as a lack of knowledge and experience.

Display Power: Your Status, Prestige, and Authority

Rank should correlate with perceptions of status, but researchers have found that when men and women have equal rank, audiences afford higher status to men. Success translates into others' perception of your power as well, but both men and women attribute a man's success to his ability and a woman's success to hard work and an easy task. In addition, audiences often perceive typically masculine behaviors, such as interrupting, controlling conversation, and occupying large amounts of space, as being more powerful.

However, women who employ power behaviors may confuse or alienate their target audiences. On the other hand, behaviors such as smiling and lingering eye contact often send mixed messages as well. One audience may perceive smiling women as expressing warmth. Another audience may assume that the same women are allowing domination when they

1. Smile.
2. Maintain eye contact (perceived as gazing adoringly).
3. Allow their space to be invaded.

If you are a man, expect to perform to the high level of expectation of your audiences. If you are a woman, expect to work harder in order to be perceived as equal to your male counterparts.

Express Confidence: The Way You Present Yourself and Your Message

The confidence with which you demonstrate your skills is the most important factor in the perception of your credibility by your audience. Men are socialized to be comfortable in front of groups, yet women's language skills are often more developed. Confidence in communication is a *major* expectation in the corporate arena.

Reality and personal experience teach us that being confident is not always easy. However, audiences tend to perceive women who do not appear confident as lacking ability. An uncomfortable man may be perceived as endearing, particularly by a female audience. (A male audience may not notice at all.)

If you are a man, your confidence and extemporaneous abilities should not preclude careful preparation. You must select and organize information based on thorough audience analysis to maintain credibility. If you are a woman, prepare and practice so that both your skills and your confidence in demonstrating those skills are the best that they can be.

A Final Thought

The problems that arise from differences in the perception of the credibility of men and women in the workplace are complex. So are the solutions. The first step is to recognize that this is not a women's issue; it is a *corporate* issue. Men, women, organizations, and businesses will benefit if men and women of equal rank, training, and expertise are afforded equal credibility.

On an individual level, we must recognize that men and women have been socialized to behave in particular ways and to expect certain behaviors from others. As male and female business communicators, we all have behavioral tendencies. As male and female audiences, we all have biases. If you believe differently, you need to raise your awareness.

Finally, as members of organizations, we have responsibilities. We must recognize both our strengths and weaknesses and those of others to create the greatest possible perception of personal and corporate credibility.

Notes

1. Research on gender differences in workplace communication predominantly includes American men and women with European backgrounds. However, we have excluded three types of gender research:
   1) Studies of senior executives—less than 3 percent of whom are women—which conclude that no differences exist
   2) Studies of freshman and sophomore college students in controlled environments
   3) Studies of intimate relationships

   The first is unrealistic for the overwhelming majority of the workplace population; the second and third have little relevance to the corporate environment.

   The material in this reference tool represents combined, reinforcing information from dozens of research studies. The following are some additional readings on gender differences:

   Aries, E., "Gender and Communication." In P. Shaver and C. Hendrick (Eds.) *Sex and Gender,* 149–176. Newbury Park, CA: Sage, 1987.

   Carr-Ruffino, N., *Managing Diversity.* Cincinnati, OH: International Thomson Publishing, 1996.

   Kenton, S. B., "Speaker Credibility in Persuasive Business Communication." *The Journal of Business Communication,* Vol. 26: 2, Spring 1989.

   Snyderman, N. L., *Necessary Journeys: Letting Ourselves Learn from Life.* New York: Hyperion, 2000.

   Tannen, D., *Talking 9 to 5.* New York: William Morrow, 1994.

   Tingley, J. C., *Genderflex: Men and Women Speaking Each Other's Language at Work.* New York: AMACOM, 1994.

   Wood, J. T., *Gendered Lives: Communication, Gender, and Culture.* Belmont, CA: Wadsworth, 1997

Formatting Written Documents

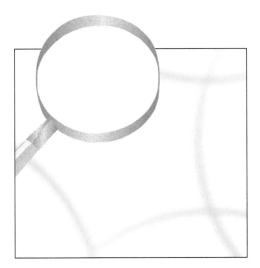

Business letters and other documents tend to follow generally accepted conventions. Proper layout and attention to details can enhance a writer's credibility and convey something about the importance of the message. When writers violate those conventions, they may appear uninformed and, thus, damage their credibility. In this reference tool, we discuss some standard ways to format business documents.

Business Letters

Listed here are the elements of standard business letters and their functions. A business letter is not the place to try out fancy fonts or experimental formats. A direct, traditional style works best. The following elements are conventional and safe and are listed in the order they appear in a standard business letter.

- **Return address/letterhead.** Type your address (or the address of the company you represent) at least one inch down from the top of the page. If you are using preprinted stationery (letterhead), do not retype the information.
- **Date.** Put the date on the first line after the return address. Spell out the month and include the date, a comma, and the year (e.g., January 31, 2002). Note: Do not put *st, th,* or *rd,* as in 1st, 4th, or 23rd, when writing the address.
- **Inside address.** Write the name, company (if appropriate), and address of the person to whom you are addressing the letter.

- **Attention line.** If the document is to be directed to a particular person or department, use an attention line (e.g., Attention: Marilyn Green, or XYYZ Corporation, Attention: Accounts Payable).

- **Salutation.** Type *Dear* followed by the person's title and name, followed by a colon (e.g., Dear Dr. Smith: or Dear Mrs. Jones:). If you are unsure of the gender of a reader (you don't want to call a man "Miss" by mistake or vice versa) write *Dear* followed by the first and last name (e.g., Dear Kelly Barrett:). Do not use a comma or semicolon. If you don't know the person who will read your letter, use a title instead (e.g., Dear Editor:). Some letter formats recommend omitting the salutation (and the complementary close, which we will discuss later), arguing that these letter elements are holdovers from another age that required more business formality.

- **Subject line/reference line.** Although not as common in letters as in memos (in which they are a standard element), a subject line can preview the content of your message for the reader. We recommend subject lines that convey a complete thought rather than ones that identify simply a one- or two-word topic. For example: "District Sales Results for March" conveys a complete thought, whereas "Sales Results" is less clear.

- **Body.** This is your actual message. Typically, each paragraph should begin so that it is even with the left margin and one line of space should appear between each section. Indenting the first line of each paragraph is still preferred by some people but is not necessary. Single spacing is normal, with double spacing between paragraphs. Use 12-point fonts (smaller ones are difficult to read for many people). Generally avoid unusual or decorative typefaces. Standard fonts such as Times New Roman, Ariel, and Palatino are standard for business writing.

- **Justification.** Use left justification for almost all business writing. Full justification (designed so that type lines up evenly on the left and right margins) is not necessary and can be distracting because of the additional spaces placed between words to make the margins even.

- **Complementary close.** Leave one line of space after your last paragraph, then use a conventional closing followed by a comma (e.g., Sincerely, Sincerely Yours, Respectfully, Yours Truly, etc.). If you have omitted the salutation in the beginning of the letter, you should also omit the complementary close.

- **Signature.** Your handwritten signature follows the complementary close with your typed name below. Allow space (four lines or more) so that you have enough room to sign your name normally. Unless you have established a personal relationship with the person to whom you are writing or unless you wish to convey friendship, use both your first and last name.

- **Typed name and position.** Type your full name below your signature. Do not include a Mr., Ms., or Mrs., but do include your organizational title if you are writing on behalf of an organization. This should appear on the next line.

- **Abbreviations.** Sometimes writers use abbreviations at the end of a letter to signify additional information. (Note that when using multiple abbreviations, each one should appear on a separate line.) The following are some common abbreviations:
  - **Copy notation.** If you wish to send a copy of the message to someone in addition to the addressee, use *Cc:* or *c:* and then name the person(s) who will receive the copy. (*Cc:* is a carryover from the old typewriter days when typists would produce a carbon copy in the typewriter. Today no one uses carbon paper, so the initial *c:* is more appropriate.)
  - **Enclosures.** Sometimes writers decide to enclose something with a letter such as product literature, price lists, a résumé, and so on. The word *enclosure* or

the abbreviation *Encl.*: serves as a reminder to include that item with the letter and draws the reader's attention to the enclosure. Generally, you should name or briefly describe the enclosure (e.g., Enclosure: Fall 2002 Price List; Encl: Benefits Pamphlet).

- **Writer's/typist's initials.** If the letter is being typed by someone other than the person who wrote and signed it, the writer's initials should be given in capital letters, followed by a slash and the typist's initials in lowercase letters (e.g., MT/fjr).

- **Page 2 (or subsequent pages) heading.** When a letter is more than one page, type the addressee's name, the page number, and the date beginning 1 inch from the top on each additional page. Leave one or two blank lines before continuing with the text.

Business Letter Layouts

Business letters commonly use two main styles, the full block style and the modified block style, shown in Figures D-1 and D-2, respectively. When using full block style, align all elements to the left margin. With modified block style, align the return address, date, closing, signature, and typed name along an imaginary line that runs down the middle of the page. Align all other elements at the left margin.

Business Envelopes

Business envelopes normally have a printed return address. You may choose to type your name above or below the address. If you are using a plain envelope for personal business, type your address (street, city, and state) in the upper-left corner. Don't crowd these lines too close to the corner of the envelope.

Memos

Memos are used for correspondence within an organization. They include four key ingredients in addition to the body of the message:

- To: line
- From: line
- date
- subject line

Keep in mind that memos often use enumeration and short sentences as discussed in Chapter 2. Also, you do not use a complementary close or signature block with a memo. Instead, you may sign or initial the memo next to your name at the top.

Memo Layouts

Most offices keep memo templates on software programs so that you can easily just begin typing in a template. Figure D-3 shows an example of a typical business memo.

company letterhead ————————

HOMETECH Corp.
100 Western Avenue
Cambridge, Massachusetts 02118

date ————————————————

January 26, 2002

inside address ————————————

Mr. Theron Bailey
BAILEY BROTHERS
23444 S. Savannah Ave.
Buford Park, GA 30322

salutation ————————————

Dear Mr. Bailey:

no indentation/left aligned ————

Quod si tam Graecis novitas invisa fuisset quam nobis, quid nunc esset vetus?

body of the letter ————————

Aut quid haberet quod legeret tereretque viritim. Ut primum positis nugari
Graecia bellis coepit et in vitium fortuna labier aequa, nunc athletarum studiis.

Nunc arsit equorum, marmoris aut eboris fabros aut aeris amavit, tibicinibus,
nunc est gavisa tragoedis, sub nutrice puella.

complementary close ——————

Sincerely,

signature ————————————

Samatha Seamour

typed name ————————————

Samantha Seamour

title and company ——————

President, HOMETECH Corp.

writer's/typist's initials ————

SS/mpt

item being sent with letter ————

Enclosure: Product brochure

copy sent to another person ————

c: Accounting Supervisor

Figure D-1
Full Block Style Letter

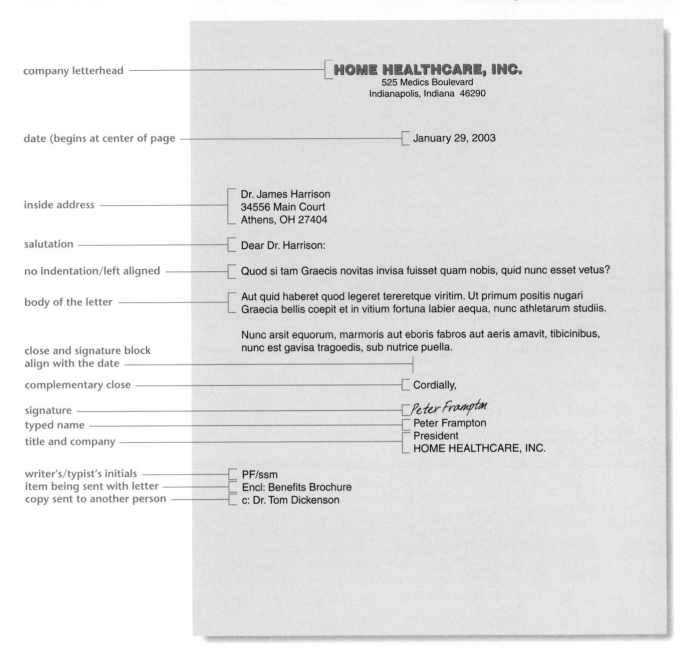

company letterhead —

HOME HEALTHCARE, INC.
525 Medics Boulevard
Indianapolis, Indiana 46290

date (begins at center of page — January 29, 2003

inside address — Dr. James Harrison
34556 Main Court
Athens, OH 27404

salutation — Dear Dr. Harrison:

no indentation/left aligned — Quod si tam Graecis novitas invisa fuisset quam nobis, quid nunc esset vetus?

body of the letter — Aut quid haberet quod legeret tereretque viritim. Ut primum positis nugari
Graecia bellis coepit et in vitium fortuna labier aequa, nunc athletarum studiis.

Nunc arsit equorum, marmoris aut eboris fabros aut aeris amavit, tibicinibus,
nunc est gavisa tragoedis, sub nutrice puella.

close and signature block
align with the date —

complementary close — Cordially,

signature — *Peter Frampton*
typed name — Peter Frampton
title and company — President
HOME HEALTHCARE, INC.

writer's/typist's initials — PF/ssm
item being sent with letter — Encl: Benefits Brochure
copy sent to another person — c: Dr. Tom Dickenson

Figure D-2
Modified Block Style Letter

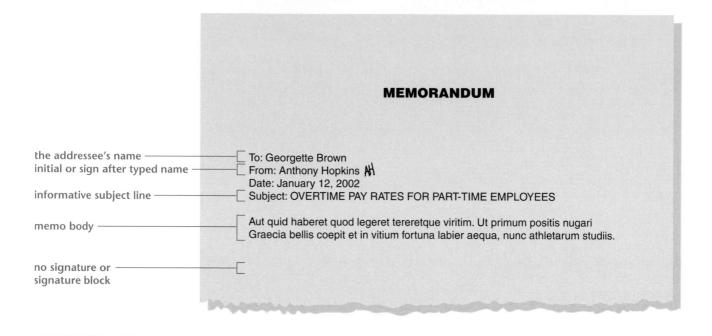

the addressee's name ——————

initial or sign after typed name ——————

informative subject line ——————

memo body ——————

no signature or
signature block

MEMORANDUM

To: Georgette Brown
From: Anthony Hopkins AH
Date: January 12, 2002
Subject: OVERTIME PAY RATES FOR PART-TIME EMPLOYEES

Aut quid haberet quod legeret tereretque viritim. Ut primum positis nugari
Graecia bellis coepit et in vitium fortuna labier aequa, nunc athletarum studiis.

Figure D-3
Typical Business Memo

E-Mail

The format for an e-mail message is set by the software being used. For example, Microsoft's popular Outlook (and virtually all other software products) includes a To, From, and Subject line. The date is automatically inserted. This format is like that used for paper memos. You may add letter elements such as a salutation and a complementary close to make the message more letter-like. E-mail also allows for easy distribution of copies using the C: or Bc: features. Bc: stands for "blind copy"—the copy is sent to another person but other receivers do not know that it has been sent to this person.

Reports

The following guidelines represent a standard report format but are not the only ways to format reports. Because of the variety of computer software available, you may want to deviate from these suggested guidelines. Learn the various features available in your own software and use them to make your reports easier to produce and more creative. Always bear in mind the importance of *accessing* key information. Here are some additional guidelines on formatting reports:

■ **Margins.** In most cases, set your top margin at 1.5 inches on the first page and 1 inch for the following pages. Set the right, left, and bottom margins at 1 inch for all pages. If your report will be bound, add 0.5 inches to the left margin to allow for the binding.

- **Pagination.** The first page is usually not numbered. All following pages should have page numbers either 0.5 inch from the top right or 0.5 inch from the bottom center.
- **Spacing.** Letters and memos are typed single spaced with double spacing between paragraphs. Long reports may be either single or double spaced. However, some people prefer 1.5-line spacing or double spacing, especially if they intend to write notes or comments in the report.
- **Headings.** Headings, like subject lines in memos, should be informative—conveying complete thoughts—rather than topical. Informative headings provide better content preview. You may place headings in a number of ways, but be sure to be consistent. Using word processing, you can create "styles" that will automatically format different level headings in the appropriate font, size, and position (left margin, centered, indented, etc.). Word processing programs will automatically set up a consistent style of fonts, spacing, and headings. Check your software instructions to learn how to use such features.
- **Quotations.** If a quotation is longer than two lines, it is indented 0.5 inch from both left and right margins. Quotations are usually single spaced and preceded and followed by a double space. Shorter quotations are placed in the text and are set off with quotation marks.
- **Listings (enumeration).** Indent listings or enumerated items 0.5 inch from the left margin. Single-space items longer than one line; indent the second and following lines under the first word, not the number; and double-space between items. Examples:

  - Bulleted or enumerated items are indented.
  - If a bulleted item runs for more than a full line, subsequent lines should be single spaced.

- **Footnotes/endnotes.** Footnotes are numbered within the text with references located at the bottom of the page on which the number appears. Endnotes are like footnotes except that the references are all located at the end of the report.
- **Page numbering.** Preliminary pages in a report such as the table of contents, a preface, or an executive summary should be numbered in lowercase Roman numerals (e.g., i, ii, iv, xi). The rest of the report uses regular numbers (except the title page). The preferred placement for page numbers is on the top right of each page.
- **Title page.** A title page is typically used for longer reports but not for memo reports or correspondence. It should include the title, the writer's name, the date, and any other information that may be helpful to a reader. An example of such other information may be: "A Research Report Requested by . . . " or "Submitted to Fulfill Course Requirement in [name of the course]."
- **Executive summary.** Formal reports often include an executive summary. This is a brief (one page or less) synopsis or abstract of the report's findings. Place the title of the report centered at the top of the page followed by the summary. Keep paragraphs short and use enumeration for easy accessing. Place this before the table of contents.
- **Table of contents.** Use a table of contents for long reports with numerous headings. Be sure that the headings on the contents page are exactly as they appear in the report. Identify the page on which the headings appear.
- **References.** A reference list or bibliography is used to identify sources cited for the report. Items appear in alphabetical order, not in the order cited in the report. The format of items is similar to footnotes. (Reference Tool B, "Researching Your

Figure D-4
Sample Title Page

AN ANALYSIS OF
CUSTOMER OPINIONS REGARDING
COMPANY EXPANSION PLANS

Prepared for:
Peter Riggins
Marketing Manager
CommCo Corporation

Prepared by:

Laresa Sweet
Marketing Intern

November 26, 2002

Topic and Documenting Your Findings," shows how to cite sources.) Check a
style guide if in doubt about a particular reference entry.

Report Layouts

Figures D-4 through D-7 show sample pages illustrating report elements and formats.

CONTENTS

Figure D-6
Sample Executive
Summary

EXECUTIVE SUMMARY

AN ANALYSIS OF
CUSTOMER OPINIONS REGARDING
COMPANY EXPANSION PLANS

Laresa Sweet
Marketing Intern

January 26, 2002

Write the summary of the report using short paragraphs and easy accessing techniques. Do not include much supporting information, rather; stick to the basic description of findings.

The idea of this part of the report is to give the busy reader a quick, boiled-down version of the report.

Figure D-7
Sample Reference Page

REFERENCES[1]

Allan, Robert. (2001) *How customers think.* New York: Pointed Press, Inc.

Benjamine, Susan J. (2002, February 23) "The time they closed Macy's," *Retail Times*, 23, pp. 43–4.

Smith, W.G. (1999) Flexibility and responsiveness in adjusting to changing customer needs: Ethnographic studies. *Personnel Journal*, 61, pp. 117–122.

For further information on layout formats for other types of documents, search online for examples. Note too that companies often have their own prescribed styles. Look at the way your organization formats documents for guidance.

Notes

1. These references are written using the American Psychological Association (APA) format. Writers may choose other styles but should be consistent with whatever format they choose.

Using Editing Symbols

Editing and proofreading symbols vary among different instructors and editors. The following are some simple symbols we have used to cover most common errors in writing. Feel free to add others, as needed, to streamline your feedback to the writer.

Add space

Agr AGREEMENT lacking

Awk AWKward writing

Capitalize

C→E? CAUSE AND EFFECT questionable

Close up words

Coh COHERENCE lacking

Connect two lines

T TENSE inconsistency

access? ACCESS key information better

WC WORD CHOICE questionable

ISS Improve SENTENCE STRUCTURE

stet Leave copy as originally typed

☐ Move right

? QUESTIONABLE CONTENT

Inappropriate Negative tone neg

DELETE word, phrase, or letters

Start new paragraph ¶

Lacking PARALLELISM par

PASSIVE voice (should be active) passive

reverse order

SPELLING error sp

spell in full

double space ds

Unclear REFERENCE ref?

Empty subject ("it", "there") exp

INSERT letter, word, punctuation ∧

Make lower CASE

Move left ☐

ENUMERATE

CHAPTER 1
Page 7: Paul Barton/Corbis/Stock Market. Page 9: Steve Niedorf/The Image Bank. Page 11: Jon Feingersh/Corbis/Stock Market. Page 14: SuperStock, Inc.

CHAPTER 2
Page 31: AP/Wide World Photos. Page 32: David De Lossy/The Image Bank. Page 38: Index Stock Imagery, Inc. Page 42: SuperStock, Inc.

CHAPTER 3
Page 53: SuperStock, Inc. Page 65: Tim Brown/Stone.

CHAPTER 4
Page 78: Juan Silva/The Image Bank. Page 79: Jose Luis Pelaez/Corbis/Stock Market. Page 83: Esbin-Anderson/The Image Works.

CHAPTER 5
Page 103: Larry Keenan/The Image Bank. Page 104: L.D. Gordon/The Image Bank. Page 109: Marc Romanelli/The Image Bank.

CHAPTER 6
Page 121: AP/Wide World Photos.

CHAPTER 7
Page 162: Gale Zucker Photography. Page 163: SuperStock, Inc.

CHAPTER 8
Page 190: Jim Cummins/Corbis/Stock Market.

CHAPTER 9
Page 199: H. Prinz/Corbis/Stock Market. Page 203: SuperStock, Inc. Page 205: SuperStock, Inc. Page 207: SuperStock, Inc.

CHAPTER 10
Page 224: John Henley/Corbis/Stock Market. Page 228: Jose Luis Pelaez/Corbis/Stock Market.

CHAPTER 11
Page 241: SuperStock, Inc. Page 247: SuperStock, Inc. Page 250: Jose Luis Pelaez/Corbis/Stock Market.

CHAPTER 12
Page 264: Jose L. Pelaez/Corbis/Stock Market. Page 268: Jon Feingersh/Corbis/Stock Market.